BEST AMERICAN
POLITICAL WRITING 2008

CLASH OF THE TITANS

The Reagan and Clinton icons of their respective parties
were in plain sight early on and, it seemed, ready to
do battle. (Illustration by Steve Brodner;
first appeared in *The New Yorker*.)

BEST AMERICAN POLITICAL WRITING 2008

EDITED BY ROYCE FLIPPIN

with an Introduction by
Todd S. Purdum

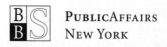

PUBLICAFFAIRS
NEW YORK

Published in the United States by PublicAffairs™, a member of the
Perseus Books Group.
Printed in the United States of America.

Book Design by Timm Bryson

Library of Congress Cataloging-in-Publication Data
    Best American political writing, 2008 / edited by Royce Flippin ;
with an introduction by Todd S. Purdum. — 1st ed.
        p. cm.
    Includes bibliographical references.
    ISBN 978–1–58648–643–3 (pbk. : alk. paper) 1. United States—
Politics and government—2001- 2. United States—Foreign
relations—2001- 3. Iraq War, 2003- 4. Afghan War, 2001- 5.
Presidents—United States—Election—2008. 6. Presidential
candidates—United States. 7. Political culture—United States. I.
Flippin, Royce.
E902.B473 2008
973.93—dc22
                        2008023470
First Edition
10 9 8 7 6 5 4 3 2 1

This book is dedicated to Alexis, Maisie, and Bailey

CONTENTS

List of Illustrations   *xi*

Acknowledgments   *xiii*

Introduction   *xv*
  Todd S. Purdum

Preface   *xix*
  Royce Flippin

The Race

Goodbye to All That: Why Obama Matters   3
  Andrew Sullivan, *The Atlantic Monthly*

One of Us, Part 2: John McCain's Last War   18
  Chris Jones, *Esquire*

One of Us, Part 3: Two Nights . . .   32
  Chris Jones, *Esquire*

The Feminist Reawakening: Hillary Clinton
and the Fourth Wave   41
  Amanda Fortini, *New York* magazine

The Choice   50
  George Packer, *The New Yorker*

The Machinery of Hope: Inside the Grass-Roots
  Field Organization of Barack Obama   66
  Tim Dickinson, *Rolling Stone*

The Iron Lady: The Clinton Campaign Returns
  from the Dead, Again   76
  Ryan Lizza, *The New Yorker*

Is John McCain Bob Dole?   85
  John Heilemann, *New York* magazine

All Aboard the McCain Express   100
  Rick Perlstein, *The Nation*

Who We Are Now

How McCain and Obama Beat the Odds:
  Delegate Math and the Emotional Logic
  of the Political Brain   111
  Drew Westen, postscript to the
  paperback edition of *The Political Brain*

The Politics of Personality Destruction   123
  Jennifer Senior, *New York* magazine

Political Civility   137
  David Mamet, *The Village Voice*

16 Ways of Looking at a Female Voter   143
  Linda Hirshman, *The New York
  Times Magazine*

The Year of Governing Dangerously   155
  David Margolick, *Vanity Fair*

Arnold Schwarzenegger Is President
  of 12% of Us   176
  Tom Junod, *Esquire*

Can You Count on Voting Machines?   188
   Clive Thompson, *The New York*
Times Magazine

So Long, Buckaroo

Inside Bush's Bunker   211
   Todd S. Purdum, *Vanity Fair*

Feast of the Wingnuts: How Economic Crackpots
   Devoured American Politics   230
   Jonathan Chait, *The New Republic*

The Economic Consequences of Mr. Bush   243
   Joseph E. Stiglitz, *Vanity Fair*

The Rove Presidency   253
   Joshua Green, *The Atlantic Monthly*

What We Talk About
When We Talk About War

Inside the Surge   277
   Jon Lee Anderson, *The New Yorker*

Anatomy of the Surge   299
   Peter D. Feaver, *Commentary*

The History Boys   309
   David Halberstam, *Vanity Fair*

After Musharraf   319
   Joshua Hammer, *The Atlantic Monthly*

The Black Sites: A Rare Look Inside the C.I.A.'s
   Secret Interrogation Program   336
   Jane Mayer, *The New Yorker*

Euphemism and American Violence   357
    David Bromwich, *The New York*
    Review of Books

Permissions   369
Contributors   373

LIST OF ILLUSTRATIONS
BY STEVE BRODNER

Frontispiece: Clash of the Titans   ii

Part 1: Stag Night at Sharkey's Redux   1

Part 2: Boy with the Straw Hat   109

Part 3: Victory Cigar   209

Part 4: War Week   275

ACKNOWLEDGMENTS

First and foremost, I'd like to thank the contributors for granting permission to reprint their work in this edition. In addition, I'd like to express my appreciation for the literary agents who represent these writers, and the permissions editors of the publications featured herein, for their invaluable help in arranging reprint rights.

I'm particularly grateful to Steve Brodner, who graciously allowed us to publish five of his superb drawings in this year's edition, and to Todd S. Purdum for contributing his eloquent introduction. I also want to thank the excellent team at PublicAffairs, which assumed the Best American Political Writing series last year. I'd especially like to thank my editor, Morgen Van Vorst, who worked with me diligently and effectively in choosing the pieces and artwork for this year's anthology and has helped to make the transition a seamless one. Thanks, too, to Melissa Raymond for overseeing the production process and to Kathy Streckfus for her copyediting skills.

Finally, I'd like to thank my wife, Alexis Lipsitz Flippin, for her love and forbearance in joining me to sift and discuss yet another year's worth of political writing!

INTRODUCTION

Todd S. Purdum

The United States is ensnared in a grim and seemingly unwinnable war half a world away. Domestic political passions run high. Accusations of un-Americanism are recklessly hurled about, even as civil liberties and constitutional protections are casually abraded. One of the most fascinating presidential campaigns in years pits a first-term statewide officeholder from Illinois (who writes his own speeches) against a bona-fide war hero (who accumulated more than his share of demerits and did not distinguish himself in his military academy class). Both have a reputation for uncommon rectitude, and the fall election will test whether either can win without proving he is unworthy of winning, as a wise (but losing) politician once put it.

That politician was Adlai E. Stevenson, who, fifty-six years ago this fall, as the first-term governor of Illinois, took on Dwight D. Eisenhower, the Supreme Allied Commander who saved the civilized world from Hitler, for the right to succeed Harry Truman. Their 1952 election battle was the last time in American history that the race for the White House was as wide open as it has been this year—with no incumbent president or vice president on either party's ticket—and the parallels between their contest and the fight of Barack Obama against John McCain are eerily obvious: the egghead vs. the egg-breaker; the poet vs. the paladin; the fresh face vs. the battle-scarred vet.

But the differences are palpable, too. Stevenson was running with the weight of twenty years of Democratic rule and its accumulated controversies on his shoulders, while McCain is burdened by public distaste for two terms of catastrophic Republican control. Obama has positioned himself as a figure above conventional politics, just as Eisenhower did when he kept both parties guessing for months about whether he was a Republican, a Democrat, or merely a kind of living god. Eisenhower captivated voters with his vague pledge to "go to Korea" (which meant get out of it), while McCain, who shares some of Ike's bipartisan patina, has vowed to stay in Iraq for years, if that's what it takes.

It remains to be seen whether Obama will be more like Stevenson, a pure and noble loser, or John F. Kennedy, a cool cat who went to school on Stevenson's mistakes. And it remains to be seen whether McCain, whose undaunted courage in the Hanoi Hilton left his body badly broken (and who would be two years older if and when he takes office than Ike was when he left it), will be more like the rise-above-it-all Eisenhower or Ike's fellow Kansan Bob Dole, who nearly lost his life as a lieutenant in Italy in World War II but seemed too damned old and cranky to wrest the presidency from that glandular phenomenon, Bill Clinton, in 1996.

Hovering over the whole scene is another figure: a pioneering First Lady who went on to an outstanding public career in her own right, winning a huge place in the hearts of many of her fellow Democrats. Like Eleanor Roosevelt, Hillary Clinton long ago rose above her husband's infidelity to make something finer for herself, and like E.R. in 1960, H.R.C. has worried this year that her party's bright young standard-bearer is not quite up to the job. But Senator Clinton's very presence on the national stage is proof of the limits of this historical ramble's relevance to current events: It was not so long ago that the prospect of a white woman (or a black man) becoming the Democratic presidential nominee was quite unthinkable.

In each presidential election cycle, it has become a cliché (or at least a truism) to say that something or other is "unprecedented." Inflation alone all but guarantees that the next election will be more expensive than the one before it; the steady breakdown of party discipline has meant that primary voters (and television news directors) have gained more and more influence over a more and more diffuse process; the rise of a 24/7 media culture has elevated trivialities to the level of great debates; and a process that once took only a few months between the parties' conventions and the general election (or eight or nine months when the primaries began in February and March) now takes the better part of two full years, if not more.

Still, as the range of provocative and insightful pieces in this anthology suggests, it seems all but certain that historians will regard the 2008 election as singular. The sheer amount of money raised by the leading candidates ($1 million a day by Barack Obama, routinely, for weeks on end), the vast size of Obama's crowds, and the intensity of the Democratic nomination fight are all a testament to the Internet's extraordinary (and, yes, unprecedented) power as a fundraising, organizing, energizing tool. More than at any time in my twenty-five years of covering politics—and my nearly fifty years of living—there is really something new under the sun.

Precisely what this year of extraordinary possibilities will produce—in Washington, or the world—is another question. For all the bitter debates of McCarthyism, the 1952 election actually produced remarkable consensus on activist government at home and internationalist government abroad: Eisenhower accepted the legacies of the New Deal and the Marshall Plan in the face of the global foe of communism. Just four years ago, President Bush's chief strategist, Karl Rove, was predicting that his reelection presaged a permanent Republican realignment. If that now seems far from likely, so does a great new day of Democratic dominance. Muddling through may be the new normal.

Neither Obama nor McCain is conventionally partisan, and each has made his name in part by railing against the destructiveness and absurdity of much of what passes for modern politics. But even in the early going, their matchup showed signs of producing conventional partisan squabbles. Would either stand much of a chance of changing the entrenched ways of Washington, the power of the special-interest money they both purport to despise, or the threat of global terrorism that they view so differently? The country may be united in opposition to George W. Bush and his policies in Iraq and elsewhere, but by most other conventional measures, voters remain closely divided. McCain would doubtless face a hostile Democratic Congress, and Obama would have nothing like the large working majorities that Franklin D. Roosevelt and Lyndon B. Johnson enjoyed in their prime.

What does seem clear enough is that this election will be a pivot point, a chance for the United States to recalibrate itself, and the world's image of it, in the face of rapidly evolving circumstances. Obama would be the fourth youngest president in our history, and McCain the very oldest, but as political personalities, either would be a decided contrast to the incumbent Decider the world has come to know so well. McCain may be Hemingway and Obama Fitzgerald, but both see the world with something of the writer's eye. Both have compelling personal narratives that reinforce and amplify their policy approaches, whether McCain's muscular nationalism and Teddy Roosevelt–style grit or Obama's promise of a new kind of politics in which small victories make big differences and aspiration is its own reward.

As Drew Westen reminds us in the insightful excerpt from his book, *The Political Brain* (page 111), politics has always been, at heart, a matter of storytelling, and voters embrace (or reject) politicians more with their hearts than with their heads. Ronald Reagan knew this instinctively, and Adlai Stevenson understood it all too well. When told at one point in his 1956 campaign that "every thinking person" in the country was for him, he replied, "That's not enough. . . . We need a majority!" From George Washington on, we have disproportionately loved our leaders, as Desdemona loved Othello, for the dangers they have passed, the obstacles they have overcome, and the dragons they set out to slay on our behalf, far more than for the ten-point plans they have promised. Our current system of selecting them may well be inhumane, inelegant, and far too prolonged, and it may provide only limited guidance about the candidates' capacity for governing. But it is the system we have made, so perhaps we deserve it.

The pieces in the pages that follow describe the state of that system, and tell the stories of the combatants, from the middle-distance perspective between current events and history that magazine writing is uniquely suited to provide. In a world full of more and more (and more unreliable) opinion masquerading as fact, and of sometimes mindless accumulation of fact substituting for meaning, the profiles, narratives, essays, and analyses gathered here offer a welcome degree of reflection. They capture the moment in which they were published, yet they already seem well positioned to stand the test of time. They plumb personality, explore technology, assay economics, and detail grave mistakes.

Perhaps more than anything, this election year, and this collection, reify that hoariest shibboleth of the national creed: that in America, any boy (or girl) can grow up to be president, and, to paraphrase Stevenson, that's just one of the risks we take.

PREFACE

Royce Flippin

The eve of the 2008 presidential election offers up a scene worthy of a Hollywood screenwriter's imagination: a lame-duck, widely unpopular Republican president limping to the end of his second term, and a wide-open race to succeed him featuring a Vietnam War hero, a first-term African American senator, and the only First Lady ever to run for the White House. The backdrop? A pugnacious but largely impotent Democratic majority in the House and Senate, the seemingly interminable armed struggle to turn Iraq and Afghanistan into working democracies, a faltering U.S. economy, and the nagging sense that Al Qaeda and its allies are still actively plotting violence against America. Something's gotta give. Change is in the air—though just what it will bring remains to be seen.

The current national mood of uncertainty, frustration, and hunger for a new direction (the most recent Gallup Poll found an unprecedented 77 percent of Americans believe the country is on the wrong track) is the raw material for the selections in *Best American Political Writing 2008*. It isn't surprising then that this year's edition is largely divided between analysis of how our country has gone astray and investigations into how we are scrambling toward what we hope will be a brighter future.

The coverage of this cataclysmic year is headed up by "The Race," a collection of articles devoted to the bruising primary battles for the Republican and Democratic presidential nominations. Andrew Sullivan's essay "Goodbye to All That: Why Obama Matters" is a fascinating rumination on Barack Obama's importance as the nation's first presidential candidate born after 1960. Chris Jones's intimate two-part profile of John McCain's ascension to the Republican nomination follows, before the spotlight shifts to Hillary Clinton with Amanda Fortini's essay on how her candidacy, and the hostility it's generated, has reinvigorated America's feminist movement. The three subsequent pieces report directly from the campaign trail, as George Packer surveys "The Choice" between Obama and Clinton, Tim Dickinson writes about Obama's unprece-dented grassroots campaign organization, and veteran political scribe Ryan Lizza captures the fierce determination of Hillary Clinton in "The Iron Lady." In conclusion, John Heilemann's thought-provoking article examines how the general election contest between McCain and Obama is likely to shape up ("Is John McCain Bob Dole?"), and Rick Perlstein takes a wry look at the right-wing punditry's belated embrace of McCain as the GOP nominee ("All Aboard the McCain Express").

"Who We Are Now" veers from the campaign trail to offer a varied selection of political perspectives. Beginning with psychologist Drew Westen, author of the assumption-shattering best-seller *The Political Brain,* we learn just how the leading presidential candidates have attempted to bond emotionally with the American public. Jennifer Senior examines why political candidates are better off hiding their true personalities, famed playwright David Mamet explains why he no longer considers himself a liberal, and professor and feminist author Linda Hirshman offers up a provocative analysis of female voting patterns. Rounding out the section are profiles of two diametrically opposed governor-ships, with David Margolick's cautionary article on Eliot Spitzer's brief and troubled tenure as New York's chief executive, published just weeks before he was forced to step down, and Tom Junod's rollicking account of how Califor-nia governor Arnold Schwarzenegger retooled his gubernatorial approach and roared his way to reelection. In closing, technology writer Clive Thompson ed-ucates us on just how hard it is to find a reliable vote-counting machine.

In "So Long, Buckaroo," contributors explore the uncertain legacy of soon-to-be-ex-president George W. Bush. Todd S. Purdum examines Bush's life in-side the White House bubble, while Jonathan Chait and economist Joseph E. Stiglitz offer a two-pronged assessment of the Bush economic program's fail-ings in their respective pieces. Joshua Green closes with a shrewd analysis of why Bush's campaign guru Karl Rove is brilliant at winning elections, but less ingenious at running a government.

"What We Talk About When We Talk About War" concentrates on Ameri-can foreign policy, with a particular focus on the conflict in Iraq. Jon Lee An-derson's "Inside the Surge" is an eyewitness account of how the recent buildup of U.S. troop strength in Iraq is playing out on the streets of Baghdad, while former Bush adviser Peter D. Feaver's "Anatomy of the Surge" provides an il-luminating view of what the Iraq occupation looks like from inside the Ad-ministration. "The History Boys," one of the last pieces written by the late

David Halberstam, pokes big holes in the Bush administration's efforts to compare George W. Bush with Harry S. Truman, another president who left office with dismal approval ratings. In "After Musharraf," foreign correspondent Joshua Hammer travels to Pakistan to assess President Pervez Musharraf's prospects of continuing as leader of that strategically important nation. "The Black Sites," by Jane Mayer, is a chilling investigation of the C.I.A.'s tactics inside its secret prisons, while "Euphemism and American Violence," by literature professor David Bromwich, challenges us to rethink the political implications of the words we use to describe our world.

This is the seventh edition of *Best American Political Writing* to see print—a series whose tenure has coincided exactly with that of George W. Bush's presidency. Next year, at long last, there will be someone else in the Oval Office to kick around. Change is in the air, and it's bracing. But no matter who the next man in the White House is, American troops will remain in Iraq and Afghanistan, the U.S. economy will likely still be sputtering, Osama bin Laden will quite probably still be at large somewhere in western Pakistan, and the Senate Democrats will almost certainly remain a few seats shy of a filibuster-proof majority. You can't have everything—and if you could, what would be left to write about?

THE RACE

STAG NIGHT AT
SHARKEY'S REDUX

A takeoff on the famous painting by George
Bellows, this time with Clinton and Obama in
the ring. McCain is ringside taking notes.
(Illustration by Steve Brodner; first
appeared in *The New Yorker*.)

1

GOODBYE TO ALL THAT: WHY OBAMA MATTERS

ANDREW SULLIVAN

The Atlantic Monthly   December 2007

As this book went to press in June 2008, the seemingly endless Democratic primary season had at last drawn to a close, with Barack Obama finally nailing down the presidential nomination. But there was nothing easy about his victory: Having piled up an insurmountable lead in pledged delegates with his string of wins midway through the process, Obama had to then outwait a series of survival maneuvers by Hillary Clinton—which included pressing to take account of the delegations from the contested Michigan and Florida primaries (both states had been "desanctioned" as punishment for moving up their primary dates in defiance of party rules, and the Democratic National Committee eventually decided to allocate a half-vote per delegate in each state) and making the case that she had "won" the popular vote (true, if you count her 328,000 to zero victory over Obama in Michigan, where his name didn't appear on the ballot).

Clinton's stubborn refusal to quit was in part a nod to her many fervent supporters, but to some, it also seemed to reflect her campaign's sense of disbelief that her "inevitable" path to the nomination had been blocked by such an unlikely (and unforeseen) adversary. In his Atlantic Monthly *article—which appeared before the first primary vote had been cast—Andrew Sullivan put a twist on the argument of so-called inevitability by noting that whatever historical forces might be at work in this election, Obama stands to benefit most from them. Born in the 1960s, he's grown up largely free of the lingering tensions spawned by that troubled decade. And if the nation is finally ready to bid adieu to the politics of the Vietnam era, as Sullivan—who's written extensively about religion and culture in American political life—believes, then Obama is the natural choice to lead the way.*

The logic behind the candidacy of Barack Obama is not, in the end, about Barack Obama. It has little to do with his policy proposals, which are very close to his Democratic rivals' and which, with a few exceptions, exist firmly within the conventions of our politics. It has little to do with Obama's considerable skills as a conciliator, legislator, or even thinker. It has even less to do with his ideological pedigree or legal background or rhetorical skills. Yes, as the many profiles prove, he has considerable intelligence and not a little guile. But so do others, not least his formidably polished and practiced opponent Senator Hillary Clinton.

Obama, moreover, is no saint. He has flaws and tics: Often tired, sometimes crabby, intermittently solipsistic, he's a surprisingly uneven campaigner. A soaring rhetorical flourish one day is undercut by a lackluster debate performance the next. He is certainly not without self-regard. He has more experience in public life than his opponents want to acknowledge, but he has not spent much time in Washington and has never run a business. His lean physique, close-cropped hair, and stick-out ears can give the impression of a slightly pushy undergraduate. You can see why many of his friends and admirers have urged him to wait his turn. He could be president in five or nine years' time—why the rush?

But he knows, and privately acknowledges, that the fundamental point of his candidacy is that it is happening now. In politics, timing matters. And the most persuasive case for Obama has less to do with him than with the moment he is meeting. The moment has been a long time coming, and it is the result of a confluence of events, from one traumatizing war in Southeast Asia to another in the most fractious country in the Middle East. The legacy is a cultural climate that stultifies our politics and corrupts our discourse.

Obama's candidacy in this sense is a potentially transformational one. Unlike any of the other candidates, he could take America—finally—past the debilitating, self-perpetuating family quarrel of the Baby Boom generation that has long engulfed all of us. So much has happened in America in the past seven years, let alone the past 40, that we can be forgiven for focusing on the present and the immediate future. But it is only when you take several large steps back into the long past that the full logic of an Obama presidency stares directly—and uncomfortably—at you.

At its best, the Obama candidacy is about ending a war—not so much the war in Iraq, which now has a momentum that will propel the occupation into the next decade—but the war within America that has prevailed since Vietnam and that shows dangerous signs of intensifying, a nonviolent civil war that has crippled America at the very time the world needs it most. It is a war about war—and about culture and about religion and about race. And in that war, Obama—and Obama alone—offers the possibility of a truce.

⤙ • ⤚

The traces of our long journey to this juncture can be found all around us. Its most obvious manifestation is political rhetoric. The high temperature—Bill O'Reilly's nightly screeds against anti-Americans on one channel, Keith Olbermann's "Worst Person in the World" on the other; MoveOn.org's "General Betray Us" on the one side, Ann Coulter's *Treason* on the other; Michael Moore's accusation of treason at the core of the Iraq War, Sean Hannity's assertion of treason in the opposition to it—is particularly striking when you examine the generally minor policy choices on the table. Something deeper and more powerful than the actual decisions we face is driving the tone of the debate.

Take the biggest foreign-policy question—the war in Iraq. The rhetoric ranges from John McCain's "No Surrender" banner to the "End the War Now" absolutism of much of the Democratic base. Yet the substantive issue is almost comically removed from this hyperventilation. Every potential president, Republican or Democrat, would likely inherit more than 100,000 occupying troops in January 2009; every one would be attempting to redeploy them as prudently as possible and to build stronger alliances both in the region and in the world. Every major candidate, moreover, will pledge to use targeted military force against Al Qaeda if necessary; every one is committed to ensuring that Iran will not have a nuclear bomb; every one is committed to an open-ended deployment in Afghanistan and an unbending alliance with Israel. We are fighting over something, to be sure. But it is more a fight over how we define ourselves and over long-term goals than over what is practically to be done on the ground.

On domestic policy, the primary issue is health care. Again, the ferocious rhetoric belies the mundane reality. Between the boogeyman of "Big Government" and the alleged threat of the drug companies, the practical differences are more matters of nuance than ideology. Yes, there are policy disagreements, but in the wake of the Bush administration, they are underwhelming. Most Republicans support continuing the Medicare drug benefit for seniors, the largest expansion of the entitlement state since Lyndon Johnson, while Democrats are merely favoring more cost controls on drug and insurance companies. Between Mitt Romney's Massachusetts plan—individual mandates, private-sector leadership—and Senator Clinton's triangulated update of her 1994 debacle, the difference is more technical than fundamental. The country has moved ever so slightly leftward. But this again is less a function of ideological transformation than of the current system's failure to provide affordable health care for the insured or any care at all for growing numbers of the working poor.

Even on issues that are seen as integral to the polarization, the practical stakes in this election are minor. A large consensus in America favors legal abortions during the first trimester and varying restrictions thereafter. Even in solidly red states, such as South Dakota, the support for total criminalization is weak. If *Roe* were to fall, the primary impact would be the end of a system more liberal than any in Europe in favor of one more in sync with the varied views that exist across this country. On marriage, the battles in the states are subsiding, as a bevy of blue states adopt either civil marriage or civil unions for gay couples, and the rest stand pat. Most states that want no recognition for same-sex couples have already made that decision, usually through state constitutional amendments that allow change only with extreme difficulty. And the one state where marriage equality exists, Massachusetts, has decided to maintain the reform indefinitely.

Given this quiet, evolving consensus on policy, how do we account for the bitter, brutal tone of American politics? The answer lies mainly with the biggest and most influential generation in America: the Baby Boomers. The divide is still—amazingly—between those who fought in Vietnam and those who didn't, and between those who fought and dissented and those who fought but never dissented at all. By defining the contours of the Boomer generation, it lasted decades. And with time came a strange intensity.

The professionalization of the battle, and the emergence of an array of well-funded interest groups dedicated to continuing it, can be traced most proximately to the bitter confirmation fights over Robert Bork and Clarence Thomas, in 1987 and 1991 respectively. The presidency of Bill Clinton, who was elected with only 43 percent of the vote in 1992, crystallized the new reality. As soon as the Baby Boomers hit the commanding heights, the Vietnam power struggle rebooted. The facts mattered little in the face of such a divide. While Clinton was substantively a moderate conservative in policy, his countercultural origins led to the drama, ultimately, of religious warfare and even impeachment. Clinton clearly tried to bridge the Boomer split. But he was trapped on one side of it—and his personal foibles only reignited his generation's agonies over sex and love and marriage. Even the failed impeachment didn't bring the two sides to their senses, and the election of 2000 only made matters worse: Gore and Bush were almost designed to reflect the Boomers' and the country's divide, which deepened further.

The trauma of 9/11 has tended to obscure the memory of that unprecedentedly bitter election, and its nail-biting aftermath, which verged on a constitutional crisis. But its legacy is very much still with us, made far worse by President Bush's approach to dealing with it. Despite losing the popular vote, Bush governed as if he had won Reagan's 49 states. Instead of cementing a coalition of the center-right, Bush and Rove set out to ensure that the new evangelical base of the Republicans would turn out more reliably in 2004. Instead of seeing the post-'60s divide as a wound to be healed, they poured acid on it.

⤙ • ⤚

With 9/11, Bush had a reset moment—a chance to reunite the country in a way that would marginalize the extreme haters on both sides and forge a national consensus. He chose not to do so. It wasn't entirely his fault. On the left, the truest believers were unprepared to give the president the benefit of any doubt in the wake of the 2000 election, and they even judged the 9/11 attacks to be a legitimate response to decades of U.S. foreign policy. Some could not support the war in Afghanistan, let alone the adventure in Iraq. As the Iraq War faltered, the polarization intensified. In 2004, the Vietnam argument returned with a new energy, with the Swift Boat attacks on John Kerry's Vietnam War record and CBS's misbegotten report on Bush's record in the Texas Air National Guard. These were the stories that touched the collective nerve of the political classes—because they parsed once again along the fault lines of the Boomer divide that had come to define all of us.

The result was an even deeper schism. Kerry was arguably the worst candidate on earth to put to rest the post-1960s culture war—and his decision to embrace his Vietnam identity at the convention made things worse. Bush, for his part, was unable to do nuance. And so the campaign became a matter of symbolism—pitting those who took the terror threat "seriously" against those who didn't. Supporters of the Iraq War became more invested in asserting the morality of their cause than in examining the effectiveness of their tactics. Opponents of the war found themselves dispirited. Some were left to hope privately for American failure; others lashed out, as distrust turned to paranoia.

It was and is a toxic cycle, in which the interests of the United States are supplanted by domestic agendas born of pride and ruthlessness on the one hand and bitterness and alienation on the other.

⤙ • ⤚

This is the critical context for the election of 2008. It is an election that holds the potential not merely to intensify this cycle of division but to bequeath it to a new generation, one marked by a new war that need not be—that should not be—seen as another Vietnam. A Giuliani-Clinton matchup, favored by the media elite, is a classic intragenerational struggle—with two deeply divisive and ruthless personalities ready to go to the brink. Giuliani represents that Nixonian disgust with anyone asking questions about, let alone actively protesting, a war. Clinton will always be, in the minds of so many, the young woman who gave the commencement address at Wellesley, who sat in on the Nixon implosion and who once disdained baking cookies. For some, her husband will always be the draft dodger who smoked pot and wouldn't admit it. And however hard she tries, there is nothing Hillary Clinton can do about it. She and Giuliani are conscripts in their generation's war. To their respective sides, they are war heroes.

In normal times, such division is not fatal, and can even be healthy. It's great copy for journalists. But we are not talking about routine rancor. And we are not talking about normal times. We are talking about a world in which Islamist terror, combined with increasingly available destructive technology, has already murdered thousands of Americans, and tens of thousands of Muslims, and could pose an existential danger to the West. The terrible failures of the Iraq occupation, the resurgence of Al Qaeda in Pakistan, the progress of Iran toward nuclear capability, and the collapse of America's prestige and moral reputation, especially among those millions of Muslims too young to have known any American president but Bush, heighten the stakes dramatically.

Perhaps the underlying risk is best illustrated by our asking what the popular response would be to another 9/11-style attack. It is hard to imagine a reprise of the sudden unity and solidarity in the days after 9/11, or an outpouring of support from allies and neighbors. It is far easier to imagine an even more bitter fight over who was responsible (apart from the perpetrators) and a profound suspicion of a government forced to impose more restrictions on travel, communications, and civil liberties. The current president would be unable to command the trust, let alone the support, of half the country in such a time. He could even be blamed for provoking any attack that came.

Of the viable national candidates, only Obama and possibly McCain have the potential to bridge this widening partisan gulf. Polling reveals Obama to be the favored Democrat among Republicans. McCain's bipartisan appeal has receded in recent years, especially with his enthusiastic embrace of the latest phase of the Iraq War. And his personal history can only reinforce the Vietnam divide. But Obama's reach outside his own ranks remains striking. Why? It's a good question: How has a black, urban liberal gained far stronger support among Republicans than the made-over moderate Clinton or the southern charmer Edwards? Perhaps because the Republicans and independents who are open to an Obama candidacy see his primary advantage in prosecuting the war on Islamist terrorism. It isn't about his policies as such; it is about his person. They are prepared to set their own ideological preferences to one side in favor of what Obama offers America in a critical moment in our dealings with the rest of the world. The war today matters enormously. The war of the last generation? Not so much. If you are an American who yearns to finally get beyond the symbolic battles of the Boomer generation and face today's actual problems, Obama may be your man.

⤙ • ⤚

What does he offer? First and foremost: his face. Think of it as the most effective potential rebranding of the United States since Reagan. Such a rebranding is not trivial—it's central to an effective war strategy. The war on Islamist terror, after all, is two-pronged: a function of both hard power and soft power. We have seen the potential of hard power in removing the Taliban and Saddam Hussein. We have also seen its inherent weaknesses in Iraq, and its profound limitations in winning a long war against radical Islam. The next president has to create a sophisticated and supple blend of soft and hard power to isolate the enemy, to fight where necessary, but also to create an ideological template that works to the West's advantage over the long haul. There is simply no other candidate with the potential of Obama to do this. Which is where his face comes in.

Consider this hypothetical. It's November 2008. A young Pakistani Muslim is watching television and sees that this man—Barack Hussein Obama—is the new face of America. In one simple image, America's soft power has been ratcheted up not a notch, but a logarithm. A brown-skinned man whose father was an African, who grew up in Indonesia and Hawaii, who attended a majority-Muslim school as a boy, is now the alleged enemy. If you wanted the crudest but most effective weapon against the demonization of America that fuels Islamist ideology, Obama's face gets close. It proves them wrong about what America is in ways no words can.

The other obvious advantage that Obama has in facing the world and our enemies is his record on the Iraq War. He is the only major candidate to have clearly opposed it from the start. Whoever is in office in January 2009 will be tasked with redeploying forces in and out of Iraq, negotiating with neighboring states, engaging America's estranged allies, tamping down regional violence. Obama's interlocutors in Iraq and the Middle East would know that he never had suspicious motives toward Iraq, has no interest in occupying it indefinitely, and foresaw more clearly than most Americans the baleful consequences of long-term occupation.

This latter point is the most salient. The act of picking the next president will be in some ways a statement of America's view of Iraq. Clinton is running as a centrist Democrat—voting for war, accepting the need for an occupation at least through her first term, while attempting to do triage as practically as possible. Obama is running as the clearer antiwar candidate. At the same time, Obama's candidacy cannot fairly be cast as a McGovernite revival in tone or substance. He is not opposed to war as such. He is not opposed to the use of unilateral force, either—as demonstrated by his willingness to target Al Qaeda in Pakistan over the objections of the Pakistani government. He does not oppose the idea of democratization in the Muslim world as a general principle or the concept of nation building as such. He is not an isolationist, as his support for the campaign in Afghanistan proves. It is worth recalling the key passages of the speech Obama gave in Chicago on October 2, 2002, five months before the war:

> I don't oppose all wars. And I know that in this crowd today, there is no shortage of patriots, or of patriotism. What I am opposed to is a dumb war. What I am opposed to is a rash war . . . I know that even a successful war against Iraq will require a U.S. occupation of undetermined length, at undetermined cost, with undetermined consequences. I know that an invasion of Iraq without a clear rationale and without strong international support will only fan the flames of the Middle East, and encourage the worst, rather than best, impulses of the Arab world, and

strengthen the recruitment arm of Al Qaeda. I am not opposed to all wars. I'm opposed to dumb wars.

The man who opposed the war for the right reasons is for that reason the potential president with the most flexibility in dealing with it. Clinton is hemmed in by her past and her generation. If she pulls out too quickly, she will fall prey to the usual browbeating from the right—the same theme that has played relentlessly since 1968. If she stays in too long, the antiwar base of her own party, already suspicious of her, will pounce. The Boomer legacy imprisons her—and so it may continue to imprison us. The debate about the war in the next four years needs to be about the practical and difficult choices ahead of us—not about the symbolism or whether it's a second Vietnam.

A generational divide also separates Clinton and Obama with respect to domestic politics. Clinton grew up saturated in the conflict that still defines American politics. As a liberal, she has spent years in a defensive crouch against triumphant post-Reagan conservatism. The mau-mauing that greeted her health-care plan and the endless nightmares of her husband's scandals drove her deeper into her political bunker. Her liberalism is warped by what you might call a Political Post-Traumatic Stress Syndrome. Reagan spooked people on the left, especially those, like Clinton, who were interested primarily in winning power. She has internalized what most Democrats of her generation have internalized: They suspect that the majority is not with them, and so some quotient of discretion, fear, or plain deception is required if they are to advance their objectives. And so the less-adept ones seem deceptive, and the more-practiced ones, like Clinton, exhibit the plasticness and inauthenticity that still plague her candidacy. She's hiding her true feelings. We know it, she knows we know it, and there is no way out of it.

Obama, simply by virtue of when he was born, is free of this defensiveness. Strictly speaking, he is at the tail end of the Boomer generation. But he is not of it.

"Partly because my mother, you know, was smack-dab in the middle of the Baby Boom generation," he told me. "She was only 18 when she had me. So when I think of Baby Boomers, I think of my mother's generation. And you know, I was too young for the formative period of the '60s—civil rights, sexual revolution, Vietnam War. Those all sort of passed me by."

Obama's mother was, in fact, born only five years earlier than Hillary Clinton. He did not politically come of age during the Vietnam era, and he is simply less afraid of the right wing than Clinton is, because he has emerged on the national stage during a period of conservative decadence and decline. And so, for example, he felt much freer than Clinton to say he was prepared to meet and hold talks with hostile world leaders in his first year in office. He has proposed sweeping middle-class tax cuts and opposed drastic reforms of Social Security, without being tarred as a fiscally reckless liberal. (Of course, such accusations are hard to make after the fiscal performance of today's "conservatives.") Even his more conservative positions—like his openness to bombing Pakistan, or his support for merit pay for public-school teachers—do not appear to emerge from a desire or need to credentialize himself with the right. He is among the first Democrats in a generation not to be afraid or ashamed of what they actually believe, which also gives them more freedom to move pragmatically to the right, if necessary. He does not smell, as Clinton does, of political fear.

There are few areas where this Democratic fear is more intense than religion. The crude exploitation of sectarian loyalty and religious zeal by Bush and Rove succeeded in deepening the culture war, to Republican advantage. Again, this played into the divide of the Boomer years—between God-fearing Americans and the peacenik atheist hippies of lore. The Democrats have responded by pretending to a public religiosity that still seems strained. Listening to Hillary Clinton detail her prayer life in public, as she did last spring to a packed house at George Washington University, was at once poignant and repellent. Poignant because her faith may well be genuine; repellent because its Methodist genuineness demands that she not profess it so tackily. But she did. The polls told her to.

Obama, in contrast, opened his soul up in public long before any focus group demanded it. His first book, *Dreams From My Father,* is a candid, haunting, and supple piece of writing. It was not concocted to solve a political problem (his second, hackneyed book, *The Audacity of Hope,* filled that niche). It was a genuine display of internal doubt and conflict and sadness. And it reveals Obama as someone whose "complex fate," to use Ralph Ellison's term, is to be both believer and doubter, in a world where such complexity is as beleaguered as it is necessary.

This struggle to embrace modernity without abandoning faith falls on one of the fault lines in the modern world. It is arguably the critical fault line, the tectonic rift that is advancing the bloody borders of Islam and the increasingly sectarian boundaries of American politics. As humankind abandons the secular totalitarianisms of the last century and grapples with breakneck technological and scientific discoveries, the appeal of absolutist faith is powerful in

both developing and developed countries. It is the latest in a long line of re-
bukes to liberal modernity—but this rebuke has the deepest roots, the widest
appeal, and the attraction that all total solutions to the human predicament
proffer. From the doctrinal absolutism of Pope Benedict's Vatican to the revival of fundamentalist Protestantism in the U.S. and Asia to the attraction for
many Muslims of the most extreme and antimodern forms of Islam, the same
phenomenon has spread to every culture and place.

You cannot confront the complex challenges of domestic or foreign policy
today unless you understand this gulf and its seriousness. You cannot lead the
United States without having a foot in both the religious and secular camps.
This, surely, is where Bush has failed most profoundly. By aligning himself with
the most extreme and basic of religious orientations, he has lost many moderate believers and alienated the secular and agnostic in the West. If you cannot
bring the agnostics along in a campaign against religious terrorism, you have
a problem.

Here again, Obama, by virtue of generation and accident, bridges this deepening divide. He was brought up in a nonreligious home and converted to
Christianity as an adult. But—critically—he is not born-again. His faith—at
once real and measured, hot and cool—lives at the center of the American religious experience. It is a modern, intellectual Christianity. "I didn't have an
epiphany," he explained to me. "What I really did was to take a set of values and
ideals that were first instilled in me from my mother, who was, as I have called
her in my book, the last of the secular humanists—you know, belief in kindness
and empathy and discipline, responsibility—those kinds of values. And I found
in the Church a vessel or a repository for those values and a way to connect
those values to a larger community and a belief in God and a belief in redemption and mercy and justice . . . I guess the point is, it continues to be both
a spiritual, but also intellectual, journey for me, this issue of faith."

The best speech Obama has ever given was not his famous 2004 convention
address, but a June 2007 speech in Connecticut. In it, he described his religious
conversion:

> One Sunday, I put on one of the few clean jackets I had, and went over
> to Trinity United Church of Christ on 95th Street on the South Side of
> Chicago. And I heard Reverend Jeremiah A. Wright deliver a sermon

called "The Audacity of Hope." And during the course of that sermon, he introduced me to someone named Jesus Christ. I learned that my sins could be redeemed. I learned that those things I was too weak to accomplish myself, he would accomplish with me if I placed my trust in him. And in time, I came to see faith as more than just a comfort to the weary or a hedge against death, but rather as an active, palpable agent in the world and in my own life.

It was because of these newfound understandings that I was finally able to walk down the aisle of Trinity one day and affirm my Christian faith. It came about as a choice and not an epiphany. I didn't fall out in church, as folks sometimes do. The questions I had didn't magically disappear. The skeptical bent of my mind didn't suddenly vanish. But kneeling beneath that cross on the South Side, I felt I heard God's spirit beckoning me. I submitted myself to his will, and dedicated myself to discovering his truth and carrying out his works.

To be able to express this kind of religious conviction without disturbing or alienating the growing phalanx of secular voters, especially on the left, is quite an achievement. As he said in 2006, "Faith doesn't mean that you don't have doubts." To deploy the rhetoric of Evangelicalism while eschewing its occasional anti-intellectualism and hubristic certainty is as rare as it is exhilarating. It is both an intellectual achievement, because Obama has clearly attempted to wrestle a modern Christianity from the encumbrances and anachronisms of its past, and an American achievement, because it was forged in the only American institution where conservative theology and the Democratic Party still communicate: the black church.

And this, of course, is the other element that makes Obama a potentially transformative candidate: race. Here, Obama again finds himself in the center of a complex fate, unwilling to pick sides in a divide that reaches back centuries and appears at times unbridgeable. His appeal to whites is palpable. I have felt it myself. Earlier this fall, I attended an Obama speech in Washington on tax policy that underwhelmed on delivery; his address was wooden, stilted, even tedious. It was only after I left the hotel that it occurred to me that I'd just been bored on tax policy by a national black leader. That I should have been struck by this was born in my own racial stereotypes, of course. But it won me over.

Obama is deeply aware of how he comes across to whites. In a revealing passage in his first book, he recounts how, in adolescence, he defused his white mother's fears that he was drifting into delinquency. She had marched into his room and demanded to know what was going on. He flashed her "a reassuring smile and patted her hand and told her not to worry." This, he tells us, was "usually an effective tactic," because people

> were satisfied as long as you were courteous and smiled and made no sudden moves. They were more than satisfied; they were relieved—such a pleasant surprise to find a well-mannered young black man who didn't seem angry all the time.

And so you have Obama's campaign for white America: courteous and smiling and with no sudden moves. This may, of course, be one reason for his still-lukewarm support among many African Americans, a large number of whom back a white woman for the presidency. It may also be because African Americans (more than many whites) simply don't believe that a black man can win the presidency, and so are leery of wasting their vote. And the persistence of race as a divisive, even explosive factor in American life was unmissable the week of Obama's tax speech. While he was detailing middle-class tax breaks, thousands of activists were preparing to march in Jena, Louisiana, after a series of crude racial incidents had blown up into a polarizing conflict.

Jesse Jackson voiced puzzlement that Obama was not at the forefront of the march. "If I were a candidate, I'd be all over Jena," he remarked. The South Carolina newspaper *The State* reported that Jackson said Obama was "acting like he's white." Obama didn't jump into the fray (no sudden moves), but instead issued measured statements on Jena, waiting till a late-September address at Howard University to find his voice. It was simultaneously an endorsement of black identity politics and a distancing from it:

> When I'm president, we will no longer accept the false choice between being tough on crime and vigilant in our pursuit of justice. Dr. King said: "It's not either/or, it's both/and." We can have a crime policy that's both tough and smart. If you're convicted of a crime involving drugs, of course you should be punished. But let's not make the punishment for crack cocaine that much more severe than the punishment for powder cocaine when the real difference between the two is the skin color of the people using them. Judges think that's wrong. Republicans think that's wrong, Democrats think that's wrong, and yet it's been approved by Republican

and Democratic presidents because no one has been willing to brave the politics and make it right. That will end when I am president.

Obama's racial journey makes this kind of both/and politics something more than a matter of political compromise. The paradox of his candidacy is that, as potentially the first African American president in a country founded on slavery, he has taken pains to downplay the racial catharsis his candidacy implies. He knows race is important, and yet he knows that it turns destructive if it becomes the only important thing. In this he again subverts a Boomer paradigm, of black victimology or black conservatism. He is neither Al Sharpton nor Clarence Thomas; neither Julian Bond nor Colin Powell. Nor is he a post-racial figure like Tiger Woods, insofar as he has spent his life trying to reconnect with a black identity his childhood never gave him. Equally, he cannot be a Jesse Jackson. His white mother brought him up to be someone else.

In *Dreams From My Father,* Obama tells the story of a man with an almost eerily nonracial childhood, who has to learn what racism is, what his own racial identity is, and even what being black in America is. And so Obama's relationship to the black American experience is as much learned as intuitive. He broke up with a serious early girlfriend in part because she was white. He decided to abandon a post-racial career among the upper-middle classes of the East Coast in order to reengage with the black experience of Chicago's South Side. It was an act of integration—personal as well as communal—that called him to the work of community organizing.

This restlessness with where he was, this attempt at personal integration, represents both an affirmation of identity politics and a commitment to carving a unique personal identity out of the race, geography, and class he inherited. It yields an identity born of displacement, not rootedness. And there are times, I confess, when Obama's account of understanding his own racial experience seemed more like that of a gay teen discovering that he lives in two worlds simultaneously than that of a young African American confronting racism for the first time.

And there are also times when Obama's experience feels more like an immigrant story than a black memoir. His autobiography navigates a new and strange world of an American racial legacy that never quite defined him at his core. He therefore speaks to a complicated and mixed identity—not a simple and alienated one. This may hurt him among some African Americans, who may fail to identify with this fellow with an odd name. Black conservatives, like

Shelby Steele, fear he is too deferential to the black establishment. Black leftists worry that he is not beholden at all. But there is no reason why African Americans cannot see the logic of Americanism that Obama also represents, a legacy that is ultimately theirs as well. To be black and white, to have belonged to a nonreligious home and a Christian church, to have attended a majority-Muslim school in Indonesia and a black church in urban Chicago, to be more than one thing and sometimes not fully anything—this is an increasingly common experience for Americans, including many racial minorities. Obama expresses such a conflicted but resilient identity before he even utters a word. And this complexity, with its internal tensions, contradictions, and moods, may increasingly be the main thing all Americans have in common.

None of this, of course, means that Obama will be the president some are dreaming of. His record in high office is sparse; his performances on the campaign trail have been patchy; his chief rival for the nomination, Senator Clinton, has bested him often with her relentless pursuit of the middle ground, her dogged attention to her own failings, and her much-improved speaking skills. At times, she has even managed to appear more inherently likable than the skinny, crabby, and sometimes morose newcomer from Chicago. Clinton's most surprising asset has been the sense of security she instills. Her husband—and the good feelings that nostalgics retain for his presidency—have buttressed her case. In dangerous times, popular majorities often seek the conservative option, broadly understood.

The paradox is that Hillary makes far more sense if you believe that times are actually pretty good. If you believe that America's current crisis is not a deep one, if you think that pragmatism alone will be enough to navigate a world on the verge of even more religious warfare, if you believe that today's ideological polarization is not dangerous, and that what appears dark today is an illusion fostered by the lingering trauma of the Bush presidency, then the argument for Obama is not that strong. Clinton will do. And a Clinton-Giuliani race could be as invigorating as it is utterly predictable.

But if you sense, as I do, that greater danger lies ahead, and that our divisions and recent history have combined to make the American polity and constitutional order increasingly vulnerable, then the calculus of risk changes. Sometimes, when the world is changing rapidly, the greater risk is caution. Close-up in this election campaign, Obama is unlikely. From a distance, he is necessary. At a time when America's estrangement from the world risks tipping into dangerous imbalance, when a country at war with lethal enemies is also increasingly at war with itself, when humankind's spiritual yearnings veer between an excess of certainty and an inability to believe anything at all, and when sectarian and racial divides seem as intractable as ever, a man who is a bridge between these worlds may be indispensable.

We may in fact have finally found that bridge to the twenty-first century that Bill Clinton told us about. Its name is Obama.

2

ONE OF US, PART 2: JOHN McCAIN'S LAST WAR

CHRIS JONES
Esquire   January 2008

In purely theatrical terms, the general election showdown between John McCain and Barack Obama promises to be an epic clash between two distinctive personalities. But the McCain campaign has never been lacking for drama: In the spring of 2007, out of money and with his staff in disarray, McCain's candidacy was declared all but finished by the nation's punditry. Yet somehow, through a combination of personal charm, dogged persistence, and unflagging vision, the former POW not only righted his campaign but went on to outpoll his leading Republican challengers decisively once the actual primary voting began.

No reporter has followed this heroic arc more closely than Chris Jones, who shadowed McCain on the campaign trail for the better part of two years. His 2006 portrait of the very early stages of McCain's presidential bid was featured in last year's edition of this anthology. In this piece, Jones picks up the story in late 2007, on the eve of the New Hampshire primary, when the candidate's fortunes have taken a clear turn for the better.

The bus is new, and so is the driver, and the driver is lost for the second time today; back in Des Moines, Amvets Post 2 had proved elusive as well. Now it's the tiny airport in Waterloo that's hiding somewhere in the corn and the failing light, twice unlucky for the man hollering in the back.

"Come on, let's go," John McCain says after the bus—with NO SURRENDER written across the side of it—gets hung up in the parking lot outside the local

American Legion, the day's last stop, at least in Iowa. He has crossed most of the state with a crusader's zeal, beginning at the crack of crow's piss in the basement VFW in Council Bluffs. That was thirteen hours ago. His bed is still eleven hundred miles away.

"Let's go," he says again. "We've got a long ride ahead of us."

At last, a wind sock hangs limp in the distance. The small plane is waiting nearby. It has ten seats, six of which will be empty. That's how light McCain's packing these days.

He takes his usual place, front right, one of the few remaining comforts of routine, with a newspaper and a magazine folded open to an article titled, "The Sunni Side of the Street." He turns on the reading lamp over his head, the light reflecting off his thin white hair.

Across the aisle from McCain, where political strategist John Weaver or campaign manager Terry Nelson might have been expected to recline, sits long-retired Marine Lieutenant Colonel Orson Swindle, strapping himself in. Forty years ago, McCain stood on Swindle's shoulders to reach one of the Hanoi Hilton's high windows, through which they communicated with other prisoners by way of a flagless semaphore. Now that the campaign has been husked to the core, Swindle has been cast again in his former role of prop. He was introduced as ugly at every stop today—"Marines by nature are pretty ugly, but this is really the ugliest marine I know," McCain said. Each time out, Swindle laughed as though he hadn't heard the line before, and along with the other veterans gathered onstage, the sorts of men and women we once named airports and schools after, he said that John McCain is the man to win us the war in Iraq, and that it's a war we need to win.

For months, mindful of poll results and his staff's urgent pleas, McCain had tried to separate himself and his candidacy from Iraq. He had to get past it, he was told often enough to make his ears bleed. While he would necessarily confess to the failures there, and he would repeat his belief that the consequences of a grander failure would be devastating, McCain dutifully tried to turn the conversation to issues of broader electoral appeal: Social Security and Medicare reform, balanced budgets, overhauling the tax system, reducing our dependence on oil. Only at sunset last night, in an airport hangar in Sioux City, backdropped by flags and bowlegged heroes, was that vain effort decisively abandoned. McCain has decided to ignore the numbers and the whispers—easier now that he has surrounded himself with apparitions—and tie his waning presidential hopes inextricably to America's fate in the Middle East. "I would rather lose a campaign than lose a war," he said today, marshaling what is left of his energy and his resources to rescue twin victories from battles begun so badly.

The plane powers up toward the runway, the generous basket of junk food sitting on the floor dancing a little on the carpet. Which reminds McCain— "Brookey, you can tell them that they don't need to order eight hundred doughnuts every time we're on the bus," he says, turning to look at press secretary Brooke Buchanan, one of five survivors from an office that had been occupied by twenty-five. This morning, a box of doughnuts the size of a crib mattress had shown up on the bus. McCain had lifted his breakfast from it, an apple fritter accompanied by a Styrofoam cup of coffee, but most of the rest of them had gone to waste, and this isn't the kind of campaign that can afford to throw out doughnuts anymore.

"Oh, they came from the event," Buchanan says. "We took those from the event."

But McCain's on a roll, suddenly seeing bridges to nowhere everywhere he looks. "Here's the twenty-seventh version of the schedule," he says, picking up tomorrow's thick manifest. "They must chop down a whole fucking forest every time they make a change. I don't know why they can't just print out one page."

It isn't long before Buchanan plugs in her iPod, dialing up some old-school rap. Apart from Too Short's faint beat and the engines, the plane goes quiet, flying east into an advancing night and Portsmouth, New Hampshire. McCain drifts off. They're restorative, these flights, like the water tables in a marathon. They are also expensive, which means McCain, his money long disappeared into the maw of his dismantled machine, has been forced to fly commercial some of the time. That's resulted in campaign events taking place via speakerphone, when US Airways decides it's not flying from D.C. to Pittsburgh after all, and it's risked McCain running as empty as his bank accounts, without time built in to catch his breath.

He's catching it now. Swindle reads. Buchanan scans tomorrow's schedule, shaking her head.

The other advantage of small planes is that they fly higher than the big ones. At forty-one thousand feet, the horizon just starts to curve, or maybe it only looks as though it does, but on this clear September evening it's beautiful either way, lit ahead by orange cities and behind by the setting sun. Inside small planes, the violet sky seems even more enormous.

McCain stirs. Buchanan worries aloud that he hasn't been eating enough. Apart from this morning's fritter and coffee, he's had a handful of potato chips and a can of Red Bull. (The barbecued chicken that came on board the bus in Des Moines was a shade of salmonella pink that could have derailed the candidate for days.) There are trays of chilled Chinese food stashed up front, fallout-shelter eats that are now dug out and served in plastic boxes on plastic trays. McCain picks at a bit of fruit, chokes back a cold egg roll. "I really don't eat well," he says. "I eat junk. I kinda get pumped up at these things and don't have much of an appetite." He consents to filling the last corner of his stomach with a fortune cookie.

He pulls the slip of paper from the cookie, reads it, and wordlessly passes it back.

The game isn't over until it's over, it reads.

McCain retrieves it and tucks it away. A short time later, the plane touches down in Portsmouth. He thanks the pilots as he ducks out the door. A van waits in the dark to take him to the night's hotel, the Sheraton down by the harbor. No one else is here to greet him.

EIGHT MONTHS AGO

McCain had tried to sleep, largely unsuccessfully, in the same hotel in the same town last April. It was the night before his campaign officially began. Announcement Day was a formality, but for most candidates it was a happy formality. For McCain, it was more a measure of how low he had been laid.

His run had been under way for more than a year, predating the midterm elections of 2006, when McCain was one of the few life rings left for floundering Republicans. Then, the man exuded uptick. While he told reporters that he hadn't made up his mind about what to do with his surging popularity, he was holding fundraisers and building an elaborate organization—even an unstoppable one, he might have hoped. But on this gray morning in Portsmouth, that all felt like such a long time ago. A lot of things, mostly bad, had happened between then and now. He woke up early, looked at the day's manifest, and pulled on a blue sweater, because a consultant had decided that sweaters made him look younger—which is important when you're seventy-one—and because his suit was too wrinkled to wear.

The buds were just breaking on the trees in nearby Prescott Park. The clouds continued rolling in over the harbor, over the Navy shipyard that provided the backdrop for a temporary stage. A band of old men wore Uncle Sam hats and played their banjos and brass; they grew red-cheeked trying to play loud enough to be heard over the rumble of idling TV trucks. A few people were holding homemade signs—VETERANS FOR McCAIN, YOUTH FOR McCAIN, AMERICA NEEDS McCAIN—all of which seemed to have been painted with the same hand. Giant spotlights were being plugged in, a thousand-watt effort to make it look like the sun was finally shining on John McCain.

Back at the hotel, however, he was just finishing up an emergency closed-door meeting of his finance committee. He was always a lousy fundraiser, and the just-announced first-quarter returns had been disappointing, placing him a distant third behind Rudy Giuliani and Mitt Romney. Worse, the $12.5 million he had collected was already spent and then some—the hundred-strong team of consultants and strategists that had been assembled, most of them veterans of the George W. Bush campaigns, was now running on McCain-style financial fumes.

Team was a word used only loosely by then. From the beginning of this, his second stab at the presidency, McCain had deemed it wise to divide the money from the politics, church and state. On one side sat Rick Davis, the campaign's chief executive officer; on the other sat Terry Nelson, the former Bush operative, and John Weaver, the lanky, laconic Texan who years earlier had first convinced McCain that he should run for president, scrawling a platform on the back of a napkin. For a long time the two sides had seemed to act in opposition to each other as often as they acted in concert. Now they weren't talking to each other at all.

Early on, Davis had projected the campaign would take in more than $100 million over the year, which was proving a wildly optimistic forecast. Some national polls placed McCain as far back as third, behind actor and then-undeclared candidate Fred Thompson and Giuliani. He was also tracking poorly with independents, the powerful swing voters who had staked him to a nineteen-point win over Bush in the New Hampshire primary in 2000. Somewhere along the way, McCain had lost his grip on underdog hearts. Week by painful week, he looked less like a straight-shooting maverick and more like the old company man, the bank robber suddenly become the bank.

Except now the bank was empty. Nelson and Weaver felt that Davis had made their job impossible: How do you map out a campaign strategy when you don't know how much money you have to spend? Davis blamed Nelson and Weaver, arguing that their mismanagement of McCain's political image had made it hard to raise enough money, and privately he told McCain as much.

In 2000, the senator had been sunk in the end by the perception, especially among religious conservatives, that he was a Republican of convenience. The bipartisanship that McCain had trumpeted as the only way to get things done in Washington had made him look too willing to compromise, casting him in a traitor's light. Later, to restore his reputation as a good soldier, McCain decided to swallow his pride and align himself strongly with the new president, including cosponsoring a Senate bill authorizing the war in Iraq. Although McCain couldn't help criticizing Bush's strategy as being short on troops and foresight—a recipe for a new Vietnam—he was careful to pin most of the blame on Donald Rumsfeld, a man even Republicans found easy to loathe. Through every botch and casualty, he remained steadfast in his public support of the president. McCain soon found himself the last man standing.

That would cost him, and he knew it. "But I don't worry about it," he said time and again. "There are far too many brave young Americans who have sacrificed too much for my political ambitions to be impacted by the popularity or the unpopularity of the war."

McCain might have survived that unpopularity—trading independents for base Republicans—except that next he called up rival and friend Ted Kennedy to talk about the snag of twelve million illegal immigrants in this country, and together they created a path for what they called earned citizenship and what some others called amnesty, and together they posed for pictures after the first successful cloture vote in the Senate, and together they climbed into an elevator and exhaled, weary with adrenaline, and alone McCain stepped out of that elevator and into an almighty, wind-driven shitstorm.

"We knew it would be a minefield, but boy howdy," Weaver says today. "We might have been overly optimistic that we could have tiptoed our way through it."

Just like that, the man whose greatest political gift was his ability to be all things to all people had pulled a nearly impossible trick: He had given everybody a reason to hate him. To the Left and Center, he was a Bush flunky and a war pig. To the Right, he was a lover of Mexicans and Kennedys.

Very few politicians can make a run based on today. They're running either on their histories or on our futures. But when his Straight Talk Express finally eased up a narrow lane into Prescott Park and the bus doors opened, John McCain found himself confronted with banjo-and-brass music and an unflattering present.

Wearing his blue sweater, he walked to the stage with his wife, Cindy, who was dressed in pink, and stumbled into his announcement speech. It had been written days earlier by Mark Salter, his Senate chief of staff and the man most responsible for McCain's public voice: a Lincoln-esque brand of rhetoric

packed with adverbs and echoes. This time, McCain tripped over the refrain—
"That's not good enough for America, and when I'm president, it won't be
good enough for me"—because the teleprompter that loomed behind the
crowd was nearly impossible to read from the stage. It was washed out by the
spotlights.

That, plus the acrimonious finance-committee meeting (it was decided that
the money would eventually come in, so the money would keep going out),
plus a nagging cold, plus the darkening skies, as well as McCain's growing feeling that he couldn't get a straight answer about anything from anybody—all of
it left him in one of those sour moods that had saddled him with a reputation
for temper. So many goddamn people around him, and no one thought to keep
his jacket pressed.

When he surrendered to a media scrum beside the bus, the last of his optimism looked squeezed out by the crush. The opening questions were about
Iraq and immigration, the issues that closed in on him like the halves of a vise.
He answered them as he had been prepared to answer them, interrupted twice
by the ringing of a cell phone on the belt of a cameraman kneeling beside him.
Then someone shouted out the start of another line of questioning: "How do
you get connected—"

"I'm already connected," McCain cut him off. "I'm already connected."

"But there seems to be a lack of enthusiasm for your candidacy. . . ."

"I haven't detected that myself. Congratulations."

And then the cameraman's phone rang for a third time—"Shall we sing
along?" said McCain, looking down at him—and then the phone rang again.

McCain measured his words. "That's your last chance," he said, and though
he managed to follow the threat with a smile, it was the sort of smile that stops
watches.

Following a short, tense drive to Concord, he headed into the Courtyard
Marriott. There, McCain went upstairs alone for a phone interview with Sean
Hannity, wondering aloud why he was reduced to radio instead of TV.

Salter filled the wait with a cigarette in the parking lot. Weaver was on his
phone, across the lobby from Cindy McCain, who stood despite a number of
empty chairs, as though if she sat down, she wasn't getting up again. She's never
been much for joining her husband on the road, and she looked like a woman
who was at the start of a long trip that she hadn't looked forward to taking.
There had been rumors in the capital, in fact, that she might even deliver one
of those cinematic it's-me-or-the-presidency ultimatums, but here she was, the

beer heiress in pearls, standing in a Courtyard Marriott in Concord, New Hampshire, watching the rain start to fall.

McCain came back downstairs and everyone returned to the bus, a splashy set of wheels with flat-screen TVs, blue leather captain's chairs, and a stainless-steel fridge and microwave in the kitchen. McCain took his customary seat, in the middle of the horseshoe in back, surrounded by reporters.

"Are we doing an out-of-doors event?" he shouted at the front of the bus, and he made a face when the wrong answer came back.

"Yeah, we'll have to fire the entire incompetent campaign staff," he said. "I'm sure I'll find many people to blame for this besides me."

SEVEN MONTHS AGO

He was in Las Vegas in early May. McCain had been looking forward to this trip for a long time. He was holding ringside tickets for the fight between Oscar De La Hoya and Floyd Mayweather at the MGM Grand on Cinco de Mayo. Cindy McCain and their youngest son, nineteen-year-old Jimmy, were flying up from Phoenix to meet him. Jimmy, a newly minted marine, was about to become the fourth generation of McCains delivered unto war. Las Vegas was part of John McCain's extended goodbye to his son. Originally, the evening's schedule was going to be clear—for one night, McCain wasn't going to be a presidential candidate or a senator; he was just going to be a husband and a father and a fight fan. But the continuing campaign budget crisis forced him to squeeze in a fundraiser beforehand at a casino nightclub called Tabú.

A reporter for the *Los Angeles Times* waited among the slot machines, hoping to ask McCain something about tribal land rights, but the senator wasn't in the mood for heaviness and was slipped through Tabú's back entrance. The nightclub was fashionably dark, with low concrete tables and big-titted waitresses dressed in black, serving lobster canapés to the guests, most of whom were comparing how good their four-figure seats were for the fight.

McCain was in such a good, backslapping humor that he didn't seem to mind having to go to work. He was buoyed by a well-reviewed performance in the first Republican debate two nights before. Improving poll numbers gave him further bounce, showing slim-to-substantial leads in all four of the early-voting states: New Hampshire, Iowa, South Carolina, and Nevada. But he was especially excited about the fight ("My heart is with De La Hoya, my head is with Mayweather") and getting the chance to spend some time with Jimmy, a light of a kid. It's chilling how much he looks like his old man, or at least how his old man used to look. White teeth, short back and sides, his slight frame wrapped in a well-cut suit, he worked the crowd like a professional. He has told friends, however, that he has no desire for a future in politics. What does it say when a son wants to follow his father into the first of his arenas but not into the second? It was hard enough to imagine that a senator's son had chosen such a dangerous path through life, kicking up the same awful fears of folded flags that every deployed soldier leaves in his wake.

Jimmy's service is the lone subject about which McCain will not answer questions—"We're proud of all our kids, is what we say." He has another son, Jack, who is a midshipman at the Naval Academy, like his father and grandfather and great-grandfather before him. McCain will talk about Jack, because Jack is safe in Annapolis. But McCain will not talk about Jimmy, whose imminent departure represented one of those rare instances when a family's and a nation's dramas unfolded on the same front line. Not since Adlai Stevenson had a presidential candidate seen his son off to war.

For the McCains, though, there had been a quiet feeling that a night such as this was inevitable, and that feeling seemed to have taken some of the nerves out of it, as though together they have been pulled toward this destiny the way the tides follow the moon. Cindy McCain has said that she would have liked for Jimmy to go to college before enlisting, but Jimmy was determined to follow his older brother into the military. Once he became Private First Class McCain—graduating in San Diego, watched by his father with pride—he reportedly signed up for infantry duty, which increased his chances of seeing combat. Those chances became a virtual lock when John McCain succeeded in his efforts to have more troops sent to Iraq, the burden of war now shared, as it had been twice before, between a McCain father and a McCain son.

Admiral John McCain Jr., who commanded Pacific forces during Vietnam, had ordered massive air strikes on Hanoi when McCain was imprisoned there. And now, with Jimmy standing in the crowd and only weeks away from deployment, John McCain kept secret whatever he had said to him in their suite on the twenty-first floor, and instead he climbed onto one of Tabú's concrete tables and said, "We can win this fight," never mentioning that it would soon include his son.

He shook some hands and posed for some pictures and was finally bundled with his family into the back of one of the MGM Grand's house limousines. The chauffeur pulled into the heavy fight traffic headed for the arena, and in the back of that car, in his own way, McCain prepared himself and his son for what awaited them. Suddenly, in the midst of so much bustle, they were alone. "This is something you'll never forget," McCain said to Jimmy, his hand on his knee. "This will be the most exciting thing you've ever seen."

The limo pulled up to a service entrance. Accompanied by a couple of heavy-weight-sized cops, McCain and company walked through the endless underground tunnels toward ringside. On the way, they ran into boxers Shane Mosley and Bernard Hopkins, business partners of De La Hoya's. McCain, his face lit up in a way it rarely is anymore by celebrity, introduced them to Jimmy like school friends. "When you're mediocre at something, you really admire the people who can do it well," he said later, referring to his own inglorious military boxing career. Now, nearing the light and sound of the arena bowl at the end of one last length of tunnel, he looked suddenly boyish. John McCain always walks fast, and Jimmy does, too, in the same perpetual hurry. That night, there really was no holding them back.

McCain emerged at the foot of the crowd, between the floor seats and the bleachers, and the cops hustled to get between him and the other fans. "No, no, that's all right," he said, stepping out from behind his protectors. "These are nice people." He shook hands on the way to his row of seats. Ron Howard and Brian Grazer sat nearby; they waved, and McCain waved back. Over there sat Will Ferrell, and Jim Carrey, and Jack Nicholson. Like every fight, the circus was as big a part of it as the blood.

Cindy was planning to take Jimmy to Caesars Palace for a nightcap afterward, but this part of the evening was between the boys. Along with the rest of the crowd, they stood and cheered when the boxers climbed up through the ropes and rolled their shoulders, and they stayed standing for the anthem and through the introductions, the electricity building, the pressure mounting, John McCain smiling at Jimmy—"Didn't I tell you?"—and Jimmy smiling back, both of them clapping and cheering, lost in the moment, anxious for the sound of the bell and the start of the fight.

FIVE MONTHS AGO

McCain had just returned from a trip to Iraq when, on the morning of Monday, July 9, he asked to meet with Terry Nelson and John Weaver. Both men thought it was going to be a strategy session, "how we could move forward." Instead, McCain erupted—"ranting, ranting, ranting," according to one aide. May's recovery had proved short-lived. The second-quarter fundraising returns were worse than the first. The immigration bill had been voted down several days before, yet the backlash was continuing unabated. ("We had told him, Just because there's a saloon fight going on doesn't mean you have to pick up a chair," Weaver says. "But that's not his nature.") He was tired of hearing about poll results and being told how he needed to distance himself from the war. And the campaign apparatus had seized to a virtual halt. It was so ugly, Rick Davis wouldn't come into the office anymore. There was even heated talk of calling it quits.

Weaver and Nelson fought back, arguing that the twin-towered campaign structure was too cumbersome for them to succeed. "The process was completely flawed," Weaver says. "Terry had done a great job for John. Unfortunately, he wasn't actually given the tools to be the campaign manager." Although all three men were close friends as well as political allies—years earlier, when Weaver was battling an apparently incurable cancer, McCain flew him and his daughter out to Arizona for a moving farewell supper—they shouted at one another until they were hoarse. "With that, I have work to do," Weaver said and slammed the door behind him.

That evening, McCain and Weaver spoke on the phone. "I thought it was a good conversation," Weaver says. "I told him I didn't want to have any more arguments." It was the last time they would speak.

The following morning, Tuesday, Weaver had fallen sick with the flu and was flat on his back in bed. His cell phone, which hadn't stopped ringing since shortly after dawn, finally coaxed him up. It was Mark Salter. McCain had come into the office at seven o'clock that morning and announced that he was replacing Terry Nelson with Rick Davis. Around the same time, Nelson, after a night of reflection, had submitted his letter of resignation. Whether he had quit or was fired was a question of minutes.

"What are you going to do?" Salter asked.

Only the week before, Weaver had moved from New York to D.C., gearing up for the meat of the campaign; "So much for being a visionary," he says. By a little after eleven o'clock that morning, Weaver had cleared out his office and said his goodbyes. "It's a sad story, there's no other way around it," Weaver says. "It wasn't an easy decision. I had a twelve-year relationship with John. I love the man, and he really does put his country first. But at the end of the day, you have to do what you think is right."

Weaver wasn't the only one who decided it was time to go. Reed Galen, McCain's deputy campaign manager, and Rob Jesmer, the campaign's political director, left later that same day. Mark Salter—who had cowritten each of

McCain's best-selling books as well as his speeches and was one of the principal architects of his political career—thought about leaving; instead, he remained in the Senate office and resigned his paid position with the campaign. Most of the crack press office—Brian Jones, Matt David, Danny Diaz—and dozens of other staff members followed.

McCain was taken aback by the scope of defection. The collapse became the talk of Washington, bringing to mind Edmund Muskie or Gary Hart. Even Bill Clinton was awed enough to weigh in: "John McCain was not well served by the people working for him," the former president said.

In response, McCain obeyed his nature and picked up a chair. "My first answer is, I did not know that President Clinton was well connected with my campaign. I had no idea that he was so intimately familiar with my campaign. My second answer is, It's my responsibility and nobody else's."

On the Senate floor that same afternoon, McCain kept railing, chiding his fellow senators about Iraq. "A lot of us are not driven by polls," he said. "A lot of us are driven by principle. And a lot of us do what is right, no matter what the polls say!"

As his voice continued to rise, he sounded more and more like a man who had grown tired of speaking to deaf ears.

NOW

John McCain greets this autumn morning from his bed at the Sheraton in Portsmouth, New Hampshire, the same hotel in the same town he has gone to sleep in and woken up in so many times before, but today there's no call for spotlights. It really is sunny outside. He climbs on board the bus—no longer the luxurious, expensive Straight Talk Express, a shabbier ride, beat-up and worn, adorned only with a McCain banner strung up in the rear window. "Frankly, I don't relish it," he says of the loss of his front-runner status. But despite his protestations, this seems to be how he likes it best of all, John McCain and a couple of old buddies—"Morning, Orson!"—and a seat in the back, shrugged free of the demands of the machine, carried on down the road instead by pink chicken and fortunes in cookies: *The game isn't over until it's over.*

"I still believe I can out-campaign anybody," he says, sounding more motivated than he has sounded in months, motivated by anger, motivated by war. Portsmouth to Rochester, Rochester to Franklin, Franklin to Concord, Concord to Hudson, Hudson to Nashua, and at every stop, before big crowds and small,

McCain grips the microphone and makes a few jokes—"I tried to enlist in the marines, but my parents were married"—before he lifts himself out of this small VFW or that smoky Legion Hall and launches into his practiced, impassioned plea.

"I think it's pretty obvious the American people ran out of patience," he says, referring to the first of his wars. "And we did pay a price for our failure. We're friends with the Vietnamese now, but we shouldn't forget that thousands were executed, hundreds of thousands were put in reeducation camps, I don't know how many fled on boats, died at sea. And in Cambodia, there was a genocide of incredible consequences. We have a tendency to forget that. But the Vietnamese never said we're going to follow them home. They had no radical extremist cause that they thought was part of the struggle between them and us. That's the difference. . . . I want us out, too, but I want us out with honor. And as terrible as the consequences of failure in Vietnam were, I don't think they are as consequential as failure in Iraq."

Whenever he talks like this, McCain almost always looks down at his right wrist, not because it's partially frozen by the wounds that war inflicted on him but because around it is a bracelet, about as thick as a ruler, with a photograph of a young soldier on it. Next to it is written:

SPC MATTHEW J. STANLEY.
ARMY 12/16/06
WOLFEBORO FALLS, NH.

The date is the day Stanley, twenty-two and newly married, was killed by a roadside bomb in Iraq. McCain was given the bracelet by Stanley's shaken mother, Lynn Savage, who took it off her wrist at a New Hampshire campaign stop a few months ago and put it on his. Today, she has joined him on the bus, and it's her turn to tell a war story, her voice trembling only a little.

"I thought maybe, if I just offered the bracelet, he might take it and remember the reason why we need to finish what we're doing and not let my son die in vain and not let thousands of others die in vain. . . . I just wanted it to be a gesture, to connect with him, so that he would understand. I'm sure he had friends who were killed during the war and he might know what their parents went through. And I thought maybe it would just be a connection, and it really was—he was very emotional when I gave it to him. That wasn't my intention. But as long as it remains a reminder for him to honor my son and all the other soldiers who have fallen, it's a wonderful thing. Never let the memories die, that's so important."

And then she will stop and smile a thin, sad smile.

This is what's left for John McCain, the man and the message stripped down to the base coat. Instead of trying to be all things to all people, he's trying to be one or two things for just a few, and maybe enough of them will hear him and think well of him for it. He's run out of the time and the money and the love that allows a man to speak of beginnings. He's finally realized that beginnings are a young man's game.

Now, like most old men, he's become obsessed with how the story will end.

After another fifty miles, after another meandering, mirthful conversation in the back of the bus, he shouts up front how long we have until the next stop.

"Twenty minutes? Oh, my God."

But the truth is, he would like to stay on this beat-up bus forever. He knows too well what will happen when it stops. "I talk to Bob Dole," he says, his voice quiet as a lake. "I was with him the last two weeks of his campaign, constantly. One of the things that was very moving—and admittedly, he didn't give great speeches and I understand that—but you'd see in the crowd these older men with the crossed skis, the 10th Mountain Division hats on. And after the speech you'd kind of see Bob go over and they'd come over, and it was fascinating to see that. It was very touching to see that. It makes me emotional even now when I think about it."

Suddenly, McCain smiles his own thin, sad smile, and his eyes brim with tears.

He has rarely attended his own military reunions; when he has, he says, he could pick out the guys who had retired by how much closer they seemed to death. Maybe that's why he's always looked ahead, always pushed forward, always tried to sell us on our futures and never on his past. Until now—until now, he never dwelled much on history, partly because he has so much of it to get lost in, mostly because he wanted to seem strong and vigorous. But now he wants to remember, and he would like for you to remember, too.

Forty years ago, John McCain was filmed in black and white, wrapped in a body cast and smoking what might have been his last cigarette. This footage was little seen until what's left of his staff—Rick Davis, Brooke Buchanan, everything cut back to the bone—convinced him it was finally time to play that card in an ad called Courageous Service. ("I'm slightly embarrassed by it," McCain says.) There he lies, all of thirty-one, interrogated by an invisible man with an Indo-French accent—What is your name, what is your rank, where were you educated, what is your official number? . . . "Six-two-four," McCain says, his smoke burning down, "seven-eight-seven." And then the screen fades to black.

The clip is powerful, because the John McCain we know today seems so far removed from that John McCain. It speaks of such long journeys. There's a subtler message hidden behind it as well: It serves to remind us, gently, that after he refused early release, he spent more time in a Vietnamese prison camp than America has spent in Iraq—that old men, and old soldiers especially, use a different abacus when making sums out of sacrifice.

Portsmouth to Rochester, Rochester to Franklin, Franklin to Concord, Concord to Hudson, Hudson to Nashua, again and again, as though on a loop, until the roads are so familiar, the memories are all you have left: John McCain would like to remind you that he nearly gave his life in service of this country; that his father and grandfather served it yesterday and that his sons are serving it today; that only seven years ago he was maverick John McCain, straight-talking John McCain, underdog John McCain; that in time measured by months rather than years, he was exactly the sort of man that many of you wished to see become the president of the United States; and that he's still out here, fighting the last big fight of his life.

3

ONE OF US, PART 3: TWO NIGHTS . . .

CHRIS JONES
Esquire   April 2008

This piece, which appeared in Esquire *three months after the preceding selection, completes Chris Jones's "One of Us" series—a trilogy profiling the soap opera–like course of John McCain's campaign for the White House. Part 1, which appeared in* The Best American Political Writing 2007, *was a portrait of the old warrior in the electoral wilderness, trying to convince people that his candidacy was for real. Part 2, on page 18, is a stirring tale of the death and rebirth of McCain's presidential hopes. In Part 3, Jones provides an eyewitness account of two key days during which those hopes became reality—and McCain found himself transformed virtually overnight from a self-styled maverick on the fringes of the Republican Party into the man who will carry the GOP's standard into the general election this November.*

They all gathered at the front of the big new plane, John McCain and his ever-expanding circle of friends and advisors, Senator Joe Lieberman of Connecticut and Governor Charlie Crist of Florida now among them, and they leaned in and listened to strategist Steve Schmidt, who was receiving the first waves of exit-poll results through his BlackBerry. It was only just past two o'clock in the afternoon on the tarmac in San Diego, but on this far-reaching day, February 5—Super Tuesday—states in the East and the Southeast were closer to calling it a night. And night was what everyone wanted to see, this night especially, maybe the night—don't even say it—that would witness the final transfiguration of McCain from perpetual outlier to the face of his party, the chosen one. The mood among McCain's entourage had been upbeat during a predawn rally in New York City and on the long cross-country flight, but now faces fell a little, and the conversation seemed intense, even anxious. A few photographers were snapping pictures of the huddle from their seats in the back. They were asked to stop. On such an open and accessible campaign, the sudden blackout raised goosebumps.

Whispers began running down the plane's aisle, growing less hushed the farther back they got. It wasn't that Mitt Romney had mounted a last-ditch recovery, which was everyone's first guess. (Although the early numbers showed McCain holding only a slim lead over Romney in his home state of Arizona, which was unthinkable.) It was that Mike Huckabee, the guy everyone had taken their eyes off of, now looked like he was making a break up the middle.

There had been an early sign that Huckabee would do better than expected, and there had been an early sign that McCain and his people were just fine about that. The plane had been chartered from JetBlue to accommodate the nearly one hundred passengers—when only months before, McCain's manifests had been reduced to four names, including his—and the TVs in the backs of the seats flashed with the news that Huckabee had surprised Romney with a win in West Virginia. There were cheers.

"We heart Huck on this plane," said Mark Salter, McCain's senior advisor and speechwriter.

They heart Huck, because they hate Romney.

It had taken time for McCain's simmering dislike of the man, stemming from an eight-year-old dispute over federal funding for the Salt Lake City Olympics, to boil over into debate spats and, finally, pitched public battles. McCain had pledged in the beginning to run a positive campaign, and, mindful of his reputation for temper, he had done his best to keep quiet, demonstrating a sometimes impressive discipline. Way back in summer-warm Iowa, he had been asked whether he wanted to comment on Romney's misfire about his five sons serving the country by helping him run for president—McCain's youngest son, Jimmy, is a marine serving in Iraq—and McCain answered only by shaking his head. Now, though, there was plenty to be said.

McCain had started the flight from New York to San Diego by asking, through the gathered press, for Romney to apologize for slighting Bob Dole, a man for whom McCain feels something like love. Dole had written a letter to Rush Limbaugh praising McCain; Romney had said that Dole was the last person he'd want writing a letter on his behalf. "It was totally inappropriate to make the comments that he did about one of the great war heroes in America," McCain said.

Salter was more pointed: "Let me tell you exactly where it's coming from. Mitt Romney is all about Mitt Romney, and nobody else. Maybe the five little Mitts. But nobody else. And so I think McCain sees something like that—who is that guy to take a shot at this guy?"

And as the day progressed, and the nerves grew taut, and the hours wore on, McCain steamed and stewed and finally said to himself, Fuck it—or fuck that guy, at least—and let the waves crash over the wall.

"He's taken at least two positions on every issue," he said.

A little later: "I just happened to see polling, I defeat both Senator Clinton and Senator Obama in a general-election matchup. Governor Romney's way down."

And after word came through that Romney accused McCain of backroom shenanigans in West Virginia, vaulting Huckabee to his surprise triumph: "Rather than blaming it on someone else, I'd suggest that he move on."

But now the plane lifted off from balmy San Diego for the short hop to Phoenix, celebrations planned, the ballroom at the Biltmore and the band booked and waiting, and here these nervous men huddled, fearing that as much as Romney had been damaged by McCain's stepped-up attacks over the previous days and weeks, perhaps it had been Huckabee, not McCain, who had benefited. To a point, that was okay—it was okay for Huckabee to win West Virginia. And he's a nice guy; let him have Arkansas. He was always going to win Arkansas.

Then came the first whoopsie reports out of Alabama, Georgia, and Tennessee—all Huck, Huck, Huck, the guy McCain liked, the guy who didn't fuel his angry engine—followed by the specter of Arizona falling, and suddenly it felt as though the plane would never touch down and the sun would never set.

⤙ • ⤚

It had felt just like that twenty-eight days ago, January 8, on that last afternoon in New Hampshire. McCain was leading in more polls than not that day, but everybody was saying it was too close to call. He'd bet his *whole* candidacy on the results of the night ahead; the afternoon was the part that everyone wanted to make disappear with a snap of their fingers. Instead, it could only be blurred with drinks and cigarettes and restless sleep on lobby couches, phone calls and hasty e-mails, lunches in the hotel bar that everybody ordered but nobody ate. On a day that represented the beginning and the end of all things, they were trapped in this awful, never-ending middle.

Eight years ago, the New Hampshire primary had marked the start of John McCain's rise, when he made up for his lack of money and lack of audience versus George W. Bush by campaigning for president door-to-door, eventually winning by 19 points. Then, he sometimes held five town-hall meetings in a day, trying to bribe folks to come inside with offers of free ice cream and still talking to empty rooms. This time around, when he saw lame-duck candidate Duncan Hunter, a congressman from California, shivering on a street corner in Manchester, reduced to waving at passing cars, McCain didn't point and laugh through the tinted windows of the Straight Talk Express. McCain knows too well how it feels to be the guy everybody else makes fun of. He didn't even have to cast back eight years to remember.

Only last July, when his once-unstoppable-seeming campaign machinery broke down and then finally collapsed, McCain had been that man on the street corner. He'd been ready to give up the ghost, because while McCain is proud, his pride is more weapon than armor. For a man who has been in uniform since he was eighteen and in politics since 1982, he can show a surprising capacity for being wounded.

One of the people who did leave the campaign then was John Weaver, McCain's longtime strategist and friend. Weaver combed McCain's hair and brushed off his jacket, because the man with the broken shoulders could not do those things for himself, and it was his defection that hurt McCain the most. "I have not talked to John in some time," McCain said in January, and he wouldn't say much more than that. The truth is, Weaver has tried to reconcile, but McCain has not answered or returned his calls. For a lot of people still out on the trail, that bitterness has cast a kind of shadow over everything. For McCain, that bitterness is gas in the tanks.

He says that he was spurred to continue his dying campaign by a reenlistment ceremony for almost six hundred soldiers in Baghdad on the Fourth of July, which he attended with one of his staunchest political allies, Senator Lindsey Graham of South Carolina. Another 161 green-card soldiers were set to receive their citizenship that day; only 159 did, because two were killed in action the previous month, dying for a country that hadn't yet awarded them a passport. Aside from coloring McCain's take on the illegal-immigration debate, the ceremony also gave him a kick in the ass. "Lindsey and I were talking," McCain said, remembering their long flight home, "and I said, We've gotta stick with this. It was very moving to see those young people willing to fight like that."

"It was one of the most moving experiences of my life," Graham said. "I know that really invigorated him."

But so, too, did the feeling that most of his own troops had abandoned him, this general without an army. McCain was ruthless in stripping what remained of his campaign staff to the core—"We knew who our friends were," Graham said—and he went on the attack, pinning what remained of his hopes on this wedge of a place, New Hampshire, which had proved so receptive to him and his ground game before.

It was a good strategy, and with McCain's limited resources, it was probably his only strategy. But it was also risky: Lose New Hampshire, lose the war.

So on the day before the primary, the tension in the back of the bus weighed heavy. This was it, and everybody knew it, and McCain was feeling nostalgic as well as nervous. He talked about the past, and he asked his staff to mirror, as closely as possible, the final day of his campaign eight years earlier. He held his one-hundredth town hall in Peterborough, where he had first dished out ice cream. He made stops in the same cities—Keene, Hanover, Concord—he had stopped in last time around, ending each of his speeches by saying, "I will never let you down," perhaps one last jab at the people who had left him for dead months earlier. Now he listened to the crowds cheering, and he remembered. He wanted so badly to remember that he made the bus stop in Portsmouth in the dark—Portsmouth, where he had held his final event in 2000 and now did again. He slept in the same hotel room, the Presidential Suite on the eighth floor of the Crowne Plaza in Nashua. The next day, he pulled on the same green sweater he had worn back then; he jingled the pennies in his pocket that he had picked up over the course of the previous week, but only if he spied them heads up; he checked the weather and was heartened that there would be drizzle in the northern part of the state, because rain had been good luck for him on Election Day.

So was watching a movie, and Cindy McCain was busy downloading a couple of his favorites for him, *Viva Zapata!* and *A Fish Called Wanda,* and he was happy about that. He was also buoyed by the midnight reports out of Dixville Notch, the remote village in the northeast corner of the state, whose seventeen voters were the first to report their primary results. He had lost there in 2000; this time, he beat Romney four to two. "A landslide," he called it, but when someone joked that it was a harbinger, he shushed them. "I'm superstitious about that, too," he told them.

Later that morning, McCain asked to go to Broad Street Elementary School, the same polling station he had visited on primary day in 2000. There, in that parking lot bordered by snowbanks, was everything that this day meant at once.

He was encouraged by the size of the crowd that engulfed him as soon as he stepped off the bus, the reporters and the voters, and their reaction to him, men reaching out their hands and women in tears. Romney had stopped by the school only minutes before, and you could have heard the snowflakes falling. He might pull this off yet. Either way, there was the sense that what this journey had been—this rollicking, old-style campaign with beat-up buses and boxes of doughnuts and 101 town halls—was finished. Even success would mean the death of something.

Back on the bus one last time, back to the Crowne Plaza, this is how the ride ended: Someone asked what question might make McCain cry, a reference to Hillary Clinton's quasi-breakdown in a diner the previous day. "How about," McCain started, "the kind of staffing that's the greatest albatross around my neck—" And here, McCain stopped and looked up at Brooke Buchanan, his long-suffering press secretary, whose jeans were falling off her, she had worked herself so thin, and then, good-naturedly but perhaps not generously to Hillary or Brooke, he put his face in his hands and feigned a good weep. "I don't know how I've been able to carry this campaign on my shoulders," he said. That was the end of New Hampshire by bus, and the start of that long afternoon.

McCain went upstairs and watched a movie and took a nap. Mark Salter pulled a table and a chair outside and sat in the sun, smoking cigarettes and writing the speech (victorious version only) that McCain would give in just a few hours. The first exit-poll results started coming in around five o'clock, and they showed him with a 5-point lead, maybe 6. The hotel lobby began to hum. In the adjacent ballroom, a man filled plastic bags with confetti.

Up in McCain's hotel suite, Cindy and their daughters Meghan and Bridget got dressed for the big night. Plates of ribs and vegetable platters were spread out on the coffee table, but McCain didn't eat much. Instead, he practiced his speech for Salter. That was the first time McCain allowed himself to claim out loud the victory he so desperately needed.

He remained nervous, though, even then. There was so much at stake, and there were so many people in New Hampshire who were undecided on his fate—McCain hated that word, *undecided*—that he still feared a jinx. And how many of his beloved independents would be lured away by Obama and into the Democratic primary instead? Until the hard numbers come in, there's really only hope and these weird, electric crackles in the air. McCain watched the news reports and tugged on a lucky rubber band that he kept around his left wrist. Salter went downstairs for another smoke.

Then, at 8:21 P.M., minutes after the polls closed, the Associated Press called it: New Hampshire for McCain. Salter butted out his cigarette and bucked it for the elevators. In the time it took to make that short dash through the hotel, Fox News called it, too, and the TVs in the lobby were obscured by raised hands and cheering. "Unbelievable, dude," Salter shouted over the noise. "The greatest political comeback in my lifetime."

Upstairs there was celebration, too, but it wasn't as raucous as downstairs. It was prideful. Now McCain was in a dark suit instead of his lucky green sweater, and he had Salter's speech rolled up in his hands, and between glances at it, he watched the TV and allowed himself his version of beaming. Lindsey Graham was there—"2008 fits John and what he has to offer like 1980 fit Reagan, that's what it comes down to," he said—and former senator Phil Gramm was there, and Cindy and the kids, and Salter and Mike Dennehy and Rick Davis and Brooke Buchanan, what was left of his once hundred-strong staff. There were whoops and hugs and handshakes, but they also spent a lot of time just looking at one another and shaking their heads: How did we get here from there?

Huckabee called, and McCain retreated into the bathroom to accept his congratulations. Romney called, too, and McCain took that call in the bedroom.

"Romney's conceded," Davis said, emerging.

"It's not the concession we want," Gramm said.

"It's good enough for tonight."

Now McCain had only to wait until the other candidates spoke to rooms cast in defeat before he could join the party downstairs. "These people have been so good to us," he said, almost marveling. "Twice."

At last, Romney came on the TV.

"Romney's going to speak here, so we better turn that down, Cindy," McCain said, pointing at the TV, but she didn't hear him, and no one else did, either.

"It will be interesting, Ron Paul bringing in third here—I would just turn that down," McCain said again, and again no one heard him.

"Another silver," Romney said.

McCain looked like he was going to throw up into the plant beside him. "That's why I wanted to turn it down," he said.

And that was the moment. That was when it happened, this great turning of prospects and moods and tactics. McCain gritted his teeth and forgot about New Hampshire, forgot about Huckabee, forgot about the beginning and the middle and saw only the end, and he found suddenly that he had all the more gas in the tanks.

◂◂ • ▸▸

McCain needed it, too, every last drop, to carry him through a disappointing loss to Romney in Michigan—"We didn't mind a fight," he said after—to a narrow win in South Carolina and to a wider win in Florida, which knocked Rudy Giuliani out of the race and into McCain's increasingly crowded corner, and then through a ridiculously punishing schedule (a single day saw stops in Chicago, Nashville, Birmingham, Atlanta, and Washington, D.C.) on the rush toward Super Tuesday, including today's last marathon leg, New York to San Diego to Phoenix, seventeen hours from rise and shine to sitting in another hotel room, jingling the pennies in his pocket, watching another TV, waiting for another twenty-one verdicts.

The exit polls were partly right: Huckabee claimed great chunks of the Southeast—better him than Romney, but still, Jesus. And then McCain began picking up states, big states, New York and New Jersey, and small states, Delaware and Connecticut, and making it a race in Massachusetts—wouldn't that have been a sweet, sharp knife to clang off Romney's ribs?—and onward west into Missouri, Oklahoma, Illinois, and running away with Arizona after all—what the hell was that about?—and then waiting, deep into the night, for the biggest and final prize, California.

He spoke before he knew he had won it. He came down to the ballroom, and he was cheered by one of the biggest crowds he had seen, and something changed once again, just as it had that night in New Hampshire. This was the beginning and the end of something, too. Except on this night, night two, it wasn't about how the rest of the country perceived John McCain; it was about how John McCain perceived himself. He's superstitious, and he's tenacious, and he's stubborn, and he's loyal, and he's vindictive, and he's combative, and he's disciplined, except when he isn't, and he's right, except when he's not, and now he would claim to have become one thing above all others, ignoring what he has been for so long in favor of what he will be.

"Although I've never minded the role of the underdog," he said, "tonight I think we must get used to the idea that we are the Republican party's front-runner. . . . And I don't really mind it one bit."

He said it quietly—even his voice was different than it had been earlier in the day, changing along with him, calmer, between breaths, sounding how he imagined he would sound as president of the United States—and the quiet became him.

And then he turned his attention to his rivals, not just that guy, *him,* but now the other one as well.

"I salute Governor Huckabee," he said.

"And I want to congratulate Governor Romney."

The difference in wording was subtle, maybe even subconscious, but it was not unimportant. It was as though even in the afterglow of victory, McCain couldn't resist moving a few more plastic tanks on the big map of the world: salute versus congratulate, respect versus hip-hip-hooray, and most important, Mike Huckabee versus Mitt Romney. Just like that, John McCain had set up a new battle in order to remove himself from an old one. Two days later, Romney would end his campaign, but McCain already seemed to have left the others behind. From now on, he was above it, he said without saying—he was ready to become that someone or something else he thinks we need him to become.

With that, he went outside, and he took a car to his condo, just down the street. He was alone with his family, no reporters, none of his new friends. It was late, and it had been a long, long day.

Now it was over.

4

THE FEMINIST REAWAKENING: HILLARY CLINTON AND THE FOURTH WAVE

AMANDA FORTINI
New York magazine   April 21, 2008

The role of gender in the heated 2008 presidential run is certain to be debated for years to come. Have the media treated Hillary Clinton unfairly because she's a woman, as Bill Clinton and others have suggested? And is her reputation as a "polarizing" candidate actually a reflection of the gulf between those who cheer the thought of the nation's first female president and those who can't stand the idea? These questions may never be fully resolved—but as Amanda Fortini makes clear, the surprising degree of male hostility encountered by the ex–First Lady during her campaign speaks to a healthy degree of sexism in "postfeminist" twenty-first-century America.

Not so long ago, it was possible for women, particularly young women, to share in the popular illusion that we were living in a postfeminist moment. There were encouraging statistics to point to: More women than men are enrolled at universities, where they typically earn higher grades; once they graduate, those who live in big cities might even receive higher salaries—at least in the early years of employment. The Speaker of the House is female, as are eight governors and 16 percent of Congress (never mind that this is 11 percent fewer than Afghanistan's parliament). Many women believed we had access to the same opportunities and experiences as men—that was the goal of the feminist movement, wasn't it?—should we choose to take advantage of them (and, increasingly, we just might not). There was, of course, the occasional gender-based slight to contend with, a comment on physical appearance, the casual office badminton played with words like *bitch* and *whore* and *slut,* but to get worked up over these things seemed pointlessly symbolic, humorless, the purview of women's-studies types. Then Hillary Clinton declared her candidacy, and the sexism in America, long lying dormant, like some feral, tranquilized animal, yawned and revealed itself. Even those of us who didn't usually concern ourselves with gender-centric matters began to realize that when it comes to women, we are not post-anything.

The egregious and by now familiar potshots are too numerous (and tiresome) to recount. A greatest-hits selection provides a measure of the misogyny: There's Republican axman Roger Stone's anti-Hillary 527 organization, Citizens United Not Timid, or CUNT. And the Facebook group Hillary Clinton: Stop Running for President and Make Me a Sandwich, which has 44,000-plus members. And the "Hillary Nutcracker" with its "stainless-steel thighs." And Clinton's Wikipedia page, which, according to *The New Republic,* is regularly vandalized with bathroom-stall slurs like "slut" and "cuntbag." And the truly horrible YouTube video of a KFC bucket that reads HILLARY MEAL DEAL: 2 FAT THIGHS, 2 SMALL BREASTS, AND A BUNCH OF LEFT WINGS. And Rush Limbaugh worrying whether the country is ready to watch a woman age in the White House (as though nearly every male politician has not emerged portly, wearied, and a grandfatherly shade of gray). And those two boors who shouted, "Iron my shirts!" from the sidelines in New Hampshire. "Ah, the remnants of sexism," Clinton replied, "alive and well." With that, she blithely shrugged off the heckling.

It was hardly a revelation to learn that sexism lived in the minds and hearts of right-wing crackpots and Internet nut-jobs, but it was something of a surprise to discover it flourished among members of the news media. The frat boys at MSNBC portrayed Clinton as a castrating scold, with Tucker Carlson commenting, "Every time I hear Hillary Clinton speak, I involuntarily cross my legs," and Chris Matthews calling her male endorsers "castratos in the eunuch chorus." Matthews also dubbed Clinton "the grieving widow of absurdity," saying, of her presidential candidacy and senatorial seat, "She didn't win there on her merit. She won because everybody felt, 'My God, this woman stood up under humiliation.'" While that may be partly true—Hillary's approval ratings soared in the wake of *l'affaire* Lewinsky—Matthews's take reduced her universally recognized political successes to rewards for public sympathy, as though Clinton's intelligence and long record of public service count for nothing. Would a male candidate be viewed so reductively? Many have argued that the media don't like Clinton simply because they don't like Clinton—even her devotees will admit she arrives with a complete set of overstuffed baggage—much in the same way they made up their mind about Al Gore back in 2000 and ganged up on him as a prissy, uptight know-it-all. But whatever is behind the vitriol, it has taken crudely sexist forms.

Even when the media did attempt to address the emergent sexism, the efforts were tepid, at best. After the laundry incident, *USA Today* ran the extenuating headline, "Clinton Responds to Seemingly Sexist Shouts." A handful of journalists pointed out the absurdity of the adverb. "If these comments were only 'seemingly' sexist, I wonder what, exactly, *indubitably* sexist remarks would sound like?" Meghan O'Rourke wrote on The XX Factor, a blog written by *Slate*'s female staffers. Many women, whatever their particular feelings about Hillary Clinton (love her, loathe her, voting for her regardless), began to feel a general sense of unease at what they were witnessing. The mask had been pulled off—or, perhaps more apt, the makeup wiped off—and the old gender wounds and scars and blemishes, rather than having healed in the past three decades, had, to the surprise of many of us, been festering all along.

Of course, we weren't delusional. Even before Tina Fey declared, "Bitch is the new black," before female outrage had been anointed a trend by the *New York Times,* many women were clued in to the numerous gender-related issues that lay, untouched and unexamined, at some subterranean level of our culture: to the way women disproportionately bear the ills of our society, like poverty and lack of health care; to the relentlessly sexist fixation on the bodies of Hollywood starlets—on the vicissitudes of their weight, on the appearance and speedy disappearance of their pregnant bellies—and the deleterious influence this obsession has on teenage girls; to the way our youth-oriented culture puts older women out to graze (rendering them what Tina Brown has called, in a nod to Ralph Ellison, "invisible women"). But who wanted to complain? It was easier—and more fun—to take the Carly Fiorina approach: to shut up and compete with the boys. Who wanted to be the statistic-wielding shrew outing every instance of prejudice and injustice? Most women prefer to think of themselves as what Caroline Bird, author of *Born Female,* has called "the loophole woman"—as the exception. The success of those women is frequently cited as evidence that feminism has met its goals. But too often, the exceptional woman is also the exception that proves the rule.

Indeed, it might be said that the postfeminist outlook was a means of avoiding an unpleasant topic. "They don't want to have the discussion," a management consultant who worked at a top firm for nearly a decade told me, referring to her female colleagues. "It's like, 'I'm trying to have a level playing field here.'" Who wanted to think of gender as a divisive force, as the root of discrimination? Perhaps more relevant, who wanted to view oneself as a victim? Postfeminism was also a form of solipsism: *If it's not happening to me, it's not happening at all.* To those women succeeding in a man's world, the problems wrought by sexism often seemed to belong to other women. But as our first serious female presidential candidate came under attack, there was a collective revelation: Even if we couldn't see the proverbial glass ceiling from where we sat, it still existed—and it was not retractable.

-+- • -+->

The women I interviewed who described a kind of conversion experience brought about by Clinton's candidacy were professionals in their thirties, forties, and fifties, and a few in their twenties. In some cases, the campaign had politicized them: Women who had never thought much about sexual politics were forwarding Gloria Steinem's now-infamous op-ed around, reiterating her claim that "gender is probably the most restricting force in American life." In other cases, it had *re*-politicized them: A few women told me they were thinking about issues they hadn't considered in any serious way since college, where women's-studies courses and gender theory were mainstays of their liberal-arts curricula. "That whole cynical part of me that has been coming to this conclusion all along was like, I knew it! We've come—not nowhere, but not as far as we thought," one said. A not insignificant number of women mentioned arguments they'd had with male friends and colleagues, who disagreed that Clinton was being treated with any bias. A high-powered film executive for a company based in New York and Los Angeles recounted a heated debate she engaged in with two of her closest male friends; she finally capitulated when they teamed up and began to shout her down. Nearly all of the women I interviewed, with the exception of those who write on gender issues professionally, refused to be named for fear of offending the male bosses and colleagues and friends they'd tangled with.

In particular, the campaign has divided women and the men they know on the subject of race. Indelicate as it seems to bring up, the oft-repeated question is, why do overtly sexist remarks slip by almost without comment, while any racially motivated insult would be widely censured? A few women told me that when they raised this issue with men, the discussion broke down, with the men arguing that racism was far more pernicious than sexism. "If you say anything about the specificity of Hillary being a woman, you're just doing the knee-jerk feminist stuff, that's the reaction," said one woman who asked not to be identified in any way. "Thinking about race is a serious issue, whereas sexism is just something for dumb feminists to think about." The point is not to determine whether it is harder to be a white woman or a black man in

America today, nor which candidate would have more symbolic value. At issue is the fact that race is, as it should be, taboo grounds for criticism, but gender remains open territory.

Why doesn't our culture take sexism seriously? Gloria Steinem has suggested that "anything that affects males is seen as more serious than anything that affects 'only' the female half of the human race." If that's true, and I'm not convinced it is, then women are also culpable. Sexism is often so subtle, threading its insidious way through many aspects of our existence, that anyone who talks about it risks sounding like an overzealous lunatic at worst—scrutinizing every interaction for gender-specific offenses, dichotomizing the world into victim and oppressor—or trivial at best. "Even the brightest movement women found themselves engaged in sullen public colloquies about the inequities of dishwashing and the intolerable humiliations of being observed by construction workers on Sixth Avenue," Joan Didion once wrote. And so, in our reluctance to appear nagging, scolding, hectoring, or petty, many of us have made a practice of enduring minor affronts, not realizing that a failure to decry the smaller indignities can foster blindness to the larger ones. We then find ourselves shocked when one of the smartest, most qualified women ever to run for public office is called "fishwife-y" by a female pundit on national television.

The post-Hillary shift in awareness, for lack of a better term—*movement* still seems a gross overstatement—has created an unusual alliance that belies the pre- and post-boomer generational divide propounded by the media. The second-wave feminists are said to have cluck-clucked at a younger generation of women, who, oblivious to past struggles, refused to join their team and vote for Clinton. (Historians generally divide the movement into three phases or "waves": the turn-of-the-century suffragists; the equal-rights activists of the sixties and seventies; and the gender and queer theorists of the nineties.) But, according to my anecdotal research, it isn't just "the hot-flash cohort," to borrow another phrase from Tina Brown, that broke for Clinton. Women in their thirties and forties—at once discomfited and galvanized by the sexist tenor of the media coverage, by the nastiness of the watercooler talk in the office, by the realization that the once-foregone conclusion of Clinton-as-president might never come to be—did, too. We haven't heard much about these women, perhaps because in this demographic, there is peer pressure to vote for Obama. A woman I interviewed described the atmosphere of Obama-Fascism in her office: "I really object to the assumption that everyone is voting for Obama in our cohort, but that's the assumption these guys talk under," she says. "They feel only idiots would vote for Hillary. There's this kind of total assumption that of course any thinking person is voting for Obama."

Old-guard feminists, for their part, seem not yet aware—or prepared to believe—that the younger generation is coming around. "Young women take a lot of things for granted," Geraldine Ferraro told me. "We sometimes joke, 'If you don't get it, give it all back.' We don't want to say, 'Look how bad it was.' But they don't know their workplaces are better because of loudmouths like me who said, 'This is not how society should be run.'" Linda Hirshman, author of *Get to Work: A Manifesto for Women of the World,* said she thinks the feminist movement, even the third wave, may have seen its final days. For another movement to reach critical mass, she said, women in society may need to experience what she calls "an accretion of insult." But with the inequities highlighted by Hillary Clinton's presidential bid reminding us of the inequities we experience on a regular basis, the insults may have, well . . . accreted.

⋖⋘ • ⋙⋗

Any woman who has spent time in the workforce likely understands what a powerful, defining force gender can be. "We used to have a saying in the women's movement," says Leslie Bennetts, author of *The Feminine Mistake.* "It takes life to make a feminist." The real divide among women of voting age is between those who have encountered gender-based hurdles and affronts as they pursued their professional ambitions and those who have not: between women in their twenties, still in college or recent graduates, and women who have worked at a job where something (money, prestige, reputation) is at stake. This may in part explain why very young women voted overwhelmingly for Barack Obama: The parity on college campuses, where women often outperform men academically, can feel like it must translate into parity in the world. I remember reading Sylvia Plath's journals in a college seminar titled Biography, Gender, and Suicide—it was straight out of a Woody Allen movie—and finding them overwrought and whiny, a bitter recitation of every domestic duty and slight. Similarly, I wondered what Hélène Cixous and her feminist poststructuralist sisters were howling about. At that point, my only experience with sexism was a high-school debate in which my coach asked me to take my hair out of a bun so that I didn't look "so severe" for the judges. (I left my hair up—and won.) To my mind, equality was the rule.

Once you get into the working world, however, even if you view that world as fundamentally equitable, you understand what it means to be bound by one's gender, for gender to always be an issue. "It's just a vibe when you're a woman and you walk into a room and you're in a position of power and you have to convince them of something," a movie producer told me. "You're constantly juggling: When you're soft, you're too soft; when you're strong, you're too strong. It's a struggle in business and a struggle in relationships. It's always a struggle." Many professional women thus empathize with Clinton. It's not so much that they've experienced such blatant sexism—in today's corporations, even the most odious boss tends to be leashed—but that they know well the ways that gender complicates the workplace, and can relate to the struggle to balance femininity and toughness. Many have faced a version of her quintessential quandary: They may be more likable, more approachable, when playing to notions of traditional femininity (mother, wife, victim), but this doesn't fly in the workplace. "To try to hide her womanliness or enhance it—that's a decision Obama would never have to make," said one woman. "I'm not saying it's harder to be a woman. It's just a choice she has to make that he doesn't."

In the public realm, women are frequently subjected to a sort of bodily litcrit, where dress and demeanor are read as symbolic of femininity or a lack thereof. We have seen this with Hillary: Her current pantsuits, her erstwhile headbands, that sliver of cleavage, have all generated much speculation. Geraldine Ferraro told me that the scrutiny hasn't changed all that much from a quarter-century ago. "When I ran for VP, they said, 'You have to wear a jacket'—I was going to wear a short-sleeved dress. They said, 'We haven't seen that with a VP candidate before,' and I said, 'I don't care, you haven't seen a woman candidate before.'" Professional women, too, experience a version of this and tend to be acutely aware of the assumptions that can arise from their choices. Do you wear the glasses to the interview, or take them off? Button up the jacket, or leave it open? Pull the hair up, or leave it down? Allow a hint of sexiness to wink at the male interviewer or recruiter or boss, or go the androgynous route? For women in clubby, male-dominated industries, like banking and consulting, the objective is often to appear more masculine (and ward off the suspicion that you will someday procreate and thus become professionally unviable). "They cultivate a hard edge, pressing to be more masculine in their manner and the way they deal with people," the management consultant told me. "They develop a reputation for being cutthroat, for being hard, even harder than men, for having exacting standards. If I think of the women I know who have gone into banking, their personalities have changed; there's a difference in their whole bearing."

But some intrinsically female characteristics are more complicated to manipulate. One's voice, for instance: Clinton's flat, nasal, and, lately, hoarse voice has not fared well against Obama's rich baritone. The pundits have repeatedly labeled her shrill—another criticism that is only ever made of a woman. The sound of a woman's voice is among the most important factors determining her success. Margaret Thatcher famously lowered her pitch on the advice of a spin doctor, and she's not the only one. A study that compared female voices between 1945 and 1993 found that, in the latter half of the century, as young women entered the workforce in increasing numbers, their voices deepened, with the average pitch decreasing about 23 hertz. Think of that "career-woman voice" donned, consciously or not, by so many working women in Manhattan. A high, reedy, or uncertain voice can stall a woman's ascent. When my former (female) boss told me I needed to work on "presentational confidence," I concentrated on making my voice, and speech, more commanding.

Another way women attempt to transcend stereotypes is through what Linda Hirshman calls "the dancing backwards in high heels thing"—or, working harder than any man presumably would. Nearly all the women I spoke to referred to the feeling that one can confound perceived gender limitations by doing a more thorough job, being smarter, better informed, better researched. I think of it as the studying-for-extra-credit approach. The idea is that we can shift the focus from the arbitrary, personal criteria by which we are evaluated—whether we have children or not, are married or not, are warm enough, or too cold, or too calculating, or overly ambitious—onto our achievements. But it doesn't necessarily happen that way, as many of us, including Hillary Clinton, have learned. It turns out that even the tendency to overprepare is gendered (to borrow a term from the women's-studies crowd) in the popular perception. Clinton is portrayed as a Tracey Flick type, as one of those girls: the ones actually studying in study hall. In real life, that gets you elected class secretary or VP of operations, but never the No. 1 spot. "Leadership" is more effortless, an *assumed* mantle of authority, confidence that doesn't need a PowerPoint presentation to back it up. But it's difficult to imagine this traditionally male archetype—embodied in Obama's easy manner and unscripted, often overly general approach—working for a woman in the same way it does for a man. "There's no way you could put his words, his message, in her mouth and get away with it," said one of the women I spoke with. "If you took his campaign message, his speeches, his everything and you put it on her, she'd be fucked."

⤙ • ⤚

None of this is to say Obama hasn't had his own stereotypes to confront during this campaign. He has faced criticism for being "too black" or "not black enough." He's had to battle the unfounded yet persistent Internet rumor that he's a radical Muslim. And when his controversial pastor evoked questions about race and patriotism, Obama promptly dealt with the matter, giving one of the most complex and sophisticated speeches a politician has ever delivered.

There has been clamoring for Clinton to make the gender equivalent of Obama's race speech. In this idealized homily, Clinton would confront the insidiousness of sexism and speak out against the societal ills that affect women; she would renounce the unfair criteria, at once more stringent and more superficial, by which women are judged. She might even address the compromises she is said to have made in her life—this is idealized, remember—and tell us why those compromises, rather than making her an inferior candidate, instead make her a stronger one, as they can be viewed as her imperfect resolutions to the dilemmas faced by many women: Do you stay with a man who has betrayed you, or divorce him? Do you keep your name, or take your husband's? Do you put your career aside for his—at least for a time?

This speech, of course, is not likely to happen. Not only because, as was pointed out on The XX Factor, women disagree on such fundamental issues as abortion and child care, or because Clinton is politically cautious and to do so would risk alienating male voters. A speech like this would open Clinton to the criticism, leveled at her several times already in this campaign, and at any female candidate who refers to her gender or acts in a particularly feminine way (by crying, for instance)—that she is "playing the gender card." It would also, sadly, only serve to reinforce the sort of stereotypes she would hope to counter: the nag, the crusading feminist, the ballbuster, the know-it-all with reams of statistics at the ready. But the fact that women are even imagining what such a speech would sound like on the national stage is significant.

As the Pennsylvania primary nears, pundits and party members are again, as they did before Ohio and Texas, calling for Clinton to step down. ("The model of female self-sacrifice is deeply embedded in our culture," notes Bennetts.) And indeed it's becoming increasingly difficult to see how this political cycle could end with her victorious. It is perhaps cold comfort to say that if she loses the nomination, her candidacy leaves behind a legacy of reawakened feminism—the fourth wave, if you will. But this is in fact what is happening.

The past few months have been like an extended consciousness-raising session, to use a retro phrase that would have once made most of us cringe. We've parsed the gender politics of the campaign with other women in the office, at parties, over e-mail, and now we're starting to parse the gender politics of our lives. This is, admittedly, depressing: *How can we be confronting the same issues, all these years later?* But it's also exciting. It feels as if a window has been opened in a stuffy, long-sealed room. There is a thrill at the collective realization. Now the question is, what next?

5

THE CHOICE

GEORGE PACKER
The New Yorker   January 28, 2008

George Packer is best known for his brilliant reporting on the Iraq conflict—a body of work that includes his highly regarded book The Assassin's Gate. *In this piece, Packer turns to the homefront as he analyzes the contrasting appeals of Hillary Clinton and Barack Obama—"two politicians . . . whose policy positions . . . are almost indistinguishable"—but who bring vastly different visions of the presidency to the table.*

In the fall of 1971, a Yale Law School student named Greg Craig sublet his apartment, on Edgewood Avenue, in New Haven, to his classmate Hillary Rodham and her boyfriend, Bill Clinton, for seventy-five dollars a month. Over the following decades, Craig and the Clintons continued to cross paths. Craig, who became a partner at the blue-chip law firm Williams & Connolly, in Washington, D.C., received regular invitations to White House Christmas parties, where Hillary always remembered to ask about his five children. In the fall of 1998, President Clinton asked him to lead the defense team that the White House was assembling for the impeachment battle. On a bookshelf in Craig's large corner office are several photographs of him with one or both Clintons, including a snapshot of the President and his lawyers—their arms folded victoriously across their chests—taken after Craig's successful presentation during the Senate trial. An inscription reads, "To Greg. We struck the right pose—and *you* struck the right chords! Thanks—Bill Clinton, 2/99."

In spite of his long history with the Clintons, Craig is an adviser to Barack Obama's campaign. "Ninety-five percent of it is because of my enthusiasm for Obama," he said last month, at his law office. "I really regard him as a fresh and exciting voice in American politics that has not been in my life since Robert Kennedy." In 1968, Craig, who is sixty-two, was campaigning for Eugene McCarthy when he heard a Bobby Kennedy speech at the University of Nebraska, and became a believer on the spot. Since then, Craig has not been inspired by any American President. As for the prospect of another Clinton Presidency, he said, "I don't discount the possibility of her being able to inspire me. But she hasn't in the past, and Obama has."

Inspiration is an underexamined part of political life and Presidential leadership. In its lowest, most common form, inspiration is simple charisma that becomes magnified by the media, as with Ronald Reagan or Bill Clinton. On rare occasions, however, a leader can become the object of an intensely personal, almost spiritual desire for cleansing, community, renewal—for what Hillary, in a 1969 commencement speech at Wellesley, called "more immediate, ecstatic, and penetrating modes of living." Somewhere between the merely great communicators and the secular saints are the exceptional politicians who, as Hillary put it then, "practice politics as the art of making what appears to be impossible possible."

Robert B. Reich, the Secretary of Labor in Clinton's first term, who now teaches at Berkeley, told me that he believes political inspiration to be "the legitimizing of social movements and social change, the empowering of all sorts of people and groups to act as remarkable change agents." Reich was once a close friend of both Clintons—he met Hillary when they were undergraduates, and began a Rhodes Scholarship the same year as Bill—but he has not endorsed a candidate, and he seems drawn to Obama, for the same reasons that attracted Craig. "Obama is to me very analogous to Robert Kennedy," Reich said. "The closer you got to him, the more you realized that his magic lay in his effect on others rather than in any specific policies. But he became a very important vehicle. He got young people very excited. He was transformative in the sense of just who he was. And a few things he said about social justice licensed people. Obama does all that, almost effortlessly."

The alternatives facing Democratic voters have been characterized variously as a choice between experience and change, between an insider and an outsider, and between two firsts—a woman and a black man. But perhaps the most important difference between these two politicians—whose policy views, after all, are almost indistinguishable—lies in their rival conceptions of the Presidency.

Obama offers himself as a catalyst by which disenchanted Americans can overcome two decades of vicious partisanship, energize our democracy, and restore faith in government. Clinton presents politics as the art of the possible, with change coming incrementally through good governance, a skill that she has honed in her career as advocate, First Lady, and senator. This is the real meaning of the remark she made during one of the New Hampshire debates: "Dr. King's dream began to be realized when President Lyndon Johnson passed the Civil Rights Act of 1964, when he was able to get through Congress something that President Kennedy was hopeful to do—the President before had not even tried—but it took a President to get it done."

In the overheated atmosphere of a closely fought primary, this historically sound statement set off a chain reaction of accusations, declarations of offense, and media hysteria, and for a few days the Democratic Party seemed poised to descend into a self-destructive frenzy of identity politics. The *Times* editorial page scolded Clinton for playing racial politics and choosing a bizarre role model in Johnson; the columnist Bob Herbert accused her of taking "cheap shots" at King. But Clinton was simply expressing her belief that the Presidency is more about pushing difficult legislation through a fractious Congress than it is about transforming society. In the recent debate before the Nevada caucus, Obama, who confessed to being disorganized, said that the Presidency has little to do with running an efficient office: "It involves having a vision for where the country needs to go . . . and then being able to mobilize and inspire the American people to get behind that agenda for change." In reply, Clinton likened the job of President to that of a "chief executive officer" who has "to be able to manage and run the bureaucracy."

Similarly, if this campaign is, among other things, a referendum on the current occupant of the White House—as elections at the end of failed Presidencies inevitably are—then its outcome will be determined partly by whether voters find George W. Bush guilty of incompetence or of demeaning American politics. Clinton is presenting herself as the candidate who is tough and knowledgeable enough to fix the broken systems of government: the intelligence agencies, the Justice Department, the legislative process, the White House itself. Last week, speaking on the phone from California, she said that a President allows advisers to oversee the running of government at his or her peril. "Otherwise, you cede too much authority, and although it may not be immediately apparent to the public, the government picks up on those signals," she said. "What we now know about how Dick Cheney basically controlled the information going to Bush means that we'll never really know how much responsibility Bush should be assumed to have taken with respect to serious decisions. The water will flow downstream, and often pool in great reservoirs of power that will then be taken advantage of by those who have been smart enough to figure out how to pull the levers. And I know from my own experience, and certainly watching how deeply involved Bill was in those areas that he thought were important, what it takes to try to get the government to respond. It's not easy. We're talking about this massive bureaucracy . . . and you have to be prepared on Day One to basically wrest the power away in order to realize the goals and vision that you have for the country."

Although Clinton didn't utter her chief rival's name, Obama seemed to be the subtext of many of her remarks, such as when she mentioned reading Michael Korda's recent biography of Eisenhower, and compared the portraits of Ike and Field Marshal Bernard Montgomery—"who was given great marks for being so brilliant and inspiring of his men, but often had a difficult time making a tough decision, often dithered about it, and claimed he needed yet more information before he could pull the trigger." If elected President, Clinton acknowledged, she would have to use unifying rhetoric and reach across partisan lines. But Clinton is less sanguine than Obama is about the possibilities of such efforts; she is readier to march ahead and let those who will follow do so. "It's also important to say, 'Look, there are certain things we have to do as a country. You may not agree, but let me explain why, and let me try to persuade you. But if I can't persuade you, we have to go forward anyway.' And I think that that kind of understanding of the combination of using the bully pulpit but also producing results—managing the government so it doesn't manage you, so it does act as an instrument of the policies you're actually implementing—will give proof to what it is I'm saying."

These rival conceptions of the Presidency—Clinton as executive, Obama as visionary—reflect a deeper difference in how the two candidates analyze what ails the country. Obama's diagnosis is more fundamental: for him, the illness precedes the Bush years and the partisan deadlock in Washington, originating in a basic failure of politicians to bring Americans together. A strong hand on the wheel won't make a difference if your car is stuck in the mud; a good leader has to persuade enough people to get out and push. Whereas Clinton echoes Churchill, who proclaimed, "Give us the tools and we will finish the job," Obama invokes Lincoln, who said, "As our case is new, so we must think anew, and act anew. We must disenthrall ourselves, and then we shall save our country."

Sidney Blumenthal, a former staff writer at this magazine, who was a senior adviser to Bill Clinton and is now a senior adviser on Hillary Clinton's campaign, describes the 2008 election as a chance to secure progressive government for years to come. "It's not a question of transcending partisanship," he said. "It's a question of *fulfilling* it. If we can win and govern well while handling multiple crises at the same time and the Congress, then we can move the country out of this Republican era and into a progressive Democratic era, for a long period of time."

Peter Wehner served in the Bush White House until August 2007, working for Karl Rove, the Administration's chief strategist. Wehner, who is now a senior fellow at the Ethics and Public Policy Center, in Washington, said that, as a candidate, Hillary Clinton would provide a "much more target-rich environment" than Obama. Republicans wouldn't need to uncover new scandals; they would simply remind voters of the not so distant Clinton wars. "Certain regions of your brain are latent," Wehner said. "But if there's a word or a sound or a memory that you hear, that region of your brain lights up again. And I have a feeling that, with Bill and Hillary Clinton, there are latent regions of the brain that will light up, and, if the Democrats don't light it up, the Republicans will. And that is going to be Clinton fatigue." As for Obama, Wehner's only complaint is that he's a liberal: "I find him to be very impressive. He would be much more difficult for Republicans to handle. He has much more breakout potential."

Advisers to Clinton told me that there is something naïve, even potentially fatal, in Obama's vision of leading the country out of its current political battles. The advisers seemed to be saying that Obama considers civility and nonpartisanship to be amulets that can stop bullets. In this view, Obama will be annihilated by what members of the Clinton campaign call "the Republican attack machine." Neera Tanden, the campaign's policy director, expressed admiration for Obama but cautioned that the general election will be brutal. "You cannot let your guard down with these guys," she said of right-wing politicians. "They take people's strengths and make them weaknesses; if you give them an inch, they'll take a mile. They're not ready to give up. They're not ready to lose the Congress and the Presidency. I don't think Grover Norquist"—the conservative lobbyist—"is sitting around thinking that's going to be great for him. His salary depends on it, at the very least. Both of the Clintons have been through it and won before. But if we don't think that the Democratic nominee, whoever it is, is going to have high negatives by the end of this process, then we're crazy."

Late last year, as the Democratic race was tightening, there was an argument within the Clinton camp over whether to go on the attack against Obama—an argument won by the proponents. When I described to Greg Craig the Clinton campaign's skepticism toward the idea of transcending partisanship, he said, "You're getting to that five percent of Hillary that I don't like—which is to see in every corner a conspiracy or an opponent that must be crushed. Look at her comment 'Now the fun part starts'"—Clinton's announcement in Iowa that she would begin attacking Obama's record. "There is a quality of playing the embattled, beleaguered victim that I find unappealing and depressing." He added, "I want a President who is looking to move the country with positive inspirational ideas rather than to fight off the bad guys and proclaim victory by defeating the forces of reaction. I would like us to inspire the forces of reaction to join us in treating people better, and lifting more vulnerable people and people in jeopardy out of their vulnerability and jeopardy."

Of course, as Craig learned during the impeachment effort—which he denounced as "a gross abuse of power"—the Republicans in Congress have shown little interest in making peace with Democrats. "Yes, but the way in which you beat them, the way in which you make progress in this country, is not by further polarizing and further dividing," Craig said. "It's by building the consensus around the positions that make sense—say, the position that we should not have forty-seven million Americans uninsured. You don't win national health insurance by turning Republicans against you. You've got to get them to join you."

Clinton's admirers counter that, as a member of the U.S. Senate, she has learned the art of compromise. In just seven years, she has mastered the power relationships and legislative labyrinths of this most difficult club. "Hillary believes in governing," Neera Tanden said. When Tanden worked as her legislative director, Clinton would call again and again from the Senate floor to gauge the effect that a new amendment would have on a bill. Such attention to minutiae is rare in a legislator. The question, though, is whether her indisputable virtues— hard work, intellectual acuity, a command of policy—are ideally suited for the White House. A senator must convince fifty to sixty fellow-politicians; a President must rouse three hundred million fellow-citizens.

◄◄ • ►►

In the nineteen-nineties, Republicans, taking aim at an all-too-human Democratic President, liked to say "character matters"—a phrase that has been bitterly reprised by Democrats during the Bush years. If there's a flaw in Hillary

Clinton's character which could keep her from becoming a successful President, or President at all, it is what Carl Bernstein, her best biographer, described to me as a tendency toward "subterfuge and eliding." In the deep and sympathetic portrait *A Woman in Charge,* Bernstein's recent biography of Clinton, a constant theme is her fear of humiliation; as the daughter of a harsh, often cruel father, she learned early to conceal any weakness and, ultimately, to protect her very humanity from exposure. In the recent Las Vegas debate, when Clinton was asked to name a weakness, all she could come up with was her impatience to get things done.

"In her personal life, she's always seemed like she had something to hide," Dee Dee Myers, who was a top adviser on Bill Clinton's 1992 campaign, and who served as White House press secretary for the first two years of his Presidency, said. "She had a difficult father, and she spent a lot of time trying to create an image of a functional family when she could have just said, 'It's my family.' The burden of perfection was upon her, and she carried it into her marriage. There's always this fear of letting people see what they already know."

In *A Woman in Charge,* Bernstein writes of Clinton, "Almost always, something holds her back from telling the whole story, as if she doesn't trust the reader, listener, friend, interviewer, constituent—or perhaps herself—to understand the true significance of events." A former Clinton administration official explained his decision to support Obama by urging me to read the two candidates' autobiographies side by side. Obama's *Dreams from My Father,* unlike Clinton's *Living History,* he said, reveals a narrator who has struggled through difficult questions of identity and resolved them, and who, as a result, is comfortable not just with himself but with the complexity and contradiction of the world. "When I'm with her, I feel she wants to impress me," the former official said. "When I'm with him, I feel he wants to know what I have to offer him."

In numerous conversations, friends of both Clintons expressed a preference for Hillary, upending the public perception that Bill is the warmer and more likable of the two. He talks; she listens, with a talent for banter that can be disarming and even whimsical. Shortly after Lissa Muscatine, a close adviser of Hillary Clinton's, went to work as a White House speechwriter, in 1993, she tried to catch the First Lady's attention as Clinton was hurrying along a corridor. "Stop—stop!" Muscatine called out. Clinton wheeled around. "Stop! in the name of love," she sang out, breaking into a boogie in the West Wing hallway. Clinton's aides are famously loyal, staying with her far longer than most staffs at the highest level of politics. Tanden, who was in her twenties when she joined Clinton's staff, in 1997, and "sort of grew up working for her," found that Clinton really wanted to know what a mid-level aide thought about policy issues. "She asks questions, and she has a very high b.s. detector on people," Tanden said. "You get in her foxhole, she gets in your foxhole." In 1999, when Muscatine underwent surgery in order to determine if she had breast cancer, the First Lady asked her to telephone as soon as she had a diagnosis. The tumor was malignant, and Muscatine was too overwhelmed by the news to call, as they had agreed. Clinton phoned her and said, "If it's O.K., I want to check back every few days. But, if you don't want to come to the phone, that's fine." Muscatine told me, "She gave me not only her support but the license not to talk to someone of her stature. That meant the world to me." Richard Holbrooke, who served as Clinton's envoy on Bosnia and as Ambassador to the United Nations, is now a foreign-policy adviser to Hillary Clinton's campaign. (He is sometimes spoken of as a potential Secretary of State.) He said of Clinton, "I like her because she's human. She has a vulnerable side. She's fighting for things she really believes in."

Several friends also describe Clinton as more committed to using power for social change than her husband—for example, during the health-care reform effort of 1993–94, she insisted on universal coverage even after President Clinton became willing to drop it. (Her intransigence, of course, helped doom the entire effort.) John Danner, who worked for Clinton during his first term as governor of Arkansas, said, "Bill's policy wonkishness, in my judgment at least, was an application of his insatiable curiosity. People confuse that with a deep caring about actually getting anything done with the political power that he'd got. Hillary has always had a tenacity and a toughness that Bill never had. In that sense, she has cared more about getting stuff done." Danner's wife, Nancy Pietrafesa, who attended Wellesley with Hillary, also worked for Bill Clinton in Arkansas. (The two couples had a falling out after Danner and Pietrafesa were fired.) Pietrafesa said that Hillary's fear of public exposure was connected to those early years in Arkansas. "To be so humiliated, and ruthlessly," Pietrafesa said. "In Arkansas, she went to a place she wasn't welcomed, big time. Everything was wrong with her. She didn't paint her toenails when she wore sandals, she didn't look like a cocktail waitress when she dressed up. Everybody really felt they could insult her with impunity."

Clinton's instinct to fight back was honed in the rough world of Arkansas politics. Once, when the two couples were talking about policy matters, Danner proposed a way to offer retail discounts to Arkansas's substantial elderly population. To the astonishment of Danner and Pietrafesa, Hillary responded, "The last thing we need to do right now is something for folks who didn't vote for Bill." She had, Danner remembered, "this binary view of the world, a little like Bush's comment 'You're with us or you're against us.'" In Pietrafesa's opinion, "Hillary needs enemies."

⤙⤙ • ⤚⤚

During the tumultuous early years of her husband's Presidency, Clinton's ambitious political goals were too often stymied by her penchant for secrecy and combativeness. In one controversy after another—Whitewater, the travel-office scandal, the Paula Jones lawsuit—she refused to compromise or be forthcoming, and allowed what might have been temporary embarrassments to become part of an endless battle that helped derail the progressive reforms on which the Clintons had campaigned, including health-care legislation.

In early 1995, not long after the Republicans' sweeping win in the midterm elections, Hillary Clinton met with a dozen advisers in the White House residence to discuss how to handle the new political reality, which would include congressional investigations on Whitewater and other matters. One argument—the one that she had always made—was to "batten down the hatches, fight to the death," in the words of an adviser who attended the meeting; another was to defuse the opposition as much as possible through openness. At one point, almost as if she were thinking aloud, Clinton suddenly said, "I need people like the people J.F.K. had around him." The adviser described the moment as "existential" for Clinton: she was saying that she wanted "people who were strong, tough, loyal, who play to win but do it in the smart, strategic way." Clinton's way had not been smart or strategic. Afterward, she grudgingly began to change her approach, withdrawing from the front lines of political battles and, as some of her aides had urged, using her platform more symbolically rather than always trying to achieve concrete results.

That year, Clinton began writing a book about children and society called *It Takes a Village*. The thing that Washington insiders remember best about the book is Hillary's failure to thank Barbara Feinman, the writer hired by Simon & Schuster, the publisher, as a collaborator. The truth, though, is more complicated, and shows Hillary to be less a Machiavellian liar than a woman whose guardedness leads to self-sabotage.

Editors at Simon & Schuster reacted to early chapters with dismay, and worried about the quality of Feinman's contributions, but they kept their reactions private. Over the summer, a manuscript emerged, but neither the publisher nor Clinton's aides—nor, especially, Hillary herself—were pleased with it. When Feinman left for vacation, Clinton, a Simon & Schuster editor, and a few key aides, working on their own time, continued on the book without her. (Feinman fulfilled the terms of her contract, and was never told by the publisher that her work was unsatisfactory.) In November, the Simon & Schuster editor spent three weeks at the White House, working intensively to expand and refine the material with the aides and with Clinton, who filled yellow legal pads with incorrigibly wonky prose, in "round, schoolgirlish handwriting," the editor told me. In private, Clinton was strikingly relaxed, padding around the Book Room and Solarium in sweatpants and Coke-bottle glasses, the editor said, calling her "buttercup." Clinton's personality, the editor found, "is refreshingly sharp and clear—but she can't show it."

It Takes a Village appeared in January, 1996, with an acknowledgments page that mentioned nobody. Clinton had apparently given in to the urge to pay her ghostwriter back (as had Simon & Schuster, which considered withholding the last portion of Feinman's hundred-and-twenty-thousand-dollar fee but quickly relented). Clinton's omission aroused the enmity of powerful friends of Feinman's at the *Washington Post,* and journalists began covering the slight, their suspicions roused by Clinton's explanation that she had forgone names in the acknowledgments for fear of leaving someone out. Hillary's triumphant return to the public eye became another embarrassment. As with so many other Clinton scandals, the press framed the story in the worst possible light, and got its essence wrong, suggesting that Feinman had written the whole book and that Clinton had stolen the credit. Instead, Clinton had micromanaged every aspect of the book's development. The episode captures her habit of undermining herself, when the worst might have been averted by a little candor and grace—a tendency that has reappeared in the past few weeks, as her campaign has responded to the shock of Obama's challenge.

⊰< • >⊱

In the Senate, Clinton seems to have taken the hard lessons of the White House years to heart, and become a far better politician. The majority of her legislative achievements, for the most part under Republican control of Congress, have been modest, and geared toward constituent service. Richard Holbrooke pointed out that Fort Drum, outside Watertown, New York, stayed open and was even expanded during a period of base closures, and said, "To her, it's one of her most important achievements. She's incredibly proud of it." A senior Democrat on the Senate staff, who declined to be named, pointed out that Clinton's focus on New York was necessary to win over her colleagues: "She demonstrated that she was a workhorse, not a show horse." Clinton has surprised Republicans by cooperating with erstwhile enemies of her husband's administration, such as Lindsey Graham, of South Carolina, who was a House impeachment manager in 1998, and Trent Lott, of Mississippi, who in 2000 expressed a hope that lightning might strike Clinton before her first day in the Senate. And she has surprised the military by becoming an expert on defense policy, as New York's first member of the Senate Armed Services Committee.

A member of Clinton's campaign told me that Obama has not held a single hearing of the Senate Foreign Relations Committee's subcommittee on European Affairs, which he chairs, implying that he is a less serious senator than she is. In fact, according to the *Boston Globe,* Obama has presided over appointment hearings, but nothing more substantive: he took over the subcommittee just as the Presidential campaign began, and all the candidates have been AWOL since then. As for the challenge to Obama's seriousness, the Senate staff member disputed it, describing him as a deeply thoughtful, well-prepared member of the committee who asks good questions and never tries to score cheap points. In the staff member's words, Obama can see all sides of an issue, whereas Clinton would be formidable across the negotiating table from, say, Iranian President Mahmoud Ahmadinejad.

In the Senate, Clinton has gone a long way toward neutralizing skeptics and antagonists by working hard, deferring to seniority, and deploying her underappreciated personal charm. At the same time, she became a Democratic leader in the Senate in part because she understood the powers of the Presidency and the need for an overarching strategy in any major conflict with the executive branch—for example, Neera Tanden said, during the fight to prevent Social Security from being privatized. Presumably, she would turn her knowledge of Congress to her advantage should she return to the White House.

"Her Senate years are when she learned," Holbrooke said. "How could she conceivably have been such a successful, bipartisan, reach-out senator, collaborating even with impeachment managers, if she hadn't learned something?" In Holbrooke's chronicle, her Senate career has instructed her in congressional power and filled the last conceivable holes in her résumé, leaving her perfectly poised for the Presidency. "Here's my view of the arc of her story," he said. "The so-called 'soft issues,' which are not soft at all—women's empowerment, H.I.V./AIDS, micro-credit, global health, foreign assistance—are things she mastered as First Lady. Her national-security qualifications are based on her five years as a member of the Senate Armed Services Committee."

There is another view of her years in the Senate, one suggested by a few associates who have grown wary of Clinton the politician: that she's learned the lessons of the nineties all too well and become the same careful centrist that electoral setbacks led her husband to become. "'Caution' is the operative word," Robert Reich said. "Essentially, Bill Clinton's agenda ended at the start of 1995, when Republicans took over Congress. What resumed in the White House was a management operation to stay relevant and to keep the Republican Congress at bay." Clinton associates expressed concern that Hillary's chief strategist and pollster was Mark Penn, the author of *Microtrends,* who is closely associated with triangulation—the cynical adoption of ideas from both sides of the political divide. And some of her actions in the Senate have had an air of opportunism; in 2005, for example, she cosponsored a bill to criminalize flag-burning. The burden of Clinton's long and intensely public political career is that she can be faulted for both excessive caution and excessive zeal. A Clinton associate put it this way to Carl Bernstein: "I'm not sure I want the circus back in town."

⤙ • ⤚

Two nights before the New Hampshire primary, Clinton was more than ninety minutes late for a rally at Winnacunnet High School, in Hampton, and the energy was rapidly seeping out of the cafeteria. The recorded-music track was on its third or fourth round of "Every Little Thing She Does Is Magic," and the standing crowd of six hundred people (with a slightly larger number in an adjacent auditorium) was no longer amused by a campaign worker tossing out "Hillary" T-shirts like a game-show host. The fearsome Clinton machine appeared to be close to breakdown. "If you're on the fence, this isn't such a good thing," a man next to me said.

Ruth Keene, a small woman of seventy-one years who wore a big blue parka, kept telling the people around us that the candidate would appear any moment. I mentioned to her that a nurse I'd met at a John McCain town-hall meeting had called Clinton "bitchy." Why did so many people dislike her so much? "Strong woman," Keene said. "I'm a bitch and proud of it. I can't talk about her with some of my friends, or it would end the friendship." As for Obama, she liked him fine, but "the Republicans would chew him up."

When Clinton finally appeared, in a black pants suit and a bright-pink blouse, there was a surge of excitement, and I noticed how many people in the room were not just female but girls. One who could not have been more than ten held a placard that said, "Hillary 2008, Sophia 2040." "I apologize for running late," Clinton said. After the loss to Obama in the Iowa caucus, she told me, New Hampshire was a matter of "do or die," and, perhaps for that reason, she almost immediately opened the floor to questions, something that she had rarely done earlier in the campaign. Whatever question the crowd threw at her, she had an informed answer, often accompanied by a multi-point plan: immigration, health care, global warming, student loans, small business, animal rights, Cuba. For well over an hour, she projected her voice across the room in the same tone, the same semi-shout, regardless of the question—even when a girl near the stage asked how her third-grade class could become more challenging. "That is really touching," Clinton said, laughing, but within half a minute she had turned away from the girl and was declaring, "We live in a much more personalized, customized world, but education is still on an industrial model."

It occurred to me that Clinton is a familiar kind of Democrat—the earnest policy junkie, like Michael Dukakis, Al Gore, or John Kerry—except that this is a wonk with a killer instinct and a passionate temperament under wraps. In our conversation, Clinton seemed to admit that she does not inspire through rhetoric and emotion. "You can also inspire through deeds," she said. "You can demonstrate determination and willingness to make difficult choices, to show backbone and courage, to confront adversity calmly and skillfully. A President, no matter how rhetorically inspiring, still has to show strength and effectiveness in the day-to-day handling of the job, because people are counting on that. So, yes, words are critically important, but they're not enough. You have to act. In my own experience, sometimes it's putting one foot in front of the other day after day." She cited her efforts on behalf of the health of workers at Ground Zero. "It's important to realize that, once the lights are off and the cheering crowds are gone, you still have to go back to the Oval Office and figure out how to solve these problems. It really does mean that the buck stops there. You can't delegate it, you can't outsource it."

In the New Hampshire cafeteria, Clinton couldn't quite make an individual connection, even when listening sympathetically to a woman in the crowd who said that she held down two jobs and still had trouble paying for her asthma medicine. When a man declared himself appalled by the Democrats' weak statements about terrorism at a televised debate, Clinton snapped, "I'm sorry you were appalled by it," and moved on. She wouldn't risk the loss of control that it might take to energize the room with humor or anger or argument, or the sort of spontaneous human touch that everyone who spends private time with her notices and likes. A number of people drifted away before she had finished.

The next morning, Obama was scheduled to appear before an overflow crowd at the opera house in Lebanon. When he walked onto the stage, which was framed by giant vertical banners proclaiming "HOPE," his liquid stride and handshake-hugs suggested a man completely at ease.

"I decided to run because of you," he told the crowd. "I'm betting on you. I think the American people are honest and generous and less divided than our politics suggests." He mocked the response to his campaign from "Washington," which everyone in the room understood to be Clinton, who had warned in the debate two nights before against "false hopes": "No, no, no! You can't do that, you're not allowed. Obama may be inspiring to you, but here's the problem— Obama has not been in Washington enough. He needs to be stewed and seasoned a little more, we need to boil the hope out of him until he sounds like us—*then* he will be ready."

The opera house exploded in laughter. "We love you," a woman shouted.

"I love you back," he said, feeding off the adoration that he had summoned without breaking a sweat. "This change thing is catching on, because everybody's talking about change. 'I'm for change.' 'Put me down for change.' 'I'm a change person, too.'"

It was the day before the primary, and Obama began to improvise a theme, almost too much in the manner of Martin Luther King: "In one day's time." It carried him through health care, schools, executive salaries, Iraq—everything that Clinton had invoked, except that this was music. Then came the peroration: "If you know who you are, who you're fighting for, what your values are, you can afford to reach out to people across the aisle. If you start off with an agreeable manner, you might be able to pick off a few folks, recruit some independents into the fold, recruit even some Republicans into the fold. If you've got the votes, you will beat them and do it with a smile on your face." It was a summons to reasonableness, yet Obama made it sound thrilling. "False hopes?

There's no such thing. This country was built on hope," he cried. "We don't need leaders to tell us what we *can't* do—we need leaders to inspire us. Some are thinking about our constraints, and others are thinking about limitless possibility." At times, Obama almost seems to be trying to escape history, presenting himself as the conduit through which people's yearnings for national transformation can be realized.

Obama spoke for only twenty-five minutes and took no questions; he had figured out how to leave an audience at the peak of its emotion, craving more. As he was ending, I walked outside and found five hundred people standing on the sidewalk and the front steps of the opera house, listening to his last words in silence, as if news of victory in the Pacific were coming over the loudspeakers. Within minutes, I couldn't recall a single thing that he had said, and the speech dissolved into pure feeling, which stayed with me for days.

In June of 1992, when Bill Clinton was running third behind President George H.W. Bush and Ross Perot, his advisers were faced with the problem of reconciling his support of the middle class with his character and biography, which, until then, the public associated with Oxford, Yale, womanizing, draft dodging, and marijuana. Their "Manhattan Project"—an effort to introduce Clinton to the country as the hardworking product of a broken family and a rough childhood—helped put him into the lead and culminated in a hugely successful campaign film shown at the Democratic Convention in New York, *The Man from Hope.*

"Hillary Clinton needs something like that," Dee Dee Myers, who worked on the Manhattan Project, said. "Too often, all we see is ambition."

Ambition, of course, is the politician's currency. "Politics has ever been about advancing yourself," Richard Holbrooke said. "The question is: Is ambition harnessed to a purpose? She has the goals to advance the national purpose, she's articulated them, she's tried to lay them out."

Blame it on the media, or blame it on the voters, but American politics requires something more. A few hours before Clinton's rally in Hampton, I watched John McCain's masterly presentation before a packed middle-school gym in Salem, which included many skeptics and independents. An accountant challenged him on his willingness to make Bush's tax cuts permanent while claiming to be a deficit hawk, telling McCain, "You're in Purgatory." The candidate shot back playfully, "Thank you very much. It's a step up from where I was last summer." He was witty, combative, humble, and blunt (while embracing Republican orthodoxy on almost every position). Unlike Clinton, he engaged questioners in lengthy back-and-forths that showed he was capable of a respectful disagreement. After hearing Clinton that evening, I thought that she might have a hard time beating McCain in November.

"I'm more reserved than people realize or accept of someone who's in the public eye, especially in the times in which we live," Clinton told me. "I think that the world is only beginning to recognize that women should be permitted the same range of leadership styles that we permit men." She went on, "I followed with great interest the election of Angela Merkel as Germany's first woman Chancellor. Many of the things that were said about her would certainly sound familiar." She laughed. Her determination to prove that a woman could be a plausible Commander-in-Chief had led her to restrain her displays of feeling, perhaps for too long. "I wasn't quite sensitive to that," she said. "Voters were saying, 'O.K., now I can look at more personal traits.'" She went on, "My friends, starting in November or December, said, 'You're not telling your story very well.'"

The day before the New Hampshire primary, Clinton, campaigning on three hours of sleep a night, spoke before undecided voters at a coffee shop in Portsmouth. Her eyes welling with tears, she said of the grueling campaign, "It's not easy, and I couldn't do it if I just didn't, you know, passionately believe it was the right thing to do. . . . I just don't want us to fall backwards." Many voters responded warmly to this candid moment. As Myers put it, "There was a flash in New Hampshire—that there's another reason that drives her, a desire to help other people." Since then, Myers said, Clinton has made the mistake of continuing to tell the public what she feels rather than showing it. During the debate in Las Vegas, she tried to explain her commitment to social change by talking about herself, not about the people she wants to help: "It is really my life's work. It is something that comes out of my own experience, both in my family and in my church—that, you know, I've been blessed." Her response displayed the awkwardness that comes from a lifelong habit of self-concealment in the face of exposure, and toughness in the face of hurt. It's a little sad and painful that this enormously accomplished and capable woman, in her sixty-first year, had to bring her mother and daughter on a "likability tour" in the days before the Iowa caucus, and found her voice—as she put it—only on the night of her upset win in New Hampshire.

"Hillary needs to connect two things," Myers said. "What's in her heart and what she wants to accomplish and why. There are many reasons to think she'd be a good President. She knows what she wants to do, she understands how the process works, she's shown an ability to work with Congress, she's become more incrementalist. But the Presidency isn't all that powerful, except as the bully pulpit. It comes down to your ability to get people to follow you, to inspire. You have to lead. Can she get people to come together, or does she remain such a polarizing figure? That's what the campaign will be about." In other words, winning the Presidency might require Clinton to transcend her own history.

6

THE MACHINERY OF HOPE: INSIDE THE GRASS-ROOTS FIELD OPERATION OF BARACK OBAMA

TIM DICKINSON
Rolling Stone   March 20, 2008

As the Democratic primary calendar approached its June 3 finish line, two facts about the race between Barack Obama and Hillary Clinton were painstakingly clear: The contest had been extremely close from start to finish, and Obama's small but definitive lead in the pledged delegate count could be ascribed almost completely to his superior campaign organization. In his article, which originally appeared in Rolling Stone *magazine, Tim Dickinson reports on how Obama's revolutionary bottom-up campaign structure came into being, and how it's changed American presidential politics forever.*

It's Presidents Day, two weeks before the Texas primary, and Adam Ukman has come to the small city of San Marcos to train precinct captains for Barack Obama. A soft-spoken native of Houston, Ukman has served on the campaign's front lines in Iowa and Utah, organizing grass-roots supporters to secure decisive victories in both states. This evening, more than eighty residents of San Marcos have crammed into a yellow clapboard recreation center on a street dotted with shacks that date from the Jim Crow era. "Our job is not to run in here to tell you how it's going to be," Ukman tells them. "This is your campaign. Not our campaign."

Anyone who has spent time around Democratic politics has heard this kind of rhetoric before. Most often, it's pure horseshit. But Ukman is not here to break in a batch of untrained organizers. He knows that there is literally hundreds of years of organizing experience in the room—all he needs to do is set it loose. There's Michael Collins, an old-school politico in a tan Stetson who chaired John F. Kennedy's campaign in West Texas in 1960. A few seats over is Sandra Tenorio, who oversaw immigration issues for Governor Ann Richards in the 1990s. And there's "Big Bob" Barton, a fixture of local party races since he worked as a volunteer for Gene McCarthy in '68. "I first voted for a Democrat more than fifty years ago," he barks out in his dry baritone. "I try not to fall in love with too many men, but this is the best damn one we've had since John Kennedy."

What Ukman is doing here in the rec center in the Hill Country of Texas is something new in American politics. Over the past year, the Obama campaign has quietly worked to integrate the online technologies that fueled the rise of Howard Dean—as well as social-networking and video tools that didn't even exist in 2004—with the kind of neighbor-to-neighbor movement-building that Obama learned as a young organizer on the streets of Chicago. "That's the magic of what they've done," says Simon Rosenberg, president of the Democratic think tank NDN. "They've married the incredibly powerful online community they built with real on-the-ground field operations. We've never seen anything like this before in American political history."

In the process, the Obama campaign has shattered the top-down, command-and-control, broadcast-TV model that has dominated American politics since the early 1960s. "They have taken the bottom-up campaign and absolutely perfected it," says Joe Trippi, who masterminded Dean's Internet campaign in 2004. "It's light-years ahead of where we were four years ago. They'll have 100,000 people in a state who have signed up on their Web site and put in their zip code. Now, paid organizers can get in touch with people at the precinct level and help them build the organization bottom up. That's never happened before. It never was *possible* before."

The meeting in San Marcos wasn't advertised in any traditional sense. Instead, the campaign posted the event on my.barackobama.com—its social-networking site affectionately known as "MyBo"—and e-mailed local residents who had donated to the campaign or surrendered their addresses as the price of admission to an Obama rally. And the volunteers who showed up won't be micromanaged by Ukman or anyone else from the campaign. They'll be able to call their own shots, from organizing local rallies to recruiting and training a crew of fellow Obama supporters to man their precincts on election day. To identify and mobilize Obama backers, they'll log on to the password-protected texasprecinctcaptains.com, download the phone numbers of targeted voters, make calls from their homes and upload the results to Austin headquarters. They'll also organize early-voting open houses—which will be publicized on MyBo—to boost turnout among core supporters. "Instead of *hoping* that your neighbors vote," Ukman tells them in an unintentional twist on the campaign's central theme, "you're going to *take* them to the polls."

This scene in the rec center is being repeated in neighborhood coffee shops, high school cafeterias and public libraries across Texas. Over the course of the three-day weekend, the Obama campaign trained 4,000 precinct captains in more than twenty communities, from El Paso to Corpus Christi. This is the same grass-roots effort that has trounced the Clinton campaign—a classic top-down operation run by high-paid consultants—in ten straight contests by an average of more than thirty points. It has evolved into the mother of all get-out-the-vote campaigns, one that has enabled Obama to collect more votes in Virginia and Wisconsin than all of the GOP candidates *combined.*

In Texas, Tenorio is hearing from fellow Richards veterans who are backing Hillary Clinton, and they're worried. "They don't have precinct captains," she says. "They don't have a local organization, and they're still trying to get names. They're really scrambling to put it together—and here we all are."

⤙ • ⤚

The Obama campaign has actually worked to tamp down media coverage of its technological advances in organizing, avoiding anything that would cast the candidate as "the next Howard Dean." In Democratic political circles, Dean's short-lived campaign still carries heavy baggage: *Howard Dean was the Internet. Howard Dean lost.*

"They've been guarded," says Peter Leyden, director of the New Politics Institute, a San Francisco–based think tank that promotes technology in politics. "It's been beautiful to watch them blending these new tools into the old-fashioned shoe-leather, door-knocking politics. But they don't talk about it. People like myself have to piece it together from its outer effects."

In recent weeks, however, the campaign has granted *Rolling Stone* rare access to its top strategists and organizers, who discussed in detail the mechanics of Obama's meteoric ascendancy. According to David Axelrod, the campaign's chief strategist, the bottom-up ethos of the campaign comes straight from the top. "When we started this race, Barack told us that he wanted the campaign to be a vehicle for involving people and giving them a stake in the kind of organizing he believed in," Axelrod says. "He is still the same guy who came to Chicago as a community organizer twenty-three years ago. The idea that we can organize together and improve our country—I mean, he really *believes* that."

To execute this vision, Obama hired as his deputy campaign manager Steve Hildebrand, a folksy veteran of South Dakota politics regarded as one of the top field strategists in the game. "We wanted to make sure we learned from Howard Dean's campaign," Hildebrand says. The most valuable lesson? "We didn't make the assumption that people signing up on our Web site meant that they were going to help the candidate or even vote for him. From the beginning, we had an initiative to take our online force offline."

Hildebrand actually flipped the equation, using the physical crowds Obama could draw to his rallies to bolster the campaign's e-mail list. In February and March of 2007, just after Obama announced his candidacy, the campaign set up huge rallies in cities from Los Angeles to Austin to Cleveland. In return for a ticket, supporters were asked only to provide their e-mail, zip code and telephone number—a practice that continues at every Obama megarally, where it has become routine for him to draw crowds in excess of 20,000.

"Events are not just an opportunity for us to put Barack in front of voters," says Hildebrand. "It's a chance for voters to be in a captive environment where we ask them to sign up and do more for Barack—to make phone calls, canvass, get out the vote. We don't want people to just come to an event—we want them to become part of this movement."

The turnout at the early rallies emboldened Obama's strategists to start imagining a truly different kind of campaign. At first, Hildebrand and Temo Figueroa, the campaign's field director, wrestled with how to harness the nationwide groundswell of support without taking their eyes off Iowa, which they considered a win-or-go-home state. But then the campaign's first-quarter fundraising numbers rolled in—$25 million. Suddenly, Hildebrand and Figueroa could afford to build the kind of fully participatory field campaign Obama had envisioned—one that set its horizons beyond Iowa and Super Tuesday. According to Hans Riemer, the campaign's youth-vote director, "The mantra was, 'If the same people show up that always show up—we're gonna lose.' We needed to build a new coalition of voters."

Riemer is no stranger to turning out young voters; he's the former political director of Rock the Vote. In most Democratic campaigns, the youth-vote co-ordinator is a symbolic post, not staffed until the general election, and often by one of the candidate's kids. Riemer, by contrast, has two deputy directors, has youth-vote staff in every state, and answers to the campaign's top brass.

"Steve Hildebrand, in shaping the campaign strategy from the outset, saw that there was an amazing opportunity here with Barack and young people," says Riemer. Turnout has been astonishing: In Iowa, as many people under thirty caucused as did senior citizens. In every contest, the youth vote has at least doubled and often tripled previous records. Riemer is quick to point out that these successes aren't just the result of the campaign organizing young people but of young people organizing themselves. "When I arrived at the Obama campaign," he says, "there were 175 Students for Barack Obama chapters already in existence"—a group that had started on Facebook in 2006 before morphing into a sophisticated grass-roots organization. "My responsibility was to nurture it and work with them on their political strategy."

As summer approached, Hildebrand and Figueroa gave the campaign's un-orthodox field operation a test run. While John Edwards and Hillary Clinton were busy barnstorming Iowa and New Hampshire, the Obama campaign sent out an e-mail asking its supporters to sign up for a day of old-fashioned door-knocking and precinct-walking across the entire country. The result: On a Sat-urday in early June—six months before anyone would cast a ballot or attend a caucus—more than 10,000 Obama supporters hit the pavement in all fifty states to persuade their neighbors to back Barack.

"That was a very important test for us," says Hildebrand. "Can we make this work offline? We said to our online supporters, 'We love you, but we need you to actually go to work in your neighborhood.' Their online support was only great if we could translate it into activity within their community."

At the same time, the campaign was developing a new high-tech toolbox to enable its supporters to keep the momentum going—both online and off. With the help of one of the founders of Facebook, the Obama campaign created MyBo, its own social-networking tool, through which supporters could or-ganize themselves however they saw fit. Today, the network claims more than half a million members and more than 8,000 affinity groups. Some are organ-ized by state (Ohioans for Obama), others by profession (Texas Business Women for Obama) and still others by groove thing (Soul Music Lovers for Obama).

"We put these tools online as a public utility," says Joe Rospars, the campaign's twenty-six-year-old director of new media, who served as one of Howard Dean's chief online organizers. "We said to our supporters, 'Have at it.'"

That move unleashed supporters to mobilize on their own—and they did, in unprecedented numbers. Before long, the campaign had transformed hundreds of thousands of online donors into street-level activists. "Obama didn't just take their money," says Donna Brazile, Al Gore's campaign manager in 2000. "He gave them seats at the table and allowed them to become players."

Equally important, Obama didn't build his machine by sucking up to the online activists who had been courted by Howard Dean—he built it from scratch. "I kind of admire that he hasn't wasted a lot of time kissing ass to make a bunch of bloggers happy," says Markos Moulitsas, founder of the influential blog *Daily Kos*. "I can't blame the guy. He's got other ways to reach people."

For Axelrod, a veteran of old-school politics, tapping the potential of the Internet meant changing the established notion of how a campaign runs. "Part of this new era of politics has been learning how to surrender command-and-control aspects of the campaign," he says. "If you really want grass-roots participation, then you have to give folks at the grass roots some autonomy to do this in their own way. We had hundreds and hundreds of thousands of people who wanted to do things. The challenge was: How do you marshal them in an organized fashion?"

⤙ • ⤚

Cuauhtémoc "Temo" Figueroa hardly looks like the kind of guy who would lead an army of grass-roots supporters. A compact forty-three-year-old with a shaved head and a stockbroker's wardrobe—gray-pinstriped dress shirt, impeccably knotted silver silk tie—Figueroa still speaks in the foulmouthed vernacular of the kickass union organizer he used to be. These days, as national field director for Obama, he serves as General Patton for the campaign's growing legions of activists.

This afternoon, Figueroa is in San Antonio, where he has been working all day recruiting Hispanic politicians who support Obama to get down to Texas. Their endorsements, he tells them straight off, don't mean shit to him. He wants them to come to the Rio Grande Valley and go to work: speaking at Elks clubs, attending church picnics and baptisms, reaching out to Spanish-language weeklies that never get any love.

"I always give people at least ten things to do," he tells me, sitting in a tamales-and-margaritas joint along the river, where he has set up a makeshift field office for the day. "Because either it'll scare them off, or they'll start doin' a handful of 'em. Right?"

Figueroa's goal is not to put supporters to work but to enable them to put themselves to work, without having to depend on the campaign for constant guidance. "We decided that we didn't want to train *volunteers*," he says. "We want to train *organizers*—folks who can fend for themselves."

To turn well-meaning students and nurses and social workers into self-sufficient organizers, the campaign has put nearly 7,000 supporters through an intensive, four-day seminar known as "Camp Obama." Starting last March, the campaign solicited applications from its most dedicated supporters and asked them to travel to Chicago on their own dime. In exchange, these "campers" would learn the art of organizing from master teachers, including Mike Kruglik, who, a quarter-century ago, helped train a fresh-faced community organizer named Barack Obama.

"Early on, there was some question as to whether this was a good investment," says Figueroa. "But all of those questions went away very quickly; you just saw how fired up people were after finishing that." Responding to demand among activists, the campaign quickly took Camp Obama on the road to Super Tuesday states: New York, Georgia, Idaho, California, Missouri, Arizona.

To staff the seminars, the campaign brought in Harvard professors, union organizers, religious leaders—each of whom was free to tweak the curriculum. "You had the best, most brilliant folks from faith-based organizing, online organizing, community-based organizing and union organizing all collectively coming together to work on Camp Obamas," says Figueroa.

The result was a network of trained organizers who became what Figueroa calls the campaign's "secret weapon." Early on, the volunteers essentially served as Obama's staff in key states where he didn't have employees. "It quadrupled the size of our operation in states that were going to be voting not only on February 5th, but February 9th, February 12th and here on March 4th," Figueroa says. "We had an anchor in those states for a long, long, long time."

Using the social-networking tools of MyBo, the volunteers began to create city- and statewide networks with names like IdahObama, groups that could be tapped later by the professional staff to organize down to the precinct level. In Maryland, the campaign was able to mobilize 3,000 volunteers in only three weeks, thanks to the months of groundwork by groups like Baltimore for Barack Obama.

A strategy that leans so heavily on the grass roots is not without risk. In February, right-wing blogs had a field day when a Fox News affiliate ran footage of a volunteer office in Houston decorated with a Che Guevara flag. But the unique structure of the Obama campaign blunts the PR fallout of such off-message moments because it offers plausible deniability: "This is a volunteer office," the campaign wrote in a press release that forced a clarification from Fox, "that is not in any way controlled by the Obama campaign."

"There's no doubt that there's a downside to the Internet," Axelrod says. "Ugly, unfiltered things circulate virally, and we've had to deal with that. But it's a great democratizing force as well."

⤛ • ⤜

Obama's army of organizers has enabled him to repeatedly outman and outwit his opponents—especially in states that vote by caucus. "The Clinton campaign is the last, antiquated vestige of the top-down model," says Trippi. "The top cannot organize caucus states; the bottom can."

As Super Tuesday approached, the Obama campaign understood that the Clinton strategy was to try to deliver a deathblow by winning big states like California, New York and New Jersey through a traditional campaign driven by thirty-second TV spots and tarmac-to-tarmac appearances by the candidate and her surrogates. The Obama team was confident that it had both the ad budget and the precinct-by-precinct support to capture delegates in states like California, whether or not they won the popular vote. They also recognized that, even with her paid staff of 700, Clinton didn't have the manpower to compete against Obama's grass-roots organizers in the caucus states.

So in the lead-up to Super Tuesday, Obama spent only a day and a half in California. "The decision was made to pull Obama out and send him to those caucus states and run up the score," says Figueroa. In Idaho, the Obama campaign ramped up its staff to twenty paid organizers split among five field offices. It also brought in the candidate to pack the Taco Bell Arena in Boise with more than 13,000 supporters—each of whom was added to the campaign's get-out-the-caucus list. The Clinton campaign, apparently, failed to hire a single staffer in the state. The result: Obama won with eighty percent of the vote, netting fifteen of the state's eighteen delegates. While Clinton was spending lavishly to win New Jersey with 600,000 votes, Obama more than offset his delegate loss there simply by mobilizing 17,000 Idahoans to caucus for him. "The Clinton campaign made a fundamental mistake by writing states off," says Hildebrand.

Having wrestled the Clinton campaign to a draw through Super Tuesday, the Obama campaign suddenly found itself in a dominant position. Thanks to the field campaign set in motion by Hildebrand and Figueroa, Obama had effective grass-roots organizations in place in each of the next ten states. Clinton, by contrast, had no plan, no money and no real grass-roots organization. Even worse for Clinton, the only state whose demographics truly favored her was Maine, a caucus. "Both campaigns thought it was better territory for her, and we were pretty nervous about it," admits Hildebrand. "She was spending a lot of time there, she had staff there." But demographics proved no match for Obama's field organization. Clinton lost Maine—by nineteen points.

"We saw early that, because of the energy that we were evoking, the caucuses would be a great opportunity for us," says Axelrod. "And not just in Iowa. So for months out, we had organizers in these caucus states, and the Clinton campaign had . . . *nothing*." By contrast, says Figueroa, "the philosophy of our campaign from the beginning was to compete for every vote. Not cede any precinct, any county, anywhere. And it got us to where we are now."

Clinton has since complained that caucuses are "dominated by activists" who "don't represent the electorate." But that bellyaching, says Trippi, "is pure cover for 'We blew it.' If you can win a precinct just by getting ten people there—and that's true—then why the hell didn't she get ten people there?"

Adds Moulitsas of *Daily Kos*, "I don't know how a candidate can say she'll be ready to lead on Day One, when she can't even organize a simple caucus."

⤙ • ⤚

In the days leading up to the Texas primary, Clinton appeared equally unprepared for the contest there. Leaks from exasperated donors made clear that the campaign, drooling over the state's large trove of Hispanic voters, was largely clueless about the complex, hybrid nature of the election in Texas. Of the state's 193 delegates, only 126 are awarded on the basis of the primary vote. But since those are apportioned on the basis of turnout in past elections, few of the delegates are available in low-voting Hispanic districts that favor Clinton.

The rest of the delegates will be decided by caucus, which begins immediately after the primary polls close on Election Night. Since the caucus is open only to those who vote in the primary, the Obama campaign is urging its supporters to cast their ballots in the state's ten-day window for early voting. "I'll tell you what we're doing—inside campaign information," Ukman tells his new precinct captains at the training in San Marcos. "The elections officials publish a list of those who voted early. With that list, we can follow up and get our people to the caucus."

As it did in Super Tuesday states, Obama's field organization in Texas has enabled his campaign staff to mobilize an army of supporters in a matter of weeks. When Figueroa arrived in San Antonio to organize volunteers, he found a group called AlamObama already up and running. "We show up last week with our organizers," Figueroa tells me, "and the AlamObama people are all like, 'Great. Welcome to the party. Here's what we're doing, here's what we need to do.' They're telling us. They're incredibly structured. And you know why? They went to Camp Obama."

No group represents the campaign machine that Obama has built better than AlamObama. A year ago, the group was nothing more than eight people who attended an informal get-together at a Borders bookstore. Today, it's a 600-member grass-roots outfit—an all-volunteer field operation that hums with the energy and efficiency of a fully staffed campaign office. "In Iowa, the campaign was on the ground for six months," says Judy Hall, a college professor who cofounded the group. "They come here, and it's like they've already been on the ground for six months. Those of us in the grass roots, we simply minded the store.

"Well," she says, reconsidering her words, "I guess we actually *built* the store—but that's what this campaign is all about."

As Hall's well-honed operation makes clear, the Obama campaign has succeeded not by attracting starry-eyed followers who place their faith in hope but by motivating committed activists who are answering a call to national service. They're pouring their lifeblood into this campaign, not because they are in thrall to a cult of personality but because they're invested in the idea that politics matter, and that their participation can turn the current political system on its ear.

In reality, it already has. "We're seeing the last time a top-down campaign has a chance to win it," says Trippi. "There won't be another campaign that makes the same mistake the Clintons made of being dependent on big donors and insiders. It's not going to work ever again."

7

THE IRON LADY: THE CLINTON CAMPAIGN RETURNS FROM THE DEAD, AGAIN

RYAN LIZZA
The New Yorker   March 17, 2008

Over the past decade, Ryan Lizza has emerged as one of America's most prolific and insightful political reporters. After a lengthy stint as political correspondent for The New Republic, *Lizza recently joined the staff of* The New Yorker, *where his series of reports on the 2008 presidential campaign has provided what amounts to a blow-by-blow account of the fights for the GOP and Democratic nominations.*

In this piece, he focuses on the candidacy that refused to die—that of the eponymous Iron Lady herself, Hillary Clinton. As Lizza observes, "Even round-the-clock cable coverage does not quite convey the drumming repetition of a campaign, and Clinton . . . is a master of this punishing, incessant rhythm." The article describes an especially delicate moment in early March, when Clinton rebounded from a string of a dozen consecutive defeats to capture the Democratic popular vote in Ohio and Texas—last-ditch victories that allowed her to stave off, for a few weeks at least, those who would have her quit the race and cede the nomination to Barack Obama, but that did little to cut into Obama's essentially unbeatable lead in the pledged delegate count.

To watch Hillary Clinton during the final two weeks of the Ohio and Texas primary campaigns, as she defiantly ignored the pronouncements of her political demise and pounded away at her opponent in one more interview, at one more rally, was to bring to mind Jason or Freddy Krueger or the sitting governor of California, those Hollywood cyborgs and zombies who, despite bullets and stakes and explosions, will not under any circumstances be vanquished. Clinton's public performances were marked by an eerily unflappable persistence as she executed an ungentle two-pronged attack: raising doubts about the readiness of her young opponent, Senator Barack Obama, to be Commander-in-Chief and challenging the depth of his commitment to the bread-and-butter concerns of the middle class. On February 25th, during a foreign-policy speech at George Washington University, she surrounded herself with six military men, including General Wesley Clark, himself a former Presidential candidate, and Major General Antonio M. Taguba, who forthrightly investigated the abuses at Abu Ghraib prison, to the despair of the Pentagon leadership. Clinton attacked Obama from both the right (he would naïvely grant a Presidential audience to the world's dictators) and the left (he would unilaterally attack terrorist enclaves in Pakistan). The charges might have been, at best, a distortion of Obama's positions, but they were surely meant to paint him as unschooled and unseasoned—Barack the Unready.

Part of the way through her fusillade, Clinton broke into a spasm of coughing—much of the campaign entourage of aides and press had been battered with the flu and other transmittable ailments—and then, briefly, she lost her voice. The audience fell silent. For a dramatic moment, it was unclear if she could continue. But Clinton righted herself and struggled through some lines about Darfur without losing her place. It was as if she had managed to suppress the coughing through sheer will. An aide slipped in from the side and handed her a cough drop, which she discreetly popped into her mouth during a burst of applause.

Two days later, aboard Clinton's chartered campaign plane (she took off in a blizzard from Cleveland and was on to Columbus), she spoke in the aisle, while reporters, some pinned against tray tables by overeager cameramen who had leaped over several seats to get a good angle, crushed in around her with their recorders. The plane began its descent, careering toward the runway. Oblivious of airline regulations, Clinton continued ticking off her anti-Obama lines: "What I feel is happening is that people are turning toward the big questions that they should have to answer in this campaign. You know, who can be the best Commander-in-Chief, who do you want in the White House answering the phone at 3 A.M.?" (The line was straight from a new Clinton television spot, in which a telephone is heard ringing, ominously, at three in the morning—a spot that belonged to a half-century tradition of scare ads involving red telephones and mushroom clouds.) The landing gear dropped, but Clinton was on to the subject of the subprime-lending crisis and home foreclosures. "Many of you are homeowners. Home values in America have dropped one-point-six trillion dollars in the last year. So everybody's wealth is disintegrating."

The runway came into view. A voice on the intercom demanded that passengers sit down and fasten their seat belts. Clinton, though, continued standing and talking calmly about why she was staying in the contest. "We're now raising on average a million dollars a day on the Internet. People have just been, you know, really rallying to my candidacy." Reporters glanced nervously out the window, but never for an instant did Clinton turn away from the cameras, lose her train of thought, or allow the imminent landing to interrupt the full ventilation of her talking points. Seconds before touchdown, an aide steered Hillary Clinton back to her seat.

◅◆ • ◆▻

Unlike Hubert Humphrey, Al Smith, or even her husband, Hillary Clinton on the campaign trail has never been able to project the image of the happy warrior. There is now, and has always been, a certain joylessness in her bearing. She has been trying to make discipline a selling point since her first "listening tour" of New York State, in the months before she ran for the United States Senate—a device designed to portray tireless commitment to voters suspicious of her carpetbagging and celebrity. After landing in Columbus, the campaign entourage headed by motorcade to Zanesville, a town of about twenty-five thousand, sixty miles away, for what was billed as an economic "summit." The ninety-minute conversation among Clinton and fourteen politicians and business and labor leaders, and Ohioans with hard-luck stories, had all the drama of a Senate committee hearing. Some no doubt found the discussion riveting, but at one point the former Ohio senator and Mercury astronaut John Glenn, a panelist, was either very deep in thought about college loans, or fast asleep. Scores of audience members were similarly benumbed and fled the event before it was over. But Clinton seemed confident about the electoral power of relentless policy tedium. It was as if the sheer display of iron-pantsed discussion would further underscore her insistent theme: the hollowness of Obama's charisma. When one speaker offered encomiums to Clinton rather than economic prescriptions, she gently reprimanded her, saying, "We're going to put a moratorium on compliments." Then, with the bonhomie of a high-school health teacher, she turned the conversation back toward government programs to help people "quit smoking, to get more exercise, to eat right, to take their vitamins."

Endurance is the unseen requirement of a successful candidate. Even round-the-clock cable coverage does not quite convey the drumming repetition of a campaign, and Clinton, for all her weaknesses, is a master of this punishing, incessant rhythm. Unlike Obama, who can seem recessive when he tires, she is intent on masking the fatigue. Even on primary day, Clinton kept at it. She spent the morning in a Houston studio, taking part in twenty television interviews reaching every major market in Texas and Ohio. Clinton was methodical. In every Texas interview, as if for the first time, she patiently mentioned her military endorsements and the work that she did thirty-six years ago in George McGovern's Presidential campaign, registering Latino voters in south Texas. (This last seemed ironic, considering that the Clinton campaign wants to portray Obama as a twenty-first-century McGovern—too soft, too naïve, and destined to lose in November.) In every Ohio interview, she raised what, in the last week of the campaign, had become a potent anti-Obama issue: the discrepancy between his public criticisms of the North American Free Trade Agreement and an Obama adviser's alleged assurances to the Canadian government that the candidate's sharp rhetoric was merely primary-season politics. "Senator Obama came to Ohio and said one thing about NAFTA, and then had a foreign government told something else," she told a Dayton radio station. Her message control was interrupted only when another prolonged coughing fit forced her to take a break during a chat with a Corpus Christi station. Her break did not last long.

Later that morning, the campaign moved to the parking lot at the J.P. Henderson Elementary School, a polling place in a heavily Hispanic corner of southeast Houston that had been transformed into a tiny set. Salsa music filled the air, about a dozen smiling Latino children were brought in, and Clinton's motorcade soon rumbled toward the school. Accompanying the candidate was a somewhat eclectic entourage: the actor Ted Danson, who wore an Irish tweed hat; his wife, the actress Mary Steenburgen, an Arkansan and longtime supporter of Bill and Hillary Clinton; Clinton's soignée aide-de-camp, Huma Abedin, who was recently profiled in *Vogue* and currently was wearing a bright-orange sweater and black boots that shimmered in the sunlight; and Anthony Weiner, the wiry Brooklyn congressman and aspiring mayor of New York. Clinton's eyes widened at the sight of the children, and with a cue from a staffer they began to chant, "Hill-ar-*ee!* Hill-are-*ee!*" Clinton bent and talked to a little girl in a black cowboy hat. The photographers swooped in for the picture of the day.

The press corps following Clinton had grown in recent days, but not for reasons that pleased the campaign. Like Vatican reporters who traveled with John Paul II less to hear his homilies than to report the details of his senescence, these reporters came, at first, for the political deathwatch. Bill Clinton himself had told Texas voters that if Texas and Ohio did not come through for Hillary, the campaign was probably finished. At the time, this seemed like further evidence that the former President had lost his political ear, that he had become more a walking minefield than an asset to his wife. But by primary day, as Hillary Clinton's resolve to stay in the race became clear, the mood in the media mob had shifted. "We have come to bury Hillary, but we may end up praising her," Tom Baldwin, of the *London Times,* said. And Mark Penn, Clinton's portly and unloved chief strategist, told me, speaking of Obama, "We broke his momentum completely. That's why, when I went to sleep Monday, I could say every single poll had moved in one direction—towards us."

By this point, Clinton had begun to see that all the work aimed at derailing Obama had paid off. As the Latino children continued their chant, she smiled and said, "I feel really good about today."

⤛ • ⤜

Later that night, at Clinton's victory party in Columbus (she won the Ohio primary with fifty-four percent of the vote), Terry McAuliffe, the chairman of the campaign and an unflaggingly high-spirited supporter of both Clintons, indulged in an impromptu we-told-you-so session. He taunted reporters for their eagerness to write off Clinton's prospects. "We came back in New Hampshire, Nevada, Super Tuesday," he said. "And we're doing it again tonight." After a long string of defeats for the Clinton forces, this was her moment of triumph. Just after MSNBC put a winning check mark next to Clinton's picture, projecting her victory in Ohio, a young female volunteer did a joyous dance with friends. "Hell yeah, baby!" she shouted. "Eat it, Barack! This is a woman's world!"

McAuliffe's agitated recap of the campaign left out some unignorable facts. He ignored that Super Tuesday, on February 5th, had widely been considered a draw. (Obama won thirteen states, Clinton won nine, and Obama emerged with a lead of more than a dozen delegates.) Nor did he mention that before March 4th Obama had won eleven straight contests—twelve counting Vermont, which he had won a few hours earlier. (Clinton was also about to win in Texas, by a margin of 51–47.) But all of these results had presented the Clinton campaign with an arithmetical dilemma. In the remaining dozen primary contests, which include the March 8th Wyoming caucus and stretch to the South Dakota primary, on June 3rd, Clinton needs to win by huge margins in order to overcome the more than hundred-delegate lead that Obama still enjoyed after March 4th. By that calculation, Clinton could reach the number of dele-

gates needed to secure the nomination only by appealing to the so-called superdelegates—elected and Party officials who aren't bound by actual voting in
the primaries and caucuses. Would it be acceptable, I asked McAuliffe, for the
superdelegates to overturn the results of the popular vote?

"You keep trying to contend the nomination is over tonight!" McAuliffe
replied loudly and happily, pointing and waving his arms. "I'm telling you we
have twelve states to go. Don't tell me about the popular vote. You call me in
June and then talk to me about it. We don't know where we're going to be. We
have a lot of states. I don't want you disenfranchising all these great states coming up. . . . Why don't you like these people?"

The next day, a Clinton adviser was more candid about what lies ahead. "Inside the campaign, people are not idiots," she told me. "Everyone can do the
math. It isn't like the Obama campaign has some special abacus. We can do
these calculations, too. Everyone recognizes how steep this hill is. But you gotta
keep your game face on."

For Clinton, it will be vital in the weeks ahead to maintain the public perception that she can still win. If the Obama campaign's strength has been its
grassroots organization—he built his delegate lead by winning in far-flung caucus states that Clinton ignored—the Clinton campaign's strength has been in
refining the art of attack. Its war room is staffed by a team of men and women
who consider themselves heirs to the celebrity operatives of Bill Clinton's 1992
campaign—in particular, James Carville, Clinton's campaign manager, and
George Stephanopoulos, his communications director. Until recently, Hillary
Clinton's communications team, led by Howard Wolfson, a pugnacious operative who has been with Clinton since her first Senate campaign, and the
equally combative Phil Singer, a former aide to Senator Charles Schumer, was
not always impressive. Through January and much of February, the campaign
never quite settled an internal debate about how aggressively to attack Obama.
In public, Hillary shifted from deferential ("I am honored to be here with
Barack Obama") to confrontational ("Shame on you, Barack Obama!"). In debates, she seemed almost to experiment with attack lines, few of which seemed
spontaneous, and Obama was deft at arguing that the attacks on him were examples of "old politics." Meanwhile, the press corps seemed uninterested in any
sustained anti-Obama focus, writing more about the history he was making
rather than the political corners he might be cutting.

By early February, Clinton's campaign seemed to be flailing. On one day, she
accused Obama of plagiarizing part of a speech (actually a few lines borrowed

at the suggestion of an Obama friend, the governor of Massachusetts), on another of reneging on a campaign-finance pledge (which would have applied only to the general election). In a series of debates (twenty in all, for anyone counting), Clinton kept accusing Obama of advocating a health-care plan—not very different from hers—that she insisted failed to insure fifteen million Americans. None of these arguments slowed Obama's victory streak, which started on February 9th with wins in Louisiana, Nebraska, Washington, and the Virgin Islands.

The Clinton campaign finally succeeded in tripping up Obama as reporters began to raise the questions put to them in daily conferences by the war-room managers: Why, as chairman of the Senate Foreign Relations Committee's Subcommittee on European Affairs, had Obama never held a hearing about NATO's role in Afghanistan? And, come to think of it, what *was* the full nature of Obama's relationship with Tony Rezko, his onetime fund-raiser and friend, who happened to be on trial in Chicago for extortion, money laundering, and fraud? There was also that curious business with the Canadians. Was it true that Obama's top economic-policy adviser, Austan Goolsbee, had told someone at the Canadian consulate that Obama was not entirely serious about renegotiating NAFTA? The Clinton campaign acted utterly shocked by this possible revelation. (Never mind that in an interview last year Clinton told me that the problem with NAFTA was "not necessarily the framework" but "the way that it was implemented and enforced.")

The attacks were working. Last week, Penn told me, "If you look at the Gallup tracking poll, we moved even after just a few days of opening a couple of basic questions on him. So it really shows that he's much weaker as a potential nominee." (The poll in question showed Obama leading nationally 50–42 on the Saturday before primary day, and the race tied, 45–45, three days later.)

The newfound strength of Clinton's war room is vital for her going forward. Her campaign realizes that if it is unable to overcome Obama's lead in pledged delegates, there may be only one other path to victory: to make the case to superdelegates—and the Party establishment—that Obama could not defeat John McCain in the general election, and that, therefore, the will of the voters should not be binding. Mark Penn has been trying to make that argument for weeks, but few paid attention while Obama was winning. (How could the Illinois senator be unelectable if he was on his way to being elected?) But people are listening now, despite polls consistently showing that Obama does better than Clinton in a head-to-head race with McCain.

≺≺ • ≻≻

Penn, regardless of the success of his tactics, has become a lonely figure in the Clinton campaign. "Mark Penn does not have many friends," one Clinton adviser told me when I asked which camp in the notoriously balkanized Clinton campaign he represented. But Penn has the two friends that matter: Bill and Hillary Clinton, who have relied on his instincts and wisdom since he was brought into the White House with Dick Morris after the Republicans, led by Newt Gingrich, took control of Congress in the 1994 midterm election. Hillary Clinton wrote in her autobiography that the weeks after that defeat were "among the most difficult of my White House years" and she "wondered how much I was to blame for the debacle: whether we had lost the election over health care." But with help from Morris and his protégé, Mark Penn, President Clinton saw his approval ratings rebound, and by the fall of 1996, after Morris resigned in the wake of his own sex—or, to be precise, toe-sucking—scandal, Penn had taken charge of Clinton's successful reelection campaign. In 1998, Bill Clinton's affair with the White House intern Monica Lewinsky was disclosed, and by that time Penn's place in the Clinton circle of friends, enablers, and strategists was fixed. He gave advice to the President throughout his impeachment ordeal and to Mrs. Clinton as she recovered from public humiliation. Penn served as the chief strategist for her successful 2000 and 2006 Senate campaigns. More than any other senior adviser, Penn has guided both Clintons through their most treacherous political troubles—and has encouraged Hillary Clinton's almost unnerving survival instincts.

Penn's poll-defying arguments about Obama's electability against McCain will be pressed ever more forcefully as both campaigns move to the dénouement of the primary season. From Penn's standpoint, Obama's freshness is his greatest vulnerability. "The GOP attack machine redefines the Democratic candidate," Penn said recently. "It's formidable. It commands a vast media network. And it has been able to skew the perceptions even of such distinguished public servants and well-respected Democrats as Al Gore and John Kerry, creating impressions of them very quickly that were out of step with reality." Hillary Clinton, he went on, "has withstood the full brunt of this kind of attack and will be able to neutralize what is likely to happen, particularly with the nominee who is not as well known through public life."

Clinton is stressing in all her appearances—another point that Penn sees as essential—that Obama will appear distinctly weaker on national-security questions in relation to McCain. (This infuriates Obama's supporters—after all, he alone among the surviving candidates opposed the invasion of Iraq.) The Clinton campaign will also press the claim that Obama will not be able to withstand heightened scrutiny of his domestic-policy views. The implication is that Obama is unacceptably liberal, while Clinton, despite the similarity of her positions and voting record, is not. "How much do Independent voters really know about Barack Obama, his voting record, and his past positions?" Penn asked recently. "Certainly less than Democrats know. In a general election the Republicans would spring into action, and quickly, if he were the nominee, roll out his full record. And the kind of Independent support that you see in places like Idaho would consequently evaporate."

Penn pushed this idea last week when he told me, "People want to have a nominee that's going to win. So a lot of the things they accepted initially may not hold up. Independent and Republican support is diminishing as they find out he's the most liberal Democratic senator"—a reference to recent rankings by the *National Journal*. "As they get more of a sense that he's not ready to be Commander-in-Chief, a lot of Independents who were supporting him are disappearing."

This electability argument—that Obama can be easily caricatured, that he's weak on national security, that he's too liberal—is not so very different from the Republican case against Obama, although the charges might be more damaging coming from a member of one's own party, especially in a bruising campaign that may last until the Convention this August in Denver. It is tempting to say that the Clinton campaign's plan is to burn the village in order to save it—that Hillary Clinton believes that Democrats, hypnotized by Obama, are making a historic mistake from which only she can rescue them. And it is tempting to add that this means the political destruction of the man who is still most likely to be the Democratic nominee.

Clinton's victories and her rhetorical tactics have challenged Obama's principled refusal to play the rough-and-ready game which he brands "old politics." Her disingenuous remark on *60 Minutes* that Obama was not a Muslim "as far as I know" was especially galling. One foreign-policy adviser, the professor and author Samantha Power, betrayed a taste of the Obama campaign's anger at Clinton when she told *The Scotsman* that Clinton was "a monster. . . . The amount of deceit she has put forward is really unattractive." (Power, who also writes for *The New Yorker,* apologized and resigned from the campaign last Friday.)

But perhaps this prospect of a grueling endgame is not as destructive as it sounds. The attacks on Obama, and Obama's counterattacks on Clinton, have been mild compared to some heard in recent elections. (Before the Iowa caucuses in 2004, a Democratic group ran an advertisement that showed an image of Osama bin Laden with a voice-over saying, "Howard Dean just cannot compete with George Bush on foreign policy." Robert Gibbs, the spokesperson for the group, is now Obama's communications director.) At the end of last week, Obama was accusing Clinton of hiding her finances, and the Clinton campaign was comparing Obama's accusations to those of Kenneth Starr, the independent counsel who investigated Bill Clinton during the Lewinsky scandal, and whose very name, among Clintonites, is synonymous with villainy.

There are two unsettled questions about Obama that a final, bitter counteroffensive from Clinton may help answer: Does Obama have the toughness required to beat John McCain, and, more important, to serve as President? And can Obama attract some of the key swing groups—especially white working-class Democrats and Latinos—who have been drawn to Clinton but are open to voting for McCain? The purpose of primaries, after all, is to answer such questions.

Clinton may be criticized for staying too long in the race and for attacking Obama in ways that his supporters will consider nefarious and desperate. But no one is entitled to a Presidential nomination. As ugly as it looks now—and as ugly as it is likely to become—if Barack Obama becomes the Democrats' nominee, he may thank Hillary Clinton for making him a better candidate.

8

IS JOHN McCAIN BOB DOLE?

JOHN HEILEMANN
   With additional reporting by Michelle Dubert
New York magazine   April 21, 2008

The common wisdom is that John McCain, in addition to his sky-high approval ratings, has another advantage in the general election: By wrapping up the GOP nomination in February, he gained a head start of several months over Barack Obama, whose campaign was forced to focus on Hillary Clinton throughout the spring. But as political correspondent John Heilemann points out, McCain faces a number of challenges, including his age (at seventy-two, he'd be the oldest man ever elected president), his campaign's surfeit of lobbyists (an issue that would lead McCain to purge his staff not long after this article appeared), his embrace of the Iraq War, and the fact that the Democrats are sure to do everything under the sun to link him to the unpopular current White House resident. Even more dangerous is the perception that McCain has lost his maverick edge, and—like Bob Dole in '96—has ascended to the Republican nomination simply because he was the next in line.

By the time John McCain trundles into the ballroom of the Fairmont hotel in Dallas, he has already had what for most men his age would have been a very full day. He has met the press at a Mexican restaurant in San Antonio. He has held a town-hall meeting at a barbecue joint in Houston. He has fielded yet another question about the "North American Union," the latest conspiracy theory from the nutters who brought us the New World Order. He has uttered the salutation "my friends" at least 40 times. And, oh yes, he has won the Republican primaries in Texas, Ohio, Rhode Island, and Vermont, dispatched that holy-rolling goober Mike Huckabee back whence he came, and secured his party's nomination for president of the United States.

So McCain is feeling pretty chuffed when he mounts the stage with his canary-yellow-suited, Barbie-blond gal, Cindy. The crowd before him is measly by Barack Obama standards, just a few hundred people, but it's plenty loud and lusty. The confetti cannons are loaded and cocked, the balloons pinned to the ceiling.

Out in the audience, Mark Salter and Steve Schmidt look twitchy. The goateed Salter is McCain's chief wordsmith; the shaven-headed Schmidt his mouthpiece. Through experience, the two men have learned that prepared addresses are not McCain's best friends—and teleprompters his mortal enemies. On a good day, McCain merely looks shifty when he's reading off a prompter, as his eyes track the flowing text; on a bad day, he stutters, stammers, yammers, making him seem . . . well, let's not go there.

As McCain begins to speak, Salter and Schmidt position themselves so they can see both their boss and the giant flat-panel on the camera riser directly in front of him. The speech is short. It's going smoothly. McCain is nearly done. "Their patience," he is saying of the American people, "is at an end for politicians who value ambition over principle, and for partisanship that is less a contest of ideas than an uncivil brawl over the spoils of power."

And then . . . *Oh, shit!*

The screen goes blank!

McCain is flying blind!

Up onstage, McCain wears a mask of misery. He shuffles some papers, blinks, smiles tightly, checks the prompter repeatedly. Schmidt and Salter, eyes bugging, heads swiveling, are in full panic mode. Ten seconds pass. Then 20, then 30, then 40 without a word from McCain. The crowd cheers and chants, filling up the dead air that threatens to throttle him on national TV—until suddenly, voilà, the text reappears and McCain picks up where he left off. Salter shakes his head. Schmidt shrugs and mops his brow. Soon they're tapping away at their BlackBerrys as if nothing momentous had occurred, let alone a near-death experience.

By the standards of the McCain campaign, of course, nothing momentous *had* occurred. Less than a year ago, the Arizona senator really was kaput—or so some of us geniuses thought. His operation was broke, his poll numbers anemic, his team in tatters, his image muddied and muddled. But today McCain stands as good a chance as any of the remaining runners of being the next resident of 1600 Pennsylvania Avenue. His approval rating, according to Gallup, is 67 percent, as high as it's ever been. In head-to-head matchups, he runs roughly even with Hillary Clinton and Barack Obama, and his prospects seem to brighten each day that the rancorous contest between his potential rivals rumbles on. "The Democrats are destroying themselves," says GOP strategist Alex Castellanos, who recently signed on with McCain. "They're engaged in killing Obama. It's like killing Santa Claus on Christmas morning—the kids won't forget or forgive."

That McCain's political resurrection owed as much to the weakness of the Republican field—not to mention blind shithouse luck—as to his talent and grit makes it no less remarkable. Yet for all the hosannas being sung to him these days, and for all the waves of fear and trembling rippling through the Democratic masses, the truth is that McCain is a candidate of pronounced and glaring weaknesses. A candidate whose capacity to raise enough money to beat back the tidal wave of Democratic moola is seriously in doubt. A candidate unwilling or unable to animate the GOP base. A candidate whose operation has never recovered from the turmoil of last summer, still skeletal and ragtag and technologically antediluvian. ("Fund-raising on the Web? You don't say. You can raise money through those tubes?") Whose cadre of confidantes contains so many lobbyists that the *Straight Talk Express* often has the vibe of a rolling

K Street clubhouse. Whose awkward positioning issues-wise was captured brilliantly by Pat Buchanan: "The jobs are never coming back, the illegals are never going home, but we're going to have a lot more wars." A candidate one senior moment—or one balky teleprompter—away from being transformed from a grizzled warrior into Grandpa Simpson. A candidate, that is, who poses an existential question for Democrats: If you can't beat a guy like this in a year like this, with a vastly unpopular Republican war still ongoing and a Republican recession looming, what precisely is the point of you?

⤛ • ⤜

The morning after McCain clinched the nomination, I hopped onboard his campaign jet and flew with him to Washington, where he was scheduled to have a congratulatory lunch with George W. Bush. (The menu? Hot dogs.) During the flight, standing in the aisle, I asked Schmidt—who channeled his ferocity on behalf of Bush in 2004, Dick Cheney in 2005, and Arnold Schwarzenegger in 2006—how McCain planned to deal with his infamous "100 years" remark about Iraq. "We trust the American people to be able to figure this out," he said in a tone, combative and stagy, that called to mind vintage James Carville. "We don't think the American people are stupid. Do you think they are stupid?"

Well, to be honest, sometimes yes and sometimes no—but that, as Schmidt was well aware, is beside the point. Equally irrelevant, in the end, is the argument raging between the McCain and Obama camps over the proper and fair interpretation of the sound bite in question. What's pertinent to the race ahead is that McCain has been unwavering in his commitment to keeping U.S. troops in Iraq for an indeterminate period of time. And that this stance puts him on the wrong side of the public on one of the two central issues on which the general election is likely to turn.

"For the past year-plus, the public has said they want to change our policy and they want to get out, and McCain has put himself squarely in the status quo corner," says the pollster Peter Hart. Indeed, according to a new Gallup survey, voters favor setting a firm timetable for troop withdrawal by a margin of 60 percent to 35 percent. "There's no way the public is going to say, 'Well, we're going to reassess things now that we see it from McCain's point of view,'" adds Hart. "His difficulty is that the public has figured this out."

McCain's difficulties may be even more pronounced on the second pivotal issue: the economy. During the New Hampshire primary, McCain blurted out the domestic equal of his "100 years" gaffe: "The issue of economics is not something I've understood as well as I should; I've got Greenspan's book," he said, though he later allowed that he had yet to crack its spine. In time, McCain would contend that he was just being momentarily glib; that he may be no economist, but he has a firm grasp of the subject. Yet repeatedly over the years, McCain—a former chair of the Senate Commerce Committee, mind you—has said things strikingly similar, to everyone from the *Wall Street Journal* to David Brooks.

Even the most loyal Republicans express concern about McCain's economics gap. "He's never been particularly fluent in or showed much intellectual interest toward economic matters," says Pete Wehner, who ran the Office of Strategic Initiatives in Bush's White House. "Can he speak fluently or compellingly about them? We'll soon see. But it would require him to lift his game."

Problematic as McCain's lack of economic fluency may be, it's only part of what plagues him. Another is the substantive ground he occupies. "People don't realize that he's Bush II on economic policy," says Mike Podhorzer, the deputy political director of the AFL-CIO. "When we tell people in focus groups where he is on health care, Social Security, and the minimum wage, they are shocked. And they immediately say, 'I have to reconsider what I think about him.'"

Painting McCain as Bush's twin will obviously be central to the Democrats' strategy this fall regardless of whether Obama or Clinton wins the nomination. As Hart notes, "McCain's single greatest weakness is that many voters believe he will be part and parcel of the policies that Bush has promulgated." Podhorzer, for his part, is already at it, having recently launched a union-financed effort designed to label him a "Bush McClone."

No sane person would assume that such efforts will be a slam-dunk, given that McCain's media-amplified image runs counter to the notion that he's a clone of anyone, let alone 43. "McCain has that reformist, maverick history that people identify him with," says Bush's former media guru Mark McKinnon, who now plays the same role for McCain. "They know he's not a typical Republican and has had his issues with the president over time, so they don't see him as in bed with the president or the Republican Party that they believe has in recent years come to represent the status quo."

The evidence buttressing McKinnon's assertion isn't hard to locate. Among independent voters, according to Gallup, McCain leads Obama by a spread of 42–29 and Clinton by 48–23. And an even more striking sign of his crossover appeal was cited by Karl Rove in a speech he gave last month in Washington.

"About twice as many Democrats support McCain as Republicans support Obama, and about three times as many Democrats support McCain as Republicans support Clinton," Rove said. "The media is all wired up about these 'Obamacans' . . . but the real story of this election is the 'McCainocrats.'"

The question is whether McCain's maverick persona, which is deeply rooted in his renegade run in the primaries eight years ago, will hold up under scrutiny. For as it should be clear to anyone paying even cursory attention, McCain 2000 and McCain 2008 are very different mammals—as evinced by his toadying to Jerry Falwell, his flip-floppy embrace of Bush's tax cuts, and his failure to offer any kind of substantial reform agenda this time around.

Then there's the fact that many people at the highest levels of McCain's campaign are lobbyists or the employees of lobbying firms. The list has included Schmidt, campaign manager Rick Davis, and one of his top strategists, the longtime K Street kingpin Charlie Black. Until recently, in fact, Black was being paid by his lobbying shop while he "volunteered" for McCain; his decision to step down from the chairmanship of his firm a couple of weeks ago—a development akin to Eliot Spitzer taking a vow of chastity—was designed to preempt criticism surrounding conflict of interest.

Even some Republican stalwarts are appalled at McCain's coziness with the influence-peddling industry. "Can you imagine a bunch of people working for Halliburton trying to elect Cheney?" says a prominent GOP consultant. "How can that be legal? Even if it is legal, it's never happened before. And it says a lot about what McCain has become. In 2000, he was the candidate of reform, of anger, of screw the system. Now he's the candidate of lobbyists, endorsements, and special deals with Beltway banks."

So if McCain is no longer the bracing iconoclast he was in 2000, who the hell is he?

"I'll tell you," this person says. "He's morphed into Bob Dole."

⋖⋅⋗

This was not my first encounter with the McCain-is-Dole meme. I had first run across it back in January, on the night of the final Republican debate, in Simi Valley, California, when McCain's crabbiness and sarcasm onstage had prompted a former GOP player now tilling the corporate field to make the comparison over dinner. As it turned out, the idea was also being promulgated sub rosa by a number of Mitt Romney's senior strategists. A few days later, on the morning of Super Duper Tuesday, it popped out of Mitt's own mouth. "There are a lot of folks that tend to think maybe John McCain's race is a bit like Bob Dole's race," Romney snarked on Fox News. "That it's the guy who's the next in line; he's the inevitable choice and we'll give it to him, and then it won't work."

Not surprisingly, McCain's people push back hard on the suggestion that their guy might be Dole Redux. "I think that in many ways he's very un-Dole-like," retorts McKinnon. "He actually has really good strategic sense. He's a very disciplined candidate in terms of delivering a message. And Dole restrained those things that people liked best about him. There's a great side of Dole that we never saw. We'll always see that with McCain."

Certainly it's true that Dole kept his sense of humor—dark, ironic, acutely subversive—largely under wraps when he was the Republican nominee in 1996. It's also true that McCain makes no effort to suppress his comic sensibilities, which are not only similar to Dole's but also to those of David Letterman, with whom he shares an affinity. Like Letterman and Dole, McCain is constantly offering a running sidelong commentary about himself and what he is doing, in the process winking, letting everyone know that, deep down, he considers it a bit of a sham. In New Hampshire, McCain routinely ended appearances on the stump by invoking Richard Daley's timeless dictum "Vote early and vote often." What other presidential candidate in history has ever left his audiences not with an applause line or a rousing crescendo but a cynical joke about politics?

As Neal Gabler argued recently in the *Times,* this is no small part of why McCain is popular with the press: He is the meta-candidate—and journalists have never met a meta they didn't like. The question, however, is whether it's the ideal approach to claiming the hearts of voters. Though Letterman is popular, Leno always thumps him in the ratings, after all. On the other hand, McCain's propensities in this regard may be the best counterweight against his increasingly geriatric bearing. "It's one of the few future-oriented things about him," says Alex Castellanos. "He's got that postmodern detachment and intolerance of bullshit that will keep you young forever."

But few of the other likenesses between McCain and Dole can be spun so benignly. There's the septuagenarian-ness (McCain is 71; Dole was 72 when he ran). There's the physical frailty, courageously earned in war, that nevertheless serves as a constant reminder of his advanced years. There's the legendary shortness of his fuse. (McCain has yet to have a full-on "Stop lying about my record" moment on the trail, but his testiness was on display the other day in a widely YouTubed confrontation on his campaign jet with the *Times*'s Elisabeth Bumiller.) There's the firm conviction, as *Time* journalist Mark Halperin has noted, that "being on *Meet the Press* is more important than going to church—actually, that being on *Meet the Press* IS going to church."

These are all superficial things, you might say, and you'd be correct. But Republicans cite deeper, more worrying commonalities between McCain and Dole. "You'd fly around with Dole in 1996 and try to talk message, and all he wanted to know was who was going to be up onstage with him at the next event," recalls an operative who worked for Dole in his pre-Viagra days. "Same deal now with McCain. He has no message outside of Iraq. What's John McCain's health plan? What's his tax plan? What's his high-tech plan? No one in a million years can tell you."

Scott Reed, Dole's campaign manager, doesn't disagree with many of these parallels. "Can't lift their arms above their heads, can't comb their own hair—yeah," he says. "Teleprompter-challenged—right." But Reed points out a salient difference between 1996 and today. "What happened with Dole was that the Democrats were able to aim both bazookas at us," he explains. "They took all their primary money and used it to create the Dole-Gingrich two-headed monster, and we were never able to get up off the mat. But the Democrats aren't able to do that now. They may never be able to do it."

Reed is right. For all the wailing and gnashing of molars among Democrats about the damage being done to Obama and Clinton by their prolonged primary tussle, the greater cost to the party may be the missed opportunity to unload on McCain this spring. To no small extent, presidential campaigns are battles that boil down to a pair of competing efforts to define the opposition. Were BHO and HRC not still endeavoring to hack each other to pieces with metaphorical meat cleavers, Democrats could be using their huge financial advantage to cast McCain in whatever mold they consider most damaging: Dubya II, Dole II, Attila the Hun II, whatever. But instead it's the GOP that's getting a head start in the definition derby—especially concerning Obama.

≪← • →≫

Back in November 2006, a few days after the midterm elections, McKinnon and I were gabbing on the phone about the hopemonger's rise. "I think Obama would be a real interesting candidate," he said. "And if it's McCain-Obama, that's a real win-win for the country. There's this great documentary on Barry

Goldwater, and it reveals that he and JFK were having conversations about how, if they were the nominees in 1964, they were going to jump on a plane and campaign together around the country—go from city to city, debating each other in a respectful way. Which is a really interesting idea, and just the sort of thing you could see McCain and Obama doing. Wouldn't that be great?"

McKinnon isn't your typical political mechanic or your standard-brand Republican. Until 1998, in fact, his résumé included only clients of the Democratic persuasion—and not just any Democrats, but the likes of Michael Dukakis and former Texas governor Ann Richards. Even after two presidential campaigns in the service of Bush, he remains a sensitive soul. So I wasn't totally surprised when he declared, "I'm gonna tell McCain that if Obama is the Democratic nominee, I'm not gonna work against him; I'm just not going to make any negative ads against Barack Obama."

A noble sentiment, to be sure, and a pledge that McKinnon continues to insist he intends to honor—though many of his friends suspect he'll find it hard to abandon ship when the moment of truth arrives. But it's not a widely shared feeling in the McCain campaign or the GOP writ large. If Obama is the nominee, you can bet the mortgage money that there will be no happy-pappy fly-arounds. (For one thing, McCain gives every indication of regarding Obama the same way that Clinton does: as a flyweight, a line-cutter, and a preening neophyte.) No, the GOP campaign against the Land of Lincolner will be unrelentingly brutal.

The contours of that campaign are already coming into view—and not just by studying the early maneuvers on the Republican side. "Our strategy will look a fair amount like the one that Hillary is running against him now," a party official says. "It'll build on two things: first, that he's way too inexperienced to be commander-in-chief, which not only polls incredibly well but has the virtue of being true; and, second, that he's way too liberal."

When it comes to experience, Republicans believe the contrast between McCain and Obama will be plain to see, and much more meaningful than it has been in the Democratic race. When it comes to liberalism, they invariably cite *National Journal*, which concluded that Obama had the most left-wing voting record in the Senate. "Is there any chance the Republicans would ever nominate the guy who's furthest to the right?" asks Reed. "Everyone throws around the L-word like it's a scarlet, but there's something there."

In the standard Republican playbook, charges of excessive liberalism are typically employed to suggest that a Democratic candidate is a pansy. And, no doubt, the party's assault on Obama will include insinuations of limp-wristedness, especially compared with McCain in the national-security arena. But Republicans have other objectives in mind, too, when they harp on Obama's purported left-wingedness.

For a start, they wish to associate him with a static, backward-looking creed. "Obama's a fantastic candidate in the sense that he understands that this could be a New Frontier election," Castellanos says. "So we need to take some of the future away from him, and it won't be hard to do. He talks a great game, but his policies are old-style, Democratic, industrial-age stuff. We just need to rip the wrapping off and show that there's nothing in the box."

Similarly, by calling Obama a liberal, the Republicans are impugning his character by calling him a phony. In his recent speech in Washington, Rove, after pummeling Obama as a liar (for what he sees as various biographical embellishments), a would-be tax raiser, and a surrender primate on Iraq, lit into him as a fraud for his pretenses of postpartisan leadership. "During the three years he's been in the Senate, anytime there has been a big bipartisan effort"—on judges, terrorist surveillance, war funding, immigration—"where was Senator Obama on any of those big fights? I'll tell you where he was. He was over there up against the wall, ironically watching everything go on and voting 'no.'"

Naturally, the Republicans' attempts to define Obama as too liberal will extend to the cultural realm. They will portray him as elitist, effete—highlighting Harvard, Hyde Park, and his gutter balls on the bowling lanes of Pennsylvania. They will tar him as arrogant, pointing to the helpful comment once coughed up by his wife: "Barack is one of the smartest people you will ever encounter who will deign to enter this messy thing called politics." (Deign to enter?) And, no doubt, they will slam him as insufficiently patriotic, calling attention to everything from his eschewal of an American-flag lapel pin to his failure to put his hand over his heart during the national anthem at a campaign event in Iowa.

Patriotism will also be the Republican entry point into the combustible realm of race. No one close to McCain believes that he intends for his campaign to exploit or exacerbate the black-white divide in any explicit way. But nor does anyone believe we've heard the last of the controversy over the Reverend Jeremiah Wright. Already a group of conservative activists have posted to YouTube a video splicing together his most incendiary comments with shots of Obama and backed by beats from Public Enemy. Expect more from the shadowy world of 527s that disgorged the Swift Boat Veterans for Truth.

It would be comforting to dismiss all this as the desperate flailing of a party in decline. But there are signs that the areas Republicans intend to target may prove soft targets. The pollster Scott Rasmussen tells me that Obama is already trailing McCain among white male voters by a whopping margin of 57–33—and that in both swing states and others, such as Virginia, that Democrats hope to capture, there has been "significant deterioration for Obama" and "a dramatic change in McCain's favor" since the Wright imbroglio erupted.

<+ • +>

What makes these developments all the more disconcerting, of course, is that they're taking place even before the GOP has sunk its teeth into Obama. Not long ago, I'm told, Bill Clinton was talking to a friend about his wife's rival and made an interesting observation. The way Republicans beat Democrats, he said, is by turning them into caricatures—citing John Kerry, Al Gore, and Dukakis as examples. The reason that he, WJC, had survived is that he'd aggressively labored to deny them the opportunity. He'd been able to say, wait a minute, I don't fit in the box you're trying to stick me in. The problem with Obama, Clinton went on, is that he's tailor-made for the container that the Republicans are devising in which to bury him.

Now, Clinton is hardly a disinterested observer here. Quite the contrary. And it's worth pointing out that his wife ain't exactly immune from caricature; the Republican cartoon of her is as vivid and damning as a Thomas Nast rendering. But the argument that Obama would be more easily crated than Hillary is really the only argument that her campaign has left to sway the remaining undecided superdelegates—though the way her people talk about it isn't usually so blunt.

Instead, they prefer to speak about the electoral map. What they will tell you privately is they believe that if Hillary were the Democratic nominee, she could be confident of holding all the states that Kerry won in 2004, and she'd be well positioned to carry Ohio, Florida, New Mexico, Nevada, and Arkansas as well. Obama, by contrast, in their judgment, would find it impossible to win either Florida or Ohio. Because of his difficulties with blue-collar whites, he would also be hard-pressed to hold Michigan—turning Virginia, Nevada, Colorado, and New Mexico into must-have states. Could Obama carry all four versus McCain, a western senator with environmental cred and an aversion to federal spending? Not bloody likely, the Clinton people claim. Thus Hillary's electability argument in a nutshell.

Castellanos agrees that Clinton would be a tougher opponent for McCain than Obama would be—but says it has little to do with the map. "We don't want the Clintons in a general election," he says. "It's bad for America, and they'll win." Why? "The Clintons don't show up at a knife fight with a gun; they show up with a missile launcher. I hope the Democrats put a stake in her heart now, or we will regret it soon."

Yet most Republican operatives believe that Obama, even with the Wright millstone draped around his neck, would be a more formidable challenger than Clinton, and their reasons boil down to three.

First, if Hillary were to win the nomination, the process by which she got there would likely hobble her. "If Hillary pulls this off, she will have undoubtedly alienated the African-American vote," Scott Reed says. "And she'll definitely have higher negative ratings than any politician in America."

Second, they point to the money—Obama's unholy capacity to amass it, that is. "By September 1, Obama could be raising $2 million a day," says a well-known Republican media savant. "That would enable them to do network-TV ad buys, which no one has done in a serious way since 1976. They could be putting up 500 points a week in places like Texas, Louisiana, Georgia—while McCain is doing nothing. That's an ugly world."

Finally, it remains the case that having Hillary's name on the ballot may be the only thing that would motivate the party's base to turn out in big numbers for McCain. "There's no doubt Obama is a less appealing figure to Republicans than he was five weeks ago," says Pete Wehner. "But Obama is not radioactive to Republicans the way Hillary Clinton is—and whatever opposition Obama elicits from the GOP, it won't be on the same intensity scale as that of Senator Clinton. Right now the Clintons are, to much of the GOP, in a category all their own."

In the end, of course, this conversation will almost certainly prove academic. With each passing hour, the Democratic nomination slips further from Clinton's grasp. On my most recent visit to the campaign's headquarters in Arlington, Virginia, it seemed for the first time that reality was setting in. Staffers were bandying about future plans—plans that didn't involve the West Wing. "That's what you do at the end of a campaign," one senior adviser said—a tacit admission the end was now in sight. As I headed for the elevator to leave, I ran into chief strategist Mark Penn. "Hiya," Penn said, and then ambled on toward communications director Howard Wolfson's office.

The next morning came the story in the *Wall Street Journal* breaking the news of Penn's fateful (and fatal) powwow with the Colombians, which must have occurred within hours of when our paths briefly crossed. And I realized that what I thought I heard as "hi" must have been a "bye."

◄◄ • ►►

On March 31, McCain set off on his weeklong "Service to America" biography tour. I caught up with him on the third day in Annapolis, Maryland, where he was slated to speak at the U.S. Naval Academy, which he entered as a plebe in 1954. After leading the pledge of allegiance at a local diner, where scrapple-scarfing patrons huddled in booths beneath a sign that read DELICIOUS PAN-CAKES, MAPLE SYRUP, MARGARINE, he arrived at a grander setting: the Navy football stadium. But no throng of midshipmen-cum-McCainiacs surrounded the candidate at the rostrum. In front of him instead were 60 folding chairs, occupied by wizened dignitaries; behind him were 35,000 seats, occupied by no one.

His speech that morning, like the others on the tour, sought to explain how a callow, shallow hellion became a man of honor. At the academy, McCain said, he was "childish" and prone to "petty acts of insubordination." But then came the horrors he suffered in Vietnam, and the lesson Annapolis had sought to teach him took hold. "It changed my life forever. I had found my cause: citizenship in the greatest nation on Earth." But McCain's next sentence—"What is lost, in a word, is citizenship"—sounded like a non sequitur, and that's because it was. Incredibly, once again, the teleprompter was at fault: It had devoured a page of his script. (Memo to McCain HQ: Hire new tech support!) But this time there was no drama: McCain just soldiered on through.

At the end of the tour, McCain's consiglieri declared it a success. "It was open-field running for us," McKinnon wrote me in an e-mail. "While the Democrats continued to attack each other and claw their way to the bottom, McCain was able to communicate a positive message and create a compelling narrative about the values he learned growing up that make him best-qualified to be president."

In truth, McCain's message reached precious few. The press coverage of the tour was perfunctory when not derisory. (Jon Stewart dubbed it the "Monsters of Nostalgia Tour," cracking that it had "all the allure of an Atlantic City senior citizens' outing without all the awkward sexual tension.") "It was a missed opportunity," says a Republican strategist with experience running a presidential campaign. "He didn't say anything. He didn't drive a message. He should have been making news every day hammering Obama's weaknesses. That Annapolis speech was ridiculous. The empty football field? What genius thought that was a good idea? The way you do these deals is you plan to drive a headline, a picture, and a story—it's a simple acronym, HPS. That's how you design every day on a national campaign. But I guess they missed the memo."

McCain's organization has been ramping up far too sluggishly in the eyes of some professional Republicans. Though its high command—the so-called Sedona Five, which consists of Black, Davis, McKinnon, Salter, and Schmidt—is well regarded, it seems stretched too thin. "It's a skeleton crew over there," said the same strategist. Astonishingly, the campaign has just four full-time finance staffers and no significant online buck-raking presence. In March, it reportedly raised just $4 million over the Web and through direct mail.

When it comes to media and strategy, however, the campaign is nearly at full speed. A best-and-brightest collection of Republican admen has been pulled together, and, maybe more significant, talent from Bush World is beginning to migrate into McCain Land. The former Republican National Committee chairman Ken Mehlman is now an informal adviser. Former Bush speechwriter Matthew Scully is onboard as well. There are even rumors that Rove, the Architect himself, is funneling ideas through the pipeline. "There's no official/formal relationship with Rove," McKinnon e-mailed coyly. "Karl is on Fox a lot. We watch a lot of Fox. Karl has become an open-source consultant." But one of the savviest Karlologists I know suspects that Rove is providing a steady stream of advice through multiple points of contact with the campaign and the national party.

The specter of another Rovean election will surely give countless Democrats a severe case of the heebie-jeebies—and it should. Obama's difficulties winning downscale whites (and especially white men) are real and potentially of enormous consequence. Some of this can be blamed on the Clintons, just as some will be attributable to whatever mischievous and malign race-baiting is practiced by Republicans this fall. Some must be laid at the doorstep of Obama and Pastor Wright. And some to the racism that, much as we might wish otherwise, remains alive in the land. But however one chooses to apportion blame, what's now quite clear is that Obama is unlikely to turn many red states, or even many purple ones, blue. The prospect of a landslide looks remote, especially against a candidate whose biography will be powerfully appealing to exactly the constituencies with which Obama is most vulnerable. "We do electoral-college projections, and over the past few weeks, every shift we've made has been in the Republican direction," says pollster Rasmussen. "A month ago, the Democrats were clearly favored. Now it's a pure toss-up."

A wealthy Democratic donor of my acquaintance likes to say, "Sometimes panic is the appropriate reaction." But for Democrats, this is not that time. Judging by almost any meaningful metric, the current political topography strongly favors the party this year. Unless Obama foolishly gets shamed into accepting public financing—and trust me, the Obama people are no fools, and they have less shame than you'd imagine—he will be the proverbial Mr. Universe at the beach, kicking sand in McCain's face when it comes to advertising and the ground game. His positions on the issues are more popular than McCain's. He can't be blamed for Bush's war or Bush's recession. He is young and vibrant and inspiring, whereas McCain is not and not and not.

And indeed, McCain's age may prove as big a hurdle for him as Obama's race is for him. According to Peter Hart's polling, 29 percent of voters say that America isn't ready to elect a president in his seventies. And among the groups who register even higher percentages of concern are women, midwesterners, and blue-collar voters. One of the central challenges that McCain will face is to prove that he isn't past his sell-by date, just another doddering member of the shuffleboard set. Watching him move through the world—a rickety little man with tiny, clawlike hands, barking out staccato platitudes—I often think of the day in 1996 when I watched Bob Dole take an errant step and fall off a stage in California, an accident that sealed his image as more AARP than C-I-C. The same danger is forever lurking for McCain.

Back in New Hampshire, McCain announced one day that he might be just a one-term president—an utterance that was variously described as an unfortunate slip or another demonstration of his refreshing candor. Please. What McCain was doing—a risky move, but not a crazy one—was not just trying to assuage concerns about his age, but turn them to his advantage. "He's got to position himself as the right guy for right now, the guy with the maturity to lead in an uncertain world," says Castellanos. "He can't be the candidate of the future, but he can be the candidate of the present who will keep you safe and give you a shot at the future."

And, hey, who knows, it might even work, for history tells us that political contests between the present and the future are always close-run things. The trouble is that McCain is no longer a man of the moment we currently share—he's an advertisement for the past. And in a contest between yesterday and tomorrow, tomorrow usually has the upper hand.

9

ALL ABOARD THE McCAIN EXPRESS

RICK PERLSTEIN
The Nation   April 21, 2008

One of the themes of the 2008 Republican presidential primary was the quest on the part of conservatives for a candidate they could embrace wholeheartedly. No one seemed to quite fit the bill: Rudy Giuliani had too many ex-wives and baggage, while Mitt Romney's attempt to repackage himself as the next Reagan succeeded only marginally. Fred Thompson offered a brief flicker of hope, until he actually started campaigning (or not). That left Baptist preacher Mike Huckabee, who garnered enough support from evangelicals and other social conservatives to be the second-to-last man standing in the race. The one thing that Rush Limbaugh and other right-wing pundits seemed to agree on was that virtually anyone would be better than that conservative apostate, John McCain. Funny how things change once a guy wins the GOP nomination. Rick Perlstein—whose body of work includes books on Barry Goldwater and Richard Nixon—analyzes the conservative elite's abrupt about-face on McCain, and suggests that the whole drama may have been more about ego (and the state of conservatism) than policy differences.

Back when the Republican presidential race was still competitive, the insults against John McCain from leading conservative voices were so extravagant they almost constituted a new literary genre. Rush Limbaugh said McCain threatened "the American way of life as we've always known it." McCain's Senate colleague Thad Cochran said, "The thought of him as President sends a cold chill down my spine." Ann Coulter charged the most unforgivable sin of all: McCain was, in fact, "a Democrat." Coulter's employer, Fox News, seconded the smear on February 7 by printing the words "John McCain (D-AZ)" under footage of the Arizona Republican.

That day was no ordinary one in the history of McCain-hate. On that afternoon, most of these figures' preferred candidate, Mitt Romney, announced at CPAC, the big annual conservative conference in Washington, that he was dropping out of the race. McCain, now the presumptive Republican nominee, was booed. The next morning the conservative magazine *Human Events* sent out a weekly roundup of its top ten stories to its e-mail list. Eight were anti-McCain jeremiads. One called the McCain ascendancy "the new Axis of Evil." Michael Reagan's article "John McCain Hates Me" posited a "huge gap that separates McCain—whose contempt for his fellow humans is patently obvious—and my dad, Ronald Reagan," and concluded, "He has contempt for conservatives who he thinks can be duped into thinking he's one of them."

Michael Reagan, for one, would not be duped. He would not defile his father's sacred memory. At least for a week. Eight days later Reagan's article for *Human Events* argued, "Assuming that John McCain will be the Republican nominee, you can bet my father would be itching to get out on the campaign trail working to elect him even if he disagreed with him on a number of issues."

Such are the strange McCain contortions Republicans have been forcing themselves into in recent weeks. Tom DeLay used to fret that he "might have to sit this one out" if McCain won the nomination. Now he's stumping for the presumptive nominee with apparent enthusiasm. At a March 1 "Reagan Day" dinner (Republicans used to call them "Lincoln Day" dinners), Texas Senator John Cornyn likened the base's swing to McCain to the grieving process: "You come to acceptance."

But what is it that made supporting a senator who has earned an 83 lifetime rating from the American Conservative Union and votes with his party 88.3 percent of the time feel like mourning in the first place? They weren't this hard, after all, on fair-weather conservatives Bob Dole in 1996 or George H.W. Bush in 1988 and 1992, were they?

Conservatism is, among many other things, a culture. The most important glue binding it together is a shared sense of cultural grievance—the conviction, uniting conservatives high and low, theocratic and plutocratic, neocon and paleocon, that someone, somewhere is looking down their noses at them with a condescending sneer. And to conservatives, McCain has been too often one of the sneerers. It is, as much as anything else, a question of *affect*. As Michael Reagan wrote, "I don't like the way he treats people. You get the impression that he thinks everybody is beneath him."

They are not entirely imagining things. Birds fly, fish swim, McCain preens: it has ever been thus. His preening has turned the thin-skinned crypt-keepers of conservatism hysterical. "McCain's apostasies," Charles Krauthammer recently wrote in the *Washington Post*, "are too numerous to count." They aren't, really. Some conservatives still call the Republican nominee "Juan" McCain, for what Reagan calls "such blatantly anti-conservative actions as his support for amnesty for illegal immigrants." But of course Reagan's sainted father, in signing the 1986 immigration bill, was a more unapologetic and effective advocate of "amnesty" than McCain ever was—and you don't hear him getting labeled "Ronaldo" Reagan. Note, also, that other supposed bugaboo of conservative ideology: pork-barrel government spending. McCain is the Senate's leading fighter against spending earmarks. If pork was what they truly cared about, he'd be a hero. But that stance has earned him no points on the "conservative" side of the ledger.

The issues aren't the issue. George Stephanopoulos once asked Tom DeLay what it was conservatives demanded of McCain, and DeLay admitted as much: "I don't think they're demanding that he change in his position," he said. "It is attitude."

━◄ • ►━

In other words: it's the ring-kissing, stupid. Consider George H.W. Bush's attitude: he all but groveled before conservatives—first calling supply-side doctrine "voodoo economics," then swallowing hard and accepting a spot as voodoo priest Reagan's running mate. Bob Dole, formerly a proud budget balancer, lay prostrate before them in accepting a 15 percent across-the-board tax cut as the cornerstone of his 1996 presidential platform, then took on movement hero Jack Kemp as his running mate.

For conservative leaders, making candidates pay them court, publicly and ostentatiously, is a colossal source of their symbolic power before their followers. It's kabuki theater, mostly. Ronald Reagan never did much to make abortion illegal. He did, however, deliver videotaped greetings, fulsome in praise for his hosts, to antiabortion rallies on the Mall. Pentecostal leaders were horrified to see George W. Bush violate what they considered biblical prophesy by giving over the Gaza Strip to the Palestinians in 2004. After they made their dismay known, Bush did not change his mind. He did, however, send top White House and National Security Council staffers to flatter them in a private meeting that concluded, according to an account one of the pastors sent to his followers, "with a heart-moving send-off of the President in his Presidential helicopter." Rings kissed, egos assuaged—and these particular Pentecostals stopped complaining about the sacrilege. The issue wasn't the issue.

For decades, the operative theory in Republican politics has been that there exists a seething mass of lockstep conservative voters controlled by leaders like these, without whose support no Republican can win a presidential election.

Michael Reagan puts it this way: "If [McCain] gets the nomination the only way he could win against Hillary or Barack Obama would be to be part of a McCain-Limbaugh ticket." But that's certainly never been reflected in any actual electoral data. Indeed, this year it appears that conservative opinion leaders are more out of touch with the masses they purport to lead than ever. According to a recent CBS poll, only 17 percent of Republicans want an uncompromising conservative as their nominee. Eighty percent of Republicans are satisfied with McCain. Sixty percent of conservative primary voters say they "want a candidate who would compromise with Democrats in order to get things done."

McCain has called their bluff. He didn't suck up to Rush Limbaugh but won the nomination anyway; he's also faring well in general election matchups. He has shown that the kingmakers have no clothes. The humiliation is hard to forgive. It has made it harder for conservative leaders to do business and turned politicians like McCain (and Arnold Schwarzenegger), in their eyes, into monsters. On Glenn Beck's CNN show, for instance, Democratic consultant Peter Fenn pointed out that the reason McCain does well with voters is that "they think he is independent."

"Yes," Beck replied, "well, so is Dr. Frankenstein."

Kind of gives the game away: in their mind, these conservative leaders create Republican Presidents. But what's the point if GOP candidates are just going to go crashing around the countryside doing whatever the hell they want?

And so the professional conservatives did their best to set loose the torch-bearing mob. Late in January, former Pennsylvania Senator Rick Santorum made call after call after call spreading the word that, yes, even a President Hillary Clinton or a President Barack Obama would be better than a President McCain. At one point, according to Democratic activist Mike Lux, who overheard an indiscreet Santorum making such calls on the New York–D.C. Metroliner, Santorum attempted to talk an interlocutor into "coming out with a terrible story about McCain from five or six years ago." Clearly the crusade to sabotage McCain didn't work. Professional conservative Monica Crowley finally admitted the obvious: "A lot of people have actually voted for McCain, and they weren't just moderates and independents. Enough Republicans have voted for him to give him the nomination—and yes, a decent number of conservatives have too."

The frustration has been palpable. There was, for instance, the incident with radio host Bill Cunningham. Cunningham had warmed up a partisan crowd before a McCain speech in Cincinnati by barking out Obama's infamous middle name, Hussein. When McCain later "learned" about the remark, he pronounced himself shocked, shocked—and said he'd never met Cunningham in his life. Republicans have been choreographing such stylized minuets for so long now—the "grassroots conservative" gets the smears "out there," the "establishment" candidate distances himself from them, everyone emerges all the stronger—that the steps have become implicit. But Cunningham pretended to have forgotten the dance. He went on TV and complained that, of course he had met McCain several times before, and that of course McCain's handlers had told him to throw the crowd "red meat."

But everyone couldn't abandon McCain. If the Democrats won the presidency, after all, the country would see, as *Human Events*'s Bret Winterble warned, "Obama socializing entire corporate sectors." Republicans were stuck with McCain. So what would happen next?

⋘ • ⋙

Conservatives started to pivot publicly in the middle of February. It may have had something to do with reports that McCain gave in to what Robert Novak identified as the negotiating terms of "elements of the Republican Party's right wing": "first, that McCain would veto any tax increase passed by a Democratic Congress; second, that he would not emulate Gerald Ford and George H.W. Bush in naming liberal Supreme Court Justices such as John Paul Stevens and David Souter." It may also have something to do with McCain's bowing down before the conservative holy grail of super-harsh enforcement-first immigration reform.

Or, if my theory is correct, the conservative turnabout may have less to do with any particular policy pledges than with an ostentatious shift in apparent attitude: a show of groveling before the professional conservatives. "I've listened and learned," ran McCain's Super Tuesday radio ads announcing he'd seen the light on immigration: "No one will be rewarded for illegal behavior." Note the language. "Listening" is precisely the word the angriest professional conservatives use most when describing McCain's attitude problem. "He promises to hear, not to listen," *Human Events* editor Jed Babbin complained. "I am appalled by his contempt for the intelligence of his listeners," Michael Reagan moaned in his column.

We may never know how these meetings went down. Something, however, seems to have shifted in those days following CPAC. Jack Kemp, the man who was made Bob Dole's 1996 running mate as a sop to conservatives, penned an open letter to right-wing talk-radio on February 11, arguing that for conservatives to sit petulantly on their hands this fall would turn over the nation to "those who would weaken our nation's defense, wave a white flag to al-Qaida, socialize our health-care system, and promote income redistribution and class warfare instead of economic growth and equality of opportunity." He even, rather comically, compared McCain to another "well-known maverick" conservatives once foolishly turned against: Winston Churchill. "He was even banned from talk radio (aka the BBC) in those days," Kemp wrote.

Then, fortuitously, in the third week of February, just as the floodgates for McCain's redemption were opening, came an exposé of his alleged favors to an attractive blond lobbyist—from dreaded bête noire of conservatives, the *New York Times.* That offered the fig leaf to erstwhile McCain-haters who wished to make the pivot to party loyalty and still save face. It was no accident, they claimed, that it had been the people Jed Babbin called in another context "the hyperliberal editors of the *New York Times*" who had engineered the man's downfall. "The *New York Times* is trying to Swift Boat McCain," trumpeted one Republican strategist. "This is the first real salvo of the general election." An RNC letter sent, among other places, to the *Human Events* e-mail list blared, "The *New York Times* has proven once again that the liberal mainstream media will do whatever it takes to put Senator Hillary Clinton or Barack Obama in the White House." MAC-LASH: TIMES SLIME BOO$TS MCCAIN, declared the *New York Post* headline on a story of the fundraising blip that ensued.

To which a citizen of the reality-based community might reasonably ask: why would the editors at the *Times*—a paper that hired McCain's most consistent and aggressive backer in the conservative opinion firmament, Bill Kristol, as a columnist—"Swiftboat" a candidate they had endorsed for the Republican nomination?

How naïve you are. "The media picked the GOP's candidate," explained Rush Limbaugh, "and is now, with utter predictability, trying to destroy him." Shock-talker Laura Ingraham helpfully elaborated: "You wait until it's pretty much beyond a doubt that he's going to be the Republican nominee, and then you let it drop." The *Times* conspiracy was so immense and manifestly evil that even McCain's sworn rival, Mike Huckabee, found it in his heart to denounce it.

So the right is finally rowing more or less in the same direction, right? Not so fast. Newsmax.com on the day of CPAC, approvingly quoting Limbaugh, added to the anti-McCain thunder this way: "We are sick and tired of how the people who seem to be triumphing in our party are precisely the people who seem to be selling this party out in terms of its ideology." Four days later, McCain's nomination guaranteed, *Newsmax*, whose e-mail list of millions of names makes it much more influential than elite outlets like *National Review* or *The Weekly Standard,* attempted an awkward 180-degree twist. It quoted the testimony of a left-wing British writer, Johann Hari—identified as an "editorial board member of The Liberal magazine," so he must be speaking for Liberal Central Command—saying that McCain's "credentials as a 'bipartisan progressive' are in fact a 'lazy, hazy myth.' 'The truth is that McCain is the candidate we should most fear.'"

See? The liberals hate him. So it's safe for us to like him.

But conservatism, like I say, is a business. You know you never get an e-mail from *Newsmax* editors without them trying to sell you something. What they were selling this time was a previous issue of their magazine with a McCain story on the cover. The piece was called "Inside McCain's Head," and it retold the far right's favorite former story about the man: that he's a Manchurian candidate whose true loyalties ultimately belong to the enemy. *Newsmax* hadn't even bothered to change the advertising copy now that former foe was friend: "In this eye-opening report on McCain *Newsmax* magazine delves into: How McCain charmed Manhattan's media elites with an exclusive fete that pundits say 'launched' his 2008 campaign for the White House. . . . Why Paul Weyrich thinks McCain isn't the right man for the White House. . . . McCain's 14-hour stints at the Las Vegas craps tables."

⊰⊱ • ⊰⊱

We like to think of the American right as a finely honed mechanism—a "conservative noise machine." And most times over the previous decade, the metaphor worked. But these days, the movement can no longer keep its stories straight. It reminds me of the McCain website the day after the *New York Times* lobbying exposé, the same day the RNC sent out its fundraising letter accusing the *Times* of electioneering for the Democrats. To anyone who might doubt that the good old conservative machine is overheating from the confusion and strain, here is proof that the noisemakers had clearly neglected to coordinate their anti-*Times* fundraising push with the McCain campaign. For there was the *Times* endorsement on its website that same day, bold as brass.

The gears of the contraption are jamming. Let the contortions of a Michael Reagan or a *Newsmax* attest to that, if nothing else. The whole machine had always been built on a series of bluffs: that once the malign hand of the liberals was removed from the executive, legislative and judicial branches, our new conservative Jerusalem would be achieved. But something remarkable occurred in the five years between 2001 and 2006: for the first time since the rise of the modern conservative movement with the nomination of Barry Goldwater in 1964, then the rise of Newt Gingrich's revolutionaries in 1994, the right had a chance to control all three branches of government—to actually run the country. Naught but obvious failures have been the result: a crashing economy, a rotting infrastructure, a failed war and a less safe world, more Americans saying their nation is on the wrong track than at any time since pollsters started measuring.

In the face of all this, the conservative movement has kept on trying to do the only thing it knows how to do: sell conservatism. Saner heads in the Republican Party, meanwhile, have done their darnedest to put forward a presidential prospect who might let the party distance itself, if only rhetorically, from the disaster that conservatism in power has proved to be.

But without "conservatism" as the core narrative, the Republican Party doesn't know how to tell any stories at all. Its confusion over how to talk about McCain is only the symptom. The conservative era is over—if you want it.

WHO WE ARE NOW

BOY WITH THE STRAW HAT

As Bush entered the debate it felt like he
was helping Obama in his opposition. After
a Diane Arbus image. (Illustration by Steve
Brodner; first appeared in *The New Yorker*.)

10

HOW McCAIN AND OBAMA BEAT THE ODDS: DELEGATE MATH AND THE EMOTIONAL LOGIC OF THE POLITICAL BRAIN

DREW WESTEN
Postscript to the paperback edition of *The Political Brain*

Whichever candidate you support in the 2008 presidential race, your choice almost certainly has little to do with his or her policy proposals. That's the startling conclusion of Drew Westen, a professor of psychology and psychiatry and behavioral science at Emory University. Westen's groundbreaking studies have found that political judgments occur primarily in the brain's emotional centers, rather than in the parts of the brain involved in logical thought. By this measure, observes Westen, "Democrats and progressives [have] been talking to the wrong parts of the brain for the better part of four decades."

By the time his influential book on the subject, The Political Brain, *appeared in print last year, Westen's thesis had already swept through the Democratic ranks. How much these fresh insights benefit the Dems at the polls this November remains to be seen. In the meantime, Westen has written a new postscript for his paperback edition in which he evaluates the performance of the 2008 presidential contenders according to the only standard that he believes ultimately matters: their emotional appeal. As Westen notes, "if you want to win voters' hearts and minds, you have to start with the heart, because otherwise they aren't going to care much what's on your mind."*

The real stories of the primaries and caucuses of 2008 were the rise and fall and rise again of three candidates: John McCain, Hillary Clinton, and Barack Obama. In July of 2007, when McCain's candidacy was plummeting, I wrote a piece for the *Huffington Post*, describing why McCain's campaign had turned moribund. And the same principles that explain his fall from grace explain his campaign's remarkable resurrection.

In politics, you have to tell coherent, emotionally compelling, memorable stories, particularly about who you are and what you stand for. What John McCain stood for—and what had earned him the respect of many Independents and even many Democrats who knew little about his record but liked the *story* of John McCain—was summarized by the name of his bus and his campaign theme: the Straight Talk Express.

That was his story. But many powerful voices in the Republican Party didn't like the plot, and McCain had seen them defeat him in 2000. So in 2006 he began to rewrite it. But it turned out to be impossible for McCain to bluff with an extreme right-wing hand when he didn't have a poker face and to embrace a president everyone knew he despised (because he'd looked into his eyes in the South Carolina primary in 2000 and seen his soul). No one was buying his new story because it flew directly in the face of the narrative that had made him so compelling.

Precisely when McCain made his pact with the devil is unclear, but the signs of the bargain were obvious by the spring of 2006. In March, at a straw poll of the Southern Republican Leadership Council, he disingenuously urged those in attendance, "if any friends here are thinking about voting for me, please don't. Just write in President Bush's name. For the next three years, with the country at war, he's our president, and the only one who must have our support today." In April, he strained credulity even among the party faithful by calling George W. Bush "one of the great presidents of the United States." That was the same month he embraced Jerry Falwell, a dramatic about-face by a man who had labeled Falwell an "agent of intolerance" just a few years earlier at a time when doing so was a sign of his straight-talking courage. The new McCain was creating a new story, but the not one he'd hoped for, and one that left his campaign in tatters: that he was willing to sell his soul for a lease on 1600 Pennsylvania Avenue.

The unfolding of that new narrative was clear on *The Daily Show,* as Jon Stewart struggled with what many in the center and the left struggled with as they watched a man they may not have agreed with on many issues, but nevertheless admired, lose the characteristic that had made him seem so admirable: "You're killing me here!" Stewart half-jokingly told McCain. "You're not freaking out on us—are you going into crazy-[conservative] base world?" McCain laughed defensively as he defenselessly responded, "I'm afraid so." In fact, McCain had recently voted to make Bush's tax cuts to the well-heeled permanent after having initially denounced them; supported the most draconian law ever proposed on abortion, a South Dakota bill that would have forced rape and incest victims to bear their rapists' babies; and expressed his support for the teaching of "intelligent design."

In March of 2007, Adam Nagourney of the *New York Times* reported on an extraordinary moment in Iowa, when McCain was asked a simple question while chatting on his bus with reporters: Did he support the distribution of condoms in Africa to fight the transmission of HIV? McCain searched for words, glanced at the ceiling, paused awkwardly with repeated silences, asked his aides to tell him what his position was, said he'd never thought about it before, and hoped his physician friend, right-wing Oklahoma Senator Tom Coburn, could help him out. When asked whether he believed sex education in the United States should teach abstinence only (the imposition of the Bush administration on public schools that wanted funding for sex education), he answered after a long pause, "Ahhh. I think I support the president's policy." When a reporter followed up, asking whether he believed contraceptives help stop the spread of HIV, he answered after another long pause, "You've stumped me." An incredulous reporter followed up, leading to the only honest moment of the press conference, when McCain answered, with a defensive laugh, "Are we on the Straight Talk Express? I'm not informed enough on it. Let me find out. You know, I'm sure I've taken a position on it in the past. I have to find out what my position was. Brian, would you find out what my position is on contraception— I'm sure I'm opposed to government spending on it. I'm sure I support the president's policies on it."

McCain's response of "Are we on the Straight Talk Express?"—like his answer to Jon Stewart's question—revealed everything the American people needed to know about John McCain: He was no longer aboard his own bus.

That McCain was able to win his party's nomination reflected, in part, the years of positive associations most Americans had to him and their difficulty making sense of (and hence willingness to forget) his two-year foray into political cowardice and opportunism because it just didn't fit with the story of his extraordinary courage as a prisoner of war in Vietnam. Our brains search for order in disorder, and when a piece of information doesn't fit, people readily forget it or rationalize it away. But McCain was also the beneficiary of two pieces of simple good luck. The first, paradoxically, was that his poll numbers tumbled so rapidly when his Straight Talk Express took a sharp right off a cliff that his campaign ran out of financial fuel, and with it went the high-priced consultants who had helped him construct a story about himself that was so manifestly untrue that no one was buying it.

The second was the absence of a strong Republican field. As a Democrat, the two candidates who worried me most in watching the first Republican primary debate—because of their nonverbal behavior, their comfort in their skin, and their ability to tell a story—were Romney and Huckabee, who turned out to be the last two contenders standing before McCain clinched the nomination. But Romney, who had been twice elected governor of Massachusetts, couldn't possibly have believed most of what he was saying on the campaign trail, and he had the misfortune of having to face television clips from his years running the most liberal state in the union that belied virtually every claim he was making to Republican primary voters about himself.

From the first time I watched Huckabee, he made me nervous, because I disliked most of what he said but I liked him anyway. The fact that many pundits found his victory in Iowa unexpected, even when his poll numbers started to climb in the weeks before the caucus, reflects what happens when you're reading the wrong cues in politics. Huckabee was the most politically intelligent of the candidates on the Republican side in 2008, with a sense of humor; a genuineness that Americans craved after eight years of an administration that has made most of us wistful for the days when an honest man like, say, Richard Nixon, inhabited the White House; and a pastor's ability to deliver a sermon.

But Huckabee had two other characteristics that derailed his candidacy, one to his right and one to his left. On the right hand, he simply wasn't angry enough. One of the biggest mistakes Democrats have made is to fail to distinguish the authoritarian fundamentalists whose political emotions center on hate, disgust, and contempt, and whose moral emotions render them antagonistic to everything Democrats stand for, from the large number of evangelical Christians who can be moved by demagogues to feel those same emotions but who are more naturally drawn to messages of love, compassion, and beneficence if someone leads them to their better angels. Huckabee was a natural for the latter but anathema to the former, as evident, for example, in his stance on immigration.

To his left, Huckabee was vulnerable because of a tendency to blurt out thoughts unbefitting of a man of his intelligence, and certainly of an American president in the twenty-first century, such as his disbelief in evolution and his suggestion that we change the Constitution to fit the Bible. The latter experiment has already been tried, and as far as most of us can tell, it doesn't seem to be working all that well in Iran (different book, same concept).

These factors, plus Rudy Giuliani's decision to enter the race once it was already over (and Fred Thompson's decision to sleep through it), conspired to give McCain a second chance, and as soon as he put the wheels back on the Straight Talk Express, it started rolling again. Just how little "issues" really mattered on the Republican side could be seen in exit polls on Super Tuesday, when Republican voters in state after state—who endorsed the most draconian positions on illegal immigration—chose the newly straight-talking McCain as their man, despite his being the Republican candidate least likely to pander to the extreme right on one of the defining issues of the Republican debates. The tension for McCain for the general election is that precisely what he needs to say to bring his party's base to the polls for him is what flies in the face of his personal story and will alienate the moderates whose votes he would need to win the presidency.

On the Democratic side, 2008 was an embarrassment of riches, at least in terms of substantial candidates with the knowledge and gravitas to lead. Hillary Clinton showed herself early to have an extraordinary intellect and a firm grasp on virtually every issue confronting the nation. No reporter, no matter how motivated with a "gotcha" question, could catch her on virtually anything (except her dogged refusal to acknowledge that her Iraq War vote was a mistake). And it is difficult to imagine a candidate who better exemplifies many of the central messages of this book than Barack Obama. Although pundits tried to dissect "what Hillary did wrong," by late February of 2008, after eleven straight primary and caucus victories for Obama, Adam Nagourney of the *New York Times* asked a simple question: Is there anything Hillary Clinton could really do to defeat Barack Obama?

Our strengths and our weaknesses tend to flow from the same wells, and Hillary's commanding debate performances were emblematic of both. She made stronger appeals to voters' values than traditional Democratic campaigns, and by late January of 2008, she was a different candidate on the stump. She couldn't match the natural charisma of Obama, but after seeing what emotion could do for her in New Hampshire, she became emotionally much more "present" as a speaker and was moving away from the megaphone-like speaking style and vocal tone that had worked poorly for her on the stump and detracted from her debate performances. And her decision to bring her daughter, Chelsea, out to campaign for her—first with her and then on her own—was just what the doctor ordered, and it clearly made a difference. Chelsea was helpful in appealing to young voters, as emphasized by traditional punditry. But more importantly,

Hillary's obviously loving relationship with her daughter flew in the face of the narrative with which she'd been successfully branded for so many years by the right—that she was cold, uncaring, and "unfeminine."

Yet even at her best, she seemed determined to run the kind of relentlessly issue-oriented campaign that offers a 10-point plan for every problem and that has led to the defeat of Democrats in election after election over the last thirty years—with the singular exception of her husband, who appealed instead to the American people with a charismatic style, a message of hope much closer to Obama's, and just enough policy to make clear that he was no lightweight. Although she was both tough and agile in her debate performances from the start, she failed to recognize—until her voice cracked in New Hampshire and signaled to voters that there was a person hiding inside that pantsuit—that what she needed more than anything was not another plan for another issue but a story of who she was and what she stood for, and a way to make a dent in the central story the right had branded her with since the early 1990s.

Her Christmas 2007 campaign ad in Iowa illustrated in microcosm the problems with her message—and with the message of Democratic campaigns at virtually every level of government for much of three decades. With *Carol of the Bells* playing in the background, a pair of scissors cuts through wrapping paper, and a pair of hands places gift cards on a series of presents. The camera focuses sequentially on the cards, which bear the inscriptions, "Universal Health Care," "Alternative Energy," "Bring Troops Home," and "Middle Class Tax Breaks." The candidate then appears on the couch amidst the pile of presents she's been wrapping, looks around the room for something missing, and asks herself, as the music stops momentarily for effect, "Where did I put 'Universal Pre-K'?" Suddenly, she finds it, and a big smile appears on her face as she utters the words, "Ach! Here it is!" and looks admiringly at the gift she imagines giving to the American people. The music then resumes.

What's wrong with this picture? Everything except the music. Perhaps most centrally, it only reinforces the story Ronald Reagan told most forcefully about Democrats, which has been repeated by Republicans ever since: that they never saw a tax they didn't want to raise or a social program they didn't want to create. Here was Hillary Clinton telling the people of Iowa what she wished for them: more government programs. The problem isn't that any of those programs, taken individually, wouldn't be worthwhile or provide real solutions to real problems that would enrich millions of people's lives. The problem is that what she was offering the people of Iowa was a bag full of issues and a bag full of government solutions, with the message, "Merry Christmas!"

Campaigns aren't won with bags full of anything. They are won by candidates who can convince voters, through their words, intonation, body language, and actions, that they share their values, that they understand people like them, and that they can inspire the nation or save it from dangers. Policies and plans should be *indicators* or *examples* of what candidates care about, which tell voters whether they share their values and would approach the nation's problems in sensible ways. Hillary's Christmas ad, like so many Democratic ads and campaigns, required voters to work too hard to know where her heart was, to find the yarn that tied together those seemingly disparate packages.

Contrast this with Barack Obama's message to Iowans that same Christmas. His ad began with a shot of the Obama family in front of their hearth, with a fire burning, stockings hanging above the fireplace, and a large Christmas tree in the background. Michelle and Barack Obama are sitting next to each other, her arm wrapped around his leg, and a child in each of their arms. Michelle begins, "We'd like to take a moment to thank you and your family for the warmth and the friendship that you've shown ours. . . ." Then Barack: "In this holiday season, we're reminded that the things that unite us as a people are more enduring than anything that sets us apart. . . . So from my family to yours, I approve *this* message" (turning to his older daughter, who says with a broad smile): "Merry Christmas," followed by the little one chirping, "Happy Holidays." The ad ends with the obviously proud parents joining their children with a warm smile, a picture-perfect family portrait of the Obama family in the home.

The ad had barely any "content" (other than Obama's signature theme of unity), no "issues," no policies, no plans. Yet it was remarkably effective. I've watched or shown it to audiences a dozen times, and by the end, I simply can't suppress a broad smile on my face, nor can anyone I've seen watch it. In part, that simply reflects the way our brains work: Smiles are literally contagious (when they're genuine), because they trigger neurons in our brain that not only detect emotions in others but lead us to experience directly what they are feeling.

But the ad was effective in several other ways as well. Most importantly, it fostered identification with Obama, something essential for a candidate whose race threatened to stand between him and the white Iowa populace. It conveyed a simple message: "I love my family, I love my wife, and I value families, just like you do."* It is difficult to watch the ad and not come away thinking, "You know, they're just like us (and their kids are really cute)." The ad erases their differentness from white Americans. And it adds a new dimension to Obama: an image of a strong, warm, loving father—just the kind of image that reassures voters in troubled times.

Although I do not know if this was intended, the ad also quietly conveyed something else very important about Obama: that he is Christian. That mattered for two reasons. First, Obama's Christianity breaks down another barrier between him and many white voters, particularly in the South. The ad implicitly says to the majority of Americans, "We worship the same God." Second, for a year the Obama campaign had let a story fester about him, largely on the Internet, that took many forms: that he was Islamic, that he put his hand on the Koran when taking his oath of office in the United States Senate, that he refused to say the Pledge of Allegiance, that he was trained at anti-American Islamic schools in Indonesia as a child—in a word, that he was not only Islamic but *foreign*, not like "us." Right-wing pundits were calling him Osama Obama and B. Hussein Obama, to make the associations to terrorists as well as to everything un-American or anti-American.

This smear campaign did substantial damage. By the winter of 2008, it was impossible to attend a focus group with swing voters anywhere in the United States without hearing a substantial minority describe him as Muslim or repeat with conviction the stories about the Pledge of Allegiance or his taking the oath of office with his hand on the Koran. It took nearly a year before he began to address this stealth attack directly, one of the few serious mistakes his campaign made. Unfortunately, the lore in Democratic campaign circles is that it's best not to address these kinds of attacks directly for fear of fanning the flames (just like some mental health professionals once believed that it's best not to ask depressed adolescents about suicidal thoughts for fear of "putting the idea in their heads"). As I show in this book, however, for reasons that are as

---

* The image of the handsome young man with his young family also unconsciously reinforced an association between Obama and another charismatic young Democratic president with young children in the White House who inspired the hope of the American people, John F. Kennedy. The obvious affection between Michelle and Barack Obama, who are gently touching throughout the ad, also triggers an implicit comparison with the Clintons, whose marital difficulties had been so public.

much neurological as political, a candidate should never allow the public to form negative associations toward him for any length of time, and certainly not a year.

The Obama campaign was, in many respects, brilliantly orchestrated, both in its ability to make its message of unity in divided times "stick" and in what political insiders call its "ground game" (e.g., getting people to the polls, understanding the complex machinery of caucuses, organizing people and events), something Obama and his lead strategist, David Axelrod, knew remarkably well how to do, with their background in community organizing. But what political pundits often forget about the Obama campaign was that it was not always electrifying, and its progress was uneven. Obama's standing in the polls was slowly but steadily slipping within a few months of the stunning speech that began his candidacy in front of the state capitol in Springfield Illinois, in January 2007. His steady decline in the polls continued through October of 2007, when Hillary Clinton broke the 50 percent mark in the national polls with Democratic voters despite a still crowded field. And as with McCain, the same principles that explain Obama's decline account for his extraordinary turnaround.

In late June 2007, I wrote a piece for the *Huffington Post,* on the day the Obama campaign announced a record-breaking fundraising quarter, called "Who Turned Out the Electricity?" I argued that if he continued to weigh down his campaign speeches and debate performances with 14-point plans to compete with the Democratic Joneses, losing his inspirational message in a morass of policies and positions instead of using his proposals as examples of where he wanted to take the country that fit his uniquely inspirational style, he would see a continued steady downward slope in the polls. Not only was the land of 14-point plans Hillary Clinton's home turf, with her encyclopedic knowledge of every issue, her years in Washington as both the most involved, accomplished First Lady in American history, and her record as a senator, but it was a no-man's land filled with the bones of fallen Democratic candidates, who had repeatedly lost to Republicans who stole the hearts of the American people while Democrats competed for their minds.

The article drew less than enthusiastic responses, given its incongruity with the news of his record-breaking fundraising quarter, although the donors who had been so enthusiastic about him were already beginning to express concerns privately about his lackluster debate performances and his inconsistent, sometimes professorial stump speeches. Their concern turned out to be well founded: For the next five months, his poll numbers did, in fact, drop steadily, as Clinton's fortunes climbed. In the June article, I described why I thought the campaign needed to change course:

> On the stump, Obama can be electrifying. And behind all that electricity is a first-rate intellect. But if you have electricity, the last thing you want to do is pull the circuit breaker and start explaining the fine points of transistors, electrons, and electrical engineering. Yet that's exactly what Obama has done in his recent debate performances. Whether the decision was his, his senior strategists', or some combination of the two, he seems to have decided to check his charisma at the door, avoid the moving imagery and oratory that electrified the electorate from the first time they saw him on the national stage, and talk about issues, positions, "marginal tax rates" (as opposed, for example, to "your taxes"), and the fine print of his health care plan.

His campaign was obviously trying to put some meat on the policy bones of his positions, in part to allay concerns about his inexperience, and in part to pacify the wonk wing of the Democratic Party and the political pundits and editorial boards who had demanded from Democratic candidates for years that they obsess on precisely the level of detail that predicts failure in general elections. I concluded in June that rather than following the traditional Democratic strategy of focusing on the minutiae of policy details and rolling out plan after plan for issue after issue, "Obama would do a lot better to take a leaf out of Reagan's book than to retrace the journey of the long list of Democrats who have drowned on the dispassionate river: Let Obama be Obama."

Months later, his campaign finally did just that. At the Jefferson-Jackson Dinner in Iowa, the Obama who had been watching Hillary Clinton's stock rise for months as he sold his own stock short stepped up to the podium and electrified the audience in a way that sent shock waves through the political world—and ultimately led to his victory in Iowa and the cascade of primaries and caucuses that followed. Newspapers in cities all over the country ran headlines such as "Obama Finally Finds His Voice," and his voice grew more confident and inspiring as the months proceeded. By the time he had racked up twelve straight primary and caucus wins after Super Tuesday, Hillary Clinton had no choice but to go negative against him, because she simply couldn't out-inspire him.

Clinton's negative campaign against Obama succeeded in breaking his momentum on March 4 in the Texas and Ohio primaries, particularly when combined with a strong message about what she would do to get an ailing economy out of a second Bush's recession—a message that strongly reinforced voters' positive associations to Bill Clinton's stewardship of the economy over his eight years in the White House. But what transpired in Texas and Ohio and over the ensuing days speaks to one of the central messages of this book, and to the way Obama's strengths and weaknesses on the campaign trail, too, flowed from the same wells: You can't win an election by ceding half the brain to the other side. No one has ever won an election by harnessing only positive emotions. Franklin Roosevelt, John F. Kennedy, Ronald Reagan, and Bill Clinton were all remarkably inspirational leaders, but none of them shied away from sharply criticizing their opponents (primarily on issues of ideology, not personality), particularly in the general elections, where such criticism doesn't risk damaging their own party's chances in November and leave voters with negative associations to the attacker. Kennedy attacked the character of his opponent in the general election (Richard Nixon) because his opponent, in fact, had problems of character relevant to his fitness for the presidency, as history would bear out. Successful campaigns are campaigns that both inspire and raise concerns about the opposition. And as I argue in this book, that's exactly what they should do, because an election is a choice, not a referendum, and because positive and negative emotions both drive voting behavior, but in psychologically and neurologically distinct ways.

Obama's relentlessly positive message of rising above politics as usual left him open to attacks that tied his campaign in knots: If he attacked back, it would threaten his master narrative, that he was above the fray and intended to set a new tone in Washington; if he didn't, he would suffer the same fate as Dukakis, Gore, Kerry, and every other Democrat who refused to respond to a strong attack with a stronger counterattack. The success or failure of his campaign would hinge on whether he could stop the bleeding after Ohio and Texas and find his way to a response that would reinforce his own story—that he had come to Washington to clean it up—while reinforcing the story that had dogged Hillary Clinton for fifteen years and worried Democratic voters about her electability. It wouldn't have been difficult to craft a message that cast every attack she made as yet one more example of the divisiveness that Obama had pledged to clean up as president. As of this writing, however, this chapter in the history of the 2008 campaign is yet to be written.

But there's another lesson in the success of Hillary's attacks, one that I address throughout this book: the fact that much of what influences voters occurs outside of conscious awareness. Voters reported in exit polls on March 4 that they thought Hillary's attacks on Obama were unfair. But precisely the same voters gave her victories in two large battleground states. People can't tell you in polls and focus groups what really influences them because they don't know. Voters may have thought Hillary went over the top, but in their guts, she had sown the seeds of serious doubts about Barack Obama, and in politics, it's the gut that's ultimately decisive.

None of this is to suggest that emotion is the only factor that accounts for the rise and fall and rise again of three extraordinary politicians, or of elections more generally. For example, the media had always loved McCain and his story, and both Hillary Clinton and Barack Obama benefited from a media transfixed by the idea of a race between a black man and a woman. As a consequence, candidates such as Joe Biden, Chris Dodd, and especially John Edwards, whose performance on the stump and in debates was routinely superb, never really got a hearing.* And as the country moves into a recession while mired in a deeply unpopular war, John McCain has an enormous cross to bear, especially after taking the baton from his unpopular predecessor.

But if there's a central message in the primary campaigns of 2008, it's that whatever accounts for who became or becomes the nominee on either side has little to do with "the issues." John McCain could certainly speak with more authority on military issues as a veteran than Mitt Romney, but their policy positions were virtually identical. Hillary Clinton and Barack Obama were about as similar as two candidates could be in their voting records in the Senate. Yet in the Wisconsin primaries, for example, voters who reported in exit polls that

---

* Whether in frustration at his inability to gain traction in the polls, the tragic events of his personal life (his wife's cancer), a strategic miscalculation, or bad advice, Edwards set aside the natural optimism and capacity to inspire that almost won him the nomination four years earlier and ran a relentlessly angry populist campaign. That approach has never won a presidential election, as voters come to associate the candidate, instead of the targets of his attacks, with negative feelings. Had Edwards aimed his anger more carefully and bookended it with humor and inspiration, he might well have gained traction. But in a year dominated by the idea of an historic candidacy—a woman or an African-American at the top of the Democratic ticket—it may simply not have been enough. Edwards may, however, have had a significant impact on the election with the success of his populist message and the resonance of his attacks on corporate malfeasance—just as Ned Lamont, while losing his race for Senate against Joe Lieberman in Connecticut in 2006, taught Democrats all over the country that they could run against the Iraq War and ultimately win an unexpected landslide election.

the most important issue to them was health care—Hillary Clinton's signature issue—broke for Obama, just as militantly anti-immigrant Republicans routinely voted for McCain.

Issues—the economy, the Iraq War, energy, immigration, health care, whatever they may be—play a major role in elections. But as every presidential election since the advent of modern polling has shown, successful candidates are the ones whose personal stories, principles, ways of talking about their virtues and concerns for the nation, and personalities capture the imagination of the public (or create enough doubt about their opponent to win despite a less than compelling story of their own). Successful candidates are those who set the emotional agenda of the electorate.

11

THE POLITICS OF PERSONALITY DESTRUCTION

JENNIFER SENIOR
New York magazine   June 11, 2007

New York *magazine's Jennifer Senior is known for her deftly drawn profiles of leading political personalities. Her account of Hillary Clinton's early tenure in the Senate was one of the selections in this anthology's inaugural 2002 edition, while her subsequent dual portrait of Hillary and Bill's preparations for a 2008 presidential run appeared in* The Best American Political Writing 2005. *(Sample prescient quote from the latter: "What* isn't *the question is whether Hillary will run. In Washington, this fact is utterly taken for granted. Rather, the question is, who'll have the nerve to wrestle the nomination away from her?") In this piece, Senior takes on the issue of politicians' personalities in general—noting that, while the public claims to crave authenticity from its political leaders, "it's also possible that phoniness, at least in certain forms, serves an important purpose . . . [and] may even be a desirable quality in politics."*

Spend enough time on the campaign trail and you really do wonder how presidential candidates manage to stay sane. Twenty-four hours into John McCain's announcement tour, the venues have already started to run together in a blur of streamers, hot-dog stands, and high-school bands playing "This Land Is Your

Land" in the same trumpet squall. The senator has received all manner of pointless tchotchkes and doodads. ("Do you know how many baseball caps a candidate gets per day?" asks Michael Deaver, the old Reagan hand.) He has said *I'm not the youngest candidate, but I am the most experienced* at least six times. Twice, he's had to smile—and act as if he found it so *original*—when his supporters gave him valedictory send-offs to the tune of "Barbara Ann," a nod to the "Bomb Iran" wisecrack he made some weeks back. And somewhere between New Hampshire and South Carolina, the Arizona senator has gotten into a tense quarrel with the press corps, who cannot *believe* that a man who bills himself as a straight talker refused, just the day before, to answer their questions about Alberto Gonzales until they'd already filed their stories—at which point he told Larry King he thought the attorney general should resign.

"Well, the fact is, I wanted yesterday's stories to be about the announcement of our campaign," says McCain when confronted about the discrepancy at a press conference. "If your tender feelings are bruised, then I apologize."

Given America's unconcern with the Geneva Conventions and McCain's own harrowing history as a prisoner of war, perhaps Mark McKinnon, an adviser to the senator, could find a more delicate metaphor when he compares the process of running for president to torture. But he's certainly onto something. "Think about it," he says. "There's sleep deprivation. You don't know when your next meal is. You have the same sensory stimuli over and over until it drives you crazy. People are asking you questions, trying to trap you. And you're watched all the time. It's designed to break you down."

It's also the last remaining freak show in the United States, which is hardly to everyone's taste. Gary Bauer, a Republican Evangelical who made a quixotic primary bid in 2000, says he had a hard enough time coping with the "butter lady" at the Iowa State Fair. "Her claim to fame was that she always brought sculptures made completely out of butter," he says. "They were displayed in a refrigerated case. And . . . well, you're going to think I'm making this up, but guess what the sculpture was that year?"

A bust of his head?

"No," he says. "That I probably could have dealt with. No, no. It was the famous painting of the Lord's Supper. The Lord's Supper! It was *humongous*. The length of this room"—he points to the opposite wall of his Arlington, Virginia, office, maybe twelve feet away—"and pretty darn deep. I'm serious. The entire scene of Christ and all the disciples. And I don't even know *how* you react to that."

When Bob Dole ran for president in 1996, he says, the journalists who followed him knew his stump speech so well they'd recite it on the plane. After two days of following McCain, I realize I could probably do the same. Already I can reel off his jokes, his favorite rhetorical questions, and, of course, his tagline: *That's not good enough for America. And when I'm president, it won't be good enough for me!*

Which raises a crucial question: If *I'm* already sick of McCain, how does McCain feel?

"I get tired of some of it," he says, as we roll along on the *Straight Talk Express.* "But there'll always be new issues, new aspects of whatever the issues are. They're always changing, when you think about it."

And this is a fine answer, a perfectly politic answer. Any man with serious presidential ambitions cannot say how anesthetizing, peculiar, or extravagantly nuts he finds certain aspects of the modern American presidential campaign. But his response was disappointing somehow, and it's only later that I realized why: It was rote. Even this question—*Golly, how can you stand it?*—John McCain had probably been asked a dozen times before.

⤙ • ⤚

Authenticity has become a dominant meme of this campaign season. From the very beginning of the 2008 cycle, both parties—or large segments of them, anyway—seemed eager to find a presidential candidate who didn't suffer from a phoniness problem. Admittedly, Democrats experienced this desire more urgently than Republicans, because the men their party ran in the past two elections looked as if they'd been specifically selected for their extra coatings of polyurethane. With Al Gore, voters at least sensed that there was another man rattling around in there somewhere—a funnier man, one who cared deeply about the environment and had a gift for explaining why we should, too—and *An Inconvenient Truth* showed this to be true. With John Kerry, the problem ran deeper: To this day, it's not clear what he's passionate about. (He was more like the random books one finds on the shelf at a summer share—palatable, but loved by no one.)

After Kerry's defeat, many Democrats thought it a sensible goal to find a nominee in 2008 who wasn't stage-managed and poll-tested within an inch of his or her life. But 2008 is supposed to be Hillary's year. And, as millions discovered this March, she looks entirely plausible in a parody of an Apple campaign based on *1984.*

Complicating matters further this cycle is the advent of YouTube. When television came along, politics may have become a scripted teleplay. But with

YouTube, it's a reality show, where the audience gets to see not only the final, blow-dried product, but the blow-drying itself (John Edwards, predictably, is the poster boy for this effect), as it happens in real time. This is a very profound change. YouTube has the power to expose the lies that make political theater possible. It has the power to show how backstage versions of our politicians can, at times, not just be unlovely but *directly contradict* the image of the person we see on television. If this new world of amateur surveillance makes candidates paranoid and self-censoring, their speech really could be like something out of *1984*—measured, state-approved, one size fits all.

This year, each primary, in a sense, is a contest between those who are fake and those who are not. One of the main sources of Barack Obama's appeal is that he's *not* Hillary, as the Apple-Orwell–*1984* mash-up so pitilessly pointed out. Rather, he seems a fellow with a low zombie quotient—someone who wrote a moving and introspective memoir, someone who sang the Muslim call to prayer for the *New York Times*' Nicholas Kristof and called it "one of the prettiest sounds on Earth at sunset." (As Kristof wrote, this isn't exactly going to endear the man to voters in Alabama.) On the Republican side, there's Mitt Romney at one extreme (high zombie quotient), Rudy Giuliani at the other (still hewing to the pro-choice line, still talking with the cheerful opinionatedness of a New York City mayor), and McCain as a kind of phoniness parable, a cautionary example of what happens when a leopard tries to change its spots. Back in early 2000, McCain lived up to the overused moniker of *maverick,* saying whatever popped into his head, including his unmistakable conviction that Jerry Falwell and his brethren were "agents of intolerance." Yet at the beginning of this cycle, when it was clear he stood a real chance of winning, the shorter odds corrupted him, prompting him to give the commencement speech at Falwell's Liberty University and make a few other cynical overtures to the conservative base. It cost him dearly among independents, according to polls. Now, with some modifications, he's back to his old self, criticizing Bush and cursing those who stand in his way. (Recently, when Senator John Cornyn gave him grief about his immigration bill, he succinctly retorted, "Fuck you.")

It's easy to blame the system, the endless fund-raising and staged events and media scrutiny that borders on the proctological, for the current epidemic of phoniness. If only, the argument goes, a system could be arranged where politicians' real selves and real ideas were always and everywhere on display, we would have the politics we deserve. But it's also possible that phoniness, at least in certain forms, serves an important purpose. It may even be a desirable quality in politics. It's certainly something we consistently choose, consciously or not.

In *The Presentation of Self in Everyday Life,* a seminal social-science book that's a de facto primer on effective political communication, sociologist Erving Goffman gives a great deal of thought to how people show themselves to the world, viewing all forms of human interaction as a kind of managed drama. "When the individual has no belief in his own act and no ultimate concern with the beliefs of his audience," he writes, "we may call him cynical, reserving the term 'sincere' for the individuals who believe in the impression fostered by their own performance." Anyone who's listened to Mitt Romney for more than ten seconds can surely grasp this distinction.

But there's a whole spectrum of behaviors, Goffman notes, between these two extremes. Sometimes sincere actors delude their audiences because their audiences want to be lied to—body-conscious women in clothing stores, patients taking placebos. Sometimes people grow into roles that were once unnatural. Sometimes they grow disenchanted with roles they once inhabited so well. And sometimes actors believe in the sincerity of their performance and its fraudulence all at once.

But whatever the circumstances, writes Goffman, part of playing a role well is learning how to suppress spontaneous reactions. In political terms, this is part of what's known as message discipline. More broadly speaking, Goffman's point is that it's important, in any performance, to maintain the line between audience and actor. As Bob Kerrey, the former Nebraska governor and senator who ran in the Democratic primary in 1992, points out, "One of the things I discovered when I became governor of Nebraska is, 'There's a *role* I gotta play here.' We didn't have to put on robes and all that, obviously. But I had to learn how to *be* this person."

But who can best learn to *be* the president? Seeking the forces that are driving the political process leading up to the election in 2008, I wanted to look at this process from the inside, from the point of view of those who've undergone it in the past or are undergoing it now. What does it do to a person to devote all his or her energies to something that can seem so ludicrous? Do you have to be a mannequin to survive a pageant? Does the process turn you into one? Exactly whom do you have to be?

⤛ • ⤜

McCain is sitting in the back of the *Straight Talk Express,* having a lively dispute with a reporter about what, precisely, Harry Reid, the majority leader of the Senate, meant when he said the war was lost.

"He meant it couldn't be won militarily," the reporter says.

"Well, that's the way wars are usually decided," McCain replies, giving her a look of deadpan exasperation. "Generally speaking." Then, gamely: "Though sometimes they are decided by a jousting match! Between two selectees! Of the opposing armies!"

For all of McCain's attempts to recast himself as a mainstream character, he remains, at bottom, an insurgent, someone whose instincts are more rebellious than political. One senses it has something to do with the five and a half years he spent in a POW camp in Vietnam—after enduring the things he did, what does he care if he pisses off people or speaks his mind? (As the late Michael Kelly was fond of noting, veterans often make interesting political candidates for this reason.) But whatever the provenance of McCain's candor, it's been in full flower recently. In addition to the recent "fuck you" incident, he told bloggers he had little patience with Mitt Romney's wifty positions on immigration: "Maybe he can get out his small varmint gun and drive those Guatemalans off his yard." He also piquantly highlighted Obama's failure, in a press release, to spell a word a president ought to know: "By the way, Senator Obama, it's 'flak' jacket, not a 'flack' jacket."

In the *Straight Talk Express,* McCain has found the vehicle, both literally and figuratively, that plays to his strengths. In the protected confines of a bus, he's free to schmooze, argue, uncork in his loony-tunes way. The problem is that this discursive quality doesn't translate well into the rigid formatting of televised debate—he looks tense, rattling through his talking points like an auctioneer—and his irreverence is positively jarring out of context. Think of the angry reaction to his "Bomb Iran" moment, or the moment on *The Daily Show* when he awkwardly joked he'd picked up an improvised explosive device at the Baghdad market. It's worth pointing out that McCain sang "Bomb Iran" to a small VFW hall of veterans like himself (in response to a very specific question: "When do we send 'em an airmail package to Tehran?"), and two days after his appearance on *The Daily Show,* he twice referred to roadblocks to immigration reform as "IEDs," rather than "obstacles." Unless you follow McCain on the campaign trail, you'd never know how war metaphors suffuse his speech.

Zephyr Teachout, the Internet philosopher and director of online organizing for Howard Dean's primary campaign in 2004, writes in an e-mail that she sees two possible directions political discourse could take in a YouTube age:

The first future, the gloomy one, is one in which constant surveillance turns our politicians into plastic people, and turns creative, thoughtful people—people who are willing to think out loud—off from pursuing public office. The second future is the one in which the current plasticness becomes so unsustainable that it goes the other way—we become much more comfortable with awkward phrasing.

Unfortunately, she concludes, the gloomy future strikes her as the more likely one. *It has something to do with the way the media—writ large, new and old—teaches us all to be strategists, not citizens, and to think poorly of someone as a strategist, not a person, for saying something stupid.*

The irony in this new, strange age of amateur surveillance is that the old media may also come to the rescue. The press at least mediates (it's not called the media for nothing), providing context for remarks and maintaining confidentiality if certain things were said off the record or in jest. It's yet another reason McCain may like the *Straight Talk Express* so much. On the bus, I ask him if YouTube is going to make him more neurotic about what he says in small settings.

"I can't be any different," he says. "This is a tough slog"—another war metaphor—"everybody knows that. You gotta be who you are. But will I make some mistakes? Absolutely. Stand by."

⤙⟵ • ⟶⤚

Paul Begala, one of the senior advisers to Bill Clinton in 1992, makes a useful observation about his former boss, and oddly enough, he invokes Goffman to do it. "Erving Goffman used to make the distinction between front-stage and backstage personas," he says. The terms are self-explanatory—front stage is who the audience sees, and backstage is who intimates see, the person we suppress while performing. "Bill Clinton has the least distance between his front stage and his backstage personas out of anyone I know."

Deaver says the same thing about Ronald Reagan. It can't be an accident that both of these men were the two most popular presidents of the late-twentieth century. Nor can it be an accident that men with more private selves—Gore, Kerry, Dole—had a harder time when they stepped into the limelight. I ask Kerry's former campaign adviser Mary Beth Cahill when the senator seemed most like himself on the campaign trail, and her answer is startling: "On the plane, I think, when he'd be in the front cabin, playing his guitar by himself." He was most like himself, in other words, when he was alone.

Yet here's a wrinkle: McCain is also the same both front stage and back. Many mavericks are. Bob Kerrey. Chuck Hagel. (Also both Vietnam vets, it should be noted.) So why do they seem like longer shots for president? What makes them different? Why don't they have the same success?

⤙ • ⤚

"They wouldn't let me be funny!" Dole is saying, then catches himself. "Well, *they.*" He leans back. He's sitting in one of the stateliest rooms in his suite at Alston & Bird, yet looking uncharacteristically informal: navy slacks and no jacket, legs stretched way out, as if lounging on a deck chair. "They kind of said, 'We don't want a comedian. This is serious business.'"

Bob Dole is not a man whose front-stage and backstage personas were the same, at least while he was in politics. Backstage, Dole was a total cut-up; front stage, he was stiff, gruff—and 1996 was a real improvement over 1988, when he made a credible primary run. (Then, his front-stage persona was perilously close to Darth Vader's, minus the wheezing.) So one of the first questions I ask when I visit him at his law office in Washington is, Why wasn't he funny on the stump? And his answer is, *They wouldn't let me.*

"I don't think anyone asked him not to be funny," explains William Lacy, a former Dole adviser. "We just saw the importance of more message discipline, of having a message every day to get across, and that's something he struggled with." The trouble with humor, explains Lacy, is that it's discursive—once Dole got rolling, there was no stopping him. That worked just fine when he first came of age politically, stopping in people's farmhouses and putting 50,000 miles on his car, but television changed all that. He never got used to it. Bob Dole the person was so alienated from Bob Dole the brand that he referred to it—referred to *himself*—in the third person.

"I had trouble staying on message, yeah, that was one of my problems," says Dole. "I'd wander into some forest somewhere and finally get back to where I was supposed to be. But after you give the same speech over and over, you don't have the enthusiasm! It's not like, *Boy, I've got a great speech here—I'm going to go out and wow the crowd!*"

Indeed, that tends to be something natural performers, like Clinton and Reagan, are far better at pulling off. To them, it doesn't feel like dreary repetition. The transaction with the crowd, not the words themselves, gives them energy.

I ask Dole about the pageantry and props that come with the territory. "Yeah, I found it hard to do a lot of those things," he says. "All the stupid things you wear—the jackets are okay, but the aprons and big tall chef's caps while you're serving chop suey or whatever it is. You look like a monkey."

He thinks some more, then remembers something. "A parade in Illinois—Wheaton, Illinois—Bob Woodward's hometown, think his father was a judge there." Dole is filled with such asides. "It wasn't that I was wearing anything. But I remember the incident well, because this lady came rushing out with her baby and handed me her baby. But I don't use my right arm. And my left is not too strong. So, uh, I'm just scared to death."

He never says what happened to the child. He simply says what happened next: "Somebody next to me got under me right away and caught the baby."

He tells this story so matter-of-factly it's easy to miss the punch line—and its implications. As a wounded World War II veteran, Dole went an entire presidential campaign giving people the impression he was afraid of small kids.

"You know, people want you to kiss the babies, hold the babies," says Dole. "It's fine. But, uh, I remember that very well. I was scared to death."

Not that Dole ever had much of a chance. The economy was thriving; Clinton's popularity was high. He says it took a toll on him sometimes, having to pretend the election was winnable. "I said at my convention that I'm the most optimistic man in America," he says. "But privately . . . you know. When you kinda have that cloud hangin' over, it doesn't look good."

Dole had to exit political life in order to bring his backstage and front-stage personas into alignment. Today, he's everything his advisers wished he were then: open about his disability, sunny, funny. Like Gore, he just needed a different kind of media experience—appearances on *Letterman,* commercials about Viagra and Pepsi—to get him there.

"I can remember the Secret Service dropping me off on Election Night," he concludes. "You know—good-bye!" He gives a little wave. "And then you say, 'What do I do tomorrow?'" He smiles, and I notice that his right arm, which he'd always taken such enormous care to hike up and close around a pen, now rests, relaxed, at his right side. The pen's still there. But the tension's gone. "But somebody has to win," he says. "And somebody has to lose."

⊰⊱ • ⊱⊰

Years ago, while they were serving together in the Senate, Bob Kerrey and John McCain both worked on the POW/MIA committee. It was an extremely sensitive assignment for both of them, but even more so for McCain, who'd been a prisoner of war. Over the course of the year, Kerrey recalls, McCain got so incensed at a fellow senator—an Iowa farmer named Chuck Grassley—he was convinced McCain was going to bodily harm him during a meeting with colleagues and staff. "I knew he wasn't going to stand up and *hit* Grassley," says Kerrey, "because when John came out of the plane in Vietnam, his arms were ripped out of his sockets, and they rebroke them several times when he was in prison. But I am thinking, *He's going to head-butt Grassley and drive the cartilage in his nose into his brain. I'm going to watch a colleague kill a colleague. That'll give me something to remember on this day.*"

McCain didn't head-butt his colleague. Instead, he kept repeating, "You know what your problem is, Senator? You don't *listen,*" until the two men were nose-to-nose. Then McCain revised his opinion: "But that's not your problem. Your problem is, you're a fucking jerk."

"John hates when I tell this story," says Kerrey. "But I *like* that anger. When he got mad, I *liked* that he became Shiva." Shiva is the Hindu god of destruction, the destroyer of worlds. "I have a very high regard for John McCain," he adds. "But in a campaign, that temperament becomes an issue."

Straight talk, in other words, may be hazardous to a political career, as welcome as it may be.

◄◄ ● ►►

Hello? Hi, Brian. When do you want to come over? I've got a meeting from 3:30 to 4:30; otherwise I'm clear . . .

I am sitting in Michael Dukakis's office at Northeastern University, where he is, ever the retail politician, answering his own phone. He finishes, looks up, and apologizes. "I loved the primary," he begins, recalling the golden days of 1988, before his campaign ended in an electoral rout. "Because I'm a guy who *loves* campaigning on the ground. I wouldn't have been made dogcatcher if I weren't a grass-roots, precinct-based sort of guy. But once you're the nominee . . . then you get security. I never had it as governor"—of Massachusetts, his day job at the time—"so I was the *last* candidate on either side to say yes to the Secret Service. And if it hadn't been for 15,000 absolutely insane Greeks in Astoria that almost trampled us to death with their enthusiasm . . ." Kitty, his wife, remembers it well. They were shaking the car with such vigor she thought they were going to turn it over. "Once you say yes to the Secret Service, a kind of walling off takes place," he says. "And I found it difficult."

During the 1988 presidential campaign, Dukakis came across as cold, academic, and overly righteous. It is shocking how different he comes across in a small setting. In his office, his style is warm and unfussy; he's a careful listener and questioner. Even the famous Velcro eyebrows make sense. They give his eyes depth.

"Now, are there ways to break through that?" he asks. "Yeah. I think the Clinton-Gore bus trips were an inspired idea. I'm sorry we didn't have those. Because on that level, you see things, people tell you about things. Drove the Secret Service crazy, but Clinton and Gore got the kind of spontaneity—the kind of *learning*—you don't get in canned events, where you're up in the plane, down, up in the plane, down."

Like Dole, Dukakis didn't have a flair for the up in the plane, down. "Part of the problem here is that most of us—I don't care whether it's Dukakis, Gore, Hart, whoever—most of us started in politics in living rooms and backyards and Legion halls," Dukakis concludes. He's talking about himself in the third person, just like Dole, as if to say, *that politician-fellow named Mike Dukakis is a different man entirely.* "And generally speaking, if I may say so, we're very good at it. But see, how do ya translate that? I can't deliver a speech off prepared text for love nor money. If I had a nickel for everybody who's come up to me since 1988 and said, 'You're nothing like the guy we were watching on television'. . . I say to them, well, that was eight seconds. Clinton—Clinton can do it in eight seconds. Reagan. I gotta spend an hour with people."

Anything short of that had the potential to result in disaster. During the second presidential debate, CNN's Bernard Shaw famously asked Dukakis whether the death penalty would be appropriate if a stranger raped and killed his wife. He gave a characteristically unemotional answer: *No, I don't, Bernard. And I think you know that I've opposed the death penalty during all of my life . . .* People say it cost him the election. Kitty herself was stunned. ("Afterwards, I turned to him in the car and said, '*What* were you *thinking*?'" she says.)

"Look, when you're opposed to the death penalty, you're asked that question a *thousand times*," Dukakis says today. "Unfortunately, I answered it as if I'd been asked it a thousand times. Folks expected more, I guess."

◄─ • ─►

"A couple weeks ago, Warren Beatty called me up and said, 'Let me ask you something: Do you think you have to be crazy to run for president?'"

This is Gary Hart, the Democratic senator who swept half the primaries in 1984 before flaming out.

"And I said, 'What do you mean? Not *crazy* crazy, right?'" he says. "And he said, 'Well, not conventionally normal.' And I began to think about that. Because I . . . I don't think I'm crazy. But I think what he was getting at was some combination of compulsion, drivenness, neuroses—who knows?"

What does he mean, *who knows?* He ran for president. What are the excesses of a presidential personality?

"Well, high energy. And a bit of . . . let's see. Whatever the sane side of messianic is. A sense that you can see farther ahead than most people. I've always felt that that was my strength, that I could see farther ahead than most people."

Whatever the sane side of messianic is. Because of its fractured grammar, this is possibly the loveliest—and truest—iteration of a campaign cliché, that a candidate for president must have a vision to convey. "And an ability to relate," he adds. "And I'll tell you how this is strange. The tagline for me throughout '83 was 'cool and aloof.' But the only reason 'cool and aloof' came about is because I was shy—instead of working a room, I'd get my back against the wall. But I'd get into a conversation, and within twenty minutes, I had the whole room around me."

How does a shy person run for president?

He gives a mild shrug. "There's a stereotypical belief that to be a politician, you have to need acclaim and gratification and acceptance," he says. "I never did. You would be amazed at the number of senators who are shy people. They hate running for office. They just force themselves. You'll do whatever it takes, if you have that sense of seeing over the horizon."

⤛ • ⤜

Hart is surely right. Given the right circumstances, a shy person can become president. But if history is any guide, it helps to be the kind of person who's amenable to the steady breaches of privacy that a president must endure.

"If you were running for office, this is what I'd say to you," says Bob Kerrey, now head of the New School. "At some point, arriving in your life is an organization called the United States Secret Service. And when the Secret Service arrives, *you can't open your own car door.* They interfere with all your neighbors; anyone who wants to get in contact with you has to deal with them. So the best advice I could ever give to a candidate is, Think about this. You might *win.*"

"The moment I remember," Kerrey continues, "is discovering that Bill Clinton *wanted* to live in 1600 Pennsylvania Avenue. He had intentionally overnighted there when Jimmy Carter was president. He knew where the living spaces were. He knew what they looked like. He had a feel for what that experience was going to be, and it made him feel good. Whereas when I got to thinking about living at 1600 Pennsylvania Avenue, it gave me the chills."

What about it?

"What about it? I was *single*."

And this suggests the biggest distinction between candidates like Kerrey and McCain versus candidates like Bill Clinton and Ronald Reagan. It's true that both have the same front-stage and backstage personas. But for people like Ronald Reagan and Bill Clinton, the front-stage persona *is* the person backstage. Clinton especially: Even when the cameras aren't rolling, he's always performing. The fantasy about Clinton is that he's exactly like you or me. But he's *nothing* like you or me. After I followed him around Africa for seven days in 2005, this, to me, was the most startling revelation. Even in the most solitary circumstances, he lit up like a Christmas tree. He *enjoyed* performing in these quiet circumstances, often repeating the same jokes and anecdotes, including ones that had already appeared in his autobiography. It was like an imaginary camera was always rolling. Everything he said seemed meant for a dais.

Reagan, though less pyrotechnic in style, had a similar openness. Deaver points out, "His whole adult life had been public." And by the time he became president, adds Ed Rollins, another one of his advisers, "having 10,000 people clapping for him didn't do anything unusual to him. Some people, the adrenaline gets them so high they ramble."

Or yelp, as was the case of Howard Dean—*Yeeeeeeeow!*

And in that yelp is the difference. For politicians like Dean, McCain, Kerrey, or (yes, sorry) Ross Perot, their backstage personas were what they trotted out front, not the other way around. For Dean, this meant we saw arrogance, hotheadedness, and a teenager's response to a screaming crowd (*Yeeeeeeeow!*) in addition to his candor and passion. With Perot, we saw a barking loony. With Kerrey, we saw ambivalence (his Senate colleagues called him "Cosmic Bob") and dread about losing his privacy. And with McCain, we see anger and irreverence.

These are all emotions we associate with private settings. They are not ones we generally haul out for public view.

Yet in almost every campaign cycle, the press has a brief romance with the candidates whose backstage personalities are also out front. They are invariably the most entertaining people as well as the most relatable. But they seldom hold up over the long haul. The rougher parts of themselves eventually start to worry us. "I would *muuuuch* rather have a phony, competent person in the White House than an incompetent, authentic person," says Kerrey. "I'm not sure the two aren't correlated: The greater competence you've got, the more you've got to be phony in order to get the job done. I *want* my president to put a mask on. When they're negotiating for a national-security agreement? Put the mask on. When they're negotiating with Congress? Put the mask on. If someone says to me a politician is phony, my response, at some point, is, 'Well, they gotta be. That's their job.'"

This front-stage–backstage distinction is a weirdly good predictor of who survives presidential races, and probably forces us to rethink what authenticity means in politics—and who, in 2008, might survive over the long haul. Obama, for instance, doesn't suffer using this guideline. Even backstage, in one-on-one interviews, he's smooth, collected, disciplined, in control.

Perhaps more surprising, though, is that Hillary doesn't necessarily suffer using this guideline either. Like many people, I used to assume that it was public life, and more specifically the unique constraints of her marriage, that made her build a carapace around herself. And I'm sure it's partly true. But people who've known Hillary a long time say her emotional life has always been opaque. As far back as Wellesley, her peers were in awe of her composure, trying to figure out who she was underneath. Though there probably is another Hillary buried somewhere in her, she's spent so long in her current role that she's more or less internalized it, the way soldiers internalize their place in the army.

Last month, the *Times* reported that Hillary has hired a communications consultant who trains his clients to "jam" and "get to cool." It's a rotten idea. Hillary may as well lead with her weakness, as she did in her Senate race, embracing the fact that she's contained but serious about the job. If she can convince the public that she isn't a cold schemer, but simply a woman of purpose and reserve—that that's who she is, front stage and back—she has a shot. (It's certainly one possible explanation for her strong poll numbers.) It might even be the ideal for the first female commander-in-chief.

McCain has the opposite problem. As exhilarating as it would be for someone as candid as he is to step into the Oval Office, voters would have to radically depart from their previous patterns to choose a man whose backstage rawness was in full frontal view. Right until September 10, New Yorkers would have said that Giuliani's backstage rawness was in full frontal view, too (as when he told a ferret-loving talk-show caller, "There is something really, really very sad about you"). But the events of September 11 recast his front-stage persona from bully to hero, and as the *Times* pointed out last week, he's been extremely disciplined on the trail, keeping his cheerful insults to a minimum. (And this may explain *his* good poll numbers.) Though many, especially New Yorkers, are still waiting for the other Rudy, the sharp-tongued and freewheeling ego-maniac (in the manner of most New York City mayors), to reappear.

One of the most stunning asides Goffman makes in *The Presentation of Self in Everyday Life* is based not on his own observation but that of Robert Ezra Park, a founder of the Chicago School of sociology. He noted that the word *person* itself comes from the Latin word *persona,* or actor's mask. "Insofar as this mask represents the conception we have formed of ourselves—the role we are striving to live up to—this mask is our truer self, the person we would like to be," Goffman quotes him as saying.

Viewed in this light, the performances our politicians give aren't necessar-ily cynical but aspirational, idealistic even: Some are using this process to be-come the person they think they're meant to be. All the butter sculptures and corn dogs and ceaseless repetition of platitudes—this bizarre, debasing torture of our candidates—may actually contribute to something positive. Phoniness may just be a kind of chrysalis, a stage a politician must pass through in order to become presidential. The trouble is, not all of them make it.

12
POLITICAL CIVILITY

DAVID MAMET
The Village Voice   March 11, 2008

"Change" has been the mantra of the 2008 political season. People may have dif-ferent ideas about what this change should entail, but there seems to be a general consensus that the various ideologies of the recent past simply aren't working, and that as a nation we need to find a new pragmatic philosophy by which to govern. That requires jettisoning not only the "government is the problem" stance of the conservative right, but also the "government is the answer" dogma that so many on the left hold dear. In his Village Voice *essay, David Mamet, one of America's leading playwrights (whose credits include the screenplay for the political spoof*

Wag the Dog), *offers himself up as the embodiment of this new zeitgeist, as he describes how he came to realize that he's not the liberal he'd always imagined himself to be.*

John Maynard Keynes was twitted with changing his mind. He replied, "When the facts change, I change my opinion. What do you do, sir?"

My favorite example of a change of mind was Norman Mailer at *The Village Voice.*

Norman took on the role of drama critic, weighing in on the New York premiere of *Waiting for Godot.*

Twentieth century's greatest play. Without bothering to go, Mailer called it a piece of garbage.

When he did get around to seeing it, he realized his mistake. He was no longer a *Voice* columnist, however, so he bought a page in the paper and wrote a retraction, praising the play as the masterpiece it is.

Every playwright's dream.

I once won one of Mary Ann Madden's "Competitions" in *New York* magazine. The task was to name or create a "10" of anything, and mine was the World's Perfect Theatrical Review. It went like this: "I never understood the theater until last night. Please forgive everything I've ever written. When you read this I'll be dead." That, of course, is the only review anybody in the theater ever wants to get.

My prize, in a stunning example of irony, was a year's subscription to *New York,* which rag (apart from Mary Ann's "Competition") I considered an open running sore on the body of world literacy—this due to the presence in its pages of John Simon, whose stunning amalgam of superciliousness and savagery, over the years, was appreciated by that readership searching for an endorsement of proactive mediocrity.

But I digress.

I wrote a play about politics (*November,* Barrymore Theater, Broadway, some seats still available). And as part of the "writing process," as I believe it's called, I started thinking about politics. This comment is not actually as jejune as it might seem. *Porgy and Bess* is a buncha good songs but has nothing to do with race relations, which is the flag of convenience under which it sailed.

But my play, it turned out, was actually about politics, which is to say, about the polemic between persons of two opposing views. The argument in my play is between a president who is self-interested, corrupt, suborned, and realistic, and his leftish, lesbian, utopian-socialist speechwriter.

The play, while being a laugh a minute, is, when it's at home, a disputation between reason and faith, or perhaps between the conservative (or tragic) view and the liberal (or perfectionist) view. The conservative president in the piece holds that people are each out to make a living, and the best way for government to facilitate that is to *stay out of the way,* as the inevitable abuses and failures of this system (free-market economics) are less than those of government intervention.

I took the liberal view for many decades, but I believe I have changed my mind.

As a child of the '60s, I accepted as an article of faith that government is corrupt, that business is exploitative, and that people are generally good at heart.

These cherished precepts had, over the years, become ingrained as increasingly impracticable prejudices. Why do I say impracticable? Because although I still held these beliefs, I no longer applied them in my life. How do I know? My wife informed me. We were riding along and listening to NPR. I felt my facial muscles tightening, and the words beginning to form in my mind: *Shut the fuck up.* "?" she prompted. And her terse, elegant summation, as always, awakened me to a deeper truth: I had been listening to NPR and reading various organs of national opinion for years, wonder and rage contending for pride of place. Further: I found I had been—rather charmingly, I thought—referring to myself for years as "a brain-dead liberal," and to NPR as "National Palestinian Radio."

This is, to me, the synthesis of this worldview with which I now found myself disenchanted: that everything is always wrong.

But in my life, a brief review revealed, everything was not always wrong, and neither was nor is always wrong in the community in which I live, or in my country. Further, it was not always wrong in previous communities in which I lived, and among the various and mobile classes of which I was at various times a part.

And, I wondered, how could I have spent decades thinking that I thought everything was always wrong *at the same time* that I thought I thought that people were basically good at heart? Which was it? I began to question what I actually thought and found that I do not think that people are basically good at heart; indeed, that view of human nature has both prompted and informed my writing for the last 40 years. I think that people, in circumstances of stress, can behave like swine, and that this, indeed, is not only a fit subject, but the only subject, of drama.

I'd observed that lust, greed, envy, sloth, and their pals are giving the world a good run for its money, but that nonetheless, people in general seem to get from day to day; and that we in the United States get from day to day under rather wonderful and privileged circumstances—that we are not and never have been the villains that some of the world and some of our citizens make us out to be, but that we are a confection of normal (greedy, lustful, duplicitous, corrupt, inspired—in short, human) individuals living under a spectacularly effective compact called the Constitution, and lucky to get it.

For the Constitution, rather than suggesting that all behave in a godlike manner, recognizes that, to the contrary, people are swine and will take any opportunity to subvert any agreement in order to pursue what they consider to be their proper interests.

To that end, the Constitution separates the power of the state into those three branches which are for most of us (I include myself) the only thing we remember from 12 years of schooling.

The Constitution, written by men with some experience of actual government, assumes that the chief executive will work to be king, the Parliament will scheme to sell off the silverware, and the judiciary will consider itself Olympian and do everything it can to much improve (destroy) the work of the other two branches. So the Constitution pits them against each other, in the attempt not to achieve stasis, but rather to allow for the constant corrections necessary to prevent one branch from getting too much power for too long.

Rather brilliant. For, in the abstract, we may envision an Olympian perfection of perfect beings in Washington doing the business of their employers, the people, but any of us who has ever been at a zoning meeting with our property at stake is aware of the urge to cut through all the pernicious bullshit and go straight to firearms.

I found not only that I didn't trust the current government (that, to me, was no surprise), but that an impartial review revealed that the faults of this president—whom I, a good liberal, considered a monster—were little different from those of a president whom I revered.

Bush got us into Iraq, JFK into Vietnam. Bush stole the election in Florida; Kennedy stole his in Chicago. Bush outed a C.I.A. agent; Kennedy left hundreds of them to die in the surf at the Bay of Pigs. Bush lied about his military service; Kennedy accepted a Pulitzer Prize for a book written by Ted Sorenson. Bush was in bed with the Saudis, Kennedy with the Mafia. Oh.

And I began to question my hatred for "the Corporations"—the hatred of which, I found, was but the flip side of my hunger for those goods and services they provide and without which we could not live.

And I began to question my distrust of the "Bad, Bad Military" of my youth, which, I saw, was then and is now made up of those men and women who actually risk their lives to protect the rest of us from a very hostile world. Is the military always right? No. Neither is government, nor are the corporations—they are just different signposts for the particular amalgamation of our country into separate working groups, if you will. Are these groups infallible, free from the possibility of mismanagement, corruption, or crime? No, and neither are you or I. So, taking the tragic view, the question was not "Is everything perfect?" but "How could it be better, at what cost, and according to whose definition?" Put into which form, things appeared to me to be unfolding pretty well.

Do I speak as a member of the "privileged class"? If you will—but classes in the United States are mobile, not static, which is the Marxist view. That is: Immigrants came and continue to come here penniless and can (and do) become rich; the nerd makes a trillion dollars; the single mother, penniless and ignorant of English, sends her two sons to college (my grandmother). On the other hand, the rich and the children of the rich can go belly-up; the hegemony of the railroads is appropriated by the airlines, that of the networks by the Internet; and the individual may and probably will change status more than once within his lifetime.

What about the role of government? Well, in the abstract, coming from my time and background, I thought it was a rather good thing, but tallying up the ledger in those things which affect me and in those things I observe, I am hard-pressed to see an instance where the intervention of the government led to much beyond sorrow.

But if the government is not to intervene, how will we, mere human beings, work it all out?

I wondered and read, and it occurred to me that I knew the answer, and here it is: We just seem to. How do I know? From experience. I referred to my own—take away the director from the staged play and what do you get? Usually a diminution of strife, a shorter rehearsal period, and a better production.

The director, generally, does not *cause* strife, but his or her presence impels the actors to direct (and manufacture) claims designed to appeal to Authority—that is, to set aside the original goal (staging a play for the audience) and indulge in politics, the purpose of which may be to gain status and influence outside the ostensible goal of the endeavor.

Strand unacquainted bus travelers in the middle of the night, and what do you get? A lot of bad drama, and a shake-and-bake Mayflower Compact. Each, instantly, adds what he or she can to the solution. Why? Each wants, and in fact needs, to contribute—to throw into the pot what gifts each has in order to achieve the overall goal, as well as status in the new-formed community. And so they work it out.

See also that most magnificent of schools, the jury system, where, again, each brings nothing into the room save his or her own prejudices, and, through the course of deliberation, comes not to a perfect solution, but a solution acceptable to the community—a solution the community can live with.

⤙ • ⤚

Prior to the midterm elections, my rabbi was taking a lot of flak. The congregation is exclusively liberal, he is a self-described independent (read "conservative"), and he was driving the flock wild. Why? Because a) he never discussed politics; and b) he taught that the quality of political discourse must be addressed first—that Jewish law teaches that it is incumbent upon each person to hear the other fellow out.

And so I, like many of the liberal congregation, began, teeth grinding, to attempt to do so. And in doing so, I recognized that I held those two views of America (politics, government, corporations, the military). One was of a state where everything was magically wrong and must be immediately corrected at any cost; and the other—the world in which I actually functioned day to day—was made up of people, most of whom were reasonably trying to maximize their comfort by getting along with each other (in the workplace, the marketplace, the jury room, on the freeway, even at the school-board meeting).

And I realized that the time had come for me to avow my participation in that America in which I chose to live, and that that country was not a school-room teaching values, but a marketplace.

"Aha," you will say, and you are right. I began reading not only the economics of Thomas Sowell (our greatest contemporary philosopher) but Milton Friedman, Paul Johnson, and Shelby Steele, and a host of conservative writers, and found that I agreed with them: a free-market understanding of the world meshes more perfectly with my experience than that idealistic vision I called liberalism.

At the same time, I was writing my play about a president, corrupt, venal, cunning, and vengeful (as I assume all of them are), and two turkeys. And I gave this fictional president a speechwriter who, in his view, is a "brain-dead liberal," much like my earlier self; and in the course of the play, they have to work it out. And they eventually do come to a human understanding of the political process. As I believe I am trying to do, and in which I believe I may be succeeding, and I will try to summarize it in the words of William Allen White.

White was for 40 years the editor of the *Emporia Gazette* in rural Kansas, and a prominent and powerful political commentator. He was a great friend of Theodore Roosevelt and wrote the best book I've ever read about the presidency. It's called *Masks in a Pageant,* and it profiles presidents from McKinley to Wilson, and I recommend it unreservedly.

White was a pretty clear-headed man, and he'd seen human nature as few can. (As Twain wrote, you want to understand men, run a country paper.) White knew that people need both to get ahead and to get along, and that they're always working at one or the other, and that government should most probably stay out of the way and let them get on with it. But, he added, there is such a thing as liberalism, and it may be reduced to these saddest of words: ". . . and yet . . . "

The right is mooing about faith, the left is mooing about change, and many are incensed about the fools on the other side—but, at the end of the day, they are the same folks we meet at the water cooler. Happy election season.

13

16 WAYS OF LOOKING AT A FEMALE VOTER

LINDA HIRSHMAN
The New York Times Magazine   February 3, 2008

Modern politics, as seen through the eyes of professional pollsters, is a statistics game: Age, gender, educational background, religious affiliation, and other attributes go a long way to predicting how a person will vote in any given election. Here, philosophy professor and self-described radical feminist Linda Hirshman— who stirred up a firestorm of controversy several years ago by arguing, in her book Get to Work *and a related article in* The American Prospect, *that professional women as a group were failing themselves and society by dropping out of the work-force en masse to raise children—crunches the numbers on women's political be-havior in and out of the voting booth.*

1. THE FEMALE THING

For months before the presidential primaries began, Senator Hillary Rodham Clinton was widely held to lead among women voters. That she would naturally appeal to her own sex accounted in no small part for her front-runner status. By the end of last year, national polls showed not only that Clinton was ahead but also that women supported her by 8 points more than men did.

But in the Iowa caucus her lead turned out, to use a Clinton phrase, to be more talk than action: 35 percent of female Iowa Democrats went for Senator Barack Obama while only 30 percent stood up for Hillary—and Obama won. Was Iowa an isolated case? Or had women voters turned their backs on Hillary?

Various explanations surfaced. A WNBC television reporter suggested that "somewhere along the line she lost the narrative of the first female president as a huge change." A blogger on the *Huffington Post* decided that what women needed wasn't change; it was the whole truth and nothing but the truth: "Women are too smart, informed and astute at reading between the lines to back a presidential candidate who isn't being straight with them—especially when she is a woman." The snarky Washington-based blog *Wonkette* proposed that maybe Hillary lacked a certain something and that Barack Obama, well, had it. "I think Chris Matthews said," the post read, "that we're all voting for Obama because we want to date him, but they were showing a picture of Obama at the time, and I heard birds singing and bells ringing and missed it."

Then in New Hampshire, things suddenly changed: 46 percent of women in the Democratic primary voted for Hillary compared with 34 percent for Obama, giving Clinton the victory. Was it the welling up? Was it the specter, three days earlier, of those male candidates piling up on her during a debate? Was it because the debate's moderator questioned how likable she was? The *Times* columnist Gail Collins briefly summed up the theories for Hillary's victory—"Do women Obama's age look at him and see the popular boy who never talked to them in high school? Did they relate to Clinton's strategy of constantly re-minding her audiences that she's been working for reform for 35 years?"—and then added her own. Hillary, she wrote, "was a stand-in for every woman who has overdosed on multitasking." As Collins saw it, women simply wanted to get their own back: "They grabbed at the opportunity to have kids/go back to school/start a business/become a lawyer. But there are days when they can't meet everybody's needs, and the men in their lives—loved ones and otherwise—make them feel like failures or towers of self-involvement. And the deal is that they can either suck it up or look like a baby."

There was one thing the commentators seemed to agree on. Women in Iowa and New Hampshire—whether they voted for or against Hillary—were doing so for the same reason: because she was a woman.

2. MIND THE GENDER GAP

In 1920, just as American women got the vote, the New York League of Women Voters tried to defeat a sitting senator, James Wadsworth Jr. The league didn't beat Wadsworth that year, but his ally Governor Nathan Miller nonetheless later denounced the league as a "menace" to "our free institutions." There is no more need for a League of Women Voters, he declared, than for a League of Men Voters. He need not have worried—women didn't begin to vote as often as men or differently from men for decades.

It wasn't until Ronald Reagan's victory in 1980 that observers first noticed the "gender gap": men supported Reagan by 8 percentage points more than women did. Of course, more women supported the incumbent, President Jimmy Carter, than did men. And ever since, women have been more likely than men to favor Democrats. Both parties have tried a variety of strategies to open or close the gender gap: nominating a woman for vice president (Geraldine Ferraro), pretending there was no difference, collecting women into smaller subgroups (soccer moms, security moms), emphasizing feminist issues (equal opportunity, reproductive rights), emphasizing economics (health, welfare, child care). A host of feminist institutions—the Democratic pro-choice political action committee Emily's List; the nonpartisan White House Project, which promotes political activity among women—have arisen to try to drive up the numbers and harness the power of the women's vote.

Despite these efforts, the gender gap has neither widened nor narrowed much. It spiked in 1996, when women supported Bill Clinton by 11 percentage points more than men did, and again in 2000, when women favored Al Gore by

12 points. But because the gap describes the difference between how many men and women vote for a single party's candidate, it doesn't necessarily tell us whether women themselves are split. In the election 28 years ago that first pointed to the existence of a so-called gender gap, women still preferred Reagan by 46 percent to Carter's 45 percent. More women may have voted for Carter than men did, but even more voted for Reagan.

3. RACE MATTERS—AND CLASS, TOO

Race factors into the gender gap in two important ways. In 2004, for example, the nonwhite female vote was 12 percent of the electorate; the nonwhite male vote was 10 percent. So when polled, women as a group were less "white" than men were—and nonwhite women are more likely to vote Democratic than white women are. Second, nonwhite women are more likely to vote Democratic than nonwhite men (75 percent to 67 percent in 2004). In other words, nonwhite women make "women" more Democratic than the nonwhite men make "men" Democratic. In 2004, 55 percent of white women actually favored George Bush.

And as it does for men, economic status can affect how women vote. In a recent national poll of Democrats and Democratic-leaning voters by the Pew Research Center, Hillary Clinton led Barack Obama among women in every category but two: self-described liberals and college graduates. Among college graduates, he is 3 points ahead. And whereas among women with incomes of more than $50,000, Clinton leads Obama by a mere 5 percentage points, among those who earn less, she leads by 36 points.

4. WINNING WOMEN ISN'T THE SAME AS WINNING

With the possible exception of 1996, women have never voted a candidate into the White House when men thought the other guy should win. (Bill Clinton's so-called gender-based victory depended on splitting the male vote with Bob Dole. In other words, women did not have to overcome fierce resistance in order to prevail.) In the 2004 election, there was a gender gap in virtually every demographic—among old folks, married people, single people, squirrel hunters—but the gender gap still did not offset the robust men's vote. If men are Republican enough, the Republicans need not care whether the women are less enthusiastic about them than men are.

5. BESIDES, WOMEN KEEP AN OPEN MIND

Still, there are ways in which women, as a group, behave differently than men. According to the Center for American Women and Politics at Rutgers University, women in 2004 made up a higher percentage of undecided and swing voters than men. In an independent survey conducted in October 2004, women accounted for 60 percent of undecided likely voters.

Just before the primary season began last month, the Norman Lear Center at the University of Southern California and Zogby International released their "National Survey on Politics and Entertainment," which juxtaposes Americans' cultural lives and their political views. They found that 62 percent of the "moderates"—those with middling and flexible positions on the issues—were women. Pollsters grouped respondents according to how they indicated their degree of agreement with certain statements. The Lear subjects clustered into three clear groups: blue, or liberal; red, or conservative; and purple, or moderate, who were 24 percent of those surveyed. Although no one was very surprised when the liberal group turned out to be 57 percent female, Johanna Blakley, deputy director of the Lear Center and a lead researcher on the project, said she found it "absolutely unbelievable" that 62 percent of the moderates were female. She had always thought of moderates as male independents, alienated from politics.

When asked to identify their party, the female moderates, it turned out, were actually more Democratic than Republican, but like most women, they voted only somewhat more for John Kerry than for George Bush in the 2004 presidential election. "They don't see the political world as legible, especially in the media," Blakley suggested. "That's why they misidentify themselves, these words don't make sense to them, they don't have a value and a weight that makes sense to them, a narrative for politics."

6. WHAT ABOUT THE MIDDLE GROUND?

When it comes to politics, it's not just that women are ambivalent; it's that, as a group, they are less interested than men are—not all women, naturally, but on average. In a 2006 University of Michigan survey, 42 percent of men responded that they were "very interested" in government and public affairs, compared with 34 percent of women. At the uninterested end, women were more likely to say that they were only "somewhat interested"—60 percent of female respondents compared with 54 percent of male respondents.

These differences—give or take a few percentage points—have persisted for at least 20 years. Studies have turned up many explanations for the difference—education, partisanship, sex-role socialization—but the interest-gap remains. The only area where the gap narrows is in local politics, where women score close to men. Not surprisingly, less interest translates into less knowledge.

In their 1996 study of Americans' political knowledge, *What Americans Know About Politics and Why It Matters,* Scott Keeter, director of survey research at the Pew organization, and his coauthor, Michael X. Delli Carpini, dean of the University of Pennsylvania's Annenberg School of Communication, reported that on average, men outscored women by more than 9 percentage points on all political questions; by 15 points when asked to name their governor; by 10 on the identity of either of their senators. (It is true that women sometimes say that don't know when they do, but this accounts for only about a quarter of the knowledge gap.)

In a separate survey done before the current election cycle, Pew asked men and women which of the Democratic candidates is Hispanic, what Mitt Romney's religion is, the name of the current speaker of the House, what position Robert Gates holds, which party has the House majority and how many U.S. troops have died in Iraq. The men outscored the women on every question, with the widest gap being the name of the secretary of defense (there was an 18 point difference between the number of men who answered correctly and the number of women who did) and the smallest that Mitt Romney is a Mormon (2 points). Many more men (13 points) knew the rough number of U.S. troop casualties in Iraq and that Nancy Pelosi is speaker of the House (6 points).

7. THE GAP THAT MATTERS

The Pew Research Center for the People and the Press has been following the gender divide in news consumption in great detail for years. This is what that gap looks like:

POLITICAL INTERESTS	MEN	WOMEN
International affairs	63 percent	37 percent
News about Washington	59 percent	41 percent
Local government	55 percent	45 percent

While men are more likely to follow international, national and local politics, women are more likely to attend to religion, health and entertainment, community, culture and the arts, crime and the weather. Men are significantly more likely than women to be regular consumers of "hard news" (32 percent of men versus 22 percent of women), and to turn to the Internet, radio news, talk radio, newspapers, political comedy shows and political talk shows. Women, by contrast, are more likely to get their news from the morning news broadcasts and network news programs. Although morning shows do offer news, they tend toward true crime, entertainment and lifestyle, and they regularly put a human-interest spin on government and foreign affairs.

Even if you factor in all the ways in which people gather news—women supposedly also get political information from the groups they join and from the people they know—and control for political affiliations, race and class, men still know more about politics than women do. The audiences for programs like *The Daily Show* and *The Rush Limbaugh Show,* those on National Public Radio and the Web sites of national newspapers all scored significantly higher on political knowledge—defined as familiarity with public figures and political policies—than those surveyed who were not part of those audiences. Of all of these outlets, only NPR has an audience that's roughly half female.

Of course, a quick glance at the numbers confirms that a lot of people, of both sexes, are hardly following the news at all. Most voters aren't policy wonks. It may well be that there's a base line of information that is "good enough" for citizenship, and knowing more makes little practical difference. But there is a strong correlation between knowledge and political participation. In most aspects of political action—candidacy, fund-raising, proselytizing, propagandizing—men predominate.

8. WHAT MAKES WOMEN TUNE OUT

A recent report assembled by the Shorenstein Center at Harvard's John F. Kennedy School of Government suggests that the absence of women in journalism and on television news programs reduces the likelihood that women will form a significant part of the audience. Most hard-core news programs have hardly any women participants at all: a 2001 White House Project study reported that on the Sunday-morning talk shows, only 11 percent of the guests were women. A follow-up study in 2005 showed the percentage had increased by only 3 points. Similarly, a 2005 Project for Excellence in Journalism study found that only one-third of news accounts cited any female sources at all.

9. PRIDE AND PREJUDICE

Not only do fewer women turn to outlets with predominantly male sources for information, but studies also tie women to what scholars call the negative-media effect. Women will sometimes back a candidate because the media they distrust are backing his or her rival.

There was a lot of speculation after the turnaround in New Hampshire that MSNBC's *Hardball* host, Chris Matthews, was at least partly responsible for Clinton's surge when he gleefully declared Hillary all but dead and buried after her Iowa loss. Although there is no way to know how many women decided to vote for Clinton in response to the news media's attacks on her, Rebecca Traister, a columnist for the online magazine *Salon* and a self-declared anti-Hillaryite, was not alone in giving voice to the impulse. "The torrent of ill-disguised hatred and resentment unleashed toward a briefly weakened Clinton," she wrote, "made me feel something that all the hectoring from feminist elders could not: guilt for not having stood up for Hillary. I can't believe I'm saying this, but had I been a New Hampshire voter on Tuesday, I would have pulled a lever for the former first lady."

10. XX MARKS THE SPOT

Historically, there is no reason to believe that women, even Democratic women, will automatically support a female candidate. As Nancy Burns, a political scientist at the University of Michigan, demonstrated in a recent article in the journal *Politics and Gender,* women, like men, have multiple commitments and connections, which pull their electoral loyalties in many directions. And because women's lives are intimately connected with those of men, women are a little harder to organize than, say, a segregated racial minority. Burns also maintained that "gender consciousness," far from helping women to organize themselves politically, has little power to generate political action, and that its influence has "waned over the last 30 years."

On the other hand, the presence of a female candidate is consistently bracing to women voters—even if they don't end up voting for her. In their book,

The Private Roots of Public Action, the political scientists Nancy Burns, Kay Lehman Schlozman and Sidney Verba found that for women, "living in a state with a statewide female politician has a significant impact on each of the components of psychological engagement with politics: political information, interest and efficacy." Women are more likely, for instance, to know the name of their state's U.S. senator or Senate candidate if a woman held or was competing for the office. Seeing themselves as part of the political arena encourages women to get involved.

Page Gardner, who founded Women's Voices Women Vote, an organization dedicated to increasing voter turnout among single women, reports that female candidates are traditionally "very motivational" to her constituency. (Single women vote less frequently than married women, by 13 percent.)

The degree to which women participated in recent primary elections suggests that a female candidate does increase turnout among women. In both the Iowa caucuses and the New Hampshire primary, 57 percent of those who voted were women, up 3 points from 2004. In Nevada, women made up nearly 60 percent of the record 116,000 Democratic caucusgoers.

11. WHEN SISTERHOOD IS POWER

Most of the data on the gender gap are gathered from research collected in the general elections. In the primaries, that gap cannot be explained simply by the fact that women tend to favor Democratic over Republican policies. To a degree, the recent primaries are taking place in virgin territory. Not only is there a female candidate in the Democratic presidential race, but a robust, viable female candidate, someone with a powerful organization, a large checkbook and a legendary campaigner at her side.

From the beginning, Mark Penn, Hillary Clinton's chief strategist, bet that women would propel Clinton to victory. Though Penn has taken a lot of flak for this statement, it would seem a solid prediction. In the New Hampshire Democratic primary, Clinton scored 17 points higher with women than she did with men. And exit polls in Nevada showed that Clinton won the backing of 51 percent of women voters, while Obama took about 38 percent. More important, in Nevada, Hillary's support among women was large enough to offset Obama's support among men, which gave her the popular vote.

Were women just waiting for a viable female candidate to form a bloc?

12. MORE SENSE THAN SENSIBILITY

Samuel L. Popkin, a political scientist at the University of California, San Diego, who has worked as a consultant to political campaigns, maintains that unless voters know how government works, they can't read the cues about their legislators' intentions and priorities and rely on "estimates of personal character instead of their attitudes about parties and issues."

Of course, recent work, like that of Drew Westen, a psychologist and the author of *The Political Brain,* suggests that voters are more driven by their emotions than by any informed summing-up of their interests. (Westen's brain studies, incidentally, were done on men.) But even if voters act, as Westen says, on their feelings toward their party and its candidate more than on their understanding of the issues, they can't begin to form those feelings if they don't know something about the parties, candidates and issues. As Popkin has noted, a party is really just shorthand for a series of issue positions—you love your party because it stands for what you stand for.

So, if women as a group know less, does that mean they are more or less emotional when it comes to voting? Perhaps there's another way to pose the question. Maybe, as Ann Lewis, the director of women's outreach for the Clinton campaign, told me recently, it's that men are the emotional ones, "more likely to get swept away in abstract ideas and symbolism," and that women are simply more practical. "They may not frame their decisions in terms of policy or party positions—not use legislative jargon—but they know what's in their family's interest," she said.

Marion Just, a political science professor at Wellesley who worked on the Kennedy School's Shorenstein report, agrees. She characterizes the female agenda as focusing mainly on "family, education, things that affect the household budget, health care." Which today, she adds, also means war and peace. Similarly, Page Gardner told me that for her single-women constituents, it's "all about economic opportunity—health, education for their children, wages, energy costs."

13. IT DOES TAKE A VILLAGE

"I understood the networks for women's issues—Emily's List, breast cancer," Ann Lewis also told me, explaining her outreach work. "Women naturally think of working with other women in network form, talking to each other about what's important." The women's outreach for Hillary started with the legendary Clinton Rolodex—Friends of Hillary—in Washington, in New York, in Arkansas, in Chicago. Once Clinton received endorsements from female elected state officials, the network spread to the endorsers' networks. "In my experience, all elected women at the state level have a network," Lewis observed, "and they are still in touch. Our campaign talks to the women who are already engaged, and then we encourage them to reach out to the ones who are less engaged."

"My goal, on Day 1," Lewis went on to say, "was to have 100 women e-mailing 100 e-mails" to their social networks, soliciting support for the candidate. The campaign has also focused on the issues they thought would attract women's support, starting with events around Equal Pay Day last spring. "The polling confirms what common sense will tell you," Lewis said. "Economics, health care, education, their own retirement."

14. OR A CYBERVILLAGE

The Obama campaign has also identified a woman-to-woman strategy. In addition to recruiting women through field offices, the Obama campaign signed up women on its Web site, creating "a 20,000-woman network." Becky Carroll, the 36-year-old national director of Women for Obama, says that that's the most important part of how they reach out to women, but that Women for Obama is not confined to traditional networking. They have "girls' nights out" where "young, professional women host cocktail parties" and book clubs around Obama's book *The Audacity of Hope.* Carroll also speaks proudly of using "new media in a very important way—a really aggressive outreach through our own blog, crossposts on hundreds of other blogs, a campaign newsletter." As a result, Carroll says, women have formed a "grass-roots movement," doing things on their own initiative.

Carroll's strategy has been to use the Internet to have voters hear directly from the Obama campaign. Certainly Obama's oratorical skill is a vivid reminder of the role of rhetoric to inspire political commitment, and he has done extremely well with young women voters, those most likely to be wired.

15. THE POLITICAL IS PERSONAL

In his essay "Federalist No. 10," James Madison worried that small republics, where politics are conducted face to face, were necessarily unstable. The constitution solved this problem by expanding the scope of representative government so that interests would be diluted. The framework turned out to be quite functional for an expanding land-based empire with a diverse population. But the system always rested on the assumption that people would work to represent their interests. The aversion of many women to big-sphere politics would seem to weaken the system and ensure that their interests will be muffled.

Yet what Samuel Popkin, the political scientist at U.C., San Diego, describes as an emphasis on personality versus issues, Page Gardner frames as marginalized citizens anxiously trying to figure out how to play the political game to get what they need—a very conventional political behavior. No less a figure than Carol Gilligan, the feminist scholar who first posited that women express themselves in a different voice, reminded me that she never said a woman's tendency to value relational connections excluded the self. "Coming forward with their own voices is key to citizenship in a democratic republic," Gilligan told me. "Women are using their emotional intelligence and relational intelligence to read the biographies to figure out if this is a trustworthy person."

And when women do come forward, they alter the political landscape. Scott Keeter, of the Pew organization, and Michael Delli Carpini, of the University of Pennsylvania, found that as knowledge increases, "both single and married men become slightly more conservative, while married women move slightly in the liberal direction and single women become quite a bit more liberal." These changes lead to a clear gender and marriage gap on domestic-welfare issues. As Keeter and Carpini concluded in their study: "A fully informed citizenry would have collective consequences, resulting in a public-opinion environment that is more ideologically diverse and slightly more liberal." It may happen sooner than we think. According to Women's Voices Women Vote, the single-female-voter demographic shifted 32 points in the five days between Iowa and New Hampshire. As their advocate Page Gardner says: "You'd better be paying attention. Because they're up for grabs."

16. BY THE NUMBERS

Since 1964, more women have voted than men have, and since 1980, they have voted at higher percentages: 54 percent of voters in the 2004 presidential election were female. If women care less about politics than men do, why do they bother? In one recent study, women said that they vote to protect their interest. Whereas men said they vote because they enjoy politics. To a campaign strategist, the female vote—if you can get it—must look like the Chinese market does to an entrepreneur. Only a modest percentage has to want your product, and you'll succeed beyond your wildest dreams.

14
THE YEAR OF GOVERNING DANGEROUSLY

DAVID MARGOLICK
Vanity Fair   January 2008

The abrupt resignation of New York governor Eliot Spitzer in March 2008, after an F.B.I. investigation uncovered his involvement with prostitutes, was a sad and stunningly swift end to a once-promising political career. Even before the scandal, however, Spitzer's combative governing style had already alienated enough foes and friends alike to put his political future in doubt—so much so that, as 2007 drew to a close, a number of national publications devoted lengthy year-end articles to the story of the new governor's rocky first year in office. In the following piece, Vanity Fair's *David Margolick reports on Spitzer's turbulent rookie year and offers up a hope—unrealized, as it turns out—that the former Sheriff of Wall Street might be able to put his gubernatorial house back in order.*

It was Inauguration Day—Day One, the day everything was supposed to change. The strains of "Fanfare for the Common Man" dissolved into the chilly Albany air, and Governor Eliot Spitzer, Princeton '81, Harvard Law School '84, rose to speak. "Like Rip van Winkle . . . New York has slept through much of the past decade while the rest of the world has passed us by," he declared as his predecessor, George Pataki, squirmed nearby. But now "the light of a new day shines down on the Empire State." (He'd ignored everyone else's counsel to hold the ceremonies indoors, and the comparatively mild weather, at least for the tundra in January, was surely another sign the gods were with him.) He promised leadership as ethical and wise as all New York. He called on his fellow citizens to enter "the arena," just as his idol, Theodore Roosevelt, had once urged, and as he himself had done. Then he went Churchillian. "Lend your sweat, your toil, and your passion to the effort of building One New York," he implored. "My fellow New Yorkers, our moment is here. Day One is now."

For all the soaring rhetoric, though, the phrase people would most remember from Eliot Spitzer's inauguration last New Year's Day came not from Eliot Spitzer at all. It came later that day, when James Taylor sang for the new governor and over a thousand guests at an arena—not the kind T.R. had in mind—nearby. That phrase, combined with Spitzer's vulgar enhancement of it, would take its place in American political lore, alongside "the only thing we have to fear is fear itself" and "Ask not what your country can do for you" and "I'm not a crook"—and would become his unofficial motto, though no one would know this for a few more weeks. "I'm a steamroller, baby," Taylor sang. "I'm bound to roll all over you."

⊰⊹ • ⊹⊱

In late January, Jim Tedisco, a Republican and the minority leader of the State Assembly, was driving to Albany on the Governor Thomas E. Dewey New York State Thruway—named for the last crime buster before Spitzer to catapult himself to the capital—when his cell phone rang. It was the governor, asking him to attend a press conference announcing ethics-reform legislation. Tedisco resisted; he'd just been excluded from some key meetings, and feared he'd merely be a prop. (Spitzer recalls it was Tedisco, dissatisfied with his treatment by the governor, who initiated the discussion.) That was when he got what's now known around Albany as the "Full Spitzer," or at least the electronic version, minus the bulging veins and spluttering that eyewitnesses get to see.

Spitzer's voice suddenly changed, Tedisco recalls: it became louder, shriller, more guttural, more menacing. In three weeks he'd done more for New York State than any governor in history, Spitzer screamed. He was having enough trouble with the other goddamned legislative leaders, he went on; Tedisco would do what he was told—or he'd be crushed. As if the point weren't sufficiently clear, Spitzer put it another way, courtesy of James Taylor. "*Listen,*" he shrieked, "*I'm a fucking steamroller, and I'll roll over you and anybody else.*"

"I was thinking to myself, My God, is this really the governor?" Tedisco recalls. "To tell you the truth, I almost drove off the thruway. . . . It's almost like an addiction he has to be confrontational," Tedisco goes on. "The only way to help him is to buy a Dale Carnegie course for better communication skills, or 10 counseling lessons on temper control." And it was all such a pity, given the high expectations for the man. "He had everything going for him," Tedisco says. "He's the one guy who could have turned this whole thing around."

Note the tenses—past and past conditional—because they're the ones that politicians, Republicans and Democrats alike, often employ these days to describe the 48-year-old Spitzer. Brilliant and energetic, he was as much crowned as elected, swept into office in the biggest landslide in New York gubernatorial history. A Democrat from New York City, he brought New Yorkers together, Republican and Democratic, upstate and down. No one seemed better equipped than the former "Sheriff of Wall Street," arguably the most influential state attorney general in American history, to get dysfunctional Albany, the captive of special interests, unstuck. Wherever Spitzer went, people wanted to follow, sometimes quite literally. At six o'clock on inauguration morning, he took a two-mile jog around Albany's Washington Park, and 200 people got up early enough to accompany him.

⤛ • ⤜

But, by any definition, Spitzer has had a rocky maiden year. As his first anniversary approaches, the State Legislature has largely ground to a halt. New York's most powerful Republican, Joseph L. Bruno, now barely speaks to him after Spitzer's office sicced the state police (and considered siccing the I.R.S.) on him. Many members of Spitzer's own party loathe him. Newspapers, even deadly rivals such as the *New York Post* and the New York *Daily News,* have turned against him. Even his great champion, the *New York Times,* has soured on him. The *Daily News's* Michael Goodwin, one of his harshest critics, wrote recently that Spitzer "seems incapable of telling the truth, admitting mistakes or working with anybody of either party," and urged New York City mayor Michael Bloomberg to challenge him in 2010. (In October, a Siena College poll showed that Bloomberg, who strenuously insists he doesn't even want the job, would beat Spitzer. In November, the same poll found that only one in four voters was prepared to reelect Spitzer, while nearly half preferred "someone else.")

Thanks largely to Spitzer and particularly to his short-lived and politically disastrous proposal to grant driver's licenses to undocumented immigrants, imperiled state Republicans feel resurrected. Spitzer's radioactivity has even spilled over into the presidential race, with Hillary Clinton, through various contradictory statements on the subject, sprinkling isotopes from the license fiasco all over herself before Spitzer withdrew the plan in mid-November. Many of the usual suspects in all the glowing Spitzer profiles that have appeared over the years have suddenly gone mute. Ask Jim Cramer of CNBC's *Mad Money,* Spitzer's pal from Harvard Law School, about the guy and he is uncharacteristically speechless.

Elite as it was, there turn out to be a few holes in the education of Eliot Spitzer. It seems he has never learned how to work well with other people. He has never unlearned how to be a prosecutor. He did not know Albany. And, until he bailed out on the license proposal, he could never admit that he was wrong—if not on the merits in that instance, then at least on the execution. His enemies describe it all with Schadenfreude, and maybe a few I-told-you-sos. Admirers speak angrily, sadly, almost elegiacally about opportunities lost, maybe irretrievably so. "It's all so frustrating, because he actually was right [about things]," says Ester Fuchs, a professor of public affairs and political science at Columbia University and lifelong student of New York politics. "He just didn't know how to do it."

⤙ • ⤚

Visit with Spitzer, though, and you sense none of this. It is as if it were still Inauguration Day, and he'd just gotten off the podium. You sense the incredible discipline and self-control and intelligence that got him so high so fast, and which, if the gods reappear, will get him out of his predicament. He is immaculate, formal, upbeat. Whatever he is feeling, whatever bruises he bears, sit in a closet somewhere: *The Picture of Eliot Spitzer.* He even says so: "I'm not great at the self-reflecting type of answers. It's not my nature."

As soon as he reached Albany, Spitzer set out to destroy Bruno, first by trying to pick off from Republicans the few seats the Democrats need to take control of the State Senate. That's just politics. So, too, was it just politics when Spitzer's aides tried to prove that Bruno, who has led the Senate for the last dozen years, was a thief, flying off regularly to partisan political events on the taxpayers' tab. What was not just politics, though, was when the governor's office used the state police to help make his case. In July, Spitzer's old nemesis, New York attorney general Andrew Cuomo, found that, while the governor's people had broken no laws, the whole thing reeked. Spitzer quickly and abjectly apologized, something he has rarely had to do. But Troopergate, as the imbroglio has been called, still hangs over him like a dark cloud. As Jacob Gershman noted recently in the *New York Sun,* Wikipedia's entry for Spitzer now devotes more lines to the scandal than to his glory years as attorney general.

At least as harmful to Spitzer has been his insistence that he had nothing to do with bringing in the state police, and that overzealous underlings were to blame. Making things worse has been his failure to testify under oath about it, or to hand over e-mails and other documents from his office. Seven of 10 New Yorkers—about the same percentage that voted for Spitzer—are calling for sworn public testimony. The state ethics commission is investigating the matter; Spitzer insists he's prepared to testify before it. (A State Senate committee is investigating, too, but Spitzer can argue, and justifiably, that it's a partisan witch hunt, and legal wrangling will likely cripple it.)

BAD BLOOD FROM THE GET-GO

Even before reaching Albany, Spitzer infuriated legislators of both parties. You don't endear yourself to people by calling their world a "cesspool," then promising to clean it up. If anything, Democrats, aching for a chief executive of their own after 12 frustrating years under the bland and unremarkable Pataki, are more put out with Spitzer than the Republicans are. One assemblyman told me that of his 107 Democratic peers 102 were disenchanted with Spitzer. Ask even friendly colleagues for the names of Spitzer's champions and long, sheepish silences follow. Spitzer has disproved John Donne: in Albany these days, he is an island. Perhaps he should bring back James Taylor—this time to sing "You've Got a Friend."

To give him his due, Spitzer has accomplished some significant things, particularly early on. He has revamped workers' compensation to increase benefits for injured workers and reduce employee costs. He has increased and restructured education spending so that tax dollars now go more consistently where they're most needed. He has lopped some $1 billion off the state's out-of-control Medicaid tab. His budget was passed almost on time—a rarity. He has secured passage of a law for the civil confinement of sexual offenders, expanded health-care coverage for uninsured children, increased legal-aid funding for indigents, and created a $600 million fund for stem-cell research.

Perhaps the negative perceptions, as one of Spitzer's advisers lamented to me, are a result of New York's tabloid mentality. Or maybe they're due to what he called "Eliot's famous A.D.D.—that hyperkinetic Eliot Spitzer get-up-at-five-A.M.-and-run" mentality, which makes him more interested in moving forward than in touting what he's already done. In any case, Spitzer's good deeds have been lost in the past few months as Troopergate, along with the license proposal, has slowed down Albany's glacial governance even further. Talk of Spitzer as eventual president, once a popular parlor game in New York Democratic circles, has largely evaporated.

A few times in his charmed life—when he got nosed out for the top job on the Horace Mann school newspaper; when he got turned down for college at Harvard; when he lost his first race for attorney general, in 1994; when he fibbed about all the money his real-estate-mogul father had used to bankroll his first two campaigns—Spitzer has faltered, but never like this. The question now is no longer how many miracles he can perform but whether he can get anything done at all. Spitzer is at one of those proverbial tipping points, poised somewhere between formidable and vulnerable, redeemable and incorrigible. His stumbles could furnish him the only ingredients he lacks—humility and empathy and wisdom, for starters—or prove they're forever beyond his reach. A great drama will now play out in Albany, one that will determine whether Spitzer is still a comer or what, in another generation, would be called a busted phenom.

Spitzer has met his predicament with a mix of defiance and contrition. Some days he's still "Zealiot," declaring that he's never backing down, that he's governing on principles rather than poll numbers, that the voters are getting precisely what he promised—and what they still want. "You don't change the world by whispering," he likes to say. Other times, he listens conspicuously. He has belatedly created a kitchen cabinet of wonks, moguls, and sages, including Robert Rubin of Clinton-administration fame. He's been making nice with legislative leaders and party powers. There have been interludes of self-awareness, such as a much-commented-upon speech at the Chautauqua Institution in August, built around theologian Reinhold Niebuhr's warnings about the perils of hubris. (The speech is predictably hung around his neck whenever he regresses, like the time shortly afterward when he told a Binghamton television reporter pressing him on Troopergate to "get a life, buddy.")

When we meet, Spitzer takes a third tack: serenity, or at least whatever serenity an intense New Yorker can muster. Spitzer is not a natural politician; he is a bit awkward, maybe even shy, and speaks too quickly—the legacy, perhaps, of all those high-powered childhood dinner conversations, in which one had to make one's points quickly or be left ignominiously behind. The realization is refreshing, even endearing: it means he actually had to work at something. At times, Spitzer seems almost gentle. When he explains his famed temper—with passion inevitably comes emotion, sometimes to excess, he says—it's hard to imagine it's ever even a problem. Of course, it's all spin, but maybe that put-on gentleness is a distant cousin of the more genuine gentleness which, friends insist, resides five layers down, alongside the self-deprecating sense of humor, both aspects of the man that few ever get to see.

⤛ • ⤜

Our session is in his New York office, a government-issue room in a utilitarian high-rise on Third Avenue, with none of those Fountainhead views of mighty Manhattan. The flat water he serves is a politically incorrect import from Maine (Poland Spring) rather than homegrown stuff from Saratoga Springs; then again, Saratoga is in Bruno's district. Spitzer rises to none of my bait; there aren't even any Quarter Spitzers this day. He is as tightly controlled as his shirt collar, which sits, behind a tie of robin's-egg blue, snugly against his neck. (Spitzer is one of those people who look no more informal without a suit jacket than with one.) I ask him what he thinks of Fredric U. Dicker, the *Post* reporter who has attacked him relentlessly, and his answer could just as easily be applied to various other antagonists and detractors, such as Andrew Cuomo, CNN's Lou Dobbs (who lambasted him almost nightly for his licensing scheme), and Rudy Giuliani. "Let me put it this way," Spitzer says with a smile. "I don't want you to think that I don't have an answer to the question, but I also think you'll understand that I'm probably clever enough not to give it to you. Plus, I'd diminish the value of my memoirs." (Characteristically, he's not keeping a journal.) His first year, he insists, went pretty much as expected; one could have foreseen that the tectonic changes he seeks "would evoke enormous pushback." He knew things would be difficult. And they are.

Though he doesn't say so himself, Spitzer clearly feels that the *Times* has forsaken him, leaving him to be eviscerated by the *Post*'s Dicker. Day after day, in dribs and drabs of 347 or 565 or 478 words on the *Post*'s second page, the paper's longtime Albany-bureau chief has gone after him, most notably with the first Troopergate story, on July 5. What drives him? Spitzer aides offer many theories: Spitzer hadn't paid him proper homage; he's doing a Republican newspaper's bidding; he's miffed that Spitzer's office leaked word about Joe Bruno's state-funded helicopter rides to the Albany *Times Union* rather than to him. More likely, it's simply that the Spitzer saga is just so damned juicy. Few stories beat those of Mr. Clean doing dirty tricks or Mr. Competent screwing up. Or of a role reversal: Utica and Syracuse and Binghamton taking down Manhattan (the Upper East Side overlooking the park, at that), Skidmore College knocking off Harvard Law School.

THE SOUL OF AN OLD MACHINE

Skidmore is where Bruno, a handsome and precisely coiffed man of 78, more elegant than you'd expect a state senator to be, went to school, after a hard-scrabble boyhood by the boxcars in Glens Falls, between Saratoga Springs and Lake George. Even without the chopper rides and police escorts, an existential clash between him and Spitzer was inevitable and, indeed, already under way. Unlike his predecessors, who tolerated the informal power sharing between the parties—each side controls one house in the Legislature—Spitzer is determined to take the State Senate from the Republicans, for the first time in four decades. He is but two seats away. Beneath the bravado and rough, roguish charm, Bruno was, at least until the past few months, a desperate man. Already under fire as the F.B.I. examines his business dealings, he is like Boss Jim Gettys, the cynical old pol in *Citizen Kane* whom Charles Foster Kane tries to take down, but who manages to take down Kane first—CANDIDATE KANE CAUGHT IN LOVE NEST. "I'm fighting for my life," Gettys explains to the betrayed Mrs. Kane. "Not just my political life. My life."

By attempting to rescue the Senate Democrats from political irrelevancy, Spitzer has turned them into the closest approximation of allies, although their loyalty, like every other Democrat's in Albany, has been tested over the past year. "He's not playing the go-along-get-along protection game that's been going on for decades," says Eric Schneiderman, a state senator from New York City. "And he's moved a smart, progressive agenda that hopefully will serve as a model for the country. A lot of Democrats have been disappointed or angry or just plain puzzled at some of the things Eliot has done, but we still believe he very much wants to do the right thing."

◂◂ • ▸▸

At first, says Bruno, he actually liked Spitzer. He liked his style: direct and straight-forward. He liked the Christmas card he got from him every year—showing Eliot and Silda Spitzer and their three lovely teenage daughters—and the bottle of jam, made at their country home in Columbia County, an hour south of Albany. He liked Spitzer's pro-business, middle-of-the-road politics. (Spitzer is no woolly liberal; he supports the death penalty, for instance.) According to Bruno, Spitzer told him that his problems as governor would be with Sheldon Silver, the Democratic Speaker of the Assembly, and not with him. (Spitzer disputes this, clarifying he anticipated he would have problems with the system and not with a particular person.) Most important, Bruno says, he thought they had a deal: he'd let Spitzer be the best chief executive New York ever had, and Spitzer would let Bruno keep his Senate majority. Together, they'd run New York.

Then, in what Bruno calls a "sneak attack," Spitzer began campaigning for Democratic senatorial candidates in the most vulnerable Republican districts prior to the 2006 election. (There never were any such deals, Spitzer counters, nor could there have been, given his obligations as leader of the state Democratic Party and his commitment to clean Albany up.) When Bruno called to complain, he says, Spitzer grew angry and abusive. "I was absolutely astounded," says Bruno. "He lost it." A honeymoon followed the inauguration, but ended in about the time it takes to drive from Albany to Niagara Falls. With various blandishments, including job offers—"bribes," Bruno calls them—Spitzer tried to entice Republican senators from Democratic-leaning districts into relinquishing their seats. Spitzer pushed for campaign-finance reform, which Bruno says gives an unfair advantage to rich, self-funding candidates like Spitzer himself. He also moved to cut Medicaid costs; the health-care workers' union happens to be one of Bruno's biggest backers.

A rhetorical war between them broke out. Bruno called Spitzer "an overgrown, rich spoiled brat." Spitzer reportedly called Bruno "an old, senile piece of shit." And the Full Spitzers followed. In one, says Bruno, Spitzer "did everything but hit his head against the wall and roll around the floor." In another, "I thought he was going to have a damned stroke." Over the phone once, Bruno says, Spitzer shouted at him, "I will knock you down, and when I knock you down, I will knock you out, and you will never get up. You will never recover." "I told him to go fuck himself, in plain English," Bruno recalls. He also urged Spitzer to enroll in "chief executives' school." "You've got to go and learn how to be a governor," he says he told him. Several times while discussing Spitzer, Bruno twirled either his index finger or a bottle of Saratoga water by his head—as if to suggest Spitzer is nuts.

Threatening to knock out a former army boxing champion, even one 30 years his senior, is odd. So, too, for that matter, is threatening to roll over Tedisco, who once played basketball against Pat Riley and still holds a number of scoring records at his college. Spitzer is just the opposite of a bully: the bigger or tougher someone is, the more tempted he is to go after him. Many say it all goes back to Spitzer's father; things might have been very different, they theorize, if only old Bernard Spitzer had let young Eliot beat him once or twice at Monopoly.

⤙ • ⤚

Lou Dobbs and Chuck Schumer, U.S. senator from New York, and Joe Bruno may all have called him a spoiled brat, but things have not been that easy for Spitzer. One's angst is no less real for being rarefied.

As all those glowing profiles detail, he grew up in an intellectual cauldron. His father, a self-made real-estate tycoon—estimated worth: $500 million— who built luxury high-rises throughout Manhattan, was demanding; meals *chez* Spitzer, where Eliot and his two older siblings (Daniel, now a brain surgeon, and Emily, a lawyer) were assigned topics to discuss, sound as brutalizing as they were nourishing. They left Eliot intellectually agile, hypercompetitive, always with something to prove. A classmate recalls that when, at 12, Spitzer enrolled in the prestigious Horace Mann School, in the Bronx, his Samsonite briefcase standing out among the backpacks, he set out to ascertain how many of the boys there were smarter than he. (By his count, there were four.)

Then it was on to Princeton, where Spitzer was president of the student body. He spent one summer digging ditches and cleaning sewage in the South, then picking tomatoes in upstate New York, just to see how the other half lived. At Harvard Law School he made the *Law Review* but starred mostly as a research assistant for celebrity lawyer and professor Alan Dershowitz, who was then appealing the conviction of Claus von Bülow. (Felicity Huffman played Spitzer in the film *Reversal of Fortune.* Hey, it's Hollywood.) He also met his wife, a North Carolinian named Silda Wall. She is at least as intelligent as and considerably more diplomatic than he. (I ask a classmate, who still marvels that he landed her, what she did for him. "She made him smile," he replies.)

He spent one year clerking for a federal judge in New York, then another at Paul, Weiss, Rifkind, Wharton & Garrison, one of New York's most prestigious and politically connected corporate firms. For six years after that, he tried cases in the Manhattan District Attorney's Office. Then he returned to private practice at an even more high-powered firm, Skadden, Arps, Slate, Meagher & Flom.

A partnership there, or maybe a sinecure in his father's business, beckoned. But to everyone's surprise—his wife's included—he decided to run in the Democratic primary for state attorney general. It was 1994, and he was 35 years old.

Using as collateral several apartments his father had given him, he took out loans totaling some $4 million to finance his campaign. Advising him was an old family friend, Dick Morris, then Bill Clinton's campaign guru, too; Morris recommended lots of commercials, which is where the money went. Caught with a toe-sucking call girl in a Washington hotel room, Morris soon fell from grace, and from Spitzer's public orbit; that he subsequently consulted for right-wingers like Jesse Helms, then became one of Connecticut's most egregious tax scofflaws, assured that Spitzer would keep his distance from him. Some nonetheless speculate that the two remain in touch; Roger Stone, the notorious Republican consultant whom Bruno brought in last May to neutralize Spitzer, says Morris commended Niebuhr's anti-hubris essay to Spitzer a decade or more ago. ("Isn't this the greatest defense for hubris you've ever seen?" Morris exclaimed, according to Stone. "Nixon should have used that!") Spitzer denies that Morris gave him the essay. "I haven't spoken to Dick in . . . two years, maybe?" he says. "A long time." Morris, who reportedly collected around $100,000 for each of Spitzer's first two campaigns, isn't talking.

Spitzer finished fourth in a field of four, having paid $33 a vote, but he impressed many. "His jaw actually juts," the *Times* marveled. Everyone saw the campaign as a well-oiled dry run, and for the next four years—from the convenient perch of a law partnership with his former boss and mentor, a Manhattan lawyer named Lloyd Constantine—he drove around the state, making contacts, spreading largesse. He won the Democratic primary in 1998. But after confessing that, contrary to his public statements and even sworn testimony, his old man really had funded both his races, he just barely won.

AN ATTORNEY GENERAL AT WAR

Despite his thin margin of victory, Spitzer compiled a dazzling record. He went after great financial institutions—huge firms, mutual funds, insurance companies, the New York Stock Exchange itself. His M.O. became familiar: find fraudulent or deceitful practices; confront wrongdoers; publicize (or leak) the cases against them and thereby wreak havoc with their stock prices; work out massive settlements that would frighten other wrongdoers into ponying up as well. Full Spitzers, filled with profanity, abuse, fury, and grandiosity—"I'm so fucking rich, they can't take me down," he told the target of one tirade, throwing in for good measure that he'd done more for poor people than anyone in the history of the state—were often in the mix. Always, the object wasn't perp walks or jail time—in this respect, he parted ways with his political doppelgänger Giuliani—but to reform entire industries. There were massive environmental cases, too; in one, out-of-state power companies pouring pollutants into New York were brought to heel.

Someone who once worked closely with Spitzer told me that to understand him properly you have to realize that on some subconscious level he feels he is "slumming." People of his pedigree normally don't seek elective office, much less state elective office. They flock to the private sector, where they amass money and power and prestige. Government service is unremunerative and grubby; if they go for it, it's only when people come to them, to be federal judges or Brahmin diplomats à la Cyrus Vance. But Spitzer entered the arena, just as Theodore Roosevelt commanded. (T.R.'s picture still hangs in his office.) With evangelical fervor, he persuaded other superstars (at least on paper: he has always been dazzled by credentials) to slum with him. As his marriage proved, he likes having smart people around, though often it turns into an intense competition. "You couldn't have a discussion without him screaming," one old associate recalls. "He'd talk really fast, agitated, spewing things at you, personal things. Even when you disagree on substance, it always becomes personal. Somehow he was belittling everything I was, not just what I believed." In this instance Congressman Charles Rangel's famous—and, in context, unflattering—description of Spitzer as "the world's smartest man" rang completely true: being a state politician "makes him want to show everyone instantaneously, notwithstanding those two chips on his shoulder, that he's a brilliant, brilliant guy."

The competitiveness colored his views of other politicians. He regarded the newly elected Bloomberg, for instance, as a fluke, winning only because of 9/11. Sure, Spitzer noted, a freshly minted senator from Illinois named Barack Obama had once been president of the *Harvard Law Review*, but that didn't prove he was brilliant, only that he was popular. And then there was Rudy. Spitzer grew miffed when the then mayor never took his calls. Only in 2002 did Giuliani initiate a conversation, urging Spitzer to go easy on Merrill Lynch, one of Spitzer's most celebrated prosecutorial targets and a new Giuliani client; even then, Giuliani was playing the 9/11 card, and Spitzer found it disgusting. The distaste was mutual: according to *The Weekly Standard*, Giuliani once said that after spending time with Spitzer he wanted to take a shower. ("I'd be curious to know when he said that, because the number of times I've actually met [Giuliani] could be counted on two or three fingers," Spitzer says.)

Attorney General Spitzer did not take on fellow politicians, brilliant or otherwise, or the real-estate industry, perhaps also for obvious reasons. He showed little interest in the more prosaic work of the office. The high-profile, high-visibility cases invigorated him most, and he courted, and catered to, and followed assiduously, the press. Mornings, his first task was to read the clips. Nothing pleased him more than landing on A1 of the *New York Times,* preferably above the fold. "He wants to do a good job," says Hank Sheinkopf, a New York political consultant who worked on Spitzer's first two campaigns. "But ultimately what he really gives a shit about is whether Harvard, Princeton, Yale, and the *New York Times* love him, because, in the back of his brain, if they don't love him, he's nobody."

There was plenty of adoration on the newsstands. "Make no mistake: Spitzer is the Democratic Party's future," Sridhar Pappu wrote in *The Atlantic.* Only the conservative business press, which saw him as an anti-capitalist menace and martinet, dissented. The "Lord High New York Executioner," the *Wall Street Journal*'s editorial page called him. With the New York Republican Party in shambles, Spitzer was the governor-in-waiting, particularly once his arch-rival, Senator Schumer, opted not to run. But was Albany a mere way station? Already, Spitzer's father, a Jewish Joe Kennedy if ever there was one, was fantasizing about nights in the Lincoln Bedroom. Once, he was asked if his son would like to be president. "It's his very nature," he replied.

⤙ • ⤚

Spitzer began his governorship aggressively, signing five executive orders—among them, one to prevent state employees from using government property for themselves. But some felt he squandered the long lead time to his inevitable victory, making his promises of sweeping change from Day One unrealistic, if not reckless. So, too, did a number of mediocre appointments, largely of cronies from his old job. "Almost Rudy-esque" was how one political person described it, referring to Giuliani's well-known penchant for taking a posse of the same old sycophants with him wherever he goes. "Clearly things had gone to his head, and he felt no need to really actively recruit fresh thinking and new talent," says someone who watched it all. Then again, getting superstars to move to Albany—"Albania," as New Yorkers consigned there like to call the capital, three hours to the north of Manhattan—isn't easy.

Legislators already put off by someone who campaigned against the "cesspool" in which they all worked were further irked when he bypassed them for critical appointments, as well as by his condescending vibes. "He felt he could walk on water," one prominent assemblyman gripes. Things got worse when Spitzer unsuccessfully tried to get the State Assembly to fill the vacant post of comptroller with his own choice, then denounced those who'd bucked him in picking one of their own. "Friendships play a role in politics. Hillary Clinton is my friend. Chuck Schumer is my friend. Eliot Spitzer is not my friend," says Democratic assemblyman Daniel O'Donnell. "I don't know who Eliot's friends are. He's not making friends. He seems to think that because it's right it should happen. That's true. But that's not how governing works." Bruno even claims that many Democrats have thanked him privately for taking Spitzer on.

Blowing gaskets and hurling threats doesn't work as well on fellow politicians as it does on corporate executives, a consultant for another major politician observes. "If you're a C.E.O. at a company and I call and I say, 'I'm going to fuck you, I'm going to destroy you, I'm going to indict your company,' and I sound totally crazy, you hang up the phone, you go see your chairman of the board, and you say, 'This guy is crazy, we need to settle,' because you're given no option," he explains. "If you're a state legislator and you get the same thing, you hang up the phone, you call the Albany *Times Union*, and you say, 'This guy is crazy,' because you don't give a shit."

OF CHOPPERS AND COPPERS

On January 31, Dicker broke the steamroller story. ("*F–ing* steamroller" is how the *Post* rendered it. The *Times* called it "a [expletive] steamroller.") It was, people around Spitzer concede, his most egregious rhetorical blunder. Say "Spitzer" to focus groups these days and it's "steamroller," not "Wall Street" or "money" or "fighting the big guys," that comes to mind. And it couldn't be just "steamroller," but "fucking steamroller," giving it a crude, salacious edge. Spitzer's communications director, Darren Dopp, said at the time that the story had been "embellished." But Constantine, now a senior adviser to Spitzer, who was with him when he said it, insists that the phrase had simply stuck in Spitzer's mind from James Taylor's performance, and that Spitzer was smiling when he said it. "He was John Wayne," he says. "It was ironic, it was partially humorous." That's not how it came across to Tedisco or, frankly, to anyone else. "What sort of an idiot, even if he *is* a fucking steamroller, *says* he's a fucking steamroller?" one Democratic assemblyman asks indignantly. Spitzer himself says he has "only the foggiest" recollection of the exchange.

In May, concerned for his perilous Senate majority and eager to make Spitzer an electoral liability to Democratic state-senatorial candidates in any way he could, Bruno brought on Roger Stone, whom *The Weekly Standard* recently described as a "political operative, Nixon-era dirty trickster, professional lord of mischief." It was Stone who helped stage the controversial "Brooks Brothers Riot" of 2000, in which well-dressed protesters descended upon Miami and helped shut down the recount. (Like Dick Morris, with whom he once worked, Stone had his brush with scandal: ads featuring photographs of him and his wife seeking sexual partners once appeared in a swingers' magazine.)

Stone's monthly fee was $20,000—roughly the cost of three round-trip rides on the state helicopter from the helipad at the Albany exit off the thruway to West 30th Street in Manhattan, the route Bruno so often took. Under the rules, though, such trips were kosher as long as they included even the merest whiff of official state business. Bruno clearly knew this, and always covered himself. Still, when James Odato of the *Times Union* asked Darren Dopp for information about Bruno's trips to New York for Republican fund-raisers, Dopp apparently saw a chance to embarrass the majority leader.

⤙ • ⤚

A Spitzer loyalist who'd come with him from the attorney general's office, Dopp began collecting materials on Bruno's trips, past, present, and future, not just airborne but also on the ground, when the state police, citing death threats Bruno said he had received, provided one of those flashing-lights escorts. Pitching in were William Howard, Spitzer's liaison to the police, and Preston Felton, the acting police superintendent.

Top senior Spitzer aides depict the whole operation as amateurish—"a bungling Keystone Kops communications exercise," one puts it—done by staffers overeager to please the boss. Dopp, they say, felt marginalized in the new administration. Howard was a holdover from Pataki, also intent on earning his spurs. And Felton wanted to remove the "acting" from his title. In fact, when Dopp proposed a press release detailing Bruno's dubious travels, Spitzer's chief of staff, Rich Baum, and chief counsel, David Nocenti, rejected the idea: they knew Bruno had met the travel regulations' porous requirements. Spitzer apparently knew enough about the scheme to agree with them.

In late June, Dopp told Odato about the travel documents he'd collected, and Odato got them through a Freedom of Information Law (FOIL) filing. On July 1 he reported on the front page of the Albany *Times Union* that, three times in May, Bruno had used taxpayer-funded aircraft and ground transportation to attend political events in New York City. (Playing dumb for the story, Dopp pledged publicly to "review this matter carefully.") Three measly flights to New York: to Dicker, who'd covered infinitely greater abuses by other politicians, the story sounded orchestrated. "Bruno Set-Up," he slugged his own piece for the next day.

⋅⋖⋅ • ⋗⋅

Despite its private conviction that Bruno had done nothing illegal, the Spitzer administration quickly asked Attorney General Andrew Cuomo to investigate. It was a risky move, given Spitzer and Cuomo's troubled history. By all accounts, they do not like each other. Spitzer refused to endorse Cuomo in his bid for governor in 2002. When Cuomo ran to succeed him as attorney general four years later, Spitzer privately preferred Cuomo's rival, Mark Green, in the Democratic primary, believing that he posed much less of a long-term threat than a Cuomo resurrected from his disastrous gubernatorial race. Moreover, Spitzer knew that despite their differing party affiliations Bruno and Cuomo are friendly; Bruno has often spoken, almost wistfully, about what a good governor Cuomo would make. ("They are still all Italians," Stone observes. "Note how the I-ties all bind and the Jews' fight: Schumer-hates-Spitzer-hates-Silver-hates-Bloomberg.") One assemblyman likened Spitzer and Cuomo to two ax murderers vying to lop off the other one's head first.

On July 5—no sense wasting a great story over the Fourth—Dicker broke word of the plot. Spitzer and his aides, he wrote, had "targeted" Bruno through an "unprecedented state police surveillance program." In a television interview, Bruno denounced Spitzer as a "Third World dictator" and his aides as "hoodlums" and "thugs." He, too, asked Cuomo to investigate. "What he's trying to do to me he's capable of doing to anyone," Bruno tells me. "He saw Bruno as the only guy standing in his way, who he couldn't roll over, who he couldn't hoodwink, that he couldn't just dismiss. So he had to get rid of me."

Noting Spitzer's sharp elbows and what the British like to call his control-freakery, even many Democrats say it's inconceivable Spitzer did not know about what Dopp and the others were up to. Henry Stern, the former New York City parks commissioner, who has chronicled Troopergate in his political newsletter, called that very notion "cockamamie." "Either he consented to the scheme or he concocted it," he says. "That he was ignorant is beyond reason." But Constantine says ignorant is exactly what Spitzer was. "If Eliot had known about it, he would have nixed it," he says. "And to the very, very limited degree he learned about something, he nixed it."

For the next two weeks, Spitzer maintained that his staff had simply responded to a FOIL request, and that the state police had followed its standard procedures. Only on July 19, he has said, did he learn otherwise. In the meantime, Cuomo's investigators were doing their work, interviewing, among others, Felton and Howard. Spitzer has said his office "fully cooperated" with Cuomo. In fact, it refused to let his investigators interview Dopp and Baum, having them submit short, unilluminating affidavits instead. It was, some in Spitzer's circle complain, the reflexive reaction from the hyper-cautious, politically tone-deaf lawyers with whom Spitzer had surrounded himself. When word leaked—apparently from Cuomo's camp—that the Spitzer folks had not been as forthcoming as the governor had claimed, there arose the telltale scent of a cover-up.

AN OLD RIVAL WEIGHS IN

On July 23—a Monday, political observers noted, giving the "Eliot Mess" story a whole newspaper week to reverberate—Cuomo released his report. Spitzer's office had broken no laws, it concluded, but it had acted improperly, thrusting the state police precisely where it did not belong: "squarely in the middle of politics." It recommended that the governor conduct a "policy and personnel review" within his office. As for Bruno, it gave him a pass. Strictly as a matter of Realpolitik, Cuomo pulled it all off masterfully: exonerating Spitzer of anything criminal, but implicating him in sleaze. "Andrew Cuomo has handled himself beautifully, superbly—exactly the way he should," says former New York City mayor Ed Koch admiringly. What must Cuomo have thought, I ask him, when his old rival landed in such hot water? Koch looks skyward and holds his hands in prayer. "In his heart of hearts, he is saying to himself, 'Thank you, God,'" Koch replies. (Cuomo not surprisingly declined comment.)

Spitzer immediately apologized for what he called his staff's "clear lapses in judgment." He suspended Dopp indefinitely without pay, throwing what was already an ineffectual P.R. team further off stride, and reassigned Howard to a job outside of the governor's office. Without cultivating the relations most politicians enjoy, Spitzer had few defenders. Some sympathizers faulted him for caving: as Alan Chartock, a Spitzer supporter who hosts a popular public-radio program in Albany, puts it, going after Joe Bruno was exactly why people sent Spitzer there in the first place. People also wondered why Spitzer had even landed in such a mess; there were so many other, less byzantine ways to go after Bruno. Besides, what was the great rush? The most vulnerable Republican state senators are mostly old men. As is Joe Bruno. The solution was as much actuarial as political.

To sense Spitzer's ordeal as the story unfolded, go to YouTube and watch his press conference of July 26, in which Dicker shouts at him, cuts him off, chastises him for his perceived evasiveness. Spitzer bites his tongue, smiles wanly, tries to keep his temper in check. Two questions Dicker never did ask Eliot Spitzer that day, Silda Spitzer already had, or so Spitzer told the *Times*: Why had he even gotten into this line of work? Would the family business really have been so bad? Spitzer conceded that the episode had undone much of what he had tried to do. His advisers tried to get him back on track, beginning with a picnic he was holding that weekend at his country house for 200 friends and donors. "Do me a favor," one told him in advance. "There will be a lot of people there who you previously thought of as blowhards. *Listen* to them. Because somewhere in all their blowhardness, there's probably a nugget of advice that might be helpful to you."

⤛ • ⤜

Somehow, Spitzer had morphed from an ethical crusader into a dissembler, and Bruno from a chiseler to a victim. Bruno's campaign was ingenious in its demonic brazenness, akin to the way in which a military malingerer like George W. Bush scored points off of John Kerry's record in Vietnam. "Unbelievably well done by them," one Spitzer adviser concedes. "They just have such balls." A lot of the credit might have gone to Stone, but he was soon gone, after someone sounding suspiciously like him left a bizarre message on Bernard Spitzer's office phone, warning him he'd soon be subpoenaed about his campaign loans to his son. "And there's not a goddamn thing your phony, psycho, piece-of-shit son can do about it," the message stated. "Bernie, your phony loans are about to catch up with you! You *will* be forced to tell the truth, and the fact that your son's a pathological liar *will . . . be . . . known . . . to all.*" Investigators traced the call to Stone's apartment at 40 Central Park South. "I was a little surprised at the crassness and, frankly, the stupidity of it all," Spitzer says. Stone says the voice belongs to an impostor, part of a nefarious plot to get him off the Spitzer case. Sure enough, Bruno promptly canned him—at least officially. "Do you think he's *really* gone?" one Spitzer insider asks me, telegraphing the suspicion that he's not.

Dopp, Baum, and Spitzer all did talk, albeit not under oath, to investigators from the office of Albany district attorney P. David Soares. Soares's September 21 report went easier on Spitzer, concluding that, even if his people had set out to smear Bruno, no one did anything illegal or, it seems, untoward: since the state police kept the records of Bruno's travels, that would logically be the place to turn for them. Spitzer's critics dismissed it as a whitewash from a Democratic prosecutor.

A Senate committee, really an arm of Bruno, Inc., is also investigating, and has asked to see Baum's and Dopp's e-mails. Spitzer's office is fighting the request. It would be ironic indeed if e-mail, the basis of so many of Spitzer's Wall Street stings, stung him. His advisers insist there's nothing from Spitzer to Dopp directing him to implement "Operation Track Bruno," or some such thing. Dopp is now ensconced with a high-powered Albany lobbyist and disinclined to dish to anyone about Spitzer, including to me, but that could change if he faces a perjury rap for possible testimony contradictions, let alone jail time.

❮❮ • ❯❯

In the end, says Constantine, Troopergate was piddling stuff. "It's rogues, but it's not rogues throwing Molotov cocktails," he says. "These are spitballs." What it really shows, he argues, is the extraordinarily high standard to which Spitzer has been held: for their own reasons, supporters and detractors alike demand perfection from him. "For you or me, we'd have to commit a felony," he says. "For him, it's just wiping his nose on his sleeve."

In September, possibly to distract people from Troopergate, possibly to please his Hispanic constituency, Spitzer announced plans to grant driver's licenses to undocumented immigrants. It made sense, promising to increase highway safety, reduce insurance premiums, and help keep tabs on a hidden population. But it was introduced with characteristic ham-handedness, with virtually no consultation with political leaders. Spitzer stepped into a firestorm, with critics, Lou Dobbs being the most vocal, charging that the plan gave cover to terrorists. Spitzer made things worse by suggesting that his opponents were all rabid right-wingers. In fact, some prominent Democrats, and even some county clerks (the ones who would actually process the licenses), were among them. So was Bloomberg, who has generally been sympathetic to Spitzer ("teething problems," he's called his difficulties). When Bloomberg voiced reservations about the proposal, Spitzer promptly called him "wrong at every level— dead wrong, factually wrong, legally wrong, morally wrong, ethically wrong." Such overheated rhetoric, and against an ally, has convinced some that Spitzer just can't turn it off.

⋖ • ⋗

When, in late October, Spitzer backed off from some elements of the licensing scheme, he only created new problems for himself. Once more, he failed to consult beforehand, blindsiding colleagues who had stuck their necks out to support the plan. Even his beloved *Times* derided him as a "rookie" and accused him of caving in. The debacle heartened Republicans; they hoped that, with a man they saw as having questionable judgment, as well as ethics, running their state, New York voters would come to think divided government isn't so bad after all. All those considerations undoubtedly led Spitzer on November 14 to chuck the proposal altogether. Predictably, the decision brought howls of betrayal from those favoring the measure and chortles from his critics. But in attempting to move on rather than digging in his heels, Spitzer showed a kind of flexibility, and insight, that even some sympathizers feared he simply didn't have. Maybe, they hoped, he could start afresh: Day 318 could be the new Day One.

State Assembly leader Sheldon Silver, with whom Spitzer has had a complicated and awkward relationship, sounds guardedly optimistic about the governor's prospects. "I really do think he's learning, and most importantly his staff is learning," he says. He can afford to be magnanimous: with all of Spitzer's difficulties, the Speaker not only has tightened his own hold on the job (there were rumors early on that Spitzer fancied replacing him with someone more pliable) but may well have regained his position as New York's most powerful Democrat.

Even if Spitzer continues to stumble, he can't be beaten without a good opponent. Bloomberg insists he's not interested, and Cuomo will certainly hang back unless something catastrophic happens. Meanwhile, acts of God or the F.B.I. or the electorate could intervene—Joe Bruno could get indicted. The Democrats could win back the State Senate (something that may be less likely with Giuliani atop the Republican ticket). Hillary Clinton could be elected president, buoying Democrats everywhere. Or something disastrous could happen, affording Spitzer a chance to shine. Look at what 9/11 did for Rudy. Perhaps it won't be necessary. Spitzer has recently brought in new, more experienced aides. He's turning more to seasoned advisers such as Constantine and, as the license debacle reveals, shows signs of listening. With three more years to go, he has the calendar on his side, and he still has the skills that got him to Albany: "He is a crafty-ass politician," one adviser notes. "The ability to get out of a jam is something that people forget about the guy." To Lieutenant Governor David Paterson, Spitzer is like George Foreman in the eighth round of his legendary 1974 fight against Muhammad Ali: on the canvas, for the first time in a career of professional perfection, in stunned disbelief. But unlike Foreman, he predicts, Spitzer will adjust, right himself, and adjust some more. Even the most intelligent people can smarten up.

And, hard sometimes as Spitzer can make it to pull for him, maybe that's what we all should hope. For far more is at stake here than just some rich kid trying to please his pop. Talented and energetic, passionate and independent, scintillating and original, Spitzer may well be Albany's best hope for a long, long time to come. Fifty years or more might pass before the planets align so spectacularly for someone again. And along with everything else he is, Spitzer remains a role model and trailblazer for all those other bests and brightests who need to be coaxed into public service, and into slumming it up in Albania.

Besides, on at least one front recently, Eliot Spitzer can claim victory. For the time being, Joe Bruno is taking private planes to New York. Or driving. Or even, occasionally, riding Amtrak.

15

ARNOLD SCHWARZENEGGER IS PRESIDENT OF 12% OF US

TOM JUNOD

Esquire   March 2008

If the previous selection was about a governor who needed to increase his charm quotient, the following piece is a hugely entertaining portrait of a governor who oozes charm from every pore—only to find that charm will only get you so far in politics if your policies aren't working. So when Arnold Schwarzenegger lost four major ballot initiatives and his approval ratings tanked midway through his first term as California's chief executive, he did what any larger-than-life Republican movie star who also happens to be married to a Kennedy would do: He reversed course and started governing the nation's most populous state not like a GOP partisan but, as Tom Junod would say, like Arnold—*installing a new Democratic chief of staff and inviting one and all to mull the Golden State's future with him over cigars in his now-legendary Sacramento smoking tent.*

It was funny. What Arnold said at the meeting of the advocates—it was funny. He didn't laugh; he hardly ever does when he says something funny. He only laughs when someone says something funny to him, and then he opens that big androidal mouth, and you feel a little bit like a lion tamer, if you're close enough—you're in the position of counting on his goodwill. He likes people who make him laugh. But because he doesn't laugh at his own jokes, you can't be sure if he's joking or not. That's the way it was at the meeting of the advocates. He didn't laugh and neither did they. But that doesn't mean what he said wasn't funny. It had to be, or else he never would have gotten away with it.

What happened was that he was making his way around the conference table in his big conference room. He was shaking hands. He was shaking the hand of each of the advocates who'd come to the meeting. This wasn't unusual—he's done this at every meeting he's ever had in the conference room. It's his method. I mean, it's not like he doesn't know who he is in relation to them—not like he doesn't know that they know who he is. And so he tries to give each of them what they came for, the Arnold experience. Of course, to some extent he gives them the Arnold experience the instant he walks in the room or opens his mouth—his face and his body and his voice are that recognizable. But then, being Arnold, he tries to give them what they want, and then mess with their expectations at the same time. And so, at the meeting of the advocates he took his walk around the table, and when he came upon a woman wearing a nice scarf, he took it in his hand. I mean, the woman is meeting Arnold Schwarzenegger for the first time, and he takes her scarf in his hand, feels it, drapes it over his thick fingers, and lets it drop. Then he says, "Cashmere—some *rich* people here."

And then he keeps going around the table, but you and everyone else in the room—the advocates—have just had your Arnold experience, which in part is the experience of saying to yourself, Did he really just *say* that? Because you see, Arnold was having a lot of meetings that week in the conference room. He was having meetings with law enforcement, he was having meetings with big-city mayors, he was having meetings with people who deliver health-care serv-ices to Californians on public assistance. He was having so many meetings that his staff resorted to a kind of shorthand when they were describing his sched-ule and took to calling the people who were coming to his Tuesday two o'clock "the advocates" without ever saying what they were advocating. Turns out they were advocates for the poor. Turns out they had arrived at the meeting deathly afraid of getting screwed, since the subject of the meeting—the subject of all his meetings that week—was the cutting he was going to have to do as a result of California's historic budget deficit. And yet what Arnold does when he comes upon the woman wearing the nice scarf is stop and *touch* it, and what he says to the advocates deathly afraid of getting screwed is, "Cashmere—some *rich* people here." And he, the richest person in the room by many orders of mag-nitude, the most famous and most powerful person in the room by many more orders of magnitude than even that, gets away with it.

It's not just because what he said is funny, either, though everyone in the room seems aware that it is, without laughing. And it's not just because it's Arnold being Arnold, delivering the Arnold experience. And it's not just be-cause he's giving the advocates shit, even though getting shit from Arnold is a major *component* of the Arnold experience. Hell, it's not even because once he sits down in his big burgundy leather chair at the head of the table and folds his hands in front of him, he levels with them right away, and says, yes, poor people are going to get screwed—but equitably, 10 percent across the board of every state agency: "Democrats are getting screwed, Republicans are getting screwed, we're all getting screwed." No, the real reason he gets away with it—the reason he gets away with everything and might yet get away with a budget that's $14 billion in the red—is that, well, he asked.

He asked the advocates to come to the capitol and sit in the conference room and get the full Arnold experience, just as he asked law enforcement and the big-city mayors and the people who provide health care for Californians on public assistance, just as he asked everyone the week he finally confirmed that he was going to declare a state of fiscal emergency for the state he governs. And no governor had ever done that before. No one had ever called everyone who was going to be affected by budget cuts to tell them how they were going to be affected by budget cuts. That's what they all said, anyway, after he asked for their input, after he told them they were getting screwed. They all said that what he was doing was unprecedented and that they were grateful for it. And it's hard to say what was more amazing—the fact that this, such a simple, such a *human* idea, had never been tried before or that the person who did finally try it was Arnold Schwarzenegger.

⤙ • ⤚

He's been governor of California for four years. That's sort of amazing in itself, considering that there was a time, recently, when the prospect of him running the most populous state in the union seemed a kind of comment on the absurdity and frivolity of American politics. And yet, even as most of us are still absorbing the fact that Arnold Schwarzenegger is the governor of California, Arnold has had this whole career as governor of California, complete with a big early run of legislative victories, a huge and consummate defeat, a bottoming out in the polls, then a comeback and a reelection and a record of accomplishment that's embarrassing—and that's to a degree meant to be embarrassing—to his equivalent in Washington, D.C. And the way that he's been able to do these things has been by developing a style of politics that may prove to be his lasting legacy, beyond the bills he's been able to push through the California legislature. We've been so desperate for a new politics—who would have ever thought that one of its sources would be the governor's office in California? Who would have ever thought it would be *him*?

I mean, okay, he's rich, sure. And he's famous, sure. And he's married into the Kennedy clan by way of Maria Shriver, sure. And he can't be elected president, because of the flaw in the Constitution barring the office to nonnatives, and therefore he doesn't have to give a shit, sure. He's still *Arnold*—and there's no way that anyone could have predicted that being Arnold would translate into being the kind of governor and the kind of politician he's been, especially since the thing everyone agrees on is that he's always Arnold, all the time. His persona has always been *this close* to being absurd, and yet he's been able to make use of it—the persona and its presumed proximity to absurdity, both—as a governor just as well as he was able to make use of it as a bodybuilder and as a movie star. Indeed, most people thought that he was using the governorship in order to rise above his persona, when in fact he was using his persona to rise above the governorship. He hasn't had to be less of himself—less, well, *Arnold*—in response to the realities of politics, though that's what some people like to think; he hasn't had to be more, either. He's simply had to prove that this person and persona he created long ago was a more expansive notion than anyone thought possible, except himself. It's an amazing American story in general, and an amazing immigrant story in particular, especially now, as he faces another crisis and is called upon not to reinvent himself, but rather to *be* himself yet again.

The crisis is pretty simple: California's broke because tax revenues have declined since the real estate market went bust, and spending hasn't. It would be a lot simpler, of course, if Californians hadn't booted Arnold's predecessor, Gray Davis, out of office last time the state went broke. It would be simpler if Arnold hadn't gotten himself elected on the promise of fixing the state's finances and if he weren't spending more money than Gray Davis when he was brought to the humiliation of a recall. It would be simpler if Arnold's success were posited on simply increasing the efficiency of state government rather than on expanding its reach with a series of popular bills and measures on stem-cell research, carbon emissions, infrastructure repair, and prison construction— if his instinct, as a man and as a politician, weren't always to go *big*. It would be simpler if his two latest big-time legislative initiatives, concerning health care and water, weren't coming into play at the exact moment he is declaring a fiscal emergency, and if he weren't so determined to keep pushing them, fiscal emergency be damned. It would be simpler if all his meetings were like the meetings he had with the advocates and the big-city mayors and all the different groups he met with in the conference room, where he was able to say he looked at the deficit "as a bump in the road and the health-care bill as something lasting forever," and to compare himself to Roosevelt, who kept on going big straight through the Great Depression. It would be simpler if the success of his health-care and water bills didn't depend on the other meetings he was having that week, the one-on-one meetings with members of the California legislature, like Don Perata, head of the Senate Democratic caucus. And it would have been a lot simpler if Perata, in particular, weren't so fond of the Kabuki.

What's the Kabuki? Well, it's an Arnold word, for sure—you haven't heard the words "the Kabuki" unless you hear them in his Austrian accent. See, the Kabuki was one of the things he didn't know about when he first became governor. "I've always been able to see ahead to the finish line when I'm negotiating," he told me one day. "It's always been that way. I see it, and then I want to get there. I get impatient. In business, that's not a problem. But in politics, a lot of people need to do the Kabuki, the song and dance. They feel cheated if you don't let them. So now if you want to do the Kabuki, okay, you can do the Kabuki. We'll get to the finish line eventually. It will just take longer."

Now, as it happens, the first time I saw Arnold Schwarzenegger, he was getting out of a meeting with Don Perata, and Perata had *started* the meeting doing the Kabuki, telling Arnold that it was not the right time for water and not the right time for health care, either, at least not until he saw the budget. Why did Arnold think this was the Kabuki? Well, for one thing, he thought Perata was playing for leverage because he wanted to be the man on water, and the only way he could do that was to hold out on health care. And then, for another . . . well, California's health-care system was broken, right? Then Arnold was going to fix it with a bill that not only was going to make sure that every single Californian had health insurance but that would also serve as a model for the national legislation sure to come. And California was drying up, right? Then Arnold was going to call for the issuance of bonds financing the construction of a new network of dams and canals. He had already seen the finish line on both these issues, and he was sure that he was on the side of history, even if history hadn't yet had the chance to take place. Hell, history was what he was *offering* Perata, and anyone else he wanted to get on his side. In the face of such belief, such optimism, such rightness, such certainty, what objection could there be but . . . the Kabuki?

Of course, I didn't know any of this at the time. I hadn't even heard him talk about the Kabuki yet. All I saw was him and Perata standing together, shaking hands—Perata a little stout, packed into a sharply tailored pinstripe suit, the thatch of hair atop his rubicund crown as blond as shredded wheat, and Arnold as always Arnold, wearing a gray suit with peak lapels, an open white shirt, and black boots emblazoned with the gubernatorial seal. And all I heard was Perata asking him if he'd flown to Sacramento that morning in the Gulfstream, and him telling Perata . . . but wait a second, did he just say that? Did he just say, "Yeah—and guess who was on it? *Gray Davis.* I wanted to talk to him about the *budget.*" Because if he did, he was definitely giving Perata shit. Oh, he was telling the truth, too, but he was telling it in such a way that the truth sounded like a Gray Davis joke, a budget joke, at a moment when Perata was using the budget to threaten his legislative agenda. And then, as I was standing there trying to parse the shit he was giving Perata, Arnold looked at me, a person he'd never met, and said, "It was a good meeting. You should have *been* there."

◄◄ • ►►

He had gotten away with it his entire life, you see—he'd gotten away with the imposition of his will. What he had in excess was one of the things the world had historically found unpalatable—the Teutonic will—and his genius had been to cast that will as a comic invention, and therefore an American one. He never had to hide his will or his ambition; he simply had to make his will and ambition an essential part of being Arnold, and then turn being Arnold into the performance of his lifetime.

You've heard of free will, of course. Well, with Arnold, there was *freed* will, and he used it, in the words of his chief of staff, "to visualize success in a way that doesn't visualize obstacles." Hell, when he came to the United States in '68, he didn't speak any English, and visualization was what he *had,* a talent for seeing the next thing. He visualized success in bodybuilding and then attained it by bending his body and then the entire sport to his will. And then he saw the next thing: "I heard that Charles Bronson was making a million dollars a movie," he told me. "That was a very big deal to an immigrant—*a million dollars a movie.* So I went to see a Charles Bronson movie. And I said, I can *do* that. And people said, No you can't—have you ever heard yourself? And I said, I can *do* that. And then I made a million dollars a movie, so the next thing became *keeping* the million. And that's how I got into business."

And that's pretty much how he became the governor of California as well. "I knew the time would come, and when the [Gray Davis] recall happened, it was *handed* to me. It was like God said, Hey, you want to circumvent the Republican primaries, because you're not conservative enough for them? Here's the recall. I was absolutely convinced that I would become governor, no matter *what*. And so I jumped in there. And I had the will to do it. When I campaigned in 2003, people said, You don't have the experience. I said, There's a storehouse of experience up in Sacramento and look at the shape the state is in. So it couldn't be experience that makes the state in good shape. What it needs is the will. The will to go and make tough decisions and the right decisions. I have the will, is what I told the people. And that's exactly what I have. I have the will."

But then, he had more than that, didn't he? There have been governors who have been rich, and there have been governors who have been famous, but there has never been a governor anywhere, ever, as rich and as famous as Arnold Schwarzenegger was when he took office in 2004. There has never been a governor who kept one of the swords from his role as Conan the Barbarian in a glass case in his office, or hung Andy Warhol's annihilatingly large blue painting of his wife on the wall behind his desk; never been a governor who was not only an icon but who possesses what one of his staffers calls a "significant private collection" of his own iconography, which he installed in the phalanx of offices housing his administration so that anyone entering them would instantly have the Arnold experience; never been a governor who not only had a persona but was willing to make use of it the way a sausage maker makes use of a hog; never been a governor who, when he said, "Well, it's all show business, anyway," knew exactly what he was talking about and had a proven record of moving people by the *millions*. He was a governor who never had to worry about people showing up, who never had to worry about people returning his call, who never felt uncomfortable being watched, since he knew that audience means opportunity.

He was a governor of and for the people, sure—he opened his office up, he invited people in, he went out into the state and saw as many Californians as he could—but he was also, from the beginning, the governor of *crowds,* and so in 2005, when his attempt to rein in spending was blocked by entrenched interests in the California legislature, he decided to go around the legislators and the lobbyists altogether. They wanted to do the Kabuki? He would show them the Kabuki. He would hold a special election so that the crowds that lined up to see him could line up and vote directly for the four initiatives he put on the ballot. The legislators were against him? The crowds would help him redraw legislative districts. The unions were against him? The crowds would help him restrict their political spending. The teachers were against him? The crowds would help him curb teacher tenure. . . .

He didn't get away with it. For the first time in his life, he didn't get away with the imposition of his will, because now for the first time in his life, his will wasn't sublimated by his performance—wasn't funny and wasn't free—but rather tethered to the interests of party and power. He was the Republican governor of the Democratic state of California, and the Republican party had tried to claim him—they tried to mold him and turn the Republican governor of California into a *real* Republican—and by the time of the special election, they succeeded all too well. He lost. All four of his ballot initiatives were comprehensively rejected, and for the first time in his life, he was comprehensively rejected as well, his approval ratings falling into the thirties. He had campaigned almost as a fantasy figure who could transcend partisanship and make California as big as he was. Now his will had been exposed as a will to power, his ambition had been exposed as partisan ambition, and the creation at the heart not only of who he was but of who he'd become—*Arnold*—had been exposed as just another Republican bully.

There are two bronze busts in the big conference room where he has his meetings. The busts belong to him, of course; they're part of his private collection, and therefore part of the Arnold experience, and therefore they represent—and are intended to represent—the polarities of Republican politics. One is Lincoln, the great American martyr, staring grimly ahead with fixed moral purpose. The other is Reagan. He's got his head tilted back, his eyes narrowed winsomely, and whatever else you may want to say about him, he's nobody's martyr—he's laughing, no matter who's getting screwed.

And that's Arnold. It's not that he doesn't feel your pain; it's that he, like Reagan, doesn't feel his own. He's either the happiest man in American politics or the happiest man in America, period. He makes governing look easy because for him it is easy—because he loves his job, and because he's determined to practice a politics that rises above politics. Like Reagan, he's not just optimistic, not just confident, not just joyful; he's figured out that optimism, confidence, and joy are what people need from him, and he's incorporated them so deeply into the performance of his job that it doesn't matter if he is performing or not—they're who he is, and who he is turns out to be both an incredibly narrow and an incredibly expansive concept. Here are some quotes culled from a single interview with David Crane, a friend of the governor's since the late seventies and now an advisor on economic policy: "He's the least angry person I know." "He's superoptimistic by nature." "He seems to like everything he does." "I've never seen him down." "He's like a very normal person that you meet in business." "He's anything but normal, and in that sense his life has not changed very much since he became governor." "He enjoys his normal, not-normal life."

There was one time he experienced guilt—as in, one time in his entire life. That's what he said one night, on his plane. He was talking about how his job continually surprised him and that one of the first surprises was how tough it was on his wife and his four children. "There is no relief," he said, "and so how do you make your family buy into that? How do you make your children understand? I never knew what guilt was. I never had any guilt. That was the first time I felt it. I felt bad that I couldn't accomplish both—pay full attention to the state and full attention to the family. It was frustrating to me, and to some degree I was angry about it—that I couldn't do it. Now, again, I've found a better way."

The better way? The better way is the plane itself. He bought a share in it, and he uses it to commute almost every day back and forth between his office in Sacramento and his home down in Brentwood. It's guilt-free—not only does he pay for it with his own money, he's also figured out some kind of charitable arrangement for his carbon offset credits. Still, it's hard to say what's more extraordinary: the fact that he's only experienced guilt once in his life or the fact that he bought into a plane to surmount it. And now that you know the parable of the plane, how do you think the other parable—the parable of the disastrous 2005 special election—ends? It was the first failure of his life, after all. Do you think he listened to the people on his staff who told him not to apologize? Do you think he martyred himself to the partisanship and the stubbornness and the political willfulness that had done him in? Or do you think he found a better way?

⤛ • ⤜

On the grounds of the capitol, twenty feet outside Arnold's office, stands a tent made of beige canvas. Though technically and legally out of doors, it has four walls, a pitched roof, and is about the size of a small hunting cabin; it is outfitted with a heater, rattan furniture, a glass table, several bowls filled with California almonds, and an array of ashtrays. The tent is to Arnold's need to smoke cigars in comfort what his plane is to his need to see his children at night: It is a better way, clearly, but it is also a better way that only he could have gotten

away with. It feels sort of *royal,* but it's also a symbol of his determined inclu-
siveness, because the tent has become the place where legislators, lobbyists,
businessmen, and activists of all stripes get a chance to meet with Arnold and
his Democratic, lesbian, cigar-smoking chief of staff.

I'm not trying to court or create controversy here, by the way. I've just never
heard Susan Kennedy referred to as anything *but* Arnold's Democratic, lesbian,
cigar-smoking chief of staff. Indeed, that he has a Democratic, lesbian, cigar-
smoking chief of staff is part of the *story*—the story of how he responded to the
special election of 2005 and the first failure of his life. His Republican staff was
part of his failure, so here's what he did: He authorized his wife to find a more
Democratic one, or at least a more heterodox one. Maria Shriver found, among
others, Susan Kennedy (no relation), who had worked for Gray Davis and had
watched, in her words, "a Democratic governor torn limb from limb by the
Democratic majority." She was out of politics and as disillusioned with the
prospect of winning as she was with the reality of losing. She was the better
way because she believed—because she needed to believe—that Arnold was
the better way. She was the better way because she believed that California
needed Arnold as much as she did and that America needed Arnold as much
as California did. She was the better way because she believed that she saw in
Arnold what the previous staff had missed—"his limitlessness"—and set about
rooting his politics in *that.*

How in the world does a governor of California base his politics on the idea
that he has no limits? Well, if you're Arnold Schwarzenegger, you simply take
the trick that's worked for you your entire life—the realization of your will
through the sublimation of your will—and adapt it to the realities of state politics. You state your ambition by taking on issues that Washington won't touch,
and then you turn those issues into bills by opening your smoking tent to
people of all parties and letting them do the Kabuki if that's what they want to
do. The health-care bill, for example—the health-care bill is a *national* bill, or
at least a model for one. "That's why," as Arnold says, "the CEOs who have come
to the table to negotiate are national CEOs, and the labor leaders who have
come to the table to negotiate are national labor leaders." And yet if the bill becomes law in California, it will become law without the support of a single Republican in the legislature. Indeed, two weeks before Christmas the Republican
governor of California had a better chance of getting lobbyists from the *tobacco*
industry to support his bill than he did legislators from his own party—and he
was planning to tax the tobacco industry in order to pay for the bill.

Okay, the tobacco lobbyists were never going to *support* the bill. But then, as Susan Kennedy said, "We don't need them to support the bill. All we need is them not spending $150 million to kill it." And so that's why they were invited to the tent. That's why they were offered the Arnold experience. He was still going to try taxing them, and they were still going to be against being taxed. "But this was probably the first time in history they were asked their opinion," he said after the meeting. "They're always considered the enemies, the villains, they create all the illnesses. But here they're being given a chance to contribute to health care. It's like us bringing in the oil companies when we passed our bill to roll back greenhouse-gas emissions. You know, environmentalists and oil companies never sit together at any event, celebrating anything. But they were all sitting there, car manufacturers, environmentalists, oil-company executives. Because we included them."

And because they all, at one time or another, came to Arnold's tent.

⋙ • ⋘

Take a look at a map of California. It's pretty big, right? And now think of how many people live there. That's a lot of damned people—12 percent of the U.S. population. And yet as large as California looks on a map, as large and pivotal a role as it plays in the electoral college, as large as its legends loom in the American psyche: Nowhere is it bigger than it is in the offices of the Arnold administration. There, it's not a state at all; it's a "nation-state," it's a "country unto itself," it's "as big as France." Hell, you know how big it is? It's as big as Arnold himself, because he's as big as it.

And so when Arnold has a week like he had the week before Christmas . . . well, the week *started* well enough, indeed historically enough, with the passage of the health-care bill he'd been negotiating in the tent for, oh, nine months or so, a first step toward guaranteeing health-care insurance for every man, woman, and child in the state. It was a party-line vote in the California Assembly—all Democrats voting yes and every single member of his party, the Republicans, voting no—and yes, the bill that was passed proposed paying for the expansion of health-care insurance by increasing the state tax on cigarettes. That was on a Monday. But then: *Perata.* He was offering no guarantees that he would bring the bill to the Senate floor until he could see the budget, until he could see how the governor could expand the state's role in the health-care system while at the same time cutting existing programs. And then:

Núñez. Assembly leader Fabian Núñez was instrumental in the passage of the health-care bill, but now he was saying of the other bill the governor was pushing, the water bill, "Water's dead." And then, on Wednesday, *Bush.* Well, really, Bush's EPA, which announced that it would not permit California and sixteen other states to set their own stringent standards for greenhouse-gas emissions. The bill that had stood as the best example of what Arnold could do for the United States from the state of California had been declared moot by an administration that had been able to do so little for the United States from Washington, D.C.

And so when Arnold has a week like that, well, he's still Arnold, isn't he? He's always Arnold, and so after he issues a statement saying that California is going to sue the EPA, he has to go back to working on his one stated goal: "to fix the state." As a goal, it sounds almost modest, almost reasonable, except that, being Arnold, he sees it as an *opportunity* to revisit most of the same spending issues that he tried to address in the 2005 special election. And since all his goals are only as modest as he is, they become part of the ongoing comedy of his limitlessness. To fix the state, he has to fix the country; to fix the country, he has to fix the country's politics; to fix the country's politics, he has to bend politics to his will; to bend politics to his will, he has to relinquish the hope of bending politics to his will; to relinquish the hope of bending politics to his will, he has to be willing to lose; to be willing to lose, he has to know that in the end he's going to win. No wonder his staff wonders if his example can translate to the rest of the country. And no wonder his Democratic, lesbian, cigar-smoking chief of staff says, "It will be the biggest tragedy in the history of American politics" if it doesn't.

⤛ • ⤜

In celebration of Christmas, there was a potluck lunch at the capitol. Members of Arnold's staff cooked for one another, and then—because they were members of Arnold's staff—judged one another, rating each dish. It was a celebration and a competition, and when Arnold stood up to speak after being introduced by Susan Kennedy as "the greatest governor in the history of California," he said he liked the annual event because it was a competition: "I like it when there are winners, and I especially like it when there are *losers.*"

And then he called an aide to his side and whispered a question in his ear: "What is his name?"

"Johnny Masterson," the aide answered. And then Arnold called Johnny Masterson to come up and stand with him near the Christmas tree, introducing him as "my new cochief of staff. Johnny's my buddy, because he is working out. Would you do something for us, Johnny? Would you flex for us for just a second. . . ."

Johnny was a small man with dark hair, a mail-room employee with Down's syndrome. Gamely and shyly, he flexed, and then, in an impulsive gesture, he threw his arms around his boss. But he wasn't big enough to hold him, his arms weren't long enough to encompass him, and Arnold suddenly looked *huge,* with Johnny's small hands clutching at the wings of his shoulders and Johnny's face pressed against his chest. And I thought: Okay, he's gotten away with this, too. He's gotten away with not knowing Johnny's name, he's gotten away with pretending he did, he's gotten away with the performance of compassion, and this was why he was good at politics. And then I looked at him, and I looked at them, and realized he'd gotten away with nothing. The disparity of scale he experienced with Johnny Masterson was what he experienced with just about everyone his entire life. It wasn't what made him transcendent; it was what he had to transcend, and now that's exactly what he went about doing, with the sheer size of his embrace.

16

CAN YOU COUNT ON VOTING MACHINES?

CLIVE THOMPSON
The New York Times Magazine   January 6, 2008

Ensuring that each voter's choices get recorded accurately and permanently is one of the most basic requirements of a functioning democracy. In practice, however, vote-counting remains an inexact science. (Remember those hanging chads in Florida?) In the following selection, Clive Thompson, who has written widely on the interface between technology and culture, reports on the dubious track record of touch-screen voting devices, and the ongoing quest for a reliable voting machine.

Jane Platten gestured, bleary-eyed, into the secure room filled with voting machines. It was 3 A.M. on November 7, and she had been working for 22 hours straight. "I guess we've seen how technology can affect an election," she said. The electronic voting machines in Cleveland were causing trouble again.

For a while, it had looked as if things would go smoothly for the Board of Elections office in Cuyahoga County, Ohio. About 200,000 voters had trooped out on the first Tuesday in November for the lightly attended local elections, tapping their choices onto the county's 5,729 touch-screen voting machines. The elections staff had collected electronic copies of the votes on memory cards and taken them to the main office, where dozens of workers inside a secure, glass-encased room fed them into the "GEMS server," a gleaming silver Dell desktop computer that tallies the votes.

Then at 10 P.M., the server suddenly froze up and stopped counting votes. Cuyahoga County technicians clustered around the computer, debating what to do. A young, business-suited employee from Diebold—the company that makes the voting machines used in Cuyahoga—peered into the screen and pecked at the keyboard. No one could figure out what was wrong. So, like anyone faced with a misbehaving computer, they simply turned it off and on again. Voilà: It started working—until an hour later, when it crashed a second time. Again, they rebooted. By the wee hours, the server mystery still hadn't been solved.

Worse was yet to come. When the votes were finally tallied the next day, 10 races were so close that they needed to be recounted. But when Platten went to retrieve paper copies of each vote—generated by the Diebold machines as they worked—she discovered that so many printers had jammed that 20 percent of the machines involved in the recounted races lacked paper copies of some of the votes. They weren't lost, technically speaking; Platten could hit "print" and a machine would generate a replacement copy. But she had no way of proving that these replacements were, indeed, what the voters had voted. She could only hope the machines had worked correctly.

As the primaries start in New Hampshire this week and roll on through the next few months, the erratic behavior of voting technology will once again find itself under a microscope. In the last three election cycles, touch-screen machines have become one of the most mysterious and divisive elements in modern electoral politics. Introduced after the 2000 hanging-chad debacle, the machines were originally intended to add clarity to election results. But in hundreds of instances, the result has been precisely the opposite: they fail unpredictably, and in extremely strange ways; voters report that their choices "flip" from one candidate to another before their eyes; machines crash or begin to count backward; votes simply vanish. (In the 80-person town of Waldenburg, Arkansas, touch-screen machines tallied zero votes for one mayoral candidate in 2006—even though he's pretty sure he voted for himself.) Most famously, in the November 2006 Congressional election in Sarasota, Florida, touch-screen machines recorded an 18,000-person "undervote" for a race decided by fewer than 400 votes.

The earliest critiques of digital voting booths came from the fringe—disgruntled citizens and scared-senseless computer geeks—but the fears have now risen to the highest levels of government. One by one, states are renouncing the use of touch-screen voting machines. California and Florida decided to get rid of their electronic voting machines last spring, and last month, Colorado decertified about half of its touch-screen devices. Also last month, Jennifer Brunner, the Ohio secretary of state, released a report in the wake of the Cuyahoga crashes arguing that touch-screens "may jeopardize the integrity of the voting process." She was so worried she is now forcing Cuyahoga to scrap its touch-screen machines and go back to paper-based voting—before the Ohio primary, scheduled for March 4. Senator Bill Nelson, a Democrat of Florida, and Senator Sheldon Whitehouse, Democrat of Rhode Island, have even sponsored a bill that would ban the use of touch-screen machines across the country by 2012.

It's difficult to say how often votes have genuinely gone astray. Michael Shamos, a computer scientist at Carnegie Mellon University who has examined voting-machine systems for more than 25 years, estimates that about 10 percent of the touch-screen machines "fail" in each election. "In general, those failures result in the loss of zero or one vote," he told me. "But they're very disturbing to the public."

Indeed, in a more sanguine political environment, this level of error might be considered acceptable. But in today's highly partisan and divided country, elections can be decided by unusually slim margins—and are often bitterly contested. The mistrust of touch-screen machines is thus equal parts technological and ideological. "A tiny number of votes can have a huge impact, so machines are part of the era of sweaty palms," says Doug Chapin, the director of Electionline.org, a nonpartisan group that monitors voting reform. Critics have spent years fretting over corruption and the specter of partisan hackers throwing an election. But the real problem may simply be inherent in the nature of computers: they can be precise but also capricious, prone to malfunctions we simply can't anticipate.

During this year's presidential primaries, roughly one-third of all votes will be cast on touch-screen machines. (New Hampshire voters are not in this group; they will vote on paper ballots, some of which are counted in optical scanners.) The same ratio is expected to hold when Americans choose their president in the fall. It is a very large chunk of the electorate. So what scares election observers is this: What happens if the next presidential election is extremely close and decided by a handful of votes cast on machines that crashed? Will voters accept a presidency decided by ballots that weren't backed up on paper and existed only on a computer drive? And what if they don't?

"The issue for me is the unknown," Platten told me when we first spoke on the phone, back in October. "There's always the unknown factor. Something—*something*—happens every election."

⤙ • ⤚

New voting technologies tend to emerge out of crises of confidence. We change systems only rarely and in response to a public anxiety that electoral results can no longer be trusted. America voted on paper in the 19th century, until ballot-box stuffing—and inept poll workers who lost bags of votes—led many to abandon that system. Some elections officials next adopted lever machines, which record each vote mechanically. But lever machines have problems of their own, not least that they make meaningful recounts impossible because they do not preserve each individual vote. Beginning in the 1960s they were widely replaced by punch-card systems, in which voters knock holes in ballots, and the ballots can be stored for a recount. Punch cards worked for decades without controversy.

Until, of course, the electoral fiasco of 2000. During the Florida recount in the Bush-Gore election, it became clear that punch cards had a potentially tragic flaw: "hanging chads." Thousands of voters failed to punch a hole clean through the ballot, turning the recount into a torturous argument over "voter intent." On top of that, many voters confused by the infamous "butterfly ballot" seem to have mistakenly picked the wrong candidate. Given Bush's microscopic margin of victory—he was ahead by only a few hundred votes statewide—the chads produced the brutal, monthlong legal brawl over how and whether the recounts should be conducted.

The 2000 election illustrated the cardinal rule of voting systems: if they produce ambiguous results, they are doomed to suspicion. The election is never settled in the mind of the public. To this date, many Gore supporters refuse to accept the legitimacy of George W. Bush's presidency; and by ultimately deciding the 2000 presidential election, the Supreme Court was pilloried for appearing overly partisan.

Many worried that another similar trauma would do irreparable harm to the electoral system. So in 2002, Congress passed the Help America Vote Act (HAVA), which gave incentives to replace punch-card machines and lever machines and authorized $3.9 billion for states to buy new technology, among other things. At the time, the four main vendors of voting machines—Diebold, ES&S, Sequoia and Hart—were aggressively marketing their new touch-screen machines. Computers seemed like the perfect answer to the hanging chad. Touch-screen machines would be clear and legible, unlike the nightmarishly unreadable "butterfly ballot." The results could be tabulated very quickly after the polls closed. And best of all, the vote totals would be conclusive, since the votes would be stored in crisp digital memory. (Touch-screen machines were also promoted as a way to allow the blind or paralyzed to vote, via audio prompts and puff tubes. This became a powerful incentive, because, at the behest of groups representing the disabled, HAVA required each poll station to have at least one "accessible" machine.)

HAVA offered no assistance or guidelines as to what type of machine to buy, and local elections officials did not have many resources to investigate the choices; indeed, theirs are some of the most neglected and understaffed offices around, because who pays attention to electoral technology between campaigns? As touch-screen vendors lobbied elections boards, the machines took on an air of inevitability. For elections directors terrified of presiding over "the next Florida," the cool digital precision of touch-screens seemed like the perfect antidote.

⤙⤙ • ⤚⤚

In the lobby of Jane Platten's office in Cleveland sits an AccuVote-TSX, made by Diebold. It is the machine that Cuyahoga County votes on, and it works like this: Inside each machine there is a computer roughly as powerful and flexible as a modern hand-held organizer. It runs Windows CE as its operating system, and Diebold has installed its own specialized voting software to run on top of Windows. When the voters tap the screen to indicate their choices, the computer records each choice on a flash-memory card that fits in a slot on the machine, much as a flash card stores pictures on your digital camera. At the end of the election night, these cards are taken to the county's election headquarters and tallied by the GEMS server. In case a memory card is accidentally lost or destroyed, the computer also stores each vote on a different chip inside the machine; election officials can open the voting machine and remove the chip in an emergency.

But there is also a third place the vote is recorded. Next to each machine's LCD screen, there is a printer much like one on a cash register. Each time a voter picks a candidate on screen, the printer types up the selections, in small, eight-point letters. Before the voter pushes "vote," she's supposed to peer down at the ribbon of paper—which sits beneath a layer of see-through plastic, to prevent tampering—and verify that the machine has, in fact, correctly recorded her choices. (She can't take the paper vote with her as proof; the spool of paper remains locked inside the machine until the end of the day.)

Under Ohio law, the paper copy *is* the voter's vote. The digital version is not. That's because the voter can see the paper vote and verify that it's correct, which she cannot do with the digital one. The digital records are, in essence, merely handy additional copies that allow the county to rapidly tally potentially a million votes in a single evening, whereas counting the paper ballots would take weeks. Theoretically speaking, the machine offers the best of all possible worlds. By using both paper and digital copies, the AccuVote promised Cuyahoga an election that would be speedy, reliable and relatively inexpensive.

Little of this held true. When the machines were first used in Cuyahoga County during the May 2006 primaries, costs ballooned—and chaos reigned. The poll workers, many senior citizens who had spent decades setting up low-tech punch-card systems, were baffled by the new computerized system and the rather poorly written manuals from Diebold and the county. "It was insane," one former poll worker told me. "A lot of people over the age of 60, trying to figure out these machines." Since the votes were ferried to the head office on small, pocket-size memory cards, it was easy for them to be misplaced, and dozens went missing.

On Election Day, poll workers complained that 143 machines were broken; dozens of other machines had printer jams or mysteriously powered down. More than 200 voter-card encoders—which create the cards that let voters vote—went missing. When the machines weren't malfunctioning, they produced errors at a stunning rate: one audit of the election discovered that in 72.5 percent of the audited machines, the paper trail did not match the digital tally on the memory cards.

This was hardly the first such incident involving touch-screen machines. So it came as little surprise that Diebold, a company once known primarily for making safes and A.T.M.'s, subsequently tried to sell off its voting-machine business and, failing to find a buyer, last August changed the name of the division to Premier Election Solutions (an analyst told *American Banker* that the voting machines were responsible for "5 percent of revenue and 100 percent of bad public relations").

Nearly a year after the May 2006 electoral disaster, Ohio's new secretary of state, Jennifer Brunner, asked the entire four-person Cuyahoga elections board to resign, and Platten—then the interim director of the board—was tapped to clean up the mess. Platten had already instituted a blizzard of tiny fixes. She added responsibilities to the position of "Election Day technician"—filled by young, computer-savvy volunteers who could help the white-haired poll workers reboot touch-screens when they crashed. She bought plastic business-card binders to hold memory cards from a precinct, so none would be misplaced. "Robocalls" at home from a phone-calling service reminded volunteers to show up. Her staff rewrote the inscrutable Diebold manuals in plain English.

The results were immediate. Over the next several months, Cuyahoga's elections ran with many fewer crashes and shorter lines of voters. Platten's candor and hard work won her fans among even the most fanatical anti-touch-screen activists. "It's a miracle," I was told by Adele Eisner, a Cuyahoga County resident who has been a vocal critic of touch-screen machines. "Jane Platten actually understands that elections are for the people." The previous board, Eisner went on to say, ridiculed critics who claimed the machines would be trouble and refused to meet with them; the new replacements, in contrast, sometimes seemed as skeptical about the voting machines as the activists, and Eisner was invited in to wander about on election night, videotaping the activity.

Still, the events of Election Day 2007 showed just how ingrained the problems with the touch-screens were. The printed paper trails caused serious headaches all day long: at one polling place, printers on most of the machines weren't functioning the night before the polls opened. Fortunately, one of the Election Day technicians was James Diener, a gray-haired former computer-and-mechanical engineer who opened up the printers, discovered that metal parts were bent out of shape and managed to repair them. The problem, he declared cheerfully, was that the printers were simply "cheap quality" (a complaint I heard from many election critics). "I'm an old computer nerd," Diener said. "I can do anything with computers. Nothing's wrong with computers. But this is the worst way to run an election."

He also pointed out several other problems with the machines, including the fact that the majority of voters he observed did not check the paper trail to see whether their votes were recorded correctly—even though that paper record is their legal ballot. (I noticed this myself, and many other poll workers told me the same thing.) Possibly they're simply lazy, or the poll workers forget to tell them to; or perhaps they're older and couldn't see the printer's tiny type anyway. And even if voters do check the paper trail, Diener pointed out, how do they know the machine is recording it for sure? "The whole printing thing is a farce," he said.

What's more, the poll workers regularly made security errors. When a touchscreen machine is turned on for the first time on Election Day, two observers from different parties are supposed to print and view the "zero tape" that shows there are no votes already recorded on the machine; a hacker could fix the vote by programming the machine to start, for example, with a negative total of votes for a candidate. Yet when I visited one Cleveland polling station at daybreak, the two checkers signed zero tapes without actually checking the zero totals. And then, of course, there were the server crashes, and the recording errors on 20 percent of the paper recount ballots.

Chris Riggall, a spokesman for Diebold, said that machine flaws were not necessarily to blame for the problems. The paper rolls were probably installed incorrectly by the poll workers. And in any case, he added, the paper trail was originally designed merely to help in auditing the accuracy of an election—it wasn't supposed to be robust enough to serve as a legal ballot, as Ohio chose to designate it. But the servers were indeed an issue of the machine's design; when his firm tested them weeks later, it found a data bottleneck that would need to be fixed with a software update.

The November 6 vote in Cuyahoga County offered a sobering lesson. Having watched Platten's staff and the elections board in action, I could see they were a model of professionalism. Yet they still couldn't get their high-tech system to work as intended. For all their diligence and hard work, they were forced, in the end, to discard much of their paper and simply trust that the machines had recorded the votes accurately in digital memory.

⤛ • ⤜

The question, of course, is whether the machines should be trusted to record votes accurately. Ed Felten doesn't think so. Felten is a computer scientist at Princeton University, and he has become famous for analyzing—and criticizing—touchscreen machines. In fact, the first serious critics of the machines—beginning 10 years ago—were computer scientists. One might expect computer scientists to be fans of computer-based vote-counting devices, but it turns out that the more you know about computers, the more likely you are to be terrified that they're running elections.

This is because computer scientists understand, from hard experience, that complex software can't function perfectly all the time. It's the nature of the beast. Myriad things can go wrong. The software might have bugs—errors in the code made by tired or overworked programmers. Or voters could do something the machines don't expect, like touching the screen in two places at once. "Computers crash and we don't know why," Felten told me. "That's just a routine part of computers."

One famous example is the "sliding finger bug" on the Diebold AccuVote-TSX, the machine used in Cuyahoga. In 2005, the state of California complained that the machines were crashing. In tests, Diebold determined that when voters tapped the final "cast vote" button, the machine would crash every few hundred ballots. They finally intuited the problem: their voting software runs on top of Windows CE, and if a voter accidentally dragged his finger downward while touching "cast vote" on the screen, Windows CE interpreted this as a "drag and drop" command. The programmers hadn't anticipated that Windows CE would do this, so they hadn't programmed a way for the machine to cope with it. The machine just crashed.

Even extremely careful programmers can accidentally create bugs like this. But critics also worry that touch-screen voting machines aren't designed very carefully at all. In the infrequent situations where computer scientists have gained access to the guts of a voting machine, they've found alarming design flaws. In 2003, Diebold employees accidentally posted the AccuVote's source code on the Internet; scientists who analyzed it found that, among other things, a hacker could program a voter card to let him cast as many votes as he liked. Ed Felten's lab, while analyzing an anonymously donated AccuVote-TS (a different model from the one used in Cuyahoga County) in 2006, discovered that the machine did not "authenticate" software: it will run any code a hacker might surreptitiously install on an easily insertable flash-memory card. After California's secretary of state hired computer scientists to review the state's machines last spring, they found that on one vote-tallying server, the default password was set to the name of the vendor—something laughably easy for a hacker to guess.

But the truth is that it's hard for computer scientists to figure out just how well or poorly the machines are made, because the vendors who make them keep the details of their manufacture tightly held. Like most software firms, they regard their "source code"—the computer programs that run on their machines—as a trade secret. The public is not allowed to see the code, so computer experts who wish to assess it for flaws and reliability can't get access to it. Felten and voter rights groups argue that this "black box" culture of secrecy is the biggest single problem with voting machines. Because the machines are not transparent, their reliability cannot be trusted.

The touch-screen vendors disagree. They point out that a small number of approved elections officials in each state and county are allowed to hold a copy in escrow and to examine it (though they are required to sign nondisclosure agreements preventing them from discussing the software publicly). Further, vendors argue, the machines are almost always tested by the government before they're permitted to be used. The Election Assistance Commission, a federal agency, this year began to fully certify four private-sector labs to stress-test machines. They subject them to environmental pressures like heat and vibration to ensure they won't break down on Election Day; and they run mock elections, to verify that the machines can count correctly. In almost all cases, if a vendor updates the software or hardware, it must be tested all over again, which can take months. "It's an extremely rigorous process," says Ken Fields, a spokesman for the voting-machine company ES&S.

If the machines are tested and officials are able to examine the source code, you might wonder why machines with so many flaws and bugs have gotten through. It is, critics insist, because the testing is nowhere near diligent enough, and the federal regulators are too sympathetic and cozy with the vendors. The 2002 federal guidelines, the latest under which machines currently in use were qualified, were vague about how much security testing the labs ought to do. The labs were also not required to test any machine's underlying operating system, like Windows, for weaknesses.

Vendors paid for the tests themselves, and the results were considered proprietary, so the public couldn't find out how they were conducted. The nation's largest tester of voting machines, Ciber Inc., was temporarily suspended after federal officials found that the company could not properly document the tests it claimed to have performed.

"The types of malfunctions we're seeing would be caught in a first-year computer science course," says Lillie Coney, an associate director with the Electronic Privacy Information Commission, which is releasing a study later this month critical of the federal tests.

In any case, the federal testing is not, strictly speaking, mandatory. The vast majority of states "certify" their machines as roadworthy. But since testing is extremely expensive, many states, particularly smaller ones, simply accept whatever passes through a federal lab. And while it's true that state and local elections officials can generally keep a copy of the source code, critics say they rarely employ computer programmers sophisticated enough to understand it. Quite the contrary: When a county buys touch-screen voting machines, its elections director becomes, as Warren Parish, a voting activist in Florida, told me, "the head of the largest I.T. department in their entire government, in charge of hundreds or thousands of new computer systems, without any training at all." Many elections directors I spoke with have been in the job for years or even decades, working mostly with paper elections or lever machines. Few seemed very computer-literate.

The upshot is a regulatory environment in which, effectively, no one assumes final responsibility for whether the machines function reliably. The vendors point to the federal and state governments, the federal agency points to the states, the states rely on the federal testing lab and the local officials are frequently hapless.

This has created an environment, critics maintain, in which the people who make and sell machines are now central to running elections. Elections officials simply do not know enough about how the machines work to maintain or fix them. When a machine crashes or behaves erratically on Election Day, many county elections officials must rely on the vendors—accepting their assurances that the problem is fixed and, crucially, that no votes were altered.

In essence, elections now face a similar outsourcing issue to that seen in the Iraq war, where the government has ceded so many core military responsibilities to firms like Halliburton and Blackwater that Washington can no longer fire the contractor. Vendors do not merely sell machines to elections departments. In many cases, they are also paid to train poll workers, design ballots and repair broken machines, for years on end.

"This is a crazy world," complained Ion Sancho, the elections supervisor of Leon County in Florida. "The process is so under control by the vendor. The primary source of information comes only from the vendor, and the vendor has a conflict of interest in telling you the truth. The vendor isn't going to tell me that his buggy software is why I can't get the right time on my audit logs."

As more and more evidence of machine failure emerges, senior government officials are sounding alarms as did the computer geeks of years ago over the growing role of private companies in elections. When I talked to Jennifer Brunner in October, she told me she wished all of Ohio's machines were "open source"—that is, run on computer code that is published publicly, for anyone to see. Only then, she says, would voters trust it; and the scrutiny of thousands of computer scientists worldwide would ferret out any flaws and bugs.

On November 6, the night of the Cuyahoga crashes, Jeff Hastings—the Republican head of the election board—sat and watched the Diebold technicians try to get the machines running. "Criminy," he said. "You've got four different vendors. Why should their source codes be private? You've privatized the essential building block of the election system."

The federal government appears to have taken that criticism to heart. New standards for testing voting machines now being implemented by the E.A.C. are regarded as more rigorous; some results are now being published online.

Amazingly, the Diebold spokesman, Chris Riggall, admitted to me that the company is considering making the software open source on its next generation of touch-screen machines, so that anyone could download, inspect or repair the code. The pressure from states is growing, he added, and "if the expectations of our customers change, we'll have to respond to that reality."

⋘ • ⋙

If you want to get a sense of the real stakes in voting-machine politics, Christine Jennings has a map to show you. It is a sprawling, wall-size diagram of the voting precincts that make up Florida's 13th district, and it hangs on the wall of her campaign office in Sarasota, where she ran for the Congressional seat in November 2006. Jennings, a Democrat, lost the seat by 369 votes to the Republican, Vern Buchanan, in a fierce fight to replace Katherine Harris. But Jennings quickly learned of an anomaly in the voting: some 18,000 people had "undervoted." That is, they had voted in every other race—a few dozen were on the ballot, including a gubernatorial contest—but abstained in the Jennings-Buchanan fight. A normal undervote in any given race is less than 3 percent. In this case, a whopping 13 percent of voters somehow decided to not vote.

"See, look at this," Jennings said, dragging me over to the map when I visited her in November. Her staff had written the size of the undervote in every precinct in Sarasota, where the undervotes occurred: 180 votes in one precinct, 338 in another. "I mean, it's huge!" she said. "It's just unbelievable." She pointed to Precinct 150, a district on the south end of Sarasota County.

Buchanan received 346 votes, Jennings received 275 and the undervote was 133. "I mean, people would walk in and vote for everything except this race?" she said. "Why?"

Jennings says she believes the reason is simple: Sarasota's touch-screen machines malfunctioned—and lost votes that could have tipped the election in her favor. Her staff has received hundreds of complaints from voters reporting mysterious behavior on the part of the machines. The specific model that Sarasota used was the iVotronic, by the company ES&S. According to the complaints, when voters tried to touch the screen for Jennings, the iVotronic wouldn't accept it, or would highlight Buchanan's name instead. When they got to the final pages of the ballot, where they reviewed their picks, the complainants said, the Jennings-Buchanan race was missing—even though they were sure they'd voted in it. The reports streamed in not merely from technophobic senior citizens but also from tech-savvy younger people, including a woman with a Ph.D. in computer science and a saleswoman who actually works for a firm that sells touch-screen devices. (Even Vern Buchanan's wife reported having trouble voting for her husband.)

If the election had been in Cuyahoga, the paper trail might have settled the story. But the iVotronic, unlike Cuyahoga's machines, does not provide a paper backup. It records votes only in digital memory: on a removable flash-memory card and on an additional flash-memory chip embedded inside the machine. Since the Jennings-Buchanan election was so close, state law called for an automatic recount. But on a paperless machine like the iVotronic, a recount is purely digital—it consists of nothing but removing the flash memory inside the machine and hitting "print" again. Jennings did, indeed, lose the recount; when they reprinted, elections workers found that the internal chips closely matched the original count (Jennings picked up four more votes). But for Jennings this is meaningless, because she says it was the screens that malfunctioned.

As evidence, she brandishes pieces of evidence she says are smoking guns. One is a memo from ES&S executives, issued in August 2006, warning that they had found a bug in the iVotronic software that produced a delay in the screen; after a voter made her choice, it would take a few seconds for the screen to display it. This, Jennings noted, could cause problems, because a voter, believing that the machine had not recorded her first touch, might push the screen again—accidentally deselecting her initial vote. Jennings also suspects that the iVotronic's hardware may have malfunctioned. An August HDNet investigation by Dan Rather discovered that the company manufacturing the touch-screens for the iVotronic had a history of production flaws. The flaw affected the calibration of the screen: When exposed to humidity—much like the weather in Florida—the screen would gradually lose accuracy.

Elections officials in Sarasota and ES&S hotly disagree that the machines were in error, noting that the calibration problems with the screens were fixed before the election. Kathy Dent, Sarasota's elections supervisor, suspects that the undervote was real—which is to say, voters intentionally skipped the race, to punish Jennings and Buchanan for waging a particularly vitriolic race. "People were really fed up," she told me. Other observers say voters were simply confused by the ballot design and didn't see the Jennings-Buchanan race.

To try to settle the question, a government audit tried to test whether the machines had malfunctioned. The state acquired a copy of the iVotronic source code from ES&S and commissioned a group of computer scientists to inspect it. Their report said they could find no flaws in the code that would lead to such a large undervote. Meanwhile, the state conducted a mock election, getting elections workers to repeatedly click the screens on iVotronic machines, voting Jennings or Buchanan. Again, no accidental undervote appeared. Early results from a separate test by an M.I.T. professor found that when voters were presented with the Sarasota ballot, over 16 percent accidentally skipped over the Jennings-Buchanan race—suggesting that poor ballot design and voter error were, indeed, part of the problem.

These explanations have not satisfied Jennings and her supporters. Kendall Coffey, one of Jennings's lawyers, has a different theory: the votes were mostly lost because of a "nonrecurring software bug"—a quirk that, like the sliding-finger bug, only crops up some of the time, propelled by voter actions that the audits did not replicate, like a voter's accidentally touching the screen in two places at once. For her part, Jennings brushes off the idea that voters were punishing her and Buchanan. Plenty of Congressional fights are nasty, she says, but they almost never yield 13 percent undervotes.

And on and on it goes. ES&S and Sarasota correctly point out that Jennings has no proof that a bug exists. Jennings correctly points out that her opponents have no proof a bug doesn't exist. This is the ultimate political legacy of touch-screen voting machines and the privatization of voting machinery generally. When invisible, secretive software runs an election, it allows for endless mistrust and muttered accusations of conspiracy. The inscrutability of the software—combined with touch-screen machines' well-documented history of weird behavior—allows critics to level almost any accusation against the machines and have it sound plausible. "It's just like the Kennedy assassination," Shamos, the Carnegie Mellon computer scientist, laments. "There's no matter of evidence that will stop people from spinning yarns."

Part of the problem stems from the fact that voting requires a level of precision we demand from virtually no other technology. We demand that the systems behind A.T.M.'s and credit cards be accurate, of course. But if they're not, we can quickly detect something is wrong: we notice that our balance is off and call the bank, or the bank notices someone in China bought $10,000 worth of clothes and calls us to make sure it's legitimate. But in an election, the voter must remain anonymous to the government. If a machine crashes and the county worries it has lost some ballots, it cannot go back and ask voters how they voted—because it doesn't know who they are. It is the need for anonymity that fuels the quest for perfection in voting machines.

Perfection isn't possible, of course; every voting system has flaws. So historically, the public—and candidates for public office—have grudgingly accepted that their voting systems will produce some errors here and there. The deep, ongoing consternation over touch-screen machines stems from something new: the unpredictability of computers. Computers do not merely produce errors; they produce errors of unforeseeable magnitude. Will people trust a system when they never know how big or small its next failure will be?

⤝⤛ • ⤜⤞

On the Friday before the November elections in Pennsylvania, I wandered into a church in a suburb of Pittsburgh. The church was going to serve as a poll location, and I was wondering: Had the voting machines been dropped off? Were they lying around unguarded—and could anyone gain access to them?

When I approached the side door of the church at 6 P.M., two women were unloading food into the basement kitchen. (They were visitors from another church who had a key to get in, but they told me they'd found the door unlocked.) I held the door for them, chatted politely, then strolled into the otherwise completely empty building. Neither woman asked why I was there.

I looked over in the corner and there they were: six iVotronic voting machines, stacked up neatly. While the women busied themselves in their car, I was left completely alone with the machines. The iVotronics had been sealed shut with numbered tamper seals to prevent anyone from opening a machine illicitly, but cutting and resealing them looked pretty easy. In essence, I could have tampered with the machines in any way I wanted, with very little chance of being detected or caught.

Is it possible that someone could hack voting machines and rig an election? Elections officials insist that they are extremely careful to train poll workers to recognize signs of machines that had been tampered with. They also claim, frequently, that the machines are carefully watched. Neither is entirely true. Machines often sit for days before elections in churches, and while churches may be wonderfully convenient polling locations, they're about as insecure a location as you could imagine: strangers are *supposed* to wander into churches. And while most poll workers do carefully check to ensure that the tamper seals on the machines are unbroken, I heard reports from poll workers who saw much more lax behavior in their colleagues.

Yet here's the curious thing: Almost no credible scientific critics of touch-screen voting say they believe any machines have ever been successfully hacked. Last year, Ed Felten, the computer scientist from Princeton, wrote a report exhaustively documenting the many ways a Diebold AccuVote-TSX could be hacked—including a technique for introducing a vote-rigging virus that would spread from machine to machine in a precinct. But Felten says the chance this has really happened is remote. He argues that the more likely danger of touch-screen machines is not in malice but in errors. Michael Shamos agrees. "If there are guys who are trying to tamper with elections through manipulation of software, we would have seen evidence of it," he told me. "Nobody ever commits the perfect crime the first time. We would have seen a succession of failed attempts leading up to possibly a successful attempt. We've never seen it."

This is a great oddity in the debate over electronic voting. When state officials in California and Ohio explain why they're moving away from touch-screen voting, they inevitably cite hacking as a chief concern. And the original, left-wing opposition to the machines in the 2004 election focused obsessively on Diebold's C.E.O. proclaiming that he would help "Ohio deliver its electoral votes" for Bush. Those fears still dominate the headlines, but in the real world of those who conduct and observe voting machines, the realistic threat isn't conspiracy. It's unreliability, incompetence and sheer error.

⤛ • ⤜

If you wanted to know where the next great eruption of voting-machine scandal is likely to emerge, you'd have to drive deep into the middle of Pennsylvania.

Tucked amid rolling, forested hills is tiny Bellefonte. It is where the elections board of Centre County has its office, and in the week preceding the November election, the elections director, Joyce McKinley, conducted a public demonstration of the county's touch-screen voting machines. She would allow anyone from the public to test six machines to ensure they worked as intended.

"Remember, we're here to observe the machines, not debate them," she said dryly. The small group that had turned out included a handful of anti-touch-screen activists, including Mary Vollero, an art teacher who wore pins saying "No War in Iraq" and "Books Not Bombs." As we gathered around, I could understand why the county board had approved the purchase of the machines two years ago. For a town with a substantial elderly population, the electronic screens were large, crisp and far easier to read than small-print paper ballots. "The voters around here love 'em," McKinley shrugged.

But what's notable about Centre County is that it uses the iVotronic—the very same star-crossed machine from Sarasota. Given the concerns about the lack of a paper trail on the iVotronics, why didn't Centre County instead buy a machine that produces a paper record? Because Pennsylvania state law will not permit any machine that would theoretically make it possible to figure out how someone voted. And if a Diebold AccuVote-TSX, for instance, were used in a precinct where only, say, a dozen people voted—a not-uncommon occurrence in small towns—then an election worker could conceivably watch who votes, in what order, and unspool the tape to figure out how they voted. (And there are no alternatives; all touch-screen machines with paper trails use spools.) As a result, nearly 40 percent of Pennsylvania's counties bought iVotronics.

Though it has gone Democratic in the last few presidential elections, Pennsylvania is considered a swing state. As the political consultant James Carville joked, it's a mix of red and blue: you've got Pittsburgh and Philadelphia at either end and Alabama in the middle.

It also has 21 electoral-college votes, a relatively large number that could decide a tight presidential race. Among election-machine observers, this provokes a shudder of anticipation. If the presidential vote is close, it could well come down to a recount in Pennsylvania. And a recount could uncover thousands of votes recorded on machines that displayed aberrant behavior—with no paper trail. Would the public accept it? Would the candidates? As Candice Hoke, the head of Ohio's Center for Election Integrity, puts it: "If it was Florida in 2000 and Ohio in 2004, everyone is saying it's going to be Pennsylvania in 2008."

The prospect of being thrust into the national spotlight has already prompted many counties to spar over ditching their iVotronics. The machines were an election issue in Centre County in November, with several candidates for county commissioner running on a pledge to get rid of the devices. (Two won and are trying to figure out if they can afford it.) And the opposition to touch-screens isn't just coming from Democrats. When the Pennsylvania Republican Rick Santorum lost his Senate seat in 2006, some Santorum voters complained that the iVotronics "flipped" their votes before their eyes. In Pittsburgh, the chief opponent of the machines is David Fawcett, the lone Republican on the county board of elections. "It's not a partisan issue," he says. "And even if it was, Republicans, at least in this state, would have a much greater interest in accuracy. The capacity for error is big, and the error itself could be so much greater than it could be on prior systems."

⤙ • ⤚

Given that there is no perfect voting system, is there at least an optimal one? Critics of touch-screen machines say that the best choice is "optical scan" technology. With this system, the voter pencils in her vote on a paper ballot, filling in bubbles to indicate which candidates she prefers. The vote is immediately tangible to the voters; they see it with their own eyes, because they personally record it. The tallying is done rapidly, because the ballots are fed into a computerized scanner. And if there's a recount, the elections officials can simply take out the paper ballots and do it by hand.

Optical scanning is used in what many elections experts regard as the "perfect elections" of Leon County in Florida, where Ion Sancho is the supervisor of elections. In the late '80s, when the county was replacing its lever machines, Sancho investigated touch-screens. But he didn't think they were user-friendly, didn't believe they would provide a reliable recount and didn't want to be beholden to a private-sector vendor. So he bought the optical-scanning devices from Unisys and trained his staff to be able to repair problems when the machines broke or malfunctioned. His error rate—how often his system miscounts a ballot—is three-quarters of a percent at its highest, and has dipped as low as three-thousandths of a percent.

More important, his paper trail prevents endless fighting over the results of tight elections. In one recent contest, a candidate claimed that his name had not appeared on the ballot in one precinct. So Sancho went into the Leon County storage, broke the security seals on the records, and pulled out the ballots. The name was there; the candidate was wrong. "He apologized to me," Sancho recalls. "And that's what you can't do with touch-screen technology. You never could have proven to that person's satisfaction that the screen didn't show his name. I like that certainty. The paper ends the discussion." Sancho has never had a legal fight over a disputed election result. "The losers have admitted they lost, which is what you want," he adds. "You have to be able to convince the loser they lost."

That, in a nutshell, is what people crave in the highly partisan arena of modern American politics: an election that can be extremely close and yet regarded by all as fair. Not only must the losing candidate believe in the loss; the public has to believe in it, too.

This is why Florida's governor, Charlie Crist, stung by the debacle in Sarasota, persuaded the state to abandon its iVotronic machines before the 2008 presidential elections and adopt optical scanning; and why, in Ohio, Cuyahoga County is planning to spend up to $12 million to switch to optical scanning in the next year (after the county paid $21 million for its touch-screens just a few years ago).

Still, optical scanning is hardly a flawless system. If someone doesn't mark a ballot clearly, a recount can wind up back in the morass of arguing over "voter intent." The machines also need to be carefully calibrated so they don't miscount ballots. Blind people may need an extra device installed to help them vote. Poorly trained poll workers could simply lose ballots. And the machines do, in fact, run software that can be hacked: Sancho himself has used computer scientists to hack his machines. It's also possible that *any* complex software isn't well suited for running elections. Most software firms deal with the inevitable bugs in their product by patching them; Microsoft still patches its seven-year-old Windows XP several times a month. But vendors of electronic voting machines do not have this luxury, because any update must be federally tested for months.

There are also serious logistical problems for the states that are switching to optical scan machines this election cycle. Experts estimate that it takes at least two years to retrain poll workers and employees on a new system; Cuyahoga County is planning to do it in only three months. Even the local activists who fought to bring in optical scanning say this shift is recklessly fast—and likely to cause problems worse than the touch-screen machines would. Indeed, this whipsawing from one voting system to the next is another danger in our modern electoral wars. Public crises of confidence in voting machines used to come along rarely, every few decades. But now every single election cycle seems to provoke a crisis, a thirst for a new technological fix. The troubles of voting machines may subside as optical scanning comes in, but they're unlikely to ever go away.

SO LONG, BUCKAROO

VICTORY CIGAR

Done at the time of the 2004 election. Bush lighting up in
celebration, not seeing the imminent ramifications of this and
many other decisions. (Illustration by Steve Brodner;
first appeared in *Rolling Stone* magazine.)

17

INSIDE BUSH'S BUNKER

TODD S. PURDUM

Vanity Fair   October 2007

By any reckoning, President George W. Bush's second term has been a rough one. Saddled with historically low approval ratings (either just above or below 30 percent, depending on which poll you read), an increasingly unpopular war, and a Congress controlled by the opposing party, the great wonder is that Bush remains as cheerful as he reportedly does. Still, as one top aide after another slips away into the private sector, Bush's last months are turning into an increasingly lonely watch. In his fascinating Vanity Fair *piece, Todd S. Purdum reports on why the presidency is an isolating job under the best of circumstances, and how George Bush's "us against them" mentality has served to cut him off even further.*

Sometime early on the morning of January 20, 2009, if recent history is a reliable guide, George W. Bush will sit down at the carved oak desk in the Oval Office and compose a note wishing his successor Godspeed. The desk is made from timbers of H.M.S. *Resolute,* a British bark that was abandoned to the ice but later salvaged by an American whaling vessel and presented to Queen Victoria in 1856 as a token of friendship. When the ship was finally decommissioned, the Queen sent a desk made from its best wood to President Rutherford B. Hayes. Since then almost every president has used the desk in one way or another. John F. Kennedy Jr. played behind the hinged door in its front, which Franklin D. Roosevelt installed to hide his leg braces and wheelchair.

In the last winter light of his tenure, what could this president, the captain of a ship that even many of his once loyal crew think of as the U.S.S. *Delusional,* possibly have to say to the man or woman who takes his place? Ronald Reagan left the first President Bush a note with the exhortation "Don't let the turkeys get you down!" The elder Bush left Bill Clinton a note promising that he would be "rooting" for him. Clinton has never revealed what he wrote to the second President Bush, but it seems safe to say that, in 2001, neither of them could have envisioned just what a failed presidency the 43rd president's would turn out to be, dragged down by war, incompetence, and corruption. The man buried in Grant's tomb may soon move up a rung.

In those moments when Bush's aides seek to show that their president is more conscientious, more reflective—in a word, deeper—than he tends to appear, they release samples of his thinking, in his own hand. ("Let freedom reign!" was his jotted response to word from Condoleezza Rice that the United States had returned sovereignty to the first of several ineffectual governments in Iraq.) But far from demonstrating Bush's depth, such exercises seem only to prove that the president, like the rest of us, has an opposable thumb. If he keeps a diary of his innermost thoughts, as even Ronald Reagan did, no one has seen it. If Bush harbors doubts about the wisdom of his course, he has not been known to confide them—he is in fact famous for being unable to admit, or even to remember, a mistake. Does he have regrets? Too few to mention: he's done it his way.

By its nature, the presidency is a lonely job. Through personality, predilection, and sheer force of will, Bush has made his presidency far lonelier than most. According to Bob Woodward, Bush told a group of Republican lawmakers in late 2005 that he would not withdraw from Iraq even if his wife, Laura, and his dog, Barney, were the only ones still supporting him. He seems determined, these days, to prove the point.

Now, with not quite a year and a half left before Bush leaves office, we have already arrived at the beleaguered endgame of his presidency. From deep inside the fortified precincts of the White House, the president projects a preternatural calm. He gives orders to nonexistent armies, which his remaining lieutenants gamely transmit: "Reform immigration!" "Overhaul the tax code!" "Privatize Social Security!" Outside the bunker, in the country that his administration now refers to as "the homeland," there is chaos and confusion. The Democrats bridged the Potomac after winning the elections last fall, and the Blue Army has now overrun most of political Washington. Its flag flies above the Capitol. More and more of the president's subordinates have been captured and interrogated, most notably the attorney general, Alberto Gonzales. Others, such as Matthew Dowd, the president's former chief campaign strategist, have managed to make good their escape—Dowd by parachuting onto the front page of the enemy *New York Times* with a detailed denunciation of Bush's policies. Independent powers that would sue for peace—the Baker-Hamilton Commission, for example—have been banished. Some loyalists, including presidential counselor Dan Bartlett, have simply fled to the safety of the private sector. For one reason or another, most of the commander in chief's senior advisers are now gone, replaced by callow upstarts and last-chance opportunists. The two most powerful advisers have been the president's second-in-command and his propaganda minister—his vice president and his political strategist—who had been at his side from the beginning and have remained close and trusted, despite the catastrophes they helped to engineer. Dick Cheney will haunt the bunker till the end, but the political strategist, Karl Rove, has quietly slipped away. The leader himself—with his lady and his loyal dog—soldiers on, in an atmosphere of disconnection and illusion. Lurid tabloid tales may hint at binge drinking and marital estrangement, although visitors report uniformly, and much to their surprise, that the president seems optimistic, unbowed, chipper, his gaze bright and steadfast. The tide is about to turn! We will prevail! But it is a hermetic and solitary existence. In the first six months of this year, the president dined outside the White House for purely personal social reasons on precisely three evenings, all in the same small swath of Northwest Washington, in the homes of old friends and aides.

So it's easy enough to imagine that Bush's frame of mind, on the morning of his successor's inauguration, will be one of isolation. As the clock winds down, with his fate inescapable, he may wander one last time through the sprawling White House complex, with its bulletproof-glass windows, its bombproof bunker, its tamperproof water supply. His whereabouts will be tracked on a small computer monitor, known as the Locator Box, in the office of his chief of staff. When he leaves the Oval Office to greet the new president in the White House residence, walking along the outdoor colonnade that leads from the West Wing, he will pass a small, lacquered wooden sign on a stand. It serves as a warning to anyone who seeks to enter his locked-down mind, or the closed world in which he lives. In gilt lettering the sign reads, NO TOURS BEYOND THIS POINT.

A HELL OF A PLACE

It isn't just a metaphor, this image of the president in a bunker. It is the fate of every president to some degree—and of this one more than any since Richard Nixon in his last days. Many factors combine to create a bunker psychology. The first, common to all modern presidencies, is the physical structure of the White House itself: appearances to the contrary, it literally is a bunker, and like any building it shapes its occupants. Another factor, again common to all presidencies, is the relentless working of time—particularly in a second term—as the buildup of problems and the departure of trusted aides create an atmosphere of vulnerability and suspicion. A third factor is the character of the man in the Oval Office. Some, like Ronald Reagan, Gerald Ford, and Bill Clinton, were temperamentally incapable of long-term bunker life. For others, like Nixon, the bunker was in some strange way the ecological niche they were born to fill. What about the current occupant? Over the past few months, I have spoken with dozens of current and former White House officials about George W. Bush and his presidency; for obvious reasons, most of them requested anonymity. They paint a picture of a president whose physical circumstances reinforce his psychological ones, and whose "My Way or the Highway" personality ultimately means that he travels alone.

Let's begin with the White House itself. A central truth about the presidential complex, easy to overlook, is that it is above all a military installation—a bristling fortress with a single first-class compartment at its heart. The president occupies a bunker from the moment he takes office. He must fight strenuously to escape it, and the tendency of the bunker is always to pull him back. Harry Truman, to whom Bush has lately taken to comparing himself, referred to the president's mansion on one occasion as a "great white sepulcher." On another he called it "a hell of a place to be alone." But Truman usually wasn't alone there. He rose regularly from his sepulcher and made a point of breaking out of his private hell.

Doing so has gotten harder. The street approach to the White House complex is cordoned off for a block in every direction, defended by rows of heavy iron bollards and retractable metal barriers implanted in the roadway. The core 18-acre White House zone is sealed by a high iron fence and a dense network of electronic sensors and alarms. Snipers patrol the White House roof. Anti-aircraft systems crown the neighboring buildings. A military presence is everywhere. Whenever the president is at work in the Oval Office, a brace of Marine guards in full-dress uniform stand at fixed posts under the West Wing portico; when he leaves, they retreat to a holding area.

The largest single component of the White House operation, in terms of personnel and budget, is also the least known: the White House Military Office. Even before the 9/11 attacks, the Military Office accounted for 2,200 of the 5,900 workers on the extended White House staff. The Military Office oversees food service in the West Wing mess and on Air Force One, for which it sends out anonymous shoppers to local grocery stores. It provides the staff of mostly

Filipino stewards who function as the president's valets. The Military Office oversees the White House Communications Agency, once a branch of the Army Signal Corps, and it coordinates all presidential transportation. Every motorcade contains a wagonload of black-clad, heavily armed Secret Service agents, known as the CAT (for "counter-assault team"), and two identical, armored black Cadillac limousines. One of them carries the president; the other is a decoy that carries the president's doctor and his personal aide and is known as "the toast car" (as in what it would be if the worst ever happened).

This is the part of the military infrastructure that the public sometimes sees. But down a stairwell in the East Wing, near the family movie theater and the visitors' office, and past the elaborate water-filtration system that purifies every drop flowing toward White House taps and tubs, is a parallel universe that no outsider so much as glimpsed until a few years ago, when several photographs were released of Vice President Dick Cheney at work there right after the World Trade Center fell. This is the Presidential Emergency Operations Center, or PEOC—the president's secure, bombproof underground redoubt. The atmosphere is kept sanitized by air locks and an independent ventilation system. Generators are on standby to provide backup electricity. Emergency escape routes lead underground from the bunker to points unknown. Besides meeting rooms, there are spartan, dormitory-style accommodations for the president, his top aides, and his family. It is here that the president's on-duty military aide—the officer who carries the "football," the briefcase containing authorization codes for launching nuclear weapons—sleeps during his 24-hour shift.

The effect on the mind of all this security—built up a brick at a time from the Cold War through the Kennedy assassination to the attempt on Ronald Reagan's life and the rise of global terrorism—cannot be overstated. "It doesn't set out to be so isolating," one former presidential aide told me. "But when you're protected by a secure package, and all these instruments and institutions and functions grow up around you, it's kind of inevitable." On his way to work, Bill Clinton, according to one of his former personal assistants, would occasionally drop by the tourist line downstairs, just for a brief infusion of the outside world—something no longer allowed the president in a post–9/11 environment.

The physical isolation of the president, any president, in the White House is extreme—palpable and oppressive even on the happiest day, in the most successful administration, during the best of times. The psychological isolation weighs more heavily still, and never more so than when a president is on the ropes. Matthew Dowd told me that he now hardly recognizes the once gregarious politician he first came to know in Texas, when Bush was governor. He said he is not sure how much of the change in the current White House atmosphere can be ascribed to Bush's personality and how much to the restrictive nature of the place, but he says, "Ultimately it rests with the president."

"It's not only the White House, and how a White House operates," Dowd adds, "but I think when you get beleaguered and you feel like you're under fire, then everybody who's not agreeing with you, or not on the program, is part of the problem."

The entire White House machine is designed to preserve, protect, and defend a president's distance from friends and enemies alike. Just knowing that plain-clothes guards lurk everywhere, even if unseen and sworn to secrecy, is guaranteed to disturb the coolest head in unpredictable ways. (One of the Kennedy family's favorite Broadway songs was the First Daughter's plaintive lament from Irving Berlin's *Mr. President,* "The Secret Service Makes Me Nervous.") Until Bill Clinton demanded a change, in 1993, the president's telephones did not even have direct-dial buttons to make outside calls. All calls to and from the president had to be routed to the switchboard, and through a communications-staff person with a designation out of a Cold War novel: Operator 1. Only a few of the president's closest friends and family members know the direct-dial numbers that will reach his office or the residence, and only a few know the private Zip Code that, in theory, makes it possible for mail to reach the president directly (though even then it must first be subjected to tests for anthrax and who knows what other threats). The current president himself pointed out, on taking office, that he would have to give up the pleasure of e-mailing with family and friends, because their idlest musings would become presidential documents, subject to scrutiny and review. (Some of Bush's closest aides, including Karl Rove, did an end run around that problem by conducting White House business on Republican National Committee e-mail accounts, which are not subject to the same recordkeeping requirements.)

⊰⊹ • ⊹⊱

Imagine, for a moment, that one of George W. Bush's oldest friends—say, his Yale classmate Roland Betts—wants to reach him. How does he go about it?

Here is roughly what might happen: Betts's name is on a short list of known presidential friends. Betts may even know the direct number of the Oval Office suite, where he might get the president's personal secretary, or the director of Oval Office operations, on the phone. She in turn might ask the advice of the president's personal aide, known in Clinton White House parlance as "the butt boy." If the president is not doing anything in particular, and the two aides agree that he might like to talk to his old friend, the call might be put through. Or they might take a number and arrange a callback, perhaps from the president's limousine on his way to a public appearance. Getting in touch is almost never a one-step process.

Now imagine that the mayor of a big American city—New Orleans, for instance—is trying to reach the president. Let's say the mayor is upset and, in a break with protocol, somehow manages to be connected to the Oval Office suite. What would happen next? First, his call would be routed to the office of Intergovernmental Affairs, the unit in the West Wing that handles presidential relations with states and municipalities. With luck, the mayor may actually know someone in that office. Maybe he blows his top and talks his way into being connected with one of the deputy chiefs of staff. Maybe, eventually, he makes it to the chief of staff himself (after asking a friendly senator or GOP fat cat to intercede). And maybe then, just maybe, the chief of staff calls the president's office. (The chief of staff is one of the tiny handful of people whose calls are always put through.) And maybe, if all goes well, the chief of staff suggests that the president call the mayor back. And if all continues to go well, after two or three missed attempts they connect, and the president says he'll see what he can do about whatever it is the mayor wants. And then the process starts all over again.

For the president—any president—to receive reliable, unvarnished, outside information about what's really going on in the world can require an enormous personal effort. Ronald Reagan and George H.W. Bush sent out handwritten notes by the thousands to keep lines open to friends and acquaintances, and to remind themselves of the utter vastness of life outside. Bill Clinton made it his business to telephone old pals and fellow pols, often late at night, to test his assumptions, ask for advice, get a reality check. He brought his friend the historian Taylor Branch to the White House for freewheeling conversations on nearly 80 occasions. Clinton also read voraciously, including his own press clippings, which sometimes enraged him. Ronald Reagan's newly released diaries suggest that he watched *Meet the Press* and *60 Minutes* more faithfully each Sunday than he went to church; more than once, while watching Jerry Lewis's annual Labor Day telethon for muscular dystrophy, he picked up the phone, asked to be connected to the number on the screen, and had trouble persuading stunned operators that it was indeed the president trying to make a pledge.

Bush's aides maintain that he keeps up with a network of friends around the country, and often frustrates White House operators by picking up the phone to dial directly. But Bush has never made a public point of demonstrating that he cares about openness or is determined to stay in touch. To the contrary, even in small, symbolic ways he has erected barriers. The Bush administration appears to be the first in history to have posted a formal dress code for anyone wanting to set foot in the West Wing: no jeans, sneakers, shorts, miniskirts, T-shirts, tank tops, or flip-flops. More seriously, the Administration has placed strict new limits on access to presidential papers, including its own. The president himself, meanwhile, has famously insisted that he ignores most newspapers and television news programs, preferring to get his information from the White House's own "objective sources," meaning the people around him. Bush also insists that he ignores polls, which Dowd, his former pollster, says is a grave mistake. "How do you, when you're sitting in a very tight, circled place, where you go from a black limousine to a helicopter to a big airplane—how do you keep in touch with what people think? One of the ways to tell what people think is, basically, by polls. For all that we can fault Clinton—and I never voted for the guy—at least he had a sense, and one of his barometers was where the American people were."

⊰⊹ • ⊹⊱

It's hard to imagine that Bush doesn't at least glance at the carefully collated daily White House news summary, a digest of the day's top stories and editorial comment stapled together in a fat, legal-size pile. At a minimum, he reads enough of it to have recommended last July that his staff check out an upbeat assessment of the Iraq war in the *Washington Post*'s Outlook section written by William Kristol, one of the war's intellectual cheerleaders. This, to be sure, is the kind of news that Bush wants to hear. When the news is something else, he may simply choose not to hear it. According to the reporter Ron Suskind, in August of 2001 a C.I.A. analyst was sent to the Bush ranch, in Texas, to brief the president about indications of an imminent threat from Al Qaeda. The president heard him out and then sent him packing with the words "All right. You've covered your ass, now."

The Bush White House has its own cable-television system, with a custom lineup of channels (Homeland Box Office, it might be called). When he travels out of town, Vice President Cheney demands, according to written instructions that recently became public, that the television sets in his hotel suite be turned on to the right-wing Fox News before he arrives. The TVs in the Bush presidential orbit are so routinely fixed on Fox that when the president gave Nancy Reagan the use of his official 747 for her husband's funeral, three years ago, she had to ask the stewards to change the channel, noting pointedly that her son Ron was affiliated with MSNBC. During the 2004 reelection campaign, presidential advance teams expelled from public events anyone they suspected might not quietly toe the party line. Since then, Bush has rarely appeared before any group, big or small, whose loyalties and questions were not prescreened and preapproved. In the course of a Bush trip to Rhode Island in June, Jarrod Holbrook, a correspondent for WPRI-TV, in Providence, twice dared to call out "Mr. President!" at an airport photo op where no one had told him that questions were off limits. Holbrook, a former Marine originally from Texas, told me he had merely intended to ask how Bush was enjoying his first visit to Rhode Island as president. A member of the White House entourage with an earpiece and security pin immediately yanked Holbrook's press credential off his belt, and disappeared with it into Air Force One. In the end, insularity becomes inertial, feeding on itself to create ever more isolation.

THE GREAT DESERTION

The isolating nature of the White House is at its most extreme in a second term. Of all the presidents lucky enough, or cursed enough, to win a second term, probably none would claim that the second time around was better. Sometimes the falloff has been pronounced. Woodrow Wilson won reelection in 1916 on the platform that "he kept us out of war," but the United States entered World War I anyway, and Wilson left office humiliated by the failure of America to join the League of Nations and brutally crippled by a stroke. Dwight D. Eisenhower's first-term achievement in ending the Korean War and presiding over a booming consumer economy faded in anxiety about Sputnik abroad, civil rights at home, and his own multiplying medical problems. Richard Nixon's travails with Watergate speak for themselves, as do Ronald

Reagan's with the Iran-contra scandal and Bill Clinton's with the Lewinsky affair and impeachment.

By any measure, the failure of George Bush's second term has been spectacular. Winning reelection in 2004, he bragged in a post-victory news conference that he had accumulated a surpassing quantity of political capital and now intended to spend it. The political capital has been squandered. Bush's grand plan to overhaul Social Security by creating private investment accounts never got off the ground. His effort to reform immigration law resulted in bitter denunciations by conservatives in his own party and a humiliating defeat in Congress. His pathetic response to Hurricane Katrina exploded any claim he might make, as the first president in history with a business degree, to managerial competence. Ever since the Democrats took control of Congress in the midterm elections, the Administration has faced slow death by subpoena on a dozen fronts. Hanging over everything has been the debacle of Iraq, a failure acknowledged everywhere in Washington except the Oval Office. The recognition of failure is so pervasive that when the president went looking for a new "czar" to oversee the war effort, he ended up with a man, Lieutenant General Douglas Lute, who had actually opposed the president's policy of "surging" more American troops into Baghdad.

The paradox of second terms—of second terms in general, and of this one most acutely—is that just when a president most needs an A Team of trusted, experienced aides around him, willing to puncture wishful thinking, he is all too apt to be surrounded by an F Troop of third- and fourth-tier appointees who have been brought in as neophytes or who had simply hung around long enough to move up the ladder.

Bush's first White House domestic-policy adviser was the capable Margaret Spellings. That job was later given to Claude Allen, who resigned in the shadow of criminal charges involving a department-store refund scam, and it is now held by Karl Zinsmeister, a stern but erratic ideologue imported from the world of right-wing think tanks. If Bush's first-term surgeon general, Dr. Richard Carmona, did not inspire confidence with his recent admission that Administration officials muzzled him on hot-button issues like the morning-after pill, then what is the country to make of Bush's current nominee for the job, Dr. James W. Holsinger Jr., who helped found a church that ministers to people who no longer wish to be gay or lesbian? How about Michael Baroody, a senior lobbyist at the National Association of Manufacturers, who was forced to withdraw as Bush's nominee to head the Consumer Product Safety Commission last spring after it came out that the association was preparing to give him a $150,000 send-off payment? (As CPSC director, he would be regulating products made by its members.) Or Henrietta Holsman Fore, nominated by Bush to replace Randall Tobias, deputy secretary of state for foreign assistance, after Tobias was forced to resign in an escort scandal? It turned out that Fore once told a college audience that she had tried to retain black employees when she was president of a small wire-products company near Los Angeles but that they preferred selling drugs; that Hispanics were lazy; and that Asians, while productive, favored professional or management jobs. (Her nomination is pending in the Senate Foreign Relations Committee.) You can multiply such examples by several score. These may not be officials at the apex of power, but the functioning of any presidency depends on people at this level, and the steady degradation of their ranks is corrosive.

—◂— • —▸—

The desertions from Bush's innermost circle have been, if anything, more pronounced. By the end of Franklin D. Roosevelt's tenure in the White House, some loyalists lamented that the aides most able to save him from trouble, or at least from himself—people such as his political adviser, Louis Howe; his secretary, Missy LeHand; and his all-purpose confidant, Harry Hopkins—were all gone from the scene. The same is true for Bush: absent now are most of the aides who knew him best, served him longest, and could give it to him straightest—people such as his old friend and former commerce secretary, Don Evans; his counselor Karen Hughes; and his longest-serving aide, Dan Bartlett. Unlike his father, who had in men such as James Baker and Brent Scowcroft genuine peers whose unvarnished advice he trusted totally, George W. Bush has never had advisers whom he regarded as true equals, so the loss of those few who came close is a calamity.

By all accounts Bush's chief of staff, Joshua Bolten, who took the job last year and freshened up the White House operation with a new press secretary and other changes, is a skilled Washington player, unafraid to give Bush bad news or challenge prevailing thinking. But, as a range of Republican insiders told me, Bolten was no match for Karl Rove. Variously nicknamed "Boy Genius" and "Turd Blossom" by Bush, Rove remained the president's chief political strategist and the dominant internal White House force (read: schoolyard bully), despite having had his wings clipped and his policy portfolio lightened by Bolten—and despite having seen his hopes for a permanent Republican majority repudiated last fall. Rove was able to interpret Bush's moods and thinking better than anyone, which gave him extraordinary power. But his effectiveness was ultimately diminished by the cloud of controversy that surrounded him, and one White House veteran told me that Republican candidates around the country had begun to shun his advice. To the surprise of many, Rove announced his resignation in August, his voice cracking in an emotional news conference with Bush. The blossom may be off the turd, but the bunker Rove helped Bush build remains very much in place.

Karen Hughes, one of the most prominent among the former Bush aides, and well known for being an effective counterforce to Rove's partisan machismo, was the first to leave the White House inner circle (in 2002, to spend more time with her family), though she remained plugged in enough to be the one to tell Bush that, whatever he thought, he *did* look defensive and impatient in his first 2004 debate against John Kerry. Matthew Dowd not only left the fold but went above it: in a front-page interview with the *New York Times* last spring, Dowd detailed chapter and verse of his disappointment with the president's policies. Nicolle Devenish Wallace, a canny, candid communications aide who once worked for Jeb Bush, was a mainstay of the reelection campaign and actually seemed to enjoy the company of journalists; she left the White House last year out of frustration with Rove's iron rule, his refusal to brook criticism, and his tendency to mock and humiliate anybody who disagreed with him.

Even more striking was the departure of counselor Dan Bartlett, the man sometimes described as the son Bush never had. Though Bartlett, who had worked for Bush since 1993, always kept a discreet and loyally low profile, he was understood to have been willing to tell the president unpleasant truths. It was Bartlett who assembled a compilation reel of post-Katrina news coverage in a last-ditch effort to make Bush understand what everyone else in America knew: that the president had a crisis on his hands. Bartlett announced his resignation in June, on his 36th birthday, looking at least half again that age, and told reporters that the birth of his third son, in January, meant it was past time for a change. Bush issued a statement praising Bartlett as a "true counselor." But there was, all the same, something grudging in Bush's body language and a poignant trace of abandonment in Bartlett's departure, which came a full year after Bolten had asked senior aides either to leave immediately or pledge to stay the remainder of Bush's term.

◄◄ • ►►

So most of the grown-ups are gone. In the end, Bush is left tethered to the most bunkered subordinate of all, Dick Cheney, who, according to the *Washington Post,* squirrels away even the most routine office documents in "man-sized Mosler safes" and who reaches down into the tiniest capillaries of the federal bureaucracy to assert his will. Bush and Cheney have always presented Cheney's lack of presidential ambition as an asset, one that has allowed Cheney to serve the president with unquestioned loyalty and singular effectiveness. The truth is precisely the opposite. As the 2008 election approaches, it is obvious that Cheney's willful political tone-deafness has become one of Bush's biggest liabilities. A vice president with his eye on the prize would operate with more astuteness and delicacy, if only for the sake of his own objectives. And a president determined to ensure his vice president's prospects could never afford to be as stubborn, as seemingly oblivious to the physics of electoral reality, as Bush has chosen to be. Despite reports of supposedly diminished influence, and of occasional losses to Defense and State on policy questions, Cheney remains the most powerful vice president in history—all the more powerful for the total privacy of his relationship with the president. One Bush-administration veteran had this to say by way of summary: "The guy scares the crap out of me."

DELUDER IN CHIEF

At a formal White House dinner last spring, President Bush made friendly small talk about one of the White House's latest technological marvels: the secure digital video-conferencing system, through which Bush can consult with far-flung aides or with world leaders such as Iraqi prime minister Nuri Kamal al-Maliki at any hour of the day or night. The picture and sound quality are so lifelike, Bush told those around him, "I can see Maliki quake when I chew him out!"

The reality of Bush's isolation in the bunker is that the reverse happens to him only rarely. Communication is a one-way street; Bush himself never gets a talking-to. "When people go in to see him now to discuss Iraq," a longtime Washington Republican who served both Ford and Reagan told me, "he has this kind of Churchillian riff that he goes into. But he doesn't really talk about it. He will *receive* people. But that doesn't mean he *hears* people."

When he was Ronald Reagan's White House political director, Ed Rollins used to arrange occasional, informal focus groups with ordinary people—truckdrivers, nurses—whose anecdotal histories were Reagan's lifeblood. Rollins sees no equivalent effort in Bush's White House. In fact, he told me, he has heard from well-known people who were brought to the White House to present their views on policy questions and instead got a piece of Bush's mind. One businessman from New York was asked to the White House to offer his views on stem-cell research—"a major C.E.O., a hospital board chairman," Rollins recalls. The man told Rollins that, after he spoke up, Bush "put his finger in my chest" in angry disagreement.

One longtime former Republican official, who held senior posts in both the first and second Bush administrations, was bluntest of all. "My question is," this former official told me, "does he expose himself to people who respectfully disagree, or thoughtfully disagree, or may have a legitimate suggestion? Not a lot, no. I think some of us are just born with a really, really active curiosity. If you're on a farm, you ask, 'How does this irrigation system work?' I think he has a very narrow curiosity. He's polite. He was raised to be polite. But you just never sense a deep curiosity. His interests are exercise and chopping wood."

⤙⤙ • ⤚⤚

At the height of the Civil War, Abraham Lincoln sought convivial company wherever he could find it. A couple of nights a week he might head to the home of his sophisticated secretary of state, William H. Seward, for talk, companionship, a change of scene. As noted, in the first six months of this year, excluding the obligatory press dinners (which he only suffers) and foreign-summit dinners (ditto), Bush left the White House to socialize only three times. According to the CBS correspondent Mark Knoller, who keeps a fastidious record of such things, Bush went out for an early Sunday-night dinner in March at the home of Karl Rove; in June, he dined at the homes of Clay Johnson, an old Yale friend who is now the deputy director of the Office of Management and Budget, and of James Langdon Jr., a lawyer and major Bush fund-raiser who headed the president's foreign-intelligence advisory board. In all three instances Bush was back at the White House by around his usual bedtime of 9:30 P.M.

By comparison, Laura Bush is a good deal more gregarious, dining out with girlfriends, attending plays and concerts at the Kennedy Center, making the occasional getaway to New York. But she keeps her own counsel, and whatever she does—or doesn't—tell her husband remains almost entirely a matter of conjecture. On the day after last fall's Republican midterm-election defeat, while the president was holding a glum news conference at the White House, Laura Bush was celebrating her sixtieth birthday with 25 friends at a lunch at the elegant Inn at Little Washington, in the Virginia countryside.

"One of the things that has been a failure of this presidency is a lack of a 'social presidency,'" Matthew Dowd says. "To me, it's one of the greatest advantages a president can have, building relationships with the opposite party, not at the time when you need their votes but in the course of everyday life, inviting people out to have dinner at Camp David, having them over to the White House. There's basically been none of that. We wear it as a badge of honor that we don't have state dinners. We think it's a good thing [that] when we go into a country, we go in there as quickly as possible. A lot of people around him think that's neat. 'He stayed on schedule; he was only here an hour and a half.' When we've needed allies, at home and abroad, we haven't had them."

Bunkers, by their nature, reinforce the tics, the traits, the tendencies of their occupants. Bush's bunker has reinforced his certitude, his self-confidence, his eerie calm, his conviction that his course is right. A few months ago a visitor inquired sympathetically about the burdens of office, and Bush would have none of it: "It's the best job in the world," he said. Under the circumstances, the effect is to make Bush look . . . well, odd. Peggy Noonan, the former speechwriter who found for the president's father some of the most effective words he ever uttered, and who has generally been a loyal supporter of the son, recently wrote that she saw Bush's relentless cheeriness in the face of bad news as "disorienting, and strange."

◄◄ • ►►

It is a staple of bunker tales: The bizarrely optimistic leader, eyes glassy with resolve. The decider. The deluder in chief. Over the last year Josh Bolten and Dan Bartlett have gone out of their way to help Bush understand and overcome the apparent disconnect. At military bases around the country, and in hotel function rooms, and occasionally in the Oval Office, he meets privately with families of troops killed in Iraq, even some who are bitterly critical of him to his face, aides say. Bolten, Bartlett, and others have invited writers and historians, by no means all of them Bush supporters, to stop in for lunch or informal discussions. These visitors tend to come away with an impression similar to Peggy Noonan's. The historian Alistair Horne told the BBC after an hour-long meeting with the president, "He looked like he'd come off a cruise in the Caribbean and seemed to have none of the worries" one might have anticipated. Irwin Stelzer, a scholar at the Hudson Institute, a right-leaning think tank in Washington, and a writer for the conservative *Weekly Standard,* was part of a small group invited to lunch with Bush last spring. He was struck, he told me, by "the kind of calm confidence that the president exhibited. I expected to see somebody under severe pressure. None of that is going on. This is a guy who's made his decisions. He seems comfortable in them. I or someone else asked him, 'How are you reacting to the pressure?' and he said, 'I just don't feel any.' He said, for instance, that 'God tells us there's good and evil, but can't tell me to put troops in Iraq; that's for me to figure out within the context of good and evil.' I don't think he has any doubt in his mind that he's made the right choice. On the other hand, he has at least enough doubts that he wants to hear other views."

A recent White House dinner guest, not a political supporter of the president's, recalled that Bush seemed to take particular comfort from Lincoln's situation in the summer of 1864, before General William Tecumseh Sherman had taken Atlanta, when some fellow Republicans were warning that Lincoln could never be reelected if he did not abandon his insistence on emancipation. Historians might well debate the appropriateness of the analogy, but the power of such examples seems palpable for Bush.

In a telephone conversation last summer, a few weeks after he left the White House, Dan Bartlett told me that "the grossest misimpression" about Bush is that he doesn't understand the depth of opposition to his policies and the intensity of public feeling on the war, and that he is somehow unwilling to hear bad news. "The irony is, for the most part that's all he gets," Bartlett says. "From the start of the day to the end of the day, it's 80–20. When things get to the president, it's usually because it's bad news. He gets a morning report that's on his desk every morning with casualty reports. And another in the middle of the day. And another before he goes to bed. The notion that everybody tiptoes around the crux of issues or controversies is patently false."

What Bush chooses to say publicly, or even privately, is another matter entirely. "My sense is that if he expressed public doubt it would crumble like a house of cards, what public support he has left," Bartlett says. "What kind of message is that? In his mind, he's just one of those people who, once he makes his mind up, he's not going to be one who's second-guessing himself." Another former senior Bush aide made the same point this way: "I don't ever get a panicked call from anybody in the White House. They don't call and say, 'Oh, my God, I need a reality check.' I think they have an extraordinary awareness of how troubled some people are by their decisions, but they work for the one person who's got his eye on how history will judge him."

Doris Kearns Goodwin, the historian who began her writing career helping Lyndon Johnson with his memoirs and went on to write in-depth accounts of the wartime presidencies of Abraham Lincoln and F.D.R., has seen this trait first-hand. In *Lyndon Johnson and the American Dream,* she wrote that the lower Johnson's popularity fell, the more he proclaimed confidence in the rightness of his decisions on Vietnam. "He had committed everything he had to Vietnam," she writes. "Regardless of all evidence, he simply had to be right. To think otherwise, to entertain even the slightest doubt, was to open himself to the pain of reliving old decisions, options and possibilities long since discarded. 'No, no, no!' Johnson shouted at me one afternoon as I tried to discuss earlier opportunities for peace. 'I will not let you take me backward in time on Vietnam. Fifty thousand American boys are dead. Nothing we say can change that fact. Your idea that I could have chosen otherwise rests upon complete ignorance. For if I had chosen otherwise, I would have been responsible for starting World War III.'"

Dowd observes that when presidents adopt such thinking they really get in trouble. "To me, it feels a lot like what they call in business 'the fallacy of sunk costs.' You've spent 75 or 80 percent of your money and you realize you've put the building in the wrong place. So you end up putting 20 percent more into a failure because you're afraid to say you misspent the 80 percent." He adds: "I know from the president and Karl that they view an admission of a mistake as a sign of weakness. Interestingly enough, the American public views that as a sign of strength. People ask me what advice I'd give a politician. I say I'd have them make a mistake every week and apologize."

The aide to both Bushes who described the current president's lack of curiosity said that it extends to the most important single act of his presidency, the decision to go to war in Iraq. "I don't think we will ever, ever really have George Bush level and say why he did this," the aide says. "I think he has drunk his Kool-Aid and that's all there is to it."

THE LAST BATTLE

"What it all comes down to," a president once said, "is the man at the desk." The words are those of the first President Bush, who memorably declared in his 1988 campaign, "I am that man." His son won the second term that the father was denied, and seemed guaranteed to have a consequential presidency, one that would count in the history books. It will count in the history books, all right. So on that January morning 15 months from now, when he sits down to compose his thoughts, what will George W. Bush, the youthful failure who succeeded beyond his family's wildest imaginings, only to fail again, say to his successor? Will he write of the burdens of the job? Will he offer guidance about the pitfalls? Will he make a joke? Will he praise the virtues of perseverance? After all, the *Resolute* itself was stuck in the Arctic ice for two full winters, until finally drifting free.

On the surface, Bush remains as confident, as cocky, as ever. At the White House press Christmas party last year, my wife, Dee Dee Myers, a former Clinton White House press secretary, to whom Bush has been unfailingly gracious over the years, shook his hand and asked how he was. "I like a challenge!" he replied, his face crinkling into a grin. Photographs of the president may tell a different story: all the compulsive exercise in the world, all the discipline, all the public projection of confidence and bonhomie, cannot keep him from looking gray and tired and haggard—and, at last, every second of his 61 years. Even so, he is not an old man. If the actuarial tables hold true, it will be his lot to see his legacy bitterly debated for many years. He professes to be at peace with the prospect.

"I guess I'm like any other political figure," he said during a rambling news conference last July, after being asked by Edwin Chen of Bloomberg News how he could hope to prosecute the war in Iraq without public support. "Everybody wants to be loved. Just sometimes the decisions you make, and the consequences, don't enable you to be loved. And so when it's all said and done, Ed, if you ever come down to visit the old, tired me down there in Crawford, I will be able to say I looked in the mirror and made decisions based upon principle, not based upon politics. And that's important to me."

⤙ • ⤚

Never mind, for the moment, that Bush's administration has been as political as any other. By some measures it has been the most politically motivated presidency of modern times, with policy on issues from science to taxes dictated by considerations of partisan advantage and ideological dogma. Bush's comment is interesting for what it says about his self-image and about how he parses his own fate. This is another staple of mythic bunker tales: the fearless leader, abandoned by the multitudes, facing the end with a remnant of his loyal band. Like a character in one of the "Left Behind" novels, Bush is waiting for the Rapture, confident that he will be saved, validated, the unpleasant earthly realities of the moment be damned. Delayed vindication may even be more satisfying, something to relish. A few months ago, when a very senior Reagan-administration official sought to counsel Bush that it was not too late to retool his presidency, reminding him that Ronald Reagan recovered from the disaster of Iran-contra to reach a 68 percent job-approval rating on his last day in office, Bush cut the official off: No, he insisted, Reagan's ratings rebounded only later, after he had left office. The official happened to be absolutely correct, but no amount of argument could dislodge Bush from his view. His eyes were on his presidential afterlife.

Ken Adelman, the Reagan-era arms-control negotiator and longtime hawk, whose distress at Bush's mishandling of the Iraq war is so intense that it has poisoned his once close friendship with Dick Cheney, is a Shakespeare buff who makes good money by lecturing on what Shakespeare can teach modern managers. I asked him if Bush reminds him of any character in Shakespeare. "Richard II," he answered instantly, explaining that Richard was surrounded by sycophantic advisers—Bushy, Bagot, and Green—and that he alienated his people with a wasteful war against Ireland, and lost his throne to Henry IV.

"Not all the water in the rough, rude sea can wash the balm off from an anointed king," Richard proclaims in defiance at one point, sounding very much like the Decider we know so well. "The breath of worldly men cannot depose the deputy elected by the Lord." But a few short passages later, Richard is reduced to acknowledging, "You have but mistook me all this while: I live with bread like you, feel want, taste grief, need friends—subjected thus, How can you say to me, I am a king?"

Every president, every person—even one as hunkered and blinkered and bunkered as George Bush—feels want, tastes grief, needs friends. Bush is hardly immune to emotion. Like all the men in his family, he is known to cry easily, if not comfortably or publicly. He has built the political and emotional prison of his bunker, policy by policy and partisan stone by partisan stone. Like all presidents, he alone holds the key. Don't count on him to turn it on January 20, 2009, when he puts down his burdens and picks up his pen.

18

FEAST OF THE WINGNUTS: HOW ECONOMIC CRACKPOTS DEVOURED AMERICAN POLITICS

JONATHAN CHAIT

The New Republic   September 10, 2007

The central tenet of the Bush administration's economic policy—the idea that the best way to boost economic growth is by cutting taxes, particularly for investment income and for the nation's wealthiest individuals—represents the culmination of "supply-side economics," a theory that's been kicking around since the days when Gerald Ford was in the White House. But as Jonathan Chait points out in his biting New Republic *essay, the supply-side concept has never been accepted by mainstream economists, and it remains not only unproven but highly suspect. That hasn't stopped a host of conservative politicians from embracing it, however.*

American politics has been hijacked by a tiny coterie of right-wing economic extremists, some of them ideological zealots, others merely greedy, a few of them possibly insane. The scope of their triumph is breathtaking. Over the course of the last three decades, they have moved from the right-wing fringe to the commanding heights of the national agenda. Notions that would have been laughed at a generation ago—that cutting taxes for the very rich is the best response to any and every economic circumstance or that it is perfectly appropriate to turn the most rapacious and self-interested elements of the business lobby into essentially an arm of the federal government—are now so pervasive, they barely attract any notice.

The result has been a slow-motion disaster. Income inequality has approached levels normally associated with Third World oligarchies, not healthy Western democracies. The federal government has grown so encrusted with business lobbyists that it can no longer meet the great public challenges of our time. Not even many conservative voters or intellectuals find the result congenial. Government is no smaller—it is simply more debt-ridden and more beholden to wealthy elites.

It was not always this way. A generation ago, Republican economics was relentlessly sober. Republicans concerned themselves with such ills as deficits, inflation, and excessive spending. They did not care very much about cutting taxes, and (as in the case of such GOP presidents as Herbert Hoover and Gerald Ford) they were quite willing to raise taxes in order to balance the budget. While many of them were wealthy and close to business, the leaders of business themselves had a strong sense of social responsibility that transcended their class interests. By temperament, such men were cautious rather than utopian.

Over the last three decades, however, such Republicans have passed almost completely from the scene, at least in Washington, to be replaced by, essentially, a cult.

All sects have their founding myths, many of them involving circumstances quite mundane. The cult in question generally traces its political origins to a meeting in Washington in late 1974 between Arthur Laffer, an economist; Jude Wanniski, an editorial page writer for the *Wall Street Journal;* and Dick Cheney, then deputy assistant to President Ford. Wanniski, an eccentric and highly excitable man, had until the previous few years no training in economics whatsoever, but he had taken Laffer's tutelage.

His choice of mentor was certainly unconventional. Laffer had been on the economics faculty at the University of Chicago since 1967. In 1970, his mentor, George Shultz, brought him to Washington to serve as a staffer in the Office of Management and Budget. Laffer quickly suffered a bout with infamy when he made a wildly unconventional calculation about the size of the 1971 Gross National Product, which was far more optimistic than estimates elsewhere. When it was discovered that Laffer had used just four indicators to arrive at his figure—most economists used hundreds if not thousands of inputs—he became a Washington laughingstock. Indeed, he turned out to be horribly wrong. Laffer left the government in disgrace and faced the scorn of his former academic colleagues yet stayed in touch with Wanniski, whom he had met in Washington, and continued to tutor him in economics.

Starting in 1972, Wanniski came to believe that Laffer had developed a blinding new insight that turned established economic wisdom on its head. Wanniski and Laffer believed it was possible to simultaneously expand the economy and tamp down inflation by cutting taxes, especially the high tax rates faced by upper-income earners. Respectable economists—not least among them conservative ones—considered this laughable. Wanniski, though, was ever more certain of its truth. He promoted this radical new doctrine through his perch on the *Wall Street Journal* editorial page and in a major article for *The Public Interest,* a journal published by the neoconservative godfather Irving Kristol. Yet

Wanniski's new doctrine, later to be called supply-side economics, had failed to win much of a following beyond a tiny circle of adherents.

That fateful night, Wanniski and Laffer were laboring with little success to explain the new theory to Cheney. Laffer pulled out a cocktail napkin and drew a parabola-shaped curve on it. The premise of the curve was simple. If the government sets a tax rate of zero, it will receive no revenue. And, if the government sets a tax rate of 100 percent, the government will also receive zero tax revenue, since nobody will have any reason to earn any income. Between these two points—zero taxes and zero revenue, 100 percent taxes and zero revenue—Laffer's curve drew an arc. The arc suggested that at higher levels of taxation, reducing the tax rate would produce more revenue for the government.

At that moment, there were a few points that Cheney might have made in response. First, he could have noted that the Laffer Curve was not, strictly speaking, correct. Yes, a zero tax rate would obviously produce zero revenue, but the assumption that a 100-percent tax rate would also produce zero revenue was, just as obviously, false. Surely Cheney was familiar with communist states such as the Soviet Union, with its 100 percent tax rate. The Soviet revenue scheme may not have represented the cutting edge in economic efficiency, but it nonetheless managed to collect enough revenue to maintain an enormous military, enslave Eastern Europe, fund ambitious projects such as Sputnik, and so on. Second, Cheney could have pointed out that, even if the Laffer Curve was correct in theory, there was no evidence that the U.S. income tax was on the downward slope of the curve—that is, that rates were then high enough that tax cuts would produce higher revenue.

But Cheney did not say either of these things. Perhaps, in retrospect, this was due to something deep in Cheney's character that makes him unusually susceptible to theories or purported data that confirm his own ideological predilections. (You can almost picture Donald Rumsfeld, years later, scrawling a diagram for Cheney on a cocktail napkin showing that only a small number of troops would be needed to occupy Iraq.) In any event, Cheney apparently found the Laffer Curve a revelation, for it presented in a simple, easily digestible form the messianic power of tax cuts.

◄- • -►

The significance of the evening was not the conversion of Cheney but the creation of a powerful symbol that could spread the word of supply-side economics. If you try to discuss economic theory with most politicians, their eyes will glaze over. But the Curve explained it all. There in that sloping parabola was the magical promise of that elusive politician's nirvana, a cost-free path to prosperity: lower taxes, higher revenues. It was beautiful, irresistible.

With astonishing speed, the message of the Laffer Curve spread through the ranks of conservatives and Republicans. Wanniski evangelized tirelessly on behalf of this new doctrine, both on the *Journal*'s editorial pages and in person. As an example of the latter, one day in 1976, he wandered by the office of a young representative named Jack Kemp. He asked to talk to Kemp for 15 minutes, but he wound up expounding on the supply-side gospel to the former NFL quarterback for the rest of the day, through dinner, and late into the night. "He took to it like a blotter," Wanniski later recalled. "I was exhausted and ecstatic. I had finally found an elected representative of the people who was as fanatical as I was."

Adherents of supply-side economics tend to describe the spread of their creed in quasi-religious terms. Irving Kristol subsequently wrote in a memoir, "It was Jude [Wanniski] who introduced me to Jack Kemp, a young congressman and a recent convert. It was Jack Kemp who, almost single-handed, converted Ronald Reagan to supply-side economics." The theological language is fitting because supply-side economics is not merely an economic program. It's a totalistic ideology. The core principle is that economic performance hinges almost entirely on how much incentive investors and entrepreneurs have to attain more wealth, and this incentive in turn hinges almost entirely on their tax rate. Therefore, cutting taxes—especially those of the rich, who carry out the decisive entrepreneurial role in the economy—is always a good idea.

But what, you may ask, about deficits, the old Republican bugaboo? Supply-siders argue either that tax cuts will produce enough growth to wipe out deficits or that deficits simply don't matter. When Reagan first adopted supply-side economics, even many Republicans considered it lunacy. ("Voodoo economics," George H.W. Bush famously called it.) Today, though, the core beliefs of the supply-siders are not even subject to question among Republicans. Every major conservative opinion outlet promotes supply-side economics. Since Bush's heresy of acceding to a small tax hike in 1990, deviation from the supply-side creed has become unthinkable for any Republican with national aspirations.

The full capitulation of the old fiscal conservatives was probably best exemplified by Bob Dole, the crusty old Kansan once thought synonymous with the traditional Midwestern conservatism of the GOP. Early on, Dole had openly scorned the supply-siders. "People who advocate only cutting taxes live in a dream world," he said in 1982. "We Republicans have been around awhile. We don't have to march in lockstep with the supply-siders." By the time he had risen high enough in the party to gain its presidential nomination, Dole had no choice but to embrace the Laffer Curve. He chose Jack Kemp, an original supply-side evangelist, as his running mate and made a 15 percent tax cut the centerpiece of his campaign.

George W. Bush's fidelity to tax-cutting runs even deeper. He took as his chief economic adviser Larry Lindsey, a fervent supply-sider whose book, *The Growth Experiment,* defended Reagan's tax cuts. He picked as his running mate yet another original supply-sider in Cheney, who summed up the new consensus by declaring (according to the former treasury secretary, Paul O'Neill), "Reagan proved deficits don't matter." Bush has poured every ounce of his political capital into cutting taxes, having signed four tax cuts during his administration; when fully phased in, they will reduce federal revenues by about $400 billion a year. Bush and his staff repeatedly tout tax cuts as an all-purpose cure. Bush can endorse even the most radical supply-side claims—"the deficit would have been bigger without the tax-relief package," he asserts regularly—without raising eyebrows. So deeply entrenched is the devotion to supply-side theory that, even in the face of large deficits and a protracted war, not a single Republican of any standing has dared broach the possibility of rolling back some of Bush's tax cuts. As Robert Bartley, the *Wall Street Journal*'s editorial page editor, boasted, "Economists still ridicule the Laffer Curve, but policymakers pay it careful heed."

Like most crank doctrines, supply-side economics has at its core a central insight that does have a ring of plausibility. The government can't simply raise tax rates as high as it wants without some adverse consequences. And there have been periods in American history when, nearly any contemporary economist would agree, top tax rates were too high, such as the several decades after World War II. And there are justifiable conservative arguments to be made on behalf of reducing tax rates and government spending. But what sets the supply-siders apart from sensible economists is their sheer monomania. You could plausibly argue that, say, Reagan's tax cuts contributed around the margins to the economic growth of the 1980s. But the supply-siders believe that, if it were not for Reagan's tax cuts, the economic malaise of the late '70s would have continued indefinitely. They believe that economic history is a function of tax rates—they insisted that Bill Clinton's upper-bracket tax hike *must* cause a recession (whoops), and they believe that the present economy is a boom not merely enhanced but brought about by the Bush tax cuts.

It doesn't take a great deal of expertise to see how implausible this sort of analysis is. All you need is a cursory bit of history. From 1947 to 1973, the U.S. economy grew at a rate of nearly 4 percent a year—a massive boom, fueling rapid growth in living standards across the board. During most of that period, from 1947 until 1964, the highest tax rate hovered around 91 percent. For the rest of the time, it was still a hefty 70 percent. Yet the economy flourished anyway. None of this is to say that those high tax rates *caused* the postwar boom. On the contrary, the economy probably expanded despite, rather than because of, those high rates. Almost no contemporary economist would endorse jacking up rates that high again. But the point is that, whatever negative effect such high tax rates have, it's relatively minor. Which necessarily means that whatever effects today's tax rates have, they're even *more* minor.

This can be seen with some very simple arithmetic. As just noted, Truman, Eisenhower, and Kennedy taxpayers in the top bracket had to pay a 91 percent rate. That meant that, if they were contemplating, say, a new investment, they would be able to keep just nine cents of every dollar they earned, a stiff disincentive. When that rate dropped down to 70 percent, our top earner could now keep 30 cents of every new dollar. That more than tripled the profitability of any new dollar—a 233 percent increase, to be exact. That's a hefty incentive boost. In 1981, the top tax rate was cut again to 50 percent. The profit on every new dollar therefore rose from 30 to 50 cents, a 67 percent increase. In 1986, the top rate dropped again, from 50 to 28 percent. The profit on every dollar rose from 50 to 72 cents, a 44 percent increase. Note that the marginal improvement of every new tax cut is less than that of the previous one. But we're still talking about large numbers. Increasing the profitability of a new investment even by 44 percent is nothing to sneeze at.

But then George Bush raised the top rate to 31 percent in 1990. This meant that, instead of taking home 72 cents on every new dollar earned, those in the top bracket had to settle for 69 cents. That's a drop of about 4 percent—peanuts, compared to the scale of previous changes. Yet supply-siders reacted hysterically. *National Review,* to offer one example, noted fearfully that, in the wake of this small tax hike, the dollar had fallen against the yen and the German mark. "It seems," its editors concluded, "that capital is flowing out of the United States to nations where 'from each according to his ability, to each according to his need' has lost its allure."

Here is where a bit of historical perspective helps. If such a piddling tax increase could really wreck such havoc on the economy, how is it possible that the economy grew so rapidly with top tax rates of 70 and 91 percent? The answer is, it's not. It's not even close to possible. All this is to say that the supply-siders have taken the germ of a decent point—that marginal tax rates matter—and stretched it, beyond all plausibility, into a monocausal explanation of the world.

⤙ • ⤚

Aside from popular articles in places like the *Journal*'s editorial page, two classic tomes defined the tenets of supply-side economics: Wanniski's *The Way the World Works* and George Gilder's 1981 manifesto, *Wealth and Poverty.* Both have had enormous influence, and both capture the feverish grandiosity that is the hallmark of the Laffer Curve acolytes. Here is what makes the rise of supply-side ideology even more baffling. One might expect that a radical ideology that successfully passed itself off as a sophisticated new doctrine would at least have the benefit of smooth, reassuring, intellectual front men, men whose very bearing could attest to the new doctrine's eminent good sense and mainstream bona fides. Yet, if you look at its two most eminent authors, good sense is not the impression you get. Let me put this delicately. No, on second thought, let me put it straightforwardly: They are deranged.

Gilder was not an economist when he wrote *Wealth and Poverty.* Until then, he was known primarily for having written a pair of anti-feminist tracts, and his notoriety derived mainly from his penchant for making comments such as "There is no such thing as a reasonably intelligent feminist." *Wealth and Poverty,* though, launched him as an eminent defender of supply-side economics just as adherents of the new creed had been catapulted into power. Gilder articulated the new philosophy of the Reagan era in admirably straightforward fashion. "To help the poor and middle classes," he wrote, "one must cut the taxes of the rich."

In reflecting the new prestige Republicans wished to see afforded the rich, Gilder defended capitalists as not merely necessary or even heroic but altruistic. "Like gifts, capitalist investments are made without a predetermined return," he wrote. In fact, while capitalists may not be sure of their exact return, they do expect to make more than they put in, which makes an investment unlike a gift in a fairly crucial way. Yet there was enough of an audience for such sentiments that Gilder's book sold more than a million copies. President Reagan handed the book to friends, and advisers such as David Stockman hailed its "Promethean" insight. *Wealth and Poverty,* reported the *New York Times,* "has been embraced by Washington with a warmth not seen since the Kennedys adopted John Kenneth Galbraith."

From the beginning, Gilder betrayed signs of erratic thought, and not merely in his misogyny. In a 1981 interview with the *Washington Post,* he declared, "ESP is important to me. I learned that it absolutely exists. A roommate and I were sharing an apartment, and another man in the building was a psychic. He taught me how to do it." In the mid-'80s, Gilder's career took an abrupt turn. He became fascinated with microprocessors and took time off to learn the physics of the new technology. This led him, by the mid-'90s, to stake out a position as the most wild-eyed of the technology utopians who flourished during that period, and he ended up publishing a newsletter that offered stock tips. Some of his pronouncements were obviously crazy even at the time. These would include his advice to short Microsoft stock in 1997, his claim that Global Crossing (now bankrupt) "will change the world economy," and general techno-giddiness, such as his claim that, because of online learning, within five years "the most deprived ghetto child in the most benighted project will gain educational opportunities exceeding those of today's suburban preppy."

In the fevered stock bubble of the 1990s, though, some of Gilder's prognostications seemed to pan out, at least for a while, and, at its peak, his newsletter attracted a subscription base worth $20 million, making him fabulously rich. In 2000, Gilder used some of his lucre to purchase *The American Spectator,* a monthly conservative magazine best known for investigating the details of President Clinton's personal indiscretions, both real and imagined. Gilder turned the *Spectator* into a shrine to Gilderism, a fusion of supply-side utopianism and techno-utopianism. He installed his cousin as editor and ran both a lengthy excerpt as well as a favorable review of his own book.

The crowning touch of Gilder's ownership was a lengthy interview with himself in the June 2001 issue. Among other musings on display were Gilder's familiar ruminations on feminism: "Christie Whitman is an upper-class American woman . . . almost none of them have any comprehension of the environment. Almost all of them are averse to science and technology and baffled by it." His financial success seemed to have propelled Gilder to even greater heights of hubris, his Promethean insights greeted by his employees with awed deference:

> TAS: In the late 1970s and early '80s, you led the intellectual debate on sexual issues from the conservative side. In the 1980s your book *Wealth and Poverty* transformed the way people thought about capitalism. And then you wandered off to study transistors. Why did you do that?
>
> Gilder: I thought I had won those debates. Whenever I actively debated anybody, they didn't have any interesting arguments anymore, so I thought I should learn something I didn't know about.

In presenting the interview with their boss, the *Spectator*'s editors promised: "An equally wide-ranging talk with George will be an annual event." Alas, it never recurred. As the tech bubble burst, Gilder and his investors found their wealth spiraling downward. Despite Gilder's frantic reassurances—"Your current qualms will seem insignificant," he promised in late 2000—his subscribers deserted him. In 2002, he confessed to *Wired* magazine that he was broke and had a lien against his home. "Most subscribers came in at the top of the market," Gilder later explained, "So the modal experience of the Gilder Technology Newsletter subscriber was to lose virtually all of his money. That stigma has been very hard to overcome."

Nonetheless, Gilder soldiers on. Today, he champions the theory of intelligent design. Once again, he can see the truth that has eluded all the so-called experts. Who could have foreseen such a tragic downfall? Actually, there was one man visionary enough to presage Gilder's fate: Gilder himself. In *Wealth and Poverty,* one of Gilder's arguments for more sympathetic treatment of the rich held that "the vast majority of America's fortunes are dissipated within two generations. . . . In a partial sense, a rich man resembles a gambler betting against the house." This is a terribly inapt description of the American economy. (It is the rare homeless shelter that caters to descendants of the Rockefeller or Morgan family fortunes.) But it turned out to be a precise description of Gilder's own fortune. Wealth and poverty, indeed.

◄◄ • ►►

As influential as Gilder and his book were, they were not nearly as influential in legitimating supply-side theory as Wanniski or his book. This isn't terribly reassuring, though, because Wanniski (who died in 2005) made Gilder look like the model of sobriety. The literary and intellectual style of *The Way the World Works* is immediately familiar to anybody who has ever sorted submissions at a political magazine. It is the manifesto of the misunderstood autodidact—an essay purporting to have interpreted history in a completely novel and completely correct way, or to have discovered the key to eternal prosperity and world peace, or some equally sweeping claim. *The Way the World Works* fits precisely into this category, except that, rather than being scrawled longhand on sheaves of notebook paper and mass-mailed to journalists, it was underwritten by the American Enterprise Institute, has been published in four editions, and features introductions attesting to its genius from such luminaries as Bartley and the columnist and ubiquitous pundit Robert Novak.

For supply-side evangelists, there is almost nothing that their theory cannot explain. For instance, in his book, Wanniski uses the Laffer Curve as a model for all of human development, beginning with young babies: "Even the infant learns to both act and think on the margin when small changes in behavior result in identifiable price changes." Parents, too, must abide by the Curve:

> The parent who does not understand that there are two tax rates that yield the same revenue is a poor political leader in the family unit, and should not be surprised if the prohibitively taxed infant rebels in one way or another—becoming an incorrigible terror (revolutionary) or withdrawing into himself (the only form of emigration open to a child).

This thought produces a footnote: "The wise ruler will never surround his adversaries with no-nos." Wanniski then runs through a number of historical rulers wise and unwise, concluding with his observation that "Kennedy's determination to box in Cuba, which included plans to assassinate Fidel Castro, left Castro no avenue but the assassination of Kennedy."

Apparently, nothing in human history defies Wanniski's attempts to involve the Laffer Curve. He goes on to write: "When Hitler came to power in 1933, fascinated with Mussolini's syndicalist style, he—like Roosevelt—left tax rates where he found them." Can you see where this is going? Yes: "Although he left the explicit tax rates high, [Germany] did chip away at the domestic and international wedges. The economy expanded, but in so distorted a fashion that it compressed the tension between agriculture and industry into an explosive problem that Hitler sought to solve through *Lebensraum,* or conquest [*sic*]." You, dear reader, may have thought that Nazi ideology led to the invasion of Poland, but, thanks to Wanniski, you can see that the underlying cause turns out to have been high taxes. (It is amazing that Bill Clinton's tax hike did not lead him to invade Canada.)

Republicans did not find these obvious signs of wingnuttery troubling. Indeed, Wanniski's book hastened his astonishingly rapid rise. Five years before he wrote his book, Wanniski knew nothing about economics. Within a few years, he had formulated a new creed and sold it to a series of powerful opinion leaders and politicians. By 1977, the Republican National Committee formally called for an across-the-board tax cut modeled on the one proposed by Wanniski's closest disciple, Kemp. The next year, Congress enacted a capital gains tax cut that he lobbied for in the halls of the Capitol and championed in the *Journal*'s columns.

Two years after the publication of his book, Wanniski found himself advising Ronald Reagan, who ran for president on ideas Wanniski had devised. But, in time, the same qualities that made him such an effective evangelist for supply-side economics—his gregariousness, his naïveté, his absolute faith in his own correctness, and his ability to persuade others of the same—did him in. Wanniski gave an interview in 1980 about the battle for Reagan's mind among his advisers, all but openly saying that the candidate was a creature of his staff. This brought about his quick expulsion from the inner circle. In 1995, fearing that the supply-side agenda was stagnating, Wanniski came up with the idea of persuading Steve Forbes, the millionaire publisher and Laffer Curve devotee, to run for president. After Wanniski lashed out at the Christian Coalition strategist Ralph Reed, though, he became a liability to the campaign he had created and was shut out. The next year, after the GOP nominee Bob Dole named his acolyte Jack Kemp to share his ticket, Wanniski again won a place of influence.

It was around this time that Wanniski's nuttiness began manifesting itself in ways that even conservatives could recognize. Wanniski began meeting with and defending Louis Farrakhan, the head of the Nation of Islam, explaining, "I expressed my belief that Jewish leaders fear he could lead the black electorate away from the Democratic Party and into opposition of support for Israel." And Farrakhan is far from the only unsavory character Wanniski embraced. He likened Slobodan Milosevic to Abraham Lincoln. He met with the lunatic conspiracy theorist and convicted felon Lyndon LaRouche and hired a number of his followers at his economic consulting firm. ("[T]hey're not trained in demand-model economics," he explained to *BusinessWeek* with undeniable logic.) And Wanniski championed Saddam Hussein, even to the point of denying that the late Iraqi dictator had ever used chemical weapons against the Kurds. ("There is no possibility that Saddam gassed his own people," he wrote.)

Such statements, combined with his erratic behavior, eventually made Wanniski an outcast within the GOP. His expulsion from the party's good graces was consecrated, in a sense, by a series of short editorial items in the conservative *Weekly Standard* in the mid-'90s, ridiculing his nutty views on Farrakhan and Iraq. But, while Wanniski himself is remembered as a nut by most conservatives, his primary doctrine has lost none of its influence. The *Standard* continues to publish editorials saying such things as "the supply-side Laffer Curve has worked." So Wanniski is now viewed as a nut on all matters save the very thing that is the font from which all his nuttiness springs. His personal influence has never been lower, but his ideological influence has never been greater. "It is no exaggeration to say that the recent history of the United States would have been far different were it not for Jude Wanniski," wrote Novak. The scary thing is that he's right.

⋖ • ⋗
•

In February 2006, the conservative journal *Policy Review* published an essay that was shockingly heretical, though perhaps unintentionally so. In it, Carles Boix of the University of Chicago argued that there is a link between democracy and economic equality:

> In an unequal society, the majority resents its diminished status. It harbors the expectation of employing elections to drastically overturn its condition. In turn, the wealthy minority fears the outcome that may follow from free elections and the assertion of majority rule. As a result, it resorts to authoritarian institutions to guarantee its social and economic advantage.

Of the many taboos that prevail among conservatives, the one forbidding any serious discussion of inequality is perhaps the strictest. Any forthright examination of this topic will lead one quickly to the realization that American society has been spreading apart rapidly for three decades and that Republican economic policies have without a doubt contributed mightily to this gulf. So conservatives usually ignore the subject of inequality, except perhaps to minimize its scale or importance.

Why, then, did *Policy Review,* which is published by the staunchly conservative Hoover Institution, open its pages to such apostasy? Well, it didn't intend to. Boix's essay (which was brilliant and widely discussed) concerned the inculcation of democracy abroad and did not deal directly with the United States. And the circumstances Boix envisioned—mainly, developing countries attempting a transition to democracy—are different from those in an advanced democracy. Americans, fortunately, do not have to worry about kleptocrats, political violence, and massive vote fraud.

But, while Boix's theory may be less applicable to the United States than it is to the Third World, it is still somewhat true. Indeed, this theory offers an uncannily precise description of what has happened in American politics over the last 30 years. The business lobbyists have turned the Republican Party into a kind of machine dedicated unwaveringly to protecting and expanding the wealth of the very rich. As it has pursued this goal ever more single-mindedly, the right has by necessity grown ever more hostile to majoritarian decision-making for the obvious reason that it's hard to enlist the public behind an agenda designed to benefit a tiny minority. The old ways of conducting politics have broken down in the face of this onslaught. The mores of the old Washington establishment—the assumption of some basic intellectual goodwill on both sides, the focus on character over substance, the belief in compromise—all developed during an era when there were few ideological differences between the parties. The old ways may have done a decent job of safeguarding the national interest when the great moderate consensus prevailed, but they have proven unequal to the challenge of a more ideological time.

All this has happened at the same time as a massive increase in income inequality, which is exactly what Boix's theory would predict. In the same essay, Boix marvels at the fortunes amassed by autocratic ruling elites throughout history:

> Rulers such as the Bourbons, the Tudors, or the Sauds seize an important part of their subjects' assets. For example, at the death of Augustus (14 A.D.), the top 1/10,000 of the Roman Empire's households received 1 percent of all income. In Mughal India around 1600 A.D., the top 1/10,000th received 5 percent of all income.

Presumably, readers looking at these numbers are supposed to gape in astonishment at the sheer inequity of those autocratic regimes. But the numbers are less astonishing when you compare them to those in the contemporary United States, which Boix does not. As of 2004, the top one-ten-thousandth of Americans earned over 3 percent of the national income—a somewhat smaller share than that earned by the Mughal elite but several times higher than that enjoyed by the wealthiest Romans.

Meanwhile, the gap between Americans and Mughals is closing rapidly. Since the late '70s, the share of national income going to the top 1 percent has doubled. The share of the top 0.1 percent has tripled, and the share of the top 0.01 percent has quadrupled. This gulf was widened precisely at the same time that the right, growing ever more plutocratic and suspicious of popular demands, was battering away at the culture of American democracy. Many people have looked at the depredations of the Bush era—the bizarre cult of personality, the anti-intellectual demagoguery, the incessant flouting of norms, the prostrate media—as the product of the president's character, or Karl Rove's machinations. But it is, in the main, the consequence of a cult-like fringe taking control of a political party and using it to wage class warfare on behalf of a tiny minority.

19

THE ECONOMIC CONSEQUENCES OF MR. BUSH

JOSEPH E. STIGLITZ
Vanity Fair   December 2007

In his piece, which provides a sequel of sorts to the preceding selection, Nobel laureate Joseph E. Stiglitz makes the case for why, in his words, "The economic effects of [George W.] Bush's presidency are more insidious than those of [Herbert] Hoover." Stiglitz's list of the Bush administration's bad decisions include massive tax cuts for the wealthiest Americans that have contributed greatly to growing inequality (and done remarkably little to stimulate the economy), misplaced spending priorities (including a lack of investment in areas critical to the nation's future), and spending policies that have led to a massive increase in the national debt. The result as he sees it? A badly hobbled economy that could well haunt the United States for generations to come.

When we look back someday at the catastrophe that was the Bush administration, we will think of many things: the tragedy of the Iraq war, the shame of Guantánamo and Abu Ghraib, the erosion of civil liberties. The damage done to the American economy does not make front-page headlines every day, but the repercussions will be felt beyond the lifetime of anyone reading this page.

I can hear an irritated counterthrust already. The president has not driven the United States into a recession during his almost seven years in office. Unemployment stands at a respectable 4.6 percent. Well, fine. But the other side of the ledger groans with distress: a tax code that has become hideously biased in favor of the rich; a national debt that will probably have grown 70 percent by the time this president leaves Washington; a swelling cascade of mortgage defaults; a record near-$850 billion trade deficit; oil prices that are higher than they have ever been; and a dollar so weak that for an American to buy a cup of coffee in London or Paris—or even the Yukon—becomes a venture in high finance.

And it gets worse. After almost seven years of this president, the United States is less prepared than ever to face the future. We have not been educating enough engineers and scientists, people with the skills we will need to compete with China and India. We have not been investing in the kinds of basic research that made us the technological powerhouse of the late 20th century. And although the president now understands—or so he says—that we must begin to wean ourselves from oil and coal, we have on his watch become more deeply dependent on both.

Up to now, the conventional wisdom has been that Herbert Hoover, whose policies aggravated the Great Depression, is the odds-on claimant for the mantle "worst president" when it comes to stewardship of the American economy. Once Franklin Roosevelt assumed office and reversed Hoover's policies, the country began to recover. The economic effects of Bush's presidency are more insidious than those of Hoover, harder to reverse, and likely to be longer-lasting. There is no threat of America's being displaced from its position as the world's richest economy. But our grandchildren will still be living with, and struggling with, the economic consequences of Mr. Bush.

REMEMBER THE SURPLUS?

The world was a very different place, economically speaking, when George W. Bush took office, in January 2001. During the Roaring '90s, many had believed that the Internet would transform everything. Productivity gains, which had averaged about 1.5 percent a year from the early 1970s through the early '90s, now approached 3 percent. During Bill Clinton's second term, gains in manufacturing productivity sometimes even surpassed 6 percent. The Federal Reserve chairman, Alan Greenspan, spoke of a New Economy marked by continued productivity gains as the Internet buried the old ways of doing business. Others went so far as to predict an end to the business cycle. Greenspan worried aloud about how he'd ever be able to manage monetary policy once the nation's debt was fully paid off.

This tremendous confidence took the Dow Jones index higher and higher. The rich did well, but so did the not-so-rich and even the downright poor. The Clinton years were not an economic Nirvana; as chairman of the president's Council of Economic Advisers during part of this time, I'm all too aware of mistakes and lost opportunities. The global-trade agreements we pushed through were often unfair to developing countries. We should have invested more in infrastructure, tightened regulation of the securities markets, and taken additional steps to promote energy conservation. We fell short because of politics and lack of money—and also, frankly, because special interests sometimes shaped the agenda more than they should have. But these boom years were the first time since Jimmy Carter that the deficit was under control. And they were the first time since the 1970s that incomes at the bottom grew faster than those at the top—a benchmark worth celebrating.

By the time George W. Bush was sworn in, parts of this bright picture had begun to dim. The tech boom was over. The NASDAQ fell 15 percent in the single month of April 2000, and no one knew for sure what effect the collapse of the Internet bubble would have on the real economy. It was a moment ripe for Keynesian economics, a time to prime the pump by spending more money on education, technology, and infrastructure—all of which America desperately needed, and still does, but which the Clinton administration had postponed in its relentless drive to eliminate the deficit. Bill Clinton had left President Bush in an ideal position to pursue such policies. Remember the presidential debates in 2000 between Al Gore and George Bush, and how the two men argued over how to spend America's anticipated $2.2 trillion budget surplus? The country could well have afforded to ramp up domestic investment in key areas. In fact, doing so would have staved off recession in the short run while spurring growth in the long run.

But the Bush administration had its own ideas. The first major economic initiative pursued by the president was a massive tax cut for the rich, enacted in June of 2001. Those with incomes over a million got a tax cut of $18,000—more than 30 times larger than the cut received by the average American. The inequities were compounded by a second tax cut, in 2003, this one skewed even more heavily toward the rich. Together these tax cuts, when fully implemented and if made permanent, mean that in 2012 the average reduction for an American in the bottom 20 percent will be a scant $45, while those with incomes of more than $1 million will see their tax bills reduced by an average of $162,000.

The Administration crows that the economy grew—by some 16 percent—during its first six years, but the growth helped mainly people who had no need of any help, and failed to help those who need plenty. A rising tide lifted all yachts. Inequality is now widening in America, and at a rate not seen in three-quarters of a century. A young male in his 30s today has an income, adjusted for inflation, that is 12 percent less than what his father was making 30 years ago. Some 5.3 million more Americans are living in poverty now than were living in poverty when Bush became president. America's class structure may not have arrived there yet, but it's heading in the direction of Brazil's and Mexico's.

THE BANKRUPTCY BOOM

In breathtaking disregard for the most basic rules of fiscal propriety, the Administration continued to cut taxes even as it undertook expensive new spending programs and embarked on a financially ruinous "war of choice" in Iraq. A budget surplus of 2.4 percent of gross domestic product (G.D.P.), which greeted Bush as he took office, turned into a deficit of 3.6 percent in the space of four years. The United States had not experienced a turnaround of this magnitude since the global crisis of World War II.

Agricultural subsidies were doubled between 2002 and 2005. Tax expenditures—the vast system of subsidies and preferences hidden in the tax code—increased more than a quarter. Tax breaks for the president's friends in the oil-and-gas industry increased by billions and billions of dollars. Yes, in the five years after 9/11, defense expenditures did increase (by some 70 percent), though much of the growth wasn't helping to fight the War on Terror at all, but was being lost or outsourced in failed missions in Iraq. Meanwhile, other funds continued to be spent on the usual high-tech gimcrackery—weapons that don't work, for enemies we don't have. In a nutshell, money was being spent everyplace except where it was needed. During these past seven years the percentage of G.D.P. spent on research and development outside defense and health has fallen. Little has been done about our decaying infrastructure—be it levees in New Orleans or bridges in Minneapolis. Coping with most of the damage will fall to the next occupant of the White House.

Although it railed against entitlement programs for the needy, the Administration enacted the largest increase in entitlements in four decades—the poorly designed Medicare prescription-drug benefit, intended as both an election-season bribe and a sop to the pharmaceutical industry. As internal documents later revealed, the true cost of the measure was hidden from Congress. Meanwhile, the pharmaceutical companies received special favors. To access the new benefits, elderly patients couldn't opt to buy cheaper medications from Canada or other countries. The law also prohibited the U.S. government, the largest single buyer of prescription drugs, from negotiating with drug manufacturers to keep costs down. As a result, American consumers pay far more for medications than people elsewhere in the developed world.

You'll still hear some—and, loudly, the president himself—argue that the Administration's tax cuts were meant to stimulate the economy, but this was never true. The bang for the buck—the amount of stimulus per dollar of deficit—was astonishingly low. Therefore, the job of economic stimulation fell to the Federal Reserve Board, which stepped on the accelerator in a historically unprecedented way, driving interest rates down to 1 percent. In real terms, taking inflation into account, interest rates actually dropped to negative 2 percent. The predictable result was a consumer spending spree. Looked at another way, Bush's own fiscal irresponsibility fostered irresponsibility in everyone else. Credit was shoveled out the door, and subprime mortgages were made available to anyone this side of life support. Credit-card debt mounted to a whopping $900 billion by the summer of 2007. "Qualified at birth" became the drunken slogan of the Bush era. American households took advantage of the low interest rates, signed up for new mortgages with "teaser" initial rates, and went to town on the proceeds.

All of this spending made the economy look better for a while; the president could (and did) boast about the economic statistics. But the consequences for many families would become apparent within a few years, when interest rates rose and mortgages proved impossible to repay. The president undoubtedly hoped the reckoning would come sometime after 2008. It arrived 18 months early. As many as 1.7 million Americans are expected to lose their homes in the months ahead. For many, this will mean the beginning of a downward spiral into poverty.

Between March 2006 and March 2007 personal-bankruptcy rates soared more than 60 percent. As families went into bankruptcy, more and more of them came to understand who had won and who had lost as a result of the president's 2005 bankruptcy bill, which made it harder for individuals to discharge their debts in a reasonable way. The lenders that had pressed for "reform" had been the clear winners, gaining added leverage and protections for themselves; people facing financial distress got the shaft.

AND THEN THERE'S IRAQ

The war in Iraq (along with, to a lesser extent, the war in Afghanistan) has cost the country dearly in blood and treasure. The loss in lives can never be quantified. As for the treasure, it's worth calling to mind that the Administration, in the run-up to the invasion of Iraq, was reluctant to venture an estimate of what the war would cost (and publicly humiliated a White House aide who suggested that it might run as much as $200 billion). When pressed to give a number, the Administration suggested $50 billion—what the United States is actually spending every few months. Today, government figures officially acknowledge that more than half a trillion dollars total has been spent by the U.S. "in theater." But in fact the overall cost of the conflict could be quadruple that amount—as a study I did with Linda Bilmes of Harvard has pointed out—even as the Congressional Budget Office now concedes that total expenditures are likely to be more than double the spending on operations. The official numbers do not include, for instance, other relevant expenditures hidden in the defense budget, such as the soaring costs of recruitment, with reenlistment bonuses of as much as $100,000. They do not include the lifetime of disability and health-care benefits that will be required by tens of thousands of wounded veterans, as many as 20 percent of whom have suffered devastating brain and spinal injuries. Astonishingly, they do not include much of the cost of the equipment that has been used in the war, and that will have to be replaced. If you also take into account the costs to the economy from higher oil prices and the knock-on effects of the war—for instance, the depressing domino effect that war-fueled uncertainty has on investment, and the difficulties U.S. firms face overseas because America is the most disliked country in the world—the total costs of the Iraq war mount, even by a conservative estimate, to at least $2 trillion. To which one needs to add these words: so far.

It is natural to wonder, What would this money have bought if we had spent it on other things? U.S. aid to all of Africa has been hovering around $5 billion a year, the equivalent of less than two weeks of direct Iraq-war expenditures. The president made a big deal out of the financial problems facing Social Security, but the system could have been repaired for a century with what we have bled into the sands of Iraq. Had even a fraction of that $2 trillion been spent on investments in education and technology, or improving our infrastructure, the country would be in a far better position economically to meet the challenges it faces in the future, including threats from abroad. For a sliver of that $2 trillion we could have provided guaranteed access to higher education for all qualified Americans.

The soaring price of oil is clearly related to the Iraq war. The issue is not whether to blame the war for this but simply how much to blame it. It seems unbelievable now to recall that Bush-administration officials before the invasion suggested not only that Iraq's oil revenues would pay for the war in its entirety—hadn't we actually turned a tidy profit from the 1991 Gulf War?—but also that war was the best way to ensure low oil prices. In retrospect, the only big winners from the war have been the oil companies, the defense contractors, and Al Qaeda. Before the war, the oil markets anticipated that the then price range of $20 to $25 a barrel would continue for the next three years or so. Market players expected to see more demand from China and India, sure, but they also anticipated that this greater demand would be met mostly by increased production in the Middle East. The war upset that calculation, not so much by curtailing oil production in Iraq, which it did, but rather by heightening the sense of insecurity everywhere in the region, suppressing future investment.

The continuing reliance on oil, regardless of price, points to one more Administration legacy: the failure to diversify America's energy resources. Leave aside the environmental reasons for weaning the world from hydrocarbons— the president has never convincingly embraced them, anyway. The economic and national-security arguments ought to have been powerful enough. Instead, the Administration has pursued a policy of "drain America first"—that is, take as much oil out of America as possible, and as quickly as possible, with as little regard for the environment as one can get away with, leaving the country even more dependent on foreign oil in the future, and hope against hope that nuclear fusion or some other miracle will come to the rescue. So many gifts to the oil industry were included in the president's 2003 energy bill that John McCain referred to it as the "No Lobbyist Left Behind" bill.

CONTEMPT FOR THE WORLD

America's budget and trade deficits have grown to record highs under President Bush. To be sure, deficits don't have to be crippling in and of themselves. If a business borrows to buy a machine, it's a good thing, not a bad thing. During the past six years, America—its government, its families, the country as a whole—has been borrowing to sustain its consumption. Meanwhile, investment in fixed assets—the plants and equipment that help increase our wealth—has been declining.

What's the impact of all this down the road? The growth rate in America's standard of living will almost certainly slow, and there could even be a decline. The American economy can take a lot of abuse, but no economy is invincible, and our vulnerabilities are plain for all to see. As confidence in the American economy has plummeted, so has the value of the dollar—by 40 percent against the euro since 2001.

The disarray in our economic policies at home has parallels in our economic policies abroad. President Bush blamed the Chinese for our huge trade deficit, but an increase in the value of the yuan, which he has pushed, would simply make us buy more textiles and apparel from Bangladesh and Cambodia instead of China; our deficit would remain unchanged. The president claimed to believe in free trade but instituted measures aimed at protecting the American steel industry. The United States pushed hard for a series of bilateral trade agreements and bullied smaller countries into accepting all sorts of bitter conditions, such as extending patent protection on drugs that were desperately needed to fight AIDS. We pressed for open markets around the world but prevented China from buying Unocal, a small American oil company, most of whose assets lie outside the United States.

Not surprisingly, protests over U.S. trade practices erupted in places such as Thailand and Morocco. But America has refused to compromise—refused, for instance, to take any decisive action to do away with our huge agricultural subsidies, which distort international markets and hurt poor farmers in developing countries. This intransigence led to the collapse of talks designed to open up international markets. As in so many other areas, President Bush worked to undermine multilateralism—the notion that countries around the world need to cooperate—and to replace it with an America-dominated system. In the end, he failed to impose American dominance—but did succeed in weakening cooperation.

The Administration's basic contempt for global institutions was underscored in 2005 when it named Paul Wolfowitz, the former deputy secretary of defense and a chief architect of the Iraq war, as president of the World Bank. Widely distrusted from the outset, and soon caught up in personal controversy, Wolfowitz became an international embarrassment and was forced to resign his position after less than two years on the job.

Globalization means that America's economy and the rest of the world have become increasingly interwoven. Consider those bad American mortgages. As families default, the owners of the mortgages find themselves holding worthless pieces of paper. The originators of these problem mortgages had already sold them to others, who packaged them, in a non-transparent way, with other assets, and passed them on once again to unidentified others. When the problems became apparent, global financial markets faced real tremors: it was discovered that billions in bad mortgages were hidden in portfolios in Europe, China, and Australia, and even in star American investment banks such as Goldman Sachs and Bear Stearns. Indonesia and other developing countries—innocent bystanders, really—suffered as global risk premiums soared, and investors pulled money out of these emerging markets, looking for safer havens. It will take years to sort out this mess.

Meanwhile, we have become dependent on other nations for the financing of our own debt. Today, China alone holds more than $1 trillion in public and private American I.O.U.'s. Cumulative borrowing from abroad during the six years of the Bush administration amounts to some $5 trillion. Most likely these creditors will not call in their loans—if they ever did, there would be a global financial crisis. But there is something bizarre and troubling about the richest country in the world not being able to live even remotely within its means. Just as Guantánamo and Abu Ghraib have eroded America's moral authority, so the Bush administration's fiscal housekeeping has eroded our economic authority.

THE WAY FORWARD

Whoever moves into the White House in January 2009 will face an unenviable set of economic circumstances. Extricating the country from Iraq will be the bloodier task, but putting America's economic house in order will be wrenching and take years.

The most immediate challenge will be simply to get the economy's metabolism back into the normal range. That will mean moving from a savings rate of zero (or less) to a more typical savings rate of, say, 4 percent. While such an increase would be good for the long-term health of America's economy, the short-term consequences would be painful. Money saved is money not spent. If people don't spend money, the economic engine stalls. If households curtail their spending quickly—as they may be forced to do as a result of the meltdown in the mortgage market—this could mean a recession; if done in a more measured way, it would still mean a protracted slowdown. The problems of foreclosure and bankruptcy posed by excessive household debt are likely to get worse before they get better. And the federal government is in a bind: any quick restoration of fiscal sanity will only aggravate both problems.

And in any case there's more to be done. What is required is in some ways simple to describe: it amounts to ceasing our current behavior and doing exactly the opposite. It means not spending money that we don't have, increasing taxes on the rich, reducing corporate welfare, strengthening the safety net for the less well off, and making greater investment in education, technology, and infrastructure.

When it comes to taxes, we should be trying to shift the burden away from things we view as good, such as labor and savings, to things we view as bad, such as pollution. With respect to the safety net, we need to remember that the more the government does to help workers improve their skills and get affordable health care the more we free up American businesses to compete in the global economy. Finally, we'll be a lot better off if we work with other countries to create fair and efficient global trade and financial systems. We'll have a better chance of getting others to open up their markets if we ourselves act less hypocritically—that is, if we open our own markets to their goods and stop subsidizing American agriculture.

―← • →―

Some portion of the damage done by the Bush administration could be rectified quickly. A large portion will take decades to fix—and that's assuming the political will to do so exists both in the White House and in Congress. Think of the interest we are paying, year after year, on the almost $4 trillion of increased debt burden—even at 5 percent, that's an annual payment of $200 billion, two Iraq wars a year forever. Think of the taxes that future governments will have to levy to repay even a fraction of the debt we have accumulated. And think of the widening divide between rich and poor in America, a phenomenon that goes beyond economics and speaks to the very future of the American Dream.

In short, there's a momentum here that will require a generation to reverse. Decades hence we should take stock, and revisit the conventional wisdom. Will Herbert Hoover still deserve his dubious mantle? I'm guessing that George W. Bush will have earned one more grim superlative.

20
THE ROVE PRESIDENCY

JOSHUA GREEN
The Atlantic Monthly   September 2007

One of the prevailing mysteries of the Bush presidency is how a team that was so effective in getting George Bush reelected could have run out of steam so quickly when it came to enacting his second-term agenda. In his article—a must-read for anyone interested in what makes the Bush White House tick—Joshua Green places much of the blame squarely on the shoulders of chief adviser Karl ("The Architect") Rove. "Rove's greatest shortcoming," he writes, "was not in conceptualizing policies but in failing to understand the process of getting them implemented, a weakness he never seems to have recognized in himself."

With more than a year left in the fading Bush presidency, Karl Rove's worst days in the White House may still lie ahead of him. I met Rove on one of his best days, a week after Bush's reelection. The occasion was a reporters' lunch hosted by *The Christian Science Monitor* at the St. Regis Hotel in Washington, a customary stop for the winning and losing campaign teams to offer battle assessments and answer questions.

Kerry's team had glumly passed through a few days earlier. Afterward his chief strategist, Bob Shrum, boarded a plane and left the country. Rove had endured a heart-stopping Election Day (early exit polls indicated a Kerry landslide) but had prevailed, and plainly wasn't hurrying off anywhere. "The Architect," as Bush had just dubbed him, had spent the week collecting praise and had now arrived—vindicated, secure of his place in history—to hold court before the political press corps.

When Rove entered the room, everyone stood up to congratulate him and shake his hand. Washington journalism has become a kind of Cult of the Consultant, so the energy in the room was a lot like it might have been if Mickey Mantle had come striding into the clubhouse after knocking in the game-winning run in the World Series. Rove was pumped.

Before taking questions, he removed a folded piece of paper from his pocket and rattled off a series of numbers that made clear how he wanted the election to be seen: not as a squeaker but a rout. "This was an extraordinary election," Rove said. "[Bush won] 59.7 million votes, and we still have about 250,000 ballots to count. Think about that—*nearly 60 million votes!* The previous largest number was Ronald Reagan in 1984, sweeping the country with 49 states. We won 81 percent of all the counties in America. We gained a percentage of the vote in 87 percent of the counties in America. In Florida, we received nearly a million votes more in this election than in the last one." Rove was officially there to talk about the campaign, but it was clear he had something much bigger in mind. So no one missed his point, he invoked Franklin Roosevelt's supremacy in the 1930s and suggested that something similar was at hand: "We've laid out an agenda, we've laid out a vision, and now people want to see results."

One of the goals of any ambitious president is to create a governing coalition just as Roosevelt did, one that long outlasts your presidency. It's the biggest thing you can aim for, and only a few presidents have achieved it. As the person with the long-term vision in the Bush administration, and with no lack of ambition either, Rove had thought long and hard about achieving this goal before ever arriving in the White House, and he has pursued it more aggressively than anyone else.

Rove has always cast himself not merely as a campaign manager but as someone with a mind for policy and for history's deeper currents—as someone, in other words, with the wherewithal not just to exploit the political landscape but to reshape it. At the *Christian Science Monitor* lunch, he appeared poised to do just that. It was already clear that Social Security privatization, a longtime Rove enthusiasm, was the first thing Bush would pursue in his second term. When things are going well for Rove, he adopts a towel-snapping jocularity. He looked supremely sure of his prospects for success.

But within a year the Administration was crumbling. Social Security had gone nowhere. Hurricane Katrina, the worsening war in Iraq, and the disastrous nomination of Harriet Miers to the Supreme Court shattered the illusion of stern competence that had helped reelect Bush. What surprised everybody was how suddenly it happened; for a while, many devotees of the Cult of Rove seemed not to accept that it had. As recently as last fall, serious journalists were churning out soaring encomiums to Rove and his methods with titles like *One Party Country* and *The Way to Win*. In retrospect, everyone should have been focusing less on how those methods were used to win elections and more on why they couldn't deliver once the elections were over.

The story of why an ambitious Republican president working with a Republican Congress failed to achieve most of what he set out to do finds Rove at center stage. A big paradox of Bush's presidency is that Rove, who had maybe the best purely political mind in a generation and almost limitless opportunities to apply it from the very outset, managed to steer the Administration toward disaster.

Years from now, when the major figures in the Bush administration publish their memoirs, historians may have a clearer idea of what went wrong than we do today. As an exercise in not waiting that long, I spent several months reading the early memoirs and talking to people inside and outside the Administration (granting anonymity as necessary), in Congress, and in lobbying and political-consulting firms that dealt directly with Rove in the White House. (Rove declined requests for an interview.) The idea was to look at the Bush years and make a first pass at explaining the consequential figure in the vortex—to answer the question, How should history understand Karl Rove, and with him, this administration?

◂◂ • ▸▸

Fifty years ago, political scientists developed what is known as realignment theory—the idea that a handful of elections in the nation's history mattered more than the others because they created "sharp and durable" changes in the polity that lasted for decades. Roosevelt's election in 1932, which brought on the New Deal and three decades of Democratic dominance in Washington, is often held up as the classic example. Modern American historians generally see five elections as realigning: 1800, when Thomas Jefferson's victory all but finished off the Federalist Party and reoriented power from the North to the agrarian South;

1828, when Andrew Jackson's victory gave rise to the modern two-party system and two decades of Jacksonian influence; 1860, when Abraham Lincoln's election marked the ascendance of the Republican Party and of the secessionist impulse that led to the Civil War; 1896, when the effects of industrialization affirmed an increasingly urban political order that brought William McKinley to power; and Roosevelt's election in 1932, during the Great Depression.

Academics debate many aspects of this theory, such as whether realignment comes in regular cycles, and whether it is driven by voter intensity or disillusionment. But historians have shown that two major preconditions typically must be in place for realignment to occur. First, party loyalty must be sufficiently weak to allow for a major shift—the electorate, as the political scientist Paul Allen Beck has put it, must be "ripe for realignment." The other condition is that the nation must undergo some sort of triggering event, often what Beck calls a "societal trauma"—the ravaging depressions of the 1890s and 1930s, for instance, or the North-South conflict of the 1850s and '60s that ended in civil war. It's important to have both. Depressions and wars throughout American history have had no realigning consequence because the electorate wasn't primed for one, just as periods of electoral unrest have passed without a realignment for lack of a catalyzing event.

Before he ever came to the White House, Rove fervently believed that the country was on the verge of another great shift. His faith derived from his reading of the presidency of a man most historians regard as a mediocrity. Anyone on the campaign trail in 2000 probably heard him cite the pivotal importance of William McKinley's election in 1896. Rove thought there were important similarities.

"Everything you know about William McKinley and Mark Hanna"—McKinley's Rove—"is wrong," he told Nicholas Lemann of *The New Yorker* in early 2000. "The country was in a period of change. McKinley's the guy who figured it out. Politics were changing. The economy was changing. We're at the same point now: weak allegiances to parties, a rising new economy." Rove was suggesting that the electorate in 2000, as in 1896, was ripe for realignment, and implying, somewhat immodestly, that he was the guy who had figured it out. What was missing was an obvious trigger. With the economy soaring (the stock-market collapse in the spring of 2000 was still months away) and the nation at peace, there was no reason to expect that a realignment was about to happen.

Instead, Rove's idea was to use the levers of government to create an effect that ordinarily occurs only in the most tumultuous periods in American history. He believed he could force a realignment himself through a series of far-reaching policies. Rove's plan had five major components: establish education standards, pass a "faith-based initiative" directing government funds to religious organizations, partially privatize Social Security, offer private health-savings accounts as an alternative to Medicare, and reform immigration laws to appeal to the growing Hispanic population. Each of these, if enacted, would weaken the Democratic Party by drawing some of its core supporters into the Republican column. His plan would lead, he believed, to a period of Republican dominance like the one that followed McKinley's election.

Rove's vision had a certain abstract conceptual logic to it, much like the Administration's plan to spread democracy by force in the Middle East. If you could invade and pacify Iraq and Afghanistan, the thinking went, democracy would spread across the region. Likewise, if you could recast major government programs to make them more susceptible to market forces, broader support for the Republican Party would ensue. But in both cases the visionaries ignored the enormous difficulty of carrying off such seismic changes.

The Middle East failure is all too well-known—the vaulting ambition coupled with the utter inability of top Administration figures to bring about their grand idea. What is less appreciated is how Rove set out to do something every bit as audacious with domestic policy. Earlier political realignments resulted from historical accidents or anomalies, conditions that were recognized and exploited after the fact by talented politicians. Nobody ever planned one. Rove didn't wait for history to happen to him—he tried to create it on his own. "It's hard to think of any analogue in American history," says David Mayhew, a Yale political scientist who has written a book on electoral realignments, "to what Karl Rove was trying to do."

⪡ • ⪢

Rove's style as a campaign consultant was to plot out well in advance of a race exactly what he would do and to stick with it no matter what. But he arrived in the White House carrying ambitions at striking variance with those of a president whose stated aims were modest and who had lost the popular vote. The prevailing view of Bush at the time seems impossibly remote today. But the notion that he wanted nothing more than "to do a few things, and do them well," as he claimed, seemed sensible enough. Nothing suggested that radical change was possible, much less likely, and the narrow margins in Congress meant that any controversial measure would require nearly flawless execution to prevail.

And yet at first it appeared that Bush might be capable of achieving big things. His first initiative, the No Child Left Behind Act, unfolded as a model of how to operate in a narrowly divided environment. Bush had made education a central theme of his campaign, an unlikely choice given that the issue strongly favors Democrats. Accountability standards had been one of his signature accomplishments as governor of Texas, and he made a persuasive pitch for them on the campaign trail. Rove likes to point out that people who named education as their top issue voted for the Democrat over the Republican 76–16 percent in the 1996 presidential election, but just 52–44 in 2000. His point is that Bush moved the electorate.

As the top political adviser in the White House, Rove orchestrated the rollout of Bush's legislative agenda. In December, even before the inauguration, he put together a conference in Austin that included key Democrats who went on to support the education bills that sailed through Congress and became the first piece of Rove's realignment. At the time, everybody assumed this was how Bush would operate—"as a uniter, not a divider," his method in Texas, where he left behind a permanent-seeming Republican majority.

It's not clear why Bush abandoned the moderate style that worked with No Child Left Behind. One of the big what-ifs of his presidency is how things might have turned out had he stuck with it (education remains the one element of Rove's realignment project that was successfully enacted). What did become clear is that Rove's tendency, like Bush's, is always to choose the most ambitious option in a list and then pursue it by the most aggressive means possible—an approach that generally works better in campaigns than in governing. Instead of modest bipartisanship, the Administration's preferred style of governing became something much closer to the way Rove runs campaigns: Steamroll the opposition whenever possible, and reach across the aisle only in the rare cases, like No Child Left Behind, when it is absolutely necessary. The large tax cut that Bush pursued and won on an almost party-line vote just afterward is a model of this confrontational style. Its limitations would become apparent.

By late summer of his first year, the early burst of achievement had slowed and Bush's approval ratings were beginning to sag. Ronald Brownstein of the *Los Angeles Times* dubbed him the "A4 president," unable even to make the front page of the newspaper. He did not seem the likely leader of a realignment.

<-- • -->

That September 11 was both a turning point for the Bush administration and an event that would change the course of American history was immediately clear. It was also clear, if less widely appreciated, that the attacks were the type of event that can instantly set off a great shifting of the geological strata of American politics. In a coincidence of epic dimensions, 9/11 provided, just when Rove needed it, the historical lever missing until then. He had been presented with exactly the sort of "societal trauma" that makes realignment possible, and with it a fresh chance to pursue his goal. Bob Woodward's trilogy on the Bush White House makes clear how neoconservatives in the Administration recognized that 9/11 gave them the opening they'd long desired to forcefully re-make the Middle East. Rove recognized the same opening.

After 9/11, any pretense of shared sacrifice or of reaching across the aisle was abandoned. The Administration could demand—and get—almost anything it wanted, easily flattening Democratic opposition, which it did with increasing frequency on issues like the PATRIOT Act and the right of Department of Homeland Security workers to unionize. The crisis atmosphere allowed the White House to ignore what normally would have been some of its most basic duties—working with Republicans in Congress (let alone Democrats) and laying the groundwork in Congress and with the American public for what it hoped to achieve. At the time, however, this didn't seem to matter.

Rove's systematic policy of sharply contrasting Republican and Democratic positions on national security was a brilliant campaign strategy and the critical mechanism of Republican victory in the 2002 midterms. But he could not foresee how this mode of operating would ultimately work at cross-purposes with his larger goal. "What Bush went out and did in 2002," a former Administration official told me, "clearly at Karl's behest, with an eye toward the permanent Republican majority, was very aggressively attack those Democrats who voted with him and were for him. There's no question that the president helped pick up seats. But all of that goodwill was squandered."

From the outset, Rove's style of pursuing realignment—through division—was in stark contrast to the way it had happened the last time. In *Franklin D. Roosevelt and the New Deal,* the historian William E. Leuchtenburg notes that Roosevelt mentioned the Democratic Party by name only three times in his entire 1936 reelection campaign. Throughout his presidency, Roosevelt had large Democratic majorities in Congress but operated in a nonpartisan fashion, as though he didn't. Bush, with razor-thin majorities—and for a time, a divided Congress—operated as though his margins were insurmountable, and sowed interparty divisions as an electoral strategy.

◄◄ • ►►

Rove never graduated from college. He dropped out of the University of Utah and campaigned for the chairmanship of the College Republicans, a national student organization whose leaders often go on to important positions in the party. He won, placing himself on a fast track to a career in politics. But he was and remains an autodidact, and a large part of his self-image depends on showing that his command of history and politics is an order of magnitude greater than other people's. Rove has a need to outdo everybody else that seems to inform his sometimes contrarian views of history. It's not enough for him to have read everything; he needs to have read everything and arrived at insights that others missed.

This aspect of Rove was on fuller-than-usual display during a speech he gave at the University of Utah, titled "What Makes a Great President," just after the Republicans swept the 2002 elections. The incumbent presidential party typically loses seats in the off-year election, so winning was a big deal to Rove, who actively involved himself in many of the campaigns. Overcoming historical precedent seemed to feed his oracular sense of himself, and during his speech and the question-and-answer period that followed he revealed a lot about how he thinks and where he imagined his party was going.

In his speech, he described a visit to the White House by the revisionist historian Forrest McDonald, who spoke about presidential greatness. Rove expressed delight at discovering a fellow McKinley enthusiast, and said that McDonald had explained in his talk, "Nobody knows McKinley is great, because history demanded little of him. He modernized the presidency, he modernized the Treasury to deal with the modern economy, he changed dramatically the policies of his party by creating a durable governing coalition for 40 years"—this last part clearly excited Rove—"and he attempted deliberately to break with the Gilded Age politics. He was inclusive, and he was the first Republican candidate for president to be endorsed by a leader in the Catholic hierarchy. The Protestant Anglo-Saxon Republicans were scandalized by his 1896 campaign, in which he paraded Portuguese fishermen and Slovak coal miners and Serbian iron workers to Canton, Ohio, to meet him. He just absolutely scandalized the country."

In this way of telling it, McKinley alone understood what everybody else was missing: A political realignment was under way, and by harnessing it, though it might "scandalize" conventional thinking, McKinley would not only carry the presidency but also bring about an unprecedented period of dominance for his party. The subtext seemed to be that Rove, too, recognized something everybody else had missed—the chance for a Republican realignment—just as he recognized the overlooked genius of William McKinley. He joked to the audience, "This tripled the size of the McKinley caucus in Washington—it was Bob Novak, me, and now Forrest McDonald."

After the speech a member of the audience asked a question that took as its premise the notion that America was evenly divided between Republicans and Democrats. Rove insisted this was not the case, pouring forth a barrage of numbers from the recent midterm elections that seemed to lay waste to the notion. "Something is going on out there," Rove insisted. "Something else more fundamental . . . But we will only know it retrospectively. In two years or four years or six years, [we may] look back and say the dam began to break in 2002."

Like his hero McKinley, he alone was the true visionary. Everyone else looked at the political landscape and saw a nation at rough parity. Rove looked at the same thing and saw an emerging Republican majority.

⋘ • ⋙

From Rove's vantage point after the 2002 elections, everything seemed to be on track. He had a clear strategy for achieving realignment and the historical conditions necessary to enact it. His already considerable influence within the Administration was growing with the Republican Party's rising fortunes, which were credited to his strategy of aggressive divisiveness on the issues of war and terrorism. But what Rove took to be the catalyst for realignment turned out to be the catalyst for his fall.

September 11 temporarily displaced much of what was going on in Washington at the time. The ease with which Republicans were able to operate in the aftermath of the attacks was misleading, and it imbued Rove, in particular, with false confidence that what he was doing would continue to work. In reality, it masked problems—bad relationships with Congress, a lack of support for Bush's broader agenda—that either went unseen or were consciously ignored. Hubris and a selective understanding of history led Rove into a series of errors and misjudgments that compounded to devastating effect.

He never appreciated that his success would ultimately depend on the sustained cooperation of congressional Republicans, and he developed a dysfunctional relationship with many of them. This wasn't clear at first. Several of the Administration's early moves looked particularly shrewd, one of them being to place the White House congressional liaisons in the office suite of the majority whip, Tom DeLay of Texas. At the time, DeLay was officially third in the Republican House leadership hierarchy, but as everyone knew, he was the capo of House Republicans and the man to see if you wanted to get something done.

Things never clicked. Republicans on the Hill say that Rove and DeLay, both formidable men who had known each other in Texas, had a less-than-amiable relationship. When I asked DeLay about their history, he let out a malevolent chuckle and told me that his very first race had pitted him against one of Rove's candidates. "They were nasty to me," DeLay recalled. "I had some payroll tax liens against me, as most small businessmen do, and I was driving a red Eldorado at the time. The taxes were paid, but they were running radio ads saying I was a deadbeat who didn't pay my taxes." DeLay still remembered the ad: "He wants to drive his red Cadillac to Washington on the backs of the taxpayers."

DeLay made a point of saying he didn't hold a grudge. ("That wouldn't be Christian of me.") But he did allow that Rove had been extremely aggressive in trying to impose his ideas on Congress. "Karl and I are sort of the same personality," he explained, "so we end up screaming at each other. But in the end you walk out of the room with an agenda." DeLay insists he didn't mind Rove's screaming, but if that's true, he belongs to a truly Christian group.

Rove's behavior toward Congress stood out. "Every once in a while Rove would come to leadership meetings, and he definitely considered himself at least an equal with the leaders in the room," a Republican aide told me. "But you have to understand that Congress is a place where a certain decorum is expected. Even in private, staff is still staff. Rove would come and chime in as if he were equal to the speaker. Cheney sometimes came, too, and was far more deferential than Rove—and he was the vice president." Other aides say Rove was notorious for interrupting congressional leaders and calling them by their first name.

Dick Armey, the House Republican majority leader when Bush took office (and no more a shrinking violet than DeLay), told me a story that captures the exquisite pettiness of most members of Congress and the arrogance that made Bush and Rove so inept at handling them. "For all the years he was president," Armey told me, "Bill Clinton and I had a little thing we'd do where every time I went to the White House, I would take the little name tag they give you and pass it to the president, who, without saying a word, would sign and date it. Bill Clinton and I didn't like each other. He said I was his least-favorite member of Congress. But he knew that when I left his office, the first schoolkid I came across would be given that card, and some kid who had come to Washington with his mama would go home with the president's autograph. I think Clinton thought it was a nice thing to do for some kid, and he was happy to do it." Armey said that when he went to his first meeting in the White House with President Bush, he explained the tradition with Clinton and asked the president if he would care to continue it. "Bush refused to sign the card. Rove, who was sitting across the table, said, 'It would probably wind up on eBay,'" Armey continued. "Do I give a damn? No. But can you imagine refusing a simple request like that with an insult? It's stupid. From the point of view of your own self-interest, it's stupid. I was from Texas, and I was the majority leader. If my expectations of civility and collegiality were disappointed, what do you think it was like for the rest of the congressmen they dealt with? The Bush White House was tone-deaf to the normal courtesies of the office."

Winning the 2002 elections earned Rove further distinction as an electoral strategist. But it didn't change the basic dynamic between the White House and Congress, and Rove drew exactly the wrong lesson from the experience, bringing the steamroller approach from the campaign trail into his work in government. Emboldened by triumph, he grew more imperious, worsening his relations with the Hill. With both houses now in Republican hands, he pressed immigration reform and Social Security privatization. A congressional aide described a Republican leadership retreat after the midterms where Rove whipped out a chart and a sheaf of poll numbers and insisted to Republican leaders that they pursue a Social Security overhaul at once. Making wholesale changes to a beloved entitlement program in the run-up to a presidential election would have been a difficult sell under the best of circumstances. Lacking goodwill in Congress and having laid no groundwork for such an undertaking, Rove didn't get a serious hearing on the issue—or on immigration, either.

A revealing pattern of behavior emerged from my interviews. Rove plainly viewed his standing as equal to or exceeding that of the party's leaders in Congress and demanded what he deemed his due. Yet he was also apparently annoyed at what came with his White House eminence, complaining to colleagues when members of Congress called him to consult about routine matters he thought were beneath his standing—something that couldn't have endeared him to the legislature.

When Bush revived immigration reform this past spring and let it be known that Rove would not take part in the negotiations, the president seemed to have belatedly grasped a basic truth about congressional relations that Armey summed up for me like this: "You can't call her ugly all year and expect her to go to the prom with you."

⧏ • ⧐

Another important misjudgment by Bush, prodded by Rove, was giving Rove too much power within the Administration. This was partly a function of Rove's desire to control policy as well as politics. His prize for winning the reelection campaign was a formal role and the title of deputy chief of staff for policy. But his power also grew because the senior policy staff in the White House was inept.

In an early scene in Ron Suskind's book *The Price of Loyalty,* Treasury Secretary Paul O'Neill, not yet alive to the futility of his endeavor, warns Dick Cheney that the White House policy process is so ineffectual that it is tantamount to "kids rolling around on the lawn." Had O'Neill lasted longer than he did (he resigned in 2002), he might have lowered his assessment. Before she left the White House in humiliation after conservatives blocked her nomination to the Supreme Court, White House Counsel Harriet Miers had also served as deputy chief of staff for policy. The president's Domestic Policy Council was run by Claude Allen, until he, too, resigned, after he was caught shoplifting at Target.

The weakness of the White House policy staff demanded Rove's constant involvement. For all his shortcomings, he had clear ideas about where the Administration should go, and the ability to maneuver. "Where the bureaucracy was failing and broken, Karl got stuff done," says a White House colleague. "Harriet was no more capable of producing policy out of the policy office she directed than you or I are capable of jumping off the roof of a building and flying to Minneapolis."

As a result, Rove not only ran the reelection campaign, he plotted much of Bush's second-term agenda, using the opportunity to push long-standing pet issues—health-savings accounts, Social Security privatization—that promised to weaken support for Democrats, by dismantling Medicare and Social Security. But this also meant committing the president to sweeping domestic changes that had no public favor and had not been a focus of the 2004 campaign, which had centered almost exclusively on the war.

Bush's reelection and Rove's assumption of a formal policy role had a bigger effect than most of Washington realized at the time. It is commonly assumed (as I assumed) that Rove exercised a major influence on White House policy before he had the title, all the time that he had it, and even after it was taken away from him in the staff shake-up last year that saw Josh Bolten succeed Andrew Card as chief of staff.

Insiders don't disagree, but say that Rove's becoming deputy chief of staff for policy was still an important development. For the purposes of comparison, a former Bush official cited the productiveness of the first two years of Bush's presidency, the period that generated not just No Child Left Behind but three tax cuts and the Medicare prescription-drug benefit. At the time, Bolten was deputy chief of staff for policy, and relations with Congress had not yet soured. "Josh was not an equal of Karl's with regard to access to the president or stature," says the official. "But he was a strong enough intellect and a strong enough presence that he was able to create a deliberative process that led to a better outcome." When Bolten left to run the Office of Management and Budget, in 2003, the balance shifted in Rove's favor, and then shifted further after the reelection. "Formalizing [Rove's policy role] was the final choke-off of any internal debate or deliberative process," says the official. "There was no offset to Karl."

Rove's greatest shortcoming was not in conceptualizing policies but in failing to understand the process of getting them implemented, a weakness he never seems to have recognized in himself. It's startling that someone who gave so much thought to redirecting the powers of government evinced so little interest in understanding how it operates. Perhaps because he had never worked in government—or maybe because his standing rested upon his relationship with a single superior—he was often ineffective at bringing into being anything that required more than a presidential signature.

⫷ • ⫸

As the September 11 mind-set began to lose its power over Washington, Rove still faced the task of getting the more difficult parts of his realignment schema through Congress. But his lack of fluency in the art of moving policy and his tendency to see the world through the divisive lens of a political campaign were great handicaps. There was an important difference between the Administration's first-term achievements and the entitlement overhauls (Social Security and Medicare) and volatile cultural issues (immigration) that Rove wanted to push through next. Cutting taxes and furnishing new benefits may generate some controversy in Washington, but few lawmakers who support them face serious political risk. (Tax cuts get Republicans elected!) So it's possible, with will and numbers alone, to pass them with the barest of majorities. Rove's mistake was to believe that this would work with everything.

Entitlement reform is a different animal. More important than reaching a majority is offering political cover to those willing to accept the risk of tampering with cherished programs, and the way to do this is by enlisting the other side. So the fact that Republicans controlled the White House and both houses of Congress after 2002—to Rove, a clinching argument for confrontation— actually *lessened* the likelihood of entitlement reform. Congressional Republicans didn't support Rove's plan in 2003 to tackle Social Security or immigration reform because they didn't *want* to pass such things on a party-line vote. History suggested they'd pay a steep price at election time.

To understand this, Rove need not have looked back any farther than the last Republican president who had attempted something on this order. Before he was president, Ronald Reagan talked about letting people opt out of the Social Security system, a precursor of the plan Rove favors. In 1981, in the full tide of victory, Reagan proposed large cuts—and the Republican Senate refused even to take them up. The mere fact that they had been put forward, however, was enough to imperil Republicans, who took significant losses in 1982.

The following year, Reagan tried again, this time cooperating with the Democratic speaker of the House, Tip O'Neill. He now understood that the only way to attain any serious change on such a sensitive issue was for both parties to hold hands and jump together. To afford each side deniability if things fell apart, the two leaders negotiated by proxy. O'Neill chose Robert Ball, a widely respected Social Security commissioner under three presidents, while Reagan picked Alan Greenspan, the future chairman of the Federal Reserve. Key senators in both parties were looped in.

As Ball and Greenspan made headway, it was really O'Neill and Reagan who were agreeing. To assure both sides political cover, the negotiations were an all-or-nothing process. The plan that was eventually settled on addressed the solvency problem by raising the retirement age (which pleased Republicans) and taxing Social Security benefits for the first time (which pleased Democrats). Unlike in 1981, Republicans in Congress weren't left exposed. Democrats couldn't attack them for raising the retirement age, because Tip O'Neill had signed on. Republicans couldn't complain about higher taxes, because Democrats had supported Ronald Reagan's plan.

At the *Christian Science Monitor* lunch just after the reelection, Rove, then at the apogee of his power, had no time for nostrums like bipartisanship or negotiation. Armed with his policy title and the aura of political genius, he pressed for the Social Security changes so far denied him. In many ways, this decision was the fulcrum of the Bush presidency. Had Bush decided not to pursue Social Security or had he somehow managed to pursue it in a way that included Democrats, his presidency might still have ended up in failure, because of Iraq. But the dramatic collapse of Rove's Social Security push foreclosed any other possibility. It left Bush all but dead in the water for what looks to be the remainder of his time in office.

Rove pursued his plan with characteristic intensity, running it out of the White House from the top down, like a political campaign, and seeking to enlist the network of grassroots activists that had carried the Bush-Cheney ticket to a second term. Bush gave Social Security prominence in his State of the Union address, then set out on a national road show to sell the idea. But after an election fought over the war, Social Security drew little interest, and in contrast to the effect Bush achieved on education in the 2000 campaign, public support didn't budge. (It actually worsened during his tour.)

Unlike Reagan, Bush did not produce a bill that could have served as a basis for negotiation—nor did he seriously consult any Democrats with whom he might have negotiated. Instead, Rove expected a bill to emerge from Congress. The strategy of a president's outlining broad principles of what he'd like in a bill and calling on Congress to draft it has worked many times in the past. But Rove had no allies in Congress, had built no support with the American public, and had chosen to undertake the most significant entitlement reform since Reagan by having Bush barnstorm the country speaking before handpicked Republican audiences with the same partisan fervor he'd brought to the presidential campaign trail—all of which must have scared the living daylights out of the very Republicans in Congress Rove foolishly counted upon to do his bidding. The problems buried for years under the war and then the presidential race came roaring back, and Bush got no meaningful support from the Hill. He was left with a flawed, unpopular concept whose motive—political gain—was all too apparent.

Within months it was clear that the Social Security offensive was in deep trouble and, worse, was dragging down Bush's popularity at a time when he needed all the support he could muster for Iraq. Every week, the political brain trust in the Bush White House gathers under Rove for what is known as the "Strategery Meeting" (an ironic nod to Bush's frequent malapropisms) to plot the course ahead. What transpires is usually a closely held secret. But two former Bush officials provided an account of one meeting in the late spring of 2005, in the middle of the Social Security push, that affords a remarkable glimpse of Rove's singularity of purpose.

He opened the meeting by acknowledging that the Social Security initiative was struggling and hurting the president's approval ratings, and then announced that, despite this, they would stay the course through the summer. He admitted that the numbers would probably continue to fall. But come September, the president would hit Democrats hard on the issue of national security and pull his numbers back up again. Winning on Social Security was so important to Rove that he was evidently willing to gamble the effectiveness of Bush's second term on what most people in the White House and Congress thought were very long odds to begin with. The gamble didn't pay off. Even before Hurricane Katrina hit New Orleans on the morning of August 29, what slim hope might have remained for Social Security was gone.

Hurricane Katrina clearly changed the public perception of Bush's presidency. Less examined is the role Rove played in the defining moment of the Administration's response: when Air Force One flew over Louisiana and Bush gazed down from on high at the wreckage without ordering his plane down. Bush advisers Matthew Dowd and Dan Bartlett wanted the president on the ground immediately, one Bush official told me, but were overruled by Rove for reasons that are still unclear: "Karl did not want the plane to land in Louisiana." Rove's political acumen seemed to be deserting him altogether.

An important theme of future Bush administration memoirs will be the opportunity cost of leading off the second term with the misguided plan to overhaul Social Security. "The great cost of the Social Security misadventure was lost support for the war," says a former Bush official. "When you send troops to war, you have no higher responsibility as president than to keep the American people engaged and maintain popular support. But for months and months after it became obvious that Social Security was not going to happen, nobody—

because of Karl's stature in the White House—could be intellectually honest in a meeting and say, 'This is not going to happen, and we need an exit strategy to get back onto winning ground.' It was a catastrophic mistake."

It strains belief to think that someone as highly attuned as Rove to all that goes on in politics could have missed the reason for Bush's reelection: He persuaded just enough people that he was the better man to manage the war. But it's also hard to fathom how the master strategist could leave his president and his party as vulnerable as they proved to be six months into the second term. The Republican pollster Tony Fabrizio says, "People who were concerned about the war, we lost. People who were concerned about the economy, we lost. People who were concerned about health care, we lost. It goes on and on. Any of those things would have helped refocus the debate or at least put something else out there besides the war. We came out of the election and what was our agenda for the next term? Social Security. There was nothing else that we were doing. We allowed ourselves as a party to be defined by—in effect, to live and die by—the war in Iraq."

That Rove ignored a political reality so clear to everyone else can be explained only by the immutable nature of his ambition: Social Security was vital for a realignment, however unlikely its success now appeared. At the peak of his influence, the only person who could have stopped him was the one person he answered to—but the president was just as fixated on his place in history as Rove was on his own.

⪡ • ⪢

Moments of precise reckoning in politics are rare outside of elections. Snapshot polls don't tell you much about whole epochs. Even voter identification can be a misleading indicator. In 1976, the post-Watergate Republican Party would have appeared to be in existential peril, when in fact it was on the verge of setting the agenda for a generation. So the question of where exactly things stand right now is more complicated than it might appear.

As he nears the end of his time in government, Rove has been campaigning for the notion that Bush has been more successful than he's being credited for. But the necessity of adopting history's longer perspective to make his argument says a great deal. Of the five policies in his realignment vision, Social Security and immigration failed outright; medical-savings accounts and the faith-based program wound up as small, face-saving initiatives after the original ambitions collapsed; and the lone success, No Child Left Behind, looks increasingly jeopardized as it comes up for renewal in Congress this year, a victim of Bush's unpopularity. Rove no longer talks about realignment—though the topic is now very popular with Democrats, who have a good shot at controlling both houses of Congress and the presidency after the next election. On the face of things, the Republican Party is in trouble. In a representative example, voters in a recent NBC–*Wall Street Journal* poll preferred that the next president be a Democrat by 52–31 percent, and delivered the most negative assessment of the Republican Party in the survey's two-decade history. In 2002, Americans were equally split along partisan lines. A recent Pew study shows that 50 percent of the public identifies as Democratic or leaning that way, while just 35 percent identifies with the GOP.

Rove is a great devotee of the historian Robert H. Wiebe, who also emphasizes the pivotal quality of the 1896 election. Wiebe thought industrialization had launched a great sorting-out process in the 1880s and '90s that reached a dramatic culmination in 1896. He argues in his book *The Search for Order, 1877–1920* that "a decade's accumulated bitterness ultimately flowed into a single national election."

It seems highly unlikely, though not impossible, that historians will one day view 2000 or 2004 as the kind of realigning election that Rove so badly wanted. Ken Mehlman, a protégé of Rove's and one of the sharper minds in the Republican Party, is adamant that the analysis that led Rove to believe realignment was at hand remains fundamentally correct. "If you look back over the last few decades, an era of politics has run its course," Mehlman told me. "Both parties achieved some of their highest goals. Democrats got civil rights, women's rights, the New Deal, and recognition of the need for a cleaner environment. Republicans got the defeat of the Soviet Union, less violent crime, lower tax rates, and welfare reform. The public agrees on this. So the issues now become: How do you deal with the terrorist threat? How do you deal with the retirement of the Baby Boomers? How do you deliver health care with people changing jobs? How do you make sure America retains its economic strength with the rise of China and India? How that plays out is something we don't know yet." As far as what's happened since 2000, Mehlman says, "the conditions remain where they were." In this view, America is still in the period of great churn, and the 1896 election hasn't happened yet.

Premised as it is on the notion that the past seven years have been a wash, Mehlman's analysis has a self-justifying tinge. At least for now, Republicans have measurably fallen behind where they were in 2000. It's hard to sift under-lying political views from temporary rage against Bush, or to anticipate what effect his presidency will have on the Republican Party's fortunes once he's gone. But the effect does seem certain to be less pronounced—less disastrous—than it is now. Considered in that context, Mehlman's analysis rings true.

When I asked Mark Gersh, one of the Democrats' best electoral analysts, for his view of how the political landscape has shifted, he basically agreed with Mehlman, and offered his own perspective on Rove's vision of realignment. "September 11 is what made them, and Iraq is what undermined them, and the truth lies in between the two—and that is that both parties are at parity," Gersh told me. "There was never any indication that the Republicans were emerging as the majority party. What was happening was that partisanship was actually hardening. Fewer people in both parties were voting for candidates of the other party." Gersh added that he doesn't believe Democrats are the ma-jority party, and he gives Republicans "at worst a 4-in–10 chance" of holding the presidency in 2008. Even if Rove didn't create a generational shift to the Re-publican Party, so far at least he does not appear to have ushered in a Demo-cratic one, either.

Nonetheless, certain painful, striking parallels between the presidencies of George Bush and William McKinley can't have been lost on Rove, even if he would be the last to admit them. Both originally campaigned almost exclu-sively on domestic issues, only to have their presidencies dominated by foreign affairs. Neither distinguished himself. *Policy inertia* is the term the historian Richard L. McCormick uses to characterize McKinley's presidency. David May-hew, the political scientist, writes in his skeptical study *Electoral Realignments,* "Policy innovations under McKinley during 1897–1901 [McKinley was assas-sinated in 1901] probably rank in the bottom quartile among all presidential terms in American history." Both sentiments could be applied to Bush.

Perhaps the strangest irony is the foreign adventure that consumed much of McKinley's presidency. Though he lacked Bush's storm-the-barricades tem-perament, McKinley launched the Spanish-American War partly at the urging of his future vice president, Teddy Roosevelt, and other hawks. As the histo-rian Eric Rauchway has pointed out, after American forces defeated the Span-ish navy in the Philippines, the U.S. occupation encountered a bloody postwar insurgency and allegations of torture committed by U.S. troops. Roosevelt, who succeeded McKinley, was hampered by questions about improper force size and commitment of troops and eventually came to rue his plight. "While I have never varied in my feeling that we had to hold the Philippines," he wrote in 1901, "I have varied very much in my feelings whether we were to be considered fortunate or unfortunate in having to hold them."

To understand Rove's record, it's useful to think of the disaster as being divided into foreign and domestic components. Rove had little say in foreign policy. Dick Cheney understood from decades of government experience how to engineer a war he'd pressed for, and still the Administration failed to reshape the Middle East. More than anyone outside the Oval Office, Rove was responsible for much of what went wrong on the domestic front—partly because he had never served in government, and he lacked Cheney's skill at manipulating it. Both men came in believing they had superior insights into history and theoretical underpinnings so strong that their ideas would prevail. But neither man understood how to see them through, and so both failed.

Rove has proved a better analyst of history than agent of historical change, showing far greater aptitude for envisioning sweeping change than for pulling it off. Cheney, through a combination of stealth and nuance, was responsible for steering the Bush administration's policy in many controversial areas: redirecting foreign policy, winning a series of tax cuts, weakening environmental regulations, asserting the primacy of the executive branch. But his interests seldom coincided with Rove's overarching goal of realignment. And Rove, forever in thrall to the mechanics of winning by dividing, consistently lacked the ability to transcend the campaign mind-set and see beyond the struggle nearest at hand. In a world made new by September 11, he put terrorism and war to work in an electoral rather than a historical context, and used them as wedge issues instead of as the unifying basis for the new political order he sought.

Why did so many people get Rove so wrong? One reason is that notwithstanding his pretensions to being a world-historic figure, Rove excelled at winning elections, which is, finally, how Washington keeps score. This leads to another reason: Journalists tend to admire tactics above all else. The books on Rove from last year dwell at length on his techniques and accept the premise of Republican dominance practically on tactical skill alone. A corollary to the Cult of the Consultant is the belief that winning an election—especially a tough one you weren't expected to win—is proof of the ability to govern. But the two are wholly distinct enterprises.

Rove's vindictiveness has also cowed his critics, at least for the time being. One reason his standing has not yet sunk as low as that of the rest of the Bush administration is his continuing ability to intimidate many of those in a position to criticize him. A Republican consultant who works downtown agreed to talk candidly for this article, but suggested that we have lunch across the river in Pentagon City, Virginia. He didn't want to be overheard. Working with Rove, he explained, was difficult enough already: "You're constantly confronting the big, booming voice of Oz."

In ways small and large, Rove has long betrayed his lack of understanding of Washington's institutional subtleties and the effective application of policy, even for the rawest political objectives. The classic example is Rove's persuading the president in 2002 to impose steep tariffs on foreign steel—a ploy he believed would win over union workers in Rust Belt swing states, ordinarily faithful Democrats, in the next presidential election. This was celebrated as a political masterstroke at the time. But within a year the tariffs were declared illegal by the World Trade Organization and nearly caused a trade war. The uproar precipitated their premature and embarrassing removal.

"It is a dangerous distraction to know as much about politics as Karl Rove knows," Bruce Reed, the domestic-policy chief in Bill Clinton's administration, told me. "If you know every single poll number on every single issue and every interest group's objection and every political factor, it can be paralyzing to try to make an honest policy decision. I think the larger, deeper problem was that they never fully appreciated that long-term success depended on making sure your policies worked."

Rove has no antecedent in modern American politics, because no president before Bush thought it wise to give a political adviser so much influence. Rove wouldn't be Rove, in other words, were Bush not Bush. That Vice President Cheney also hit a historic high-water mark for influence says a lot about how the actual president sees fit to govern. All rhetoric about "leadership" aside, Bush will be viewed as a weak executive who ceded far too much authority. Rove's failures are ultimately his.

Bush will leave behind a legacy long on ambition and short on positive results. History will draw many lessons from his presidency—about the danger of concentrating too much power in the hands of too few, about the risk of commingling politics and policy beyond a certain point, about the cost of constricting the channels of information to the Oval Office. More broadly, as the next group of presidential candidates and their gurus eases the current crew from the stage, Rove's example should serve as a caution to politicians and journalists.

The Bush administration made a virtual religion of the belief that if you act boldly, others will follow in your wake. That certainly proved to be the case with Karl Rove, for a time. But for all the fascination with what Rove was doing and thinking, little attention was given to whether or not it was working and why. This neglect encompasses many people, though one person with far greater consequences than all the others. In the end, the verdict on George W. Bush may be as simple as this: He never questioned the big, booming voice of Oz, so he never saw the little man behind the curtain.

WHAT WE TALK ABOUT WHEN WE TALK ABOUT WAR

WAR WEEK

One week in March posed an interesting confluence of events.
(Illustration by Steve Brodner; first appeared in *Comix Nation*.)

21

INSIDE THE SURGE

JON LEE ANDERSON

The New Yorker   November 19, 2007

Five years after the American-led invasion of Iraq, the official statistics tell the story of just how bloody the invasion and subsequent occupation have been: over 4,000 U.S. soldiers killed (plus another 300 from other coalition nations); at least another 30,000 G.I.s wounded, many of them with permanent, severe disabilities; and hundreds of thousands of Iraqi civilians killed or wounded—all at a cost to American taxpayers of some $9 billion a month, according to the Congressional Budget Office. From the statements of politicians in both parties, it appears that our military will be in Iraq for years to come, no matter who our next president is. Meanwhile, determining the actual state of affairs in the country is maddeningly difficult. Has the tide finally turned in our favor, as President Bush, John McCain, and other proponents of staying the course are claiming? Certainly, the violence in Iraq has subsided following the recent "surge" of an additional 30,000 U.S. troops into the conflict. But as this report by Jon Lee Anderson from the front lines of Baghdad makes clear, the question of whether the surge has really made Iraq more stable is, like the future of Iraq itself, still very much up in the air.

Joint Security Station Thrasher, in the western Baghdad suburb of Ghazaliya, is housed in a Saddam-era mansion with twenty-foot columns and a fountain, now dry, that looks like a layer cake of concrete and limestone. The mansion and two adjacent houses have been surrounded by blast walls. J.S.S Thrasher was set up last March, and is part of the surge in troops engineered by General David Petraeus, the American commander in Iraq. Moving units out of large bases and into Joint Security Stations—small outposts in Baghdad's most dangerous districts—has been crucial to Petraeus's counterinsurgency strategy, and Thrasher is now home to a hundred American soldiers and a few hundred Iraqis. This fall, on the roof of the mansion, amid sandbags, communications gear, and exercise equipment protected by a sniper awning, Captain Jon Brooks, Thrasher's commander, pointed out some of the local landmarks. "This site was selected because it was the main body drop in Ghazaliya," he said, indicating a grassy area nearby. "There were up to eleven bodies a week. Most were brutally mutilated."

The Mother of All Battles Mosque, with its unmistakable phalanx of minarets shaped like Scud missiles, is nearby. Saddam Hussein hid in Ghazaliya during the American bombing in the first Gulf War, and built the mosque to show his gratitude to the neighborhood. ("Ghazaliya used to have—still does—a lot of retired Saddam military people," Brooks said.) In April 2004, wounded gunmen taking part in the battle for Falluja took refuge in the mosque. Ghazaliya borders the eastern edge of Anbar province, the center of the Sunni insurgency, and it became a strategic gateway to Baghdad for insurgents and foreign jihadis. On a previous visit to Ghazaliya, in December 2003, I had met insurgents at a safe house in the neighborhood. They told me that they were intent on killing Americans. Since those days, with few exceptions, Ghazaliya had been a no-go area for Westerners, including journalists, who ran the risk of being kidnapped and killed. American patrols in Ghazaliya were regularly ambushed.

Captain Brooks is twenty-eight, of medium height and a stocky build, with close-cropped brown hair. From the roof, he pointed to where Sergeant Robert Thrasher, for whom the J.S.S. was named, had been killed by a sniper, last February. At the time, the company was working out of Camp Victory, the American base encompassing a large swath of Baghdad, including the airport. Thrasher was twenty-three; he had joined the Army out of high school.

Despite the insurgency's influence, Ghazaliya remained, at first, what it had been for decades—a middle-class Baghdad neighborhood in which sectarian tensions were more or less held in check. The vast majority of the estimated hundred thousand residents were Sunni, but, Brooks said, "there were a lot of professionals, college-educated Sunnis, and Shias, too, and mosques for both." The neighborhood changed after February 2006, when Sunni militants bombed the ninth-century Askariya shrine, in Samarra, one of the Shiites' holiest sites, and sectarian violence flared up across Iraq. Shiite militias, foremost among them the Mahdi Army, pushed deeper into Ghazaliya from Shulla, a poor, sprawling Shiite neighborhood just to the north. The Sunnis responded by turning to hard-line insurgents and to the foreign jihadis of Al Qaeda in Mesopotamia, whom the U.S. Army called Al Qaeda in Iraq.

"You had Sunni extremists in the area before Samarra. After Samarra, though, Al Qaeda in Iraq came on strong," Captain Brooks said. "They had death squads. They systematically selected people because of the locations of their houses, or their relationships. They brutally tortured them, killed them, and dumped their bodies." Shia families, and many Sunnis—those who had the financial means—fled the neighborhood. By the beginning of this year, southern Ghazaliya was under the de facto control of Al Qaeda in Mesopotamia, while the northern part of the neighborhood was besieged by Shiite militiamen. "Twenty dollars and a phone card could get you an I.E.D. placed," Captain Brooks said, referring to the improvised explosive devices that have caused the majority of American military deaths in Iraq. "The people realized they had let something in that they couldn't control."

President Bush, after securing Secretary of Defense Donald Rumsfeld's resignation, in November, gave his new war team—Secretary of Defense Robert Gates and General Petraeus—an opportunity to change the strategy in Iraq, and in February the surge began. The plan called for thirty thousand extra troops; estimates of the actual number run as high as fifty thousand. Thirty-four Joint Security Stations were opened in Baghdad, three of them in Ghazaliya: the first, J.S.S. Casino, in northern Ghazaliya; next, in the southwest, J.S.S. Thrasher; and, last May, J.S.S. Maverick, in the southeast.

Brooks pointed to a large house with broken windows across from the base. His men called it the Cannister-Round House, because when they were first moving in snipers had fired on them from inside, and they responded by lobbing tank shells into the house. "We don't get shot at anymore," he said. Brooks's men began the manpower-intensive work of conducting systematic patrols by day and aggressive raids at night; William Bushnell, a sergeant in Brooks's company, was killed on one of those patrols in April. Previously, Brooks's men had headed back to the heavily fortified Camp Victory after roving through Ghazaliya. With the surge, the Americans became a permanent presence in the neighborhood. After they moved in, the U.S. Army erected twenty miles of concrete walls in Ghazaliya, both to separate Shiite and Sunni residents from each other and to establish secure perimeters. Brooks said that his unit's success had been made possible by his colleagues at J.S.S. Casino, who kept Shiite militiamen from Shulla out of the neighborhood.

By midsummer, Ghazaliya's violence had abated significantly. This fall, when I stood on the roof of J.S.S. Thrasher at night, I occasionally saw explosions in the distance, fireballs flaring up in the sky. One night, a large blast shook the building, followed by automatic-weapons fire that momentarily illuminated the streets. But most of the explosions were so far away from Ghazaliya that they could not even be heard. The number of bodies found in the neighbor-hood had fallen steeply, "to practically zero, to pre-Samarra levels," Brooks said. His company had not lost any more men. When Petraeus spoke before Congress in September, he cited Ghazaliya as an example of the progress the military was making in Iraq.

The new strategy is also meant to prepare the ground for Iraqi security forces to replace the Americans, and all the Joint Security Stations, as the name suggests, involve Americans and Iraqis. But the Iraqis do not all belong to the official, government forces. With American assistance, several hundred armed Sunni volunteers called the Ghazaliya Guardians were gradually assuming police duties. Such U.S.-approved Sunni forces had begun to sprout up everywhere. Many of them, to the dismay of some Shiites, included former insurgents. An official with one of the major Shiite political parties told me, "Some of these armed groups were, until yesterday, hostile forces that attacked the Iraqi government, Coalition forces, and anyone who was involved in the government. They were considered terrorists. What happened?"

It was a question I heard often in Iraq. Colonel J.B. Burton is a good-natured bull of a man who commands the First Infantry's Dagger Brigade, covering most of northwest Baghdad, with fourteen J.S.S.s, including the three in Ghazaliya. "We began by asking ourselves the question: What is facilitating the entry of Al Qaeda into an area populated by moderate secular Arabs?" Colonel Burton said. The answer, he said, was fear of Shiite militias. "I think we're in a time of increasing opportunity to bring in people who want to be part of the solution. It's done by talking to people. Hell, it's no different than Tullahoma, Tennessee, where I'm from. It's sitting on the back porch, drinking tea, listening to the crickets, and talking." Colonel Burton went on, "You're talking with people who've pulled a trigger against American forces? Hell, yeah! Because we're fighting a common enemy—Al Qaeda."

His brigade's mission, Burton said, was "to defeat Al Qaeda and effect the transition to Iraqi authorities, and that's full-spectrum operations, which means everything from fighting terrorism to fixing sewage lines." Whether those goals could be accomplished ultimately hinged on political progress toward national reconciliation among Iraqis, Burton said. "We're in a window that's very narrow, and we have some important decisions to make. Which way Iraq goes will depend on what we do."

At Thrasher, Captain Brooks told me, "The new buzzword is 'sustainability.' We've learned from our experiences—for sustainable development here we need security. If they can have a local security force that can do the job, then that allows us to return home."

⤛ • ⤜

Ghazaliya is not the only area of Iraq in which the landscape has changed. On my previous visit to the country, ten months before, the violence seemed uncontrollable, with mass abductions and killings taking place in broad daylight. Most of the Iraqis I knew spoke bitterly about how the Americans and Iraq's political leaders were safely ensconced in the Green Zone, while mayhem raged around them. According to the Pentagon, in February the war took the lives of nearly two thousand Iraqi civilians; by October, that number had dropped to under a thousand. As with all body-count statistics in Iraq, these figures are disputed, but no one denies that the violence has waned considerably. The deaths of American soldiers have also fallen sharply, from a high of a hundred and twenty-six last May, as the surge intensified, to thirty-eight last month. For the moment, at least, it looked as if the surge might be working.

In a sense, the surge was belated emergency triage. Some of Baghdad's most dangerous Sunni neighborhoods, like Ghazaliya and Amiriya, have been tackled, but much of Diyala province, stretching from Baghdad northeast to the Iranian border, and Kirkuk, which has become a flashpoint because of Kurdish claims to the city and its oil resources, remain horrific battlegrounds. On October 29th, the same day that the decapitated bodies of twenty men were found outside Baquba, in Diyala, a suicide bomber on a bicycle killed twenty-nine policemen in the city.

And there has yet to be any significant U.S. troop presence in Baghdad's Shiite slums, such as Sadr City and Shulla, which are controlled by Shiite militiamen. Many of them claim to be members of the Mahdi Army, led by Moqtada al-Sadr, whose political brinkmanship and tactical use of violence have been an enduring source of bewilderment to the Pentagon's war planners. Indeed, analysts credit much of the recent drop in Iraqi civilian deaths not to the surge but to Sadr's decision, in August, to order the Mahdi Army, which is believed to have been responsible for much of the Shiite-on-Sunni sectarian killing in and around Baghdad, to "freeze" its activities for six months. Sadr's apparent aim was to ward off an escalation of a two-day gun battle between the Mahdi and another Shiite militia, and to reassert his control over his men.

The surge also coincided with the so-called Sunni Awakening, the decision by some Anbar tribesmen to ally themselves with the Americans and to fight against Al Qaeda in Mesopotamia—a shift that was not foreseen in Petraeus's plan. Sunnis in other areas have since joined them, though many have not; Al Qaeda in Mesopotamia is still active, and foreign jihadis remain in the country. On September 13th, Abu Risha, the Sunni tribal leader regarded as the catalyst of the alliance, whom President Bush had met in Anbar ten days before, was assassinated. Abu Risha was an influential and charismatic figure, and although his brother stepped in to take his place, most of the Iraqis I spoke to viewed his death as a serious loss and wondered how long his brother would survive. Still, there was hope that Al Qaeda might eventually be neutralized, thus removing at least one vicious aspect of the multifaceted war.

Some combination of the surge, the Sunni Awakening, and Sadr's freeze has helped to stabilize troubled areas of the capital and Anbar; it is unclear whether the gains can be expanded upon—or even sustained—with fewer troops, but further increases alone will not win the war. And no more troop additions are planned; instead, President Bush has promised to withdraw, by next July, almost as many troops as were brought in for the surge. Iraq's future, for the moment, is in limbo. The best one can say, perhaps, is that the U.S. has bought or borrowed a little space to work with. But there have been costs, some more obvious than others.

◂┼ • ┼▸

A few days before General Petraeus testified before Congress, I met with Sheikh Zaidan al-Awad, a prominent Sunni tribal leader from Anbar. The last time I had seen him, in 2004, he was full of hostile bluster about the U.S., and made no secret of his identification with the "resistance," as he described the hard-line Sunni insurgents. Sheikh Zaidan was a fugitive, suspected by the Americans of being a sponsor of the insurgency, and he was living in voluntary exile in Jordan. But when we spoke this fall, in an apartment in Amman, Zaidan told me that he had recently met for informal talks with American military and intelligence officials, because he approved of what they were now doing—allowing Sunni tribesmen to police themselves.

I asked Zaidan what sort of deal had led to the Sunni Awakening. "It's not a *deal*," he said, bristling. "People have come to realize that our fate is tied to the Americans', and theirs to ours. If they are successful in Iraq, it will depend on

Anbar. We always said this. Time was lost. America was lost, but now it's woken up; it now holds a thread in its hand. For the first time, they're doing something right."

Zaidan said that Anbar's Sunni tribes no longer had any need to exact blood vengeance on U.S. forces. "We've already taken our revenge," he said. "We're the ones who've made them crawl on their stomachs, and now we're the ones to pick them up." He added, "Once Anbar is settled, we must take control of Baghdad, and we will." There would have to be a lot more fighting before the capital was taken back from the Shiites, he said. "The Anbaris will take charge of the purge. What the whole world failed to do in Anbar, we have done overnight. Baghdad will be a lot easier."

Many of the players in Iraq seemed, like Zaidan, to be positioning themselves for the next battle. While the Shiites issued warnings about the Sunnis' intentions, nearly all the talk among the Americans was of the Mahdi Army and its reputed sponsor, Iran, which Petraeus accused of waging a "proxy war" in Iraq; there were dismissive references to Al Qaeda as a spent force.

Colonel Burton said, "Al Qaeda is relatively easy to fight. You just fight them, deny them access." The Mahdi Army, he said, "was harder." By all accounts, the Mahdi Army and other Shiite militias had penetrated the Iraqi security forces, and Sadr's political party was an on-again, off-again partner in Prime Minister Nuri al-Maliki's Shiite-dominated coalition government. "We began investigating the Iraqi security forces and began to target them, their leaders, and members of the Iraqi government," Burton said. (One notorious case of official involvement in sectarian killings concerns the former deputy health minister and the ministry's security chief. In February, the men, who are Shiites and loyalists of Moqtada al-Sadr, were arrested on charges of organizing the murders of hundreds of Sunnis in Baghdad's hospitals—including patients, their relatives, and medical staff.)

Referring to the Mahdi Army by the acronym of its Arabic name, Jaish al-Mahdi, Colonel Burton said, "I talk to some of these JAM guys, you know. I have e-mail contact with some of them. Recently, a JAM sheikh in Khadamiya told me that if I released three of his guys there'd be no more attacks on U.S. forces there." He raised his eyebrows.

The Shiite authorities' control over many government services meant that there was a great deal of institutional discrimination against Sunni communities. When I was there, for example, Ghazaliya residents complained of receiving half as much electricity a day as a neighboring Shiite area. The Americans were doing a lot of politicking to alleviate the situation, but it hadn't been easy. "On the Shia side, there's lots of money moving around, and essential services are doing really well," Burton said. "But on the Sunni side—not so well."

The new strategy, like most of the previous strategies employed in Iraq, had the drawback of having been imposed by the Americans. Many of the Shiite politicians in Iraq's government were angry about the U.S. decision to wall off Baghdad neighborhoods and to recruit and arm Sunni volunteer organizations without consulting them. There were fears that the U.S. was simply arming a new set of militias—undermining the authority of the fragile coalition government. This may have been part of the goal. Iraq, with a hundred and seventy thousand U.S. troops on its soil, is not a sovereign country, and the U.S. uses its military power to shape the Iraqi political scene. By strengthening the hand of the Sunnis, the U.S. effectively forced the Maliki government to incorporate more Sunnis into the security forces—a step toward national reconciliation.

Shiite political parties and militias are so interwoven that a Shiite equivalent of the Sunni Awakening seems unlikely—it would probably require a split within the Shiite community, a civil war within a civil war. Iran would also be a major factor. Given Sadr's alleged close links to Iranian hard-liners, and the growing hostility between Iran and the United States, his future moves are virtually impossible to predict. A largely covert conflict is already taking place between Iran and the United States. Iran has intervened in Iraq by providing financial and military support for Shiite militia groups, and, more directly, by sending agents and officials there. Iraq's Shiite leaders have long had close ties to Iran, where many of them lived in exile during Saddam's rule, and they and the Kurds have, without visible success, sought greater cooperation between Iran and the U.S. over security in Iraq. Many Sunnis, meanwhile, are distrustful of any dealings with Iran, and are unabashed about their hostility.

Sheikh Zaidan offered a vision of how the conflict in Iraq could escalate to the advantage of the Sunnis: "I think America will be able to start a Shia-Shia civil war in the south—with the Arab Shia, the tribes, being supported by the U.S., and the Persian Shiites supported by Iran." He said that this would be an opportunity for the Americans to "cut off the head of Iran's government and its militias in Iraq." The Sunnis could help in this fight, he suggested.

The likelihood of Zaidan's scenario being played out depends, to a large extent, on how the Iranians, the Americans, and the Iraqi Shiites choose to shape their ongoing competition for influence. Political moderates may broker a settlement. But Zaidan's views are shared by many in the Sunni community, where extremist positions still have a hold. At one roadblock in Ghazaliya, I spoke with a Ghazaliya Guardian, a twenty-six-year-old Sunni who identified himself as Officer Ahmed. He told me that he thought a purge of Shiites from power in Baghdad, such as that proposed by Zaidan, was a good idea. When I asked Officer Ahmed how his neighborhood had gone from being a bastion of the insurgency to a model of cooperation, his response was vague. "When the Ghazaliya Guardians started, the terrorists disappeared," he said. "We don't know where they are now." He had been elsewhere during the fighting, he said, and returned only when it was over.

I found the young Guardian's story of the recent past—in which he had merely tried to keep his head down until things blew over—unconvincing. In most of my conversations with the Iraqis working with the Americans, their true motivations struck me as unknowable. The Americans, no doubt driven by an urgent need to establish greater security, to be able to draw down troops, seemed all too willing to take their new allies at face value.

◄◄← • →►►

At J.S.S. Thrasher, Brooks and his men conducted raids several times a week, usually after dark. The raids were generally the result of tips from residents who called in to a hot line manned twenty-four hours a day by Iraqi interpreters, known as Terps; during daily patrols, Brooks's men passed out flyers with the phone number. "We say, 'If anyone threatens you, give a call.' The foot patrols are key: when you see someone walking down your street, when you see a face—it's different," Brooks said. "As a tank commander, I found it funny—the first thing I had to do was tell my tankers to get out and walk."

Brooks said that he had wanted to be a tank commander ever since he was a boy ("I love tanks"). After high school, in Springdale, Arkansas, he had gone to the New Mexico Military Institute, in Roswell, and afterward joined the Kansas Army National Guard. He was in the U.S. Armor Officer Basic Course during the attacks of September 11th, and in 2003 was sent to Iraq. He was eleven months into his second fifteen-month deployment. Brooks and his men had been told that they might be home for Christmas, but nobody was getting his hopes up too much yet.

One night, I went along on a raid, which Brooks designated Operation Muttonchops, because the main target was a man with a lot of facial hair. We drove from Thrasher in a Bradley Fighting Vehicle. The Americans had superimposed their own lexicon on the neighborhood's geography, to make it comprehensible to themselves. Just as Ghazaliya had been divided into three areas—Casino, Thrasher, and Maverick—all the major road arteries were referred to in Pentagonese: Red Falcon, Caradine, Vernon, Cecil, R.P.G. Alley, High Tension Road, and so forth. Few of the American soldiers knew how the locals referred to those same streets.

When the hydraulic rear hatch of the Bradley opened, I saw Iraqi and American soldiers running here and there, shouting, guns drawn. I followed some soldiers into a house. In the kitchen, a young American in full combat gear was bending over a man who was lying face down on the floor. The soldier cursed as he struggled to tie the man's hands behind his back with plastic handcuffs. A couple of half-eaten plates of food were on a table, along with a mobile phone, which rang repeatedly. In an adjacent room, another prone man was being trussed. A teen-age Iraqi, the younger brother of the two men, entered the kitchen and began to object; the American soldier handcuffed him as well. Pushing the teen-ager's face toward the floor, the soldier shouted, in English, "Shut the fuck up! Move your fucking head!"

A middle-aged woman in a flower-patterned smock emerged, sobbing, as the three brothers were moved outside. They were made to kneel, their cuffed hands behind their heads. A masked Terp held a photograph up next to each of the men's faces. As American soldiers inspected the teen-ager, who had peach fuzz on his chin, one muttered, "*This* isn't Muttonchops."

The three men were shoved down the street aggressively by the young soldier. (He was the only soldier I saw behave in that way; later, when he began berating women in another home, an officer told him to cool down.) After further consultation between the Americans and their masked Terps, it was decided that none of the three detainees were targets of the raid. Their handcuffs were cut, and they were told to go home.

The Americans now turned their attention to three other men, who were seated on a curb. One was a chubby adolescent. With him was a thin, scraggly-bearded youth in his early twenties and a man in his thirties. They explained that they had been sitting outside in the cool air, chatting and smoking. Their families, with several small children, were roused from bed. The Americans released the boy—he was fourteen years old—into his father's custody, but decided to take the two other men back to Thrasher.

I climbed into the Bradley, along with the older of the detainees, who was seated on the bench across from me. His hands had been bound, and he was trembling. The gunner of the Bradley leaned back, grabbed the detainee's T-shirt, and forced it over his head, like a hood. The disoriented man sat stiffly upright, and held his mouth open against the cloth around his face, as if to help himself breathe.

◄◄ • ►►

As it happened, an Iraqi whom I knew well had begun working for the Americans at a base under Colonel Burton's jurisdiction. I will call him Karim. He is a Shiite, and lives in a mixed Baghdad neighborhood just east of Ghazaliya. Karim said that he and a friend, whom I will call Amar (other names in their account have also been changed), had called in more than forty American raids, which had resulted in the capture of several dozen terrorists.

Karim said that, at first, he had welcomed the Mahdi Army, because it offered a measure of protection against Sunni extremists. But the militia had transformed itself into something like a Mafia organization, extorting money and abducting and murdering his neighbors—Shiites and Sunnis alike. The Mahdi Army men in their neighborhood, who regarded Karim and Amar as friends, had no idea that they were turning them in. Then Karim told me that it wasn't only the Mahdi Army that he was deceiving but the Americans, too.

Amar was a lifelong friend of Karim's. Three months earlier, Amar and his older brother, Jafaar, had been riding in the van of a friend, Sayeed, when a group of gunmen hailed them. Amar recognized them as Mahdi Army men, and assumed that they were coming to say hello. As Sayeed braked, the car was riddled with gunfire. Amar crouched as low as he could, as the Mahdi Army men emptied their Kalashnikovs. He was unhurt, but Jafaar and Sayeed were dead.

That night, Amar told Karim that, at the morgue, he had sworn over his brother's body to take revenge. He had vowed to kill a hundred Mahdi men—ten for each of Jafaar's fingers. His mother, Um Jafaar, supported him, and begged Karim to help her son. He agreed.

Their first concern was to make sure that the Mahdi militiamen didn't suspect them. During Jafaar's funeral procession, they shouted angry denunciations of a Sunni tribe that lived nearby. Word soon spread that Jafaar's family and friends blamed the Sunnis for his death.

Karim and Amar also decided that it would be easier to carry out the killings if they won the Americans' trust. Karim went to a nearby U.S. military base, and spoke to a captain. "I told the captain, 'You help me, I help you. I love my country, my neighbors. The Mahdi have killed many of my friends, and American soldiers, too. I want to cooperate.'" Karim gave the captain the names of two of the men who had killed Jafaar. The captain said that, if they were detained, Karim would get some money. He refused: "If I take it, it makes me a spy, and I am a gentleman, not a spy."

Karim put the captain in touch with Amar, who directed American soldiers to the houses where the two gunmen were staying. The operation was a success. "They found many guns and pistols," Karim said. "They took them, investigated, and they were convinced about what they were—killers. One was young, fifteen or sixteen, and had killed five or six people. He was just starting out. He is now in Bucca"—a U.S. prison camp in southern Iraq.

"Then the killing started," Karim told me. Their first victim was the father of the younger gunman. When I asked him whether the father had anything to do with Jafaar's killing, he looked nonplussed, and said no, but that the man had been an intelligence officer under Saddam, and had probably killed people, too. (In Iraq's tribal vendettas, male relatives are often seen as legitimate targets.) The father was now working as a taxi-driver. Karim told Amar's sister to wave him down as he left his house, and ask to be dropped off at a warehouse on the outskirts of a Sunni district. "Amar and I followed," he said. "She got out, and crossed the street. I told Amar, 'Do it now.'"

Amar drove in front of the taxi-driver, cutting him off. "Amar got out of the car and he shot him in the face. I had put five dumdums and four normal bullets in the gun, a SIG Sauer. One dumdum is enough to kill one man. I told him to shoot only four and keep some back, just in case, but he shot them all." (Afterward, according to Karim, Amar apologized. "He said, 'I couldn't help it. I became crazy.'")

Next, they went to a Sunni sheikh whom Karim knew, whose brother was in the insurgency. The brother and his men kidnapped six Mahdi militiamen, including four who had been in the group that killed Jafaar. They took them to a house in Mansour, a Sunni district, where Karim and Amar met them. "They were tied up and their heads were covered. Amar beat them too much—not me," Karim said. "We were pretending to be Sunni mujahideen. We told them, 'If you tell the truth we release you, but if not we will kill you.' Of course, this was not the truth."

The men said that Sayeed had been their target; Jafaar just happened to be in the car. "They said they had killed Sayeed because he was a member of Badr"—the military wing of the Islamic Supreme Council of Iraq, a major rival of the Mahdi Army—"and worked with Americans. But this is not true. They killed him because he was rich and didn't respect the Mahdi Army. They were jealous."

Karim told me that he left before the interrogation was over, and didn't talk to Amar until the next day. "When I saw him, he kissed me. He said, 'I left three bodies near the train track, and two in Canal Street, to be taken to the morgue.'

"I said, 'No. 6, where is he?' Amar said, 'The sheikh's brother took him, because he thinks he killed his cousin.'"

The killing continued. After fifteen days, they went to Um Jafaar, Amar's mother. "I told her who was dead and who was in jail. She was very happy," Karim said. "Then she said, 'Do you want me to be completely comforted?'" Um Jafaar asked them to bring her parts of the dead men's bodies. Amar did what she asked.

"One man, he cut off his ear when he was still alive," Karim said. "But I swear that Amar has never killed anyone who was innocent."

Karim said that Amar had killed eighteen or twenty men. "After a while, I told Amar to stop this. My wife, also, was angry with me. I didn't like to do this, either, but we had to. We had to kill these guys, because they were killing too many people. When some of them were killed, my neighbors celebrated—sometimes even the Mahdi Army guys did."

Karim mentioned the American captain with whom Amar worked. "Amar is a friend of the captain, but he doesn't know about this." He added, "Amar was friends of the Mahdi—*real* friends. I have to be honest with you. If not for Jafaar's killing, he still would be."

Amar told Karim that he would not stop killing until he reached his goal of a hundred victims. "He is hungry for killing now," Karim said. "Sometimes I think maybe he *has* gone a little crazy."

⤛ • ⤜

In the next days, I confirmed that Amar was working with the American military; I also heard that he had been employed by a large private military contractor. Amar's case underscores one of the many dangers of fighting a war in a land where the culture and the language are incomprehensible to most of the soldiers. The U.S. military can do little without the assistance of local allies at every level, from collaborators like Amar to political leaders. Paradoxically, it is during the Americans' well-armed raids that their vulnerability in Iraq is most acutely on display. The Americans are always accompanied by their spectral Terps. They often act on tips whose sources are opaque, without knowing what lies behind them. Among the Iraqis I met who were working with the Americans, motives seemed to range from the pecuniary—a job and a good wage—to the patriotic, or a combination of both. But, in great measure, their ultimate loyalties must be taken on faith.

There have been some well-publicized embarrassments, such as when the U.S. Marines named a former Iraqi general to lead a militia, the so-called Falluja Brigade, to combat insurgents there in 2004. The general, it turned out, had been accused of involvement in Saddam-era atrocities against the Kurds. He was quickly replaced; months later, the brigade fell under suspicion of aiding insurgents, and was disbanded.

Amar's killing spree may not pose that sort of problem for the U.S. military—assuming that his victims really are all "bad guys." In wars, killing acquires a kind of perverse logic, and at times can come to be seen as part of the solution. Colonel Burton made it clear to me that he hadn't been sorry to hear that in the area under his command a notorious Shiite militia leader had been, as he put it, "whacked": "If he is gone, then it means that a big area that was influenced by him has been lifted from his control." Burton acknowledged, however, that the assassination of the Shiite militia leader had sparked a series of sectarian revenge killings; the neighborhood had to be placed under a "no-move policy." (I learned that the militia leader had been killed by the same man who had helped Amar kidnap six of his victims—the ones they had tortured before killing.)

Later, I told Colonel Burton that I had heard about Iraqis working with the U.S. who engaged in revenge killings. He responded, "Let me put it this way: I know that we do work with people who have provided information that has led to the capture of criminals and weapons caches. They have also called us and said they know where we can find the remains of people that we're looking for. There is a form of justice in Iraq that is traditional, but we do our best to get ahead of it."

Tribal vendettas have been an underlying feature of the Iraq war since it began. Amar's story may be unusual in the scale of his ambitions—a hundred men for his brother—but such crimes are common. At least some of the initial impetus for Iraq's insurgency came in the spring of 2003, when American troops in Falluja shot and killed seventeen demonstrators, and kinsmen of the dead sought revenge by killing Americans. In tribal families, it is often the matriarch who encourages the vendetta, as Amar's mother did.

Um Jafaar is a handsome, elderly woman. When I arrived at her home, with Karim, she was wearing a black abaya, and I noticed blue tribal tattoos on her chin and her hands. She invited me to sit down on a couch, and sat next to me in an armchair. Jafaar's three young daughters were watching us. When I asked Um Jafaar if she wanted revenge for her son's death, she got up from her chair, came over, and kissed the top of my head.

"Yes, I want revenge," she said. "I am a mother, and I lost my son for nothing." She began weeping, great wracking sobs. When she recovered, Um Jafaar pointed to her granddaughters. "Look, they have no father," she said. "Why?"

Um Jafaar went on to tell me that she took the body parts of Amar's victims, wrapped in cloth, to his grave, in the holy city of Najaf, and buried them there. "I talk to my son, I tell him, 'Here, this is from those who killed you, I take revenge.'" Moving one hand in a horizontal circle, she said, "I put them around the grave. So far, I have taken one hand, one eye, an Adam's apple, toes, fingers, ears, and noses." (Karim told me that the hand had made the house stink for days.) I asked her how many Mahdi men Amar had killed. "I don't know: eighteen, twenty? But still my heart hurts. Even if we kill all of them, I won't have comfort," she said.

"The Americans catch them and put them in jail," Um Jafaar went on. "This is not a solution, they have to be killed!" She turned to me: "Tell the American forces I am ready to fight with them against the Jaish al-Mahdi. I am a woman but I am ready. When you come here, we will sacrifice everything for you, because *you* did not kill my son. I pray for the Americans—even if they are Christians and Jews—and to the Prophet Muhammad, to protect you."

A few days earlier, Um Jafaar told me, she had been at the funeral of a Mahdi fighter, and had heard one of his comrades vow to avenge him: "He said, 'If before I decapitated them at the neck, now I will do it at their mouths.'" She made a hacking motion across her mouth.

Karim's cell phone rang. He answered it, and began speaking in Arabic. Afterward, he told me that it was Amar, who was out on an American patrol. "They have caught two Jaish al-Mahdi, and the Americans' Terps are making them dance at gunpoint," Karim said, laughing.

I asked if I could meet Amar. Karim said that he would see.

<-- • -->

J.S.S. Maverick, in the southeast corner of Ghazaliya, was the quietest of the neighborhood's three Joint Security Stations. When I visited, in September, it had been two months since the last I.E.D. explosion. There was still danger but a certain tedium had set in to the soldiers' routines. "They hate the daily shit, like all soldiers do," an officer told me. "But they love not getting shot at or blown up by I.E.D.s every day"—which, until midsummer, was how it had been in Ghazaliya. "It's like going from cocaine to weed," he said.

I drove through Maverick with a crew in a Humvee. There were no people on the streets, and the senior soldier in the unit said, "I don't like it. Makes me expect something to go boom." The Humvee cut across a field, and halted where a suspicious-looking metal cannister lay in our path; the driver gave it a wide berth. As we made our way, very slowly because of the armored Humvee's weight—six tons—we approached a street that was covered in raw sewage. "Doo-doo water!" one of the men yelled. "Ooooh!" the others in the Humvee shouted in disgusted unison.

That evening, units from Maverick went on a "census mission"—part of a program aimed at creating a central register with the biometric profile of every military-age man living within its area, to help identify infiltrators. Iraqi police closed off either end of the street, as Americans and Terps searched each house. The residents seemed to know what was expected of them. The men came forward politely and handed over their identification cards; an Army man took their photographs with an iris-scanning camera.

In theory, operations like this represent the advantage of moving U.S. soldiers into neighborhoods like Ghazaliya, where they can build relationships and glean intelligence, and that night's census was civil enough. But the constant raids and patrols can also alienate local residents, and reinforce the impression of the Americans as a coercive force with the overweening power to invade the homes of Iraqis, and detain them at will. The Army's tactics can become the catalyst that leads Iraqis to the insurgency.

Maverick's area of Ghazaliya did not yet have a contingent of Guardians, and so the soldiers were using the Iraqi National Police, which is predominantly Shiite, as their auxiliaries. The national police in Ghazaliya, however, were suspected of being under the control of the Mahdi Army. The local police commander had recently been arrested and charged with helping carry out kidnappings and murders. A new police commander, Lieutenant Colonel Ahsin al-Khazragee, had been appointed, but the detachment remained a matter of concern. "No one trusts 'em," Lieutenant Matthew Holtzendorff, who led the census mission, told me. (The complaints go in both directions: while I was there, a truck belonging to Kellogg, Brown, and Root, the military contractor, had ploughed through barriers manned by the national police in Maverick's area, killing one policeman and badly injuring another, and then sped on without stopping. An Army officer told me that the incident was being investigated; K.B.R., when asked for comment, denied any knowledge of it.)

On the way back to Maverick, the convoy drove past a group of sullen-looking Iraqi police at a barricade, then pulled up in front of a well-tended middle-class home. A young boy opened the door, smiling when he saw Lieutenant Holtzendorff. We went inside, and were greeted warmly by a man in his thirties whom I will call Sabah, and who worked as a civil engineer inside the Green Zone. A few months earlier, Holtzendorff had saved Sabah from being kidnapped by the Iraqi police detachment down the street—the ones we had just passed. They had beaten him badly, and, most likely, had planned to kill him. Holtzendorff made a point of visiting Sabah regularly, to make it clear that he was under American protection.

Sabah was sweating, and he chain-smoked. He anxiously asked Holtzendorff where he had been; it had been two weeks since his previous visit. Holtzendorff explained that he had been called away, but said that he had asked his men to stop by every few days. They had, hadn't they? Sabah nodded and smiled, but his hands shook. After thirty minutes or so, despite Sabah's entreaties to stay longer, Holtzendorff stood up, promising to return.

Later, I discussed Sabah's case with one of the unit's officers. Developing a nonsectarian national police force is an essential part of the U.S. military's plan to disengage its own troops, but, as the officer saw it, the police were still part of the problem. "Please don't print my name, or Petraeus will kill me," he said. "The national police are supposed to be our salvation; all our hopes are pinned on them!" He added, "Balancing the Shia and the Sunni—the politics of it— that's the hardest part of my job. 'Hunt bad guy, kill bad guy'—O.K., that's what I'm trained to do. But they don't train you for this."

⤙ • ⤚

Colonel Ahsin, the newly appointed police chief in Maverick's area, is a punctilious man in his late thirties; when I joined him for an evening walkabout, on a street a few blocks from Maverick, I picked up the aroma of cologne. Ahsin was accompanied by Major Robert O'Brien, the American officer in charge of Maverick's National Police Transition Team, or N.P.T.T.s, known by all as Nip-its.

Three bodyguards moved around Colonel Ahsin like a protective fan. As we headed down the street, a mixture of homes and shops, Ahsin made a great display of courteousness to the stall keepers. At one stand, he popped a sweet-meat in his mouth. He bent down to tousle the hair of some small boys. As he walked on, an older man approached, and the bodyguards immediately huddled around him. The man complained that an Iraqi police car had collided with his car. Ahsin listened and then, in a loud voice, called out, "Maaa-jor!"

O'Brien trotted over, saying deferentially, "*Na'm, sayyidi*?" ("Yes, sir?"). Colonel Ahsin told O'Brien that he wanted to have the offending policeman arrested. "*Na'm, sayyidi*," O'Brien said, scribbling in his notebook. As we proceeded, this scene was repeated again and again: Ahsin gave orders to O'Brien, who obsequiously wrote them down. At one point, O'Brien smiled in my direction, and said, "This is the magic. Yeah!"

Later, I asked O'Brien what he knew about Colonel Ahsin. "All I know is that he was thirteen years in the special forces with Saddam's Army, and joined the national police in 2004," O'Brien said. They had known each other only a week and a half, but he thought that Ahsin was "fantastic."

I said that Ahsin seemed to enjoy the role of the Big Man.

O'Brien flashed me a look. "Look, it works," he said quietly. "That's what I want. I *want* him to take charge. Some advisers want to take command, and we need them to." He paused. "It's like surfing, except that here we're surfing on top of a shit tidal wave, and we're just trying not to fall in." O'Brien laughed. "Saddam Hussein once said that the trick of counterinsurgency is to separate the people from the insurgents. That's what we're trying to do here. If the people like what you do more than what the others do, then you have a chance."

⤚ • ⤙

The Americans hoped that the Ghazaliya Guardians, the Sunni volunteer group, would serve as a new police force. Here, too, there were complications: General Petraeus had singled out the Guardians as a positive development, but the Shiites had a very different view. "The policy adopted by the Iraqi government, along with the Coalition, has been to *disband* armed militia groups," an official of the Islamic Supreme Council of Iraq said. He acknowledged that Iraq's security force was a "weak and sick body," ridden with militias, and needed to be reformed. "But the solution is not to bring new forces onto the scene, ones that people have doubts about."

The Americans, the Shiite official said, were arming the Sunni volunteers without adequately looking into their backgrounds. "There are a lot of stories now that some of those involved in the Awakening were known to be very dangerous criminals in their areas," he said. He mentioned hard-line insurgent groups like the 1920 Revolution Brigades and the Islamic Army, whose members have joined volunteer groups. "Now they're walking around armed, with uniforms and badges that allow them to go into places normally permitted only to Iraqi security forces." He added, "There must be mechanisms put into place to insure that these people's loyalties are to Iraq and its government—before they get stronger and have their own controlled territories."

On a clear morning in late September, about a dozen members of the Ghazaliya Guardians mustered at a small public marketplace to meet Captain Brooks. Dressed in matching cream-colored shirts, khaki pants, and beige baseball caps, they resembled security guards for a golf course. Their only noticeable insignia were small shoulder badges showing the Iraqi flag. (Colonel Burton had told me, "The guys in Ghazaliya, now, they're militaristic, pretty well dressed, pretty professional; a lot of them are former Iraqi Army guys.") Their leader, a portly middle-aged man with a notebook, greeted Captain Brooks attentively.

This was an important day for the Guardians. After three months under Iraqi Army supervision, they were about to be allowed to man roadblocks on their own—just the sort of transition that the Shiite official worried about. Their leader conducted Brooks to several spots around the intersection, which he proposed as the Guardians' checkpoints. At the first, Brooks said, "You wouldn't want to fight from here; you need a place you can retreat to." The Guardian pointed to a row of buildings, and suggested that it might be an ideal place for a Guardian office, where his men could rest. Brooks said, "I don't want you hunkered down," and that, instead, they should set up a stall in the market, with an awning.

As Captain Brooks walked around, a shopkeeper came up to him and pointed to the sewage in the street. Brooks said that he would send in the "suck truck" to remove it. Another man complained about electricity, and a third said that the neighborhood needed a water truck, "to keep the dust down." Brooks rolled his eyes. "I can fix a lot of things," he said. "But I can't do much about dust."

After he moved on, Brooks was approached by a woman who said that her son, a member of the Guardians, had recently been arrested. She had heard nothing more of him since.

As she was speaking, gunshots rang out from the other side of the market-place: a Guardian had fired off warning shots when a vehicle did not heed his command to halt. Brooks sent his men over with orders to check out the position: "See if it can be fixed so people have more time to react." Turning back to the woman, he told her that he would try and find out about her son. He said that, in a few days, an office would open nearby, where residents could get information about detainees.

It was now midday; the heat was intense, and Brooks was getting impatient. He was besieged by another group of shopkeepers, who complained about a trash-strewn field next to their stalls. Brooks pointed to a large wire-mesh basket; it was one of several that his soldiers had placed in vacant lots around Ghazaliya. He noted that it was nearly empty, and that garbage had been dumped all around it. He challenged them: "Why should I care about your garbage if the people here don't?"

We climbed back into the Humvee and drove off. As we were leaving the marketplace, Brooks yelled for the driver to stop, and leaped out of the Humvee, cursing loudly. He strode up to a man who sat under a tree behind a table that was laden with chocolate, potato chips, cigarettes, and some cheap plastic toys. Brooks grabbed a plastic pistol and a toy AK–47 off the table and brandished them in the face of the vender. "What are these?" he shouted. The vender, who had smiled anxiously as Brooks approached, now crumpled with apprehension. "They're just toys, for babies," he said placatingly, still forcing himself to smile. A tall masked Terp named Leo was translating for Brooks.

"You're an idiot!" Brooks shouted. Leo said something to the man in Arabic. "What do you think will happen if one of my soldiers sees this pointed at him at night?" Brooks waved the toy pistol in the man's face. "You will kill more children in this area than Al Qaeda!" Brooks demanded a reply. Leo spoke again to the vender, who said that he was not the only person selling toy guns; there was a stall in front of Ghazaliya's municipal offices. "Everyone sells them," he said.

Brooks listened stonily. Then he stepped back and spat on the ground in front of the vender's table. Shaking a fist, he said, "You make me sick, you killer of children," and wheeled around to leave. Stopping a few feet away, he turned back again and kicked a cloud of dust toward the vender. "Let's go!" he shouted. Brooks was silent for the return journey to J.S.S. Thrasher.

Back at the base, I asked Leo about the exchange. He said that he had not translated "exactly" what Captain Brooks had said: "His words were very insulting, you know. If I had told him exactly, the man would have been very offended."

⤛ • ⤜

Several days after I saw Um Jafaar, Karim arranged a meeting for me with Amar. A stocky man in his mid-thirties, Amar had a close-shaven head and a lumpy, fleshy face with a thick mustache. There was an unnervingly serene air about him, and I found it difficult to look him in the eye for very long.

Amar spoke in a matter-of-fact monotone. "Jafaar had ten fingers; each one of his fingers was worth ten Jaish al-Mahdi guys," he said. "So I decided to take my revenge against a hundred of them. So far, I have taken my revenge against twenty."

Did he count those he had helped the Americans capture? I asked.

Amar shook his head. "Some are now in prison," he said. "If they are released, I will kill them. If they are not released, I will kill their brothers or their fathers. Today, I have one in my mind." He and Karim spoke in Arabic for a moment. Turning to me, Karim said, "Yes, this man deserves it. He's killed, like, three hundred people in Baghdad."

Amar mentioned a nearby neighborhood. "I take most of the people and kill them there," he said. "It's two minutes from Hay al-Adil, a Sunni district. The Jaish al-Mahdi think the people of Hay al-Adil are killing them." Amar smiled wanly. "They come with me, as my friends. They trust me, the Jaish al-Mahdi." Amar said that he would also invite the Mahdi men to a warehouse he owned—"to eat or to drink, or to race pigeons. I make up different stories." Once there, he usually put a drug in their tea or sprinkled it on dates he offered them. "They fall asleep, then I shoot them in the head." Sometimes, he slit their throats.

"Americans are too honorable, too clean," he said. "They have to kill these people. They are dirty. Anyway, if they don't kill them, I will. But helping the Americans arrest them helps them not suspect me."

Before Jafaar's death, Amar had made mistakes—drinking, women. In seeking revenge, he had become closer to God, and that, he said, had kept him going. "God wants me to kill these people. It is *haram* to kill cats, but it is good to kill the Jaish al-Mahdi," he said. "They have strangled honest Sunni people in front of me. I feel no difference between me and the Sunni; I feel very angry about that. The Mahdi are not like they were before; they kill Shia or Sunni, for whatever reason. If I go to Hell, I will be comfortable, because I took my revenge." He added, "Honestly, it was only after the first one that I didn't sleep well, because I had not killed before. But afterward it felt normal."

Last week, I spoke again to Karim. He told me that something had happened—there was now reason to believe that the Mahdi Army had become aware of Amar's involvement in the killings. Karim was urging him to leave Baghdad, at least for a while. If he didn't, there was a good chance that he would be a target. For the moment, though, Amar was simply lying low.

◄◄ • ►►

One afternoon, sitting with Captain Brooks in Thrasher's rooftop gym, I asked if he felt that what he was doing in Iraq was appreciated by the people back home. "Oh, yeah," he said. Turning to one of his N.C.O.s, who was seated nearby, smoking a cigar, he asked, "What do you think, Sergeant Cochran?"

Lowering his voice, Cochran replied, "When that bullet goes by my head, all the politics goes right out the window. My only thought is to get my men out of there alive."

"Thanks for quoting *Black Hawk Down,* Sergeant Cochran," Brooks drawled. Turning back to me, he said, "When I went home the last time, we went skiing in Colorado. Everywhere we went, people thanked me. One man said, 'I don't support the war but I support the soldiers.' I can accept that. We have a system that allows freedom of speech. Hell, I put on the uniform to defend that."

Brooks seemed to feel that what he and his men were doing in Iraq was worthwhile. He felt that, for now, the country needed the U.S. military, as much for its peacekeeping duties as for its combat role. "In the Sunni population, there is still fear of Shia militias, and fear that violence will start again," Captain Brooks said. "We've seen efforts by Al Qaeda in Iraq to reignite sectarian violence, but, to the people's credit, nothing really reignited, and has not yet." He knocked on a wooden table in front of him. "There's still a lot of work to be done on national reconciliation in this area. Ghazaliya is a microcosm of what Iraq faces as a whole. The Iraq Study Group said national reconciliation was essential, and I agree. Until Iraqis work out the Sunni-Shia sectarian issues, they're going to have a very tough time making meaningful or lasting progress."

I asked Brooks if he planned to stay in the Army after his tour ended. He gave me a candid look, and said he hadn't made up his mind yet. "I want to go on vacation when I get home and then decide," he said.

When I asked how long he thought the U.S. would remain in Iraq, Brooks thought for a while, and said, "I'm not just blowing smoke up your ass, but it really depends on what the U.S. civilian-controlled government decides its goals are and what it tells the military to do."

Brooks continued, "Things are going well. Just about everything we wanted to achieve on a local level, we've achieved. It's counterinsurgency, it's different from what one would normally associate with war—i.e., 'victory is won.' I feel that winning will be a point you never realize that you're there—that at some indeterminate point you'll look back and realize that you've won."

22

ANATOMY OF THE SURGE

PETER D. FEAVER
Commentary   April 2008

One of the toughest challenges facing political journalists is to inform readers about the thinking and motivations behind various policy decisions. For numerous reasons, government officials are often reluctant to share their reasoning processes with the press, especially if the policy under discussion is controversial. The following article from Commentary *is a refreshing exception to this rule, since the author is an insider himself. Here, Peter D. Feaver, a professor of political science and public policy at Duke University who spent two years as a member of the government team shaping U.S. policy in Iraq, offers up his account of how things appear from within the Administration, looking out.*

Over the past sixteen months, the United States has altered its trajectory in Iraq. We are no longer headed toward a catastrophic defeat and may be on the path to a remarkable victory. As a result, the next President, Democrat or Republican, may well find it easier to adopt the broad contours of this administration's current strategy than to jeopardize progress by changing course abruptly.

That would be an ironic, but satisfying, outcome to the tortuous journey on which the Bush administration's policy toward Iraq, and this nation's views of Iraq, have been traveling over the past three years.

The Administration's description of the long-term American goal—a democratic Iraq that can defend itself, govern itself, and sustain itself, and will be an ally in the war on terror—has remained consistent from the time the war was launched in 2003 until now. What has shifted, due to sobering experience, is its sense of how long it might take to achieve this goal: a time frame that has stretched from months, to years, and even to decades.

I witnessed the shift first-hand. For two years, from June 2005 to July 2007, I left my teaching position at Duke to join the National Security Council staff as a special adviser for strategic planning, and in that capacity I worked closely on Iraq policy. By the middle of 2005, it was painfully obvious to everyone involved that the only *decisive* outcome that could be achieved during President Bush's tenure was the triumph of our enemies, America's withdrawal, and Iraq's descent into a hellish chaos as yet undreamed of.

The challenge, therefore, was to develop and implement a workable strategy that could be handed over to Bush's successor. Although important progress could be made on that strategy during Bush's watch, ultimately it would be carried through by the next President. This was the reality behind the course followed by the Administration in 2005–2006, and it remains the reality behind the new and different course the Administration has been following since 2007.

This new and different strategy, now called the "surge" but at one point called by insiders the "bridge," emerged out of a growing recognition over 2006 that our critics were right about one thing: our Iraq policy was not working. At the same time, however, and whether knowingly or ignorantly, many of those same critics were insisting that the answer lay in pursuing precisely the same strategy we already had in place. That is, they were telling us that we needed (a) to push Iraqi government officials to come together politically and (b) to train Iraqi troops so that they could take over from American forces. We had been doing exactly these things for a year, and we had been driven to the brink.

This was no solution at all. The results on the ground in Iraq made it clear that, without a dramatic change, the President would be leaving his successor with an untenable mess, if not the prospect of a catastrophic American rout. A review of Administration policy was therefore launched that led to the dramatic course revision we have seen unfolding over the past year-and-a-half.

This month, the military leader of the surge, General David Petraeus, and America's chief diplomat in Iraq, Ambassador Ryan Crocker, will present their second report to Congress on the surge and its effects. Prudent and circumspect men, they will surely not advance bold claims on behalf of the policy the United States has been following under their leadership. But I expect they will speak more optimistically about the future than many thought possible eighteen months ago. Their testimony will demonstrate that, at last, the United States has a sustainable strategy for Iraq with a reasonable chance of success, and one that George W. Bush will be able to turn over with confidence to the next incumbent of the White House.

How we got here is a story in itself.

⇤ • ⇥

In the summer of 2005, General George Casey, the theater commander in Iraq, was pressing a military campaign whose primary goal was the training and maturing of Iraqi security forces. At the same time, Iraqis had designed a national constitution that would be the subject of a countrywide referendum in October, to be followed (assuming the constitution's ratification) by national elections in December.

Here at home, Administration policy was inundated by criticisms on every front. Much of it was reckless, but not all of it. From "skeptical supporters" of the war like Senator John McCain and the military analyst Fred Kagan came the charge that the number of American "boots on the ground" was far from sufficient to accomplish the mission. Although our military commanders in Iraq kept assuring the White House that this was not the case, the criticism flitted like Banquo's ghost in the background of every internal discussion about the war.

Some Democrats in the "loyal opposition"—i.e., those who were not simply advocating an irresponsible strategy of defeat and withdrawal—made the same point, but more often they took a different tack. Charging that the Administration had no strategy beyond "staying the course," they proposed instead that the United States pressure the Iraqis to bring the sullen and disaffected Sunni minority into the political sphere. This would siphon support from the insurgency. In addition, the Pentagon needed to accelerate the training of Iraqi security forces to handle more of the load against the enemies of the new Iraq. And the State Department had to lean on Iraq's neighbors to do more to help.

This counsel seemed maddeningly sensible to us. It was, to the letter, the Administration's strategy at that very moment. Still, exasperating though it may have been to be told that we should do what we were actually doing, this line of criticism also seemed to contain potentially good news. Perhaps, we thought, we could find common ground with these Democratic critics—their number included Senators Hillary Clinton, Joseph Biden, and Carl Levin—and forge a consensus on how to move forward.

That was the background to a decision in the fall of 2005 to release an unclassified version of General Casey's campaign plan, along with a document explaining how all elements of American power were being mobilized to assist in its realization. The full document was called the National Strategy for Supporting Iraq, the name of which changed somewhere along the way to the National Strategy for Victory in Iraq (NSVI). There was nothing new here. The release of the NSVI, bolstered by a series of frank presidential addresses, was simply an attempt to make public a number of details about our approach and offer a reasonable response to our reasonable critics.

The effort was doomed. It was overtaken by political events or, rather, by one specific event: a press conference, on November 17, 2005, by John Murtha, a Democratic congressman from Pennsylvania.

Murtha was a veteran of the Vietnam war and a hawk on defense spending—someone generally thought to be at home with the old "Scoop" Jackson wing of the Democratic party. When it came to Iraq, he turned out to be something else. "Our military has accomplished its mission and done its duty," Murtha summarily declared at his press conference, and now it was time to bring the troops home—as soon as possible, but no later than in six months.

Murtha was not calling for a gradual transition to Iraqi control. To the contrary, he was advocating the wholesale abandonment of Iraq. As he well knew, moreover, six months would be the fastest possible withdrawal under the most optimistic timetable, with our forces working 24 hours a day, seven days a week, to pull out all of the equipment and materiel we had brought in over the previous three years. This was not a brief for haste but rather a recipe for panic.

Unlike those critics who lambasted our policy and then commended it to our attention, Murtha was presenting an unambiguous alternative. The left wing of the Democratic party and its supporters in Moveon.org had finally found a spokesman with credentials on national security to make the most extreme case for the war's end.

The media lauded the Murtha plan, but they did not examine it closely. I spent hours with reporters in a futile effort to persuade them to show Murtha the respect of subjecting his scheme—including his bizarre notion of redeploying troops 5,000 miles away on the island of Okinawa in the Sea of Japan—to the same level of scrutiny they lavished upon Administration policy. One key reporter told me, "We don't scrutinize Murtha's plan because none of us takes it seriously."

Inside the White House, we joked bitterly that the only way we could get people to see the flaws in Murtha's proposal would be to offer it as our own.

◄◄ • ►►

In the end, however, even if we had managed to secure some kind of bipartisan support for our strategy, it would have made little difference. Over the course of 2006, the National Strategy for Victory in Iraq collapsed.

We had assumed that steady political movement would drain Sunni support for the insurgency by giving Sunnis a stake in the new Iraq—and that such political progress could be completed before the safety of the Iraqi population had been secured. Alas, the stunningly successful constitutional referendum of October 2005 and the national election two months later were followed by a dreadful stalemate. It took Sunnis nearly six weeks to acknowledge that the vote had been free and fair, and then squabbling within the Shiite community paralyzed its politicians in turn. Month after month, the nascent Iraqi political class found itself unable to form and seat a government. Almost a half-year of political momentum was forgone.

No less worrisome was the discovery that the Iraqi security forces were not yet in any condition to shoulder an increasing portion of the burden—to "stand up" so that coalition forces could "stand down." At the same time, the security challenge became far grimmer. In February, Al Qaeda terrorists blew up the Golden Dome mosque in Samarra, one of the holiest Shiite shrines in Iraq. Shiite militia groups responded just as the terrorists had hoped, launching retaliatory strikes against Sunni citizens. A bloody pattern—sectarian atrocity, sectarian reprisal, sectarian counter-reprisal—took hold. Each week, attack levels reached new heights. Since even the vastly more capable U.S. forces seemed unable to tamp down the violence, there was no chance that fledgling Iraqi security forces might do so any time soon.

With the situation deteriorating throughout the spring, the Administration might have begun the full-fledged reconsideration of the National Strategy for Victory that it would conduct later in the year. But suddenly the existing strategy appeared to receive a boost. After months of wrangling, the Iraqis finally installed a unity government under the leadership of the little-known Nouri al-Maliki. And U.S. special forces killed Abu Musab al-Zarqawi, the charismatic leader of Al Qaeda in Iraq and the mastermind behind its strategy of fomenting civil war between Sunnis and Shiites. Hope rekindled that the chaos could be brought under control.

But the boost proved illusory. General Casey launched a new effort to regain control of the capital, but within weeks it foundered when several of the Iraqi units on which it depended simply failed to show up for the fight. A revised version of the Casey plan likewise came a cropper when the new Maliki government interfered with efforts to go after rogue Shiite militias that were now rivaling Al Qaeda in Iraq in wreaking havoc.

Over the summer, doubts began to grow among White House officials working on Iraq; by September the NSC staff initiated a quiet but thorough review of strategy with an eye to developing a new way forward. The review, which soon expanded beyond the confines of the National Security Council, became a matter of public knowledge after Secretary of Defense Donald Rumsfeld's departure in November, the day after the landslide Democratic victory in the midterm elections. The election underscored the fact that, at a minimum, the Administration would have to reposition the Iraq mission in the minds of the American people. Our review confirmed that it would take more than a change of face to rescue the possibility of victory—it would take an entirely new strategy.

The idea was for our proposed change in course to be completed in time to take advantage of the release of another document. This was the much-awaited report of the Iraq Study Group, a bipartisan commission cochaired by former Secretary of State James Baker and former Congressman Lee Hamilton. Inside the White House, we hoped that the report's recommendations would be palatable enough to blend with whatever new approach the President decided to adopt. The long-sought holy grail—a bipartisan consensus on the way forward in Iraq—seemed again within reach.

‹‹– • –››

It was not to be. While sharply criticizing the lack of progress thus far, the Baker-Hamilton commission essentially recommended back to us an accelerated version of the strategy envisioned by the NSVI: stand them up so we can stand down. While there was still some support inside the Administration for continuing on that path, the interagency team on which I served was of a different mind. The situation in Iraq had eroded beyond the point envisioned by the Baker-Hamilton report; under the horrific conditions now at play, we concluded, Iraq's security forces were far more likely to crack under the strain than to "stand up." And those forces were the essential glue of a stable, unified future. If they went the way of Humpty Dumpty, neither they nor the new Iraq could ever be put back together again.

The Baker-Hamilton report did offer theoretical support for a short-term surge of military forces—something the President and the interagency team were also looking at very closely—but this was mentioned only in a brief passage and was far from the document's central thrust. The White House never succeeded in shifting the conventional wisdom in Washington that Baker-Hamilton provided an alternative to current policy. Nor, unfortunately, were we ready with our own genuine alternative when the Baker-Hamilton report was released on December 6, 2006. That put paid to the idea that we could use the occasion as a means of securing bipartisan support for a new approach. By the time the President announced the surge in January, the climate had turned frostier still.

By then, the leadership of the newly triumphant Democrats on Capitol Hill had already determined that the war was irretrievably lost and that the only responsible course was to get out as quickly as possible. Signaling the emphasis the Democrats meant to place on ending our involvement in Iraq quickly, Nancy Pelosi, the new speaker of the House, sought to make Jack Murtha her principal deputy.

As for the President's new strategy, the Democrats labeled it "an escalation"—no doubt because polls and focus groups showed that this would make it seem least palatable to the American public. The Administration countered with the proposition that we were sending "reinforcements." The media settled on "surge." Each of these labels had the unfortunate side-effect of obscuring the many other changes contained in the new strategy and focusing attention exclusively on the increase in military troops—certainly the gutsiest element in terms of our domestic politics but by no means the only important one.

Week after week, the Democrats attempted to use their control of Congress to suffocate the surge in its cradle. Various proposals were advanced to hobble General Petraeus and render implementation impossible. In April, just as the 30,000 new surge troops were entering the country, Senate Majority Leader Harry Reid declared peremptorily: "This war is lost, and this surge is not accomplishing anything."

Reid was wrong. While the political standoff in Washington worsened, the situation in Iraq began to improve. Not right away or all at once, of course. In fact, to judge by the measures of greatest salience to the American media, the situation only eroded in the first half of 2007. Attacks rose in number, as did American fatalities. But Petraeus was steadily refining and adapting the new strategy, and his efforts became especially productive after the full complement of new forces was on the ground and the "surge in operations" could begin in earnest by the beginning of June.

By September 2007, when Petraeus and Crocker gave their first report to Congress, the trend line toward success was discernible. Still, the matter remained debatable—to the point where Senator Clinton felt confident enough to inform Petraeus and Crocker on national television that "the reports you provided to us require the willing suspension of disbelief" and to characterize the two men as "the de facto spokesmen of what many of us consider to be a failed policy."

A few months after that showdown, however, the progress was all but indisputable. By now, indeed, we can see that the surge has bought precious time for the United States and the nascent Iraqi state to progress meaningfully toward five specific objectives.

First is extirpating the inciters of sectarian violence: Al Qaeda in Iraq among the Sunnis and the rogue militias among the Shiites. Second is building up a larger, more capable, and more integrated Iraqi Security Force than existed in 2006.

At the same time, Iraqis are being given the opportunity to create the means of political accommodation locally and from the "bottom up," in ways that reflect the realities of life inside the highly complex mosaic of their country. The achievement of this third goal is the precursor to the fourth, which is to make the central, "top down" government in Baghdad more responsive to the nation's eighteen provinces by opening its pocketbook for projects that will improve the economic and living conditions of the country's citizenry at large.

The final goal is, perhaps, the trickiest: pushing Iraqi politicians to pass legislation on a number of important measures, including the sharing of oil revenues, the funding of infrastructure projects, the reform of de-Baathification laws, and the like. These are the notorious "benchmarks" mentioned by the President in his January 2007 speech and subjected to much derision by skeptics.

A year after Bush first announced the new strategy, progress on the first three objectives has exceeded everyone's expectations, even those who helped design the surge. Al Qaeda in Iraq has been gravely wounded. The rogue elements within the Shiite militias are being pruned away. The Iraq Security Force is growing in size and reliability. And, following the decision of Sunni tribes to turn on Al Qaeda and throw in their lot with the United States and the new Iraq, local political accommodation is proceeding at a remarkable pace.

There has also been some movement toward linking the Iraqi parliament's spending to the needs of localities, but so far this is less impressive. As for the benchmarks on political reconciliation from the top down, it is useful to recall that we once thought such political change should precede everything else. That approach did not work. Our new strategy was based on the contrary assumption that security came first, and that parliamentary progress would lag significantly behind other elements. Of course, this has hardly prevented the President's critics from seizing on the failure of the Iraqi government to have completed all of its benchmarks as putative evidence of the surge's overall failure. Even here, however, there has been a measure of progress on the ground: in February, for example, the Iraqi parliament passed legislation addressing several key benchmarks, notably including de-Baathification reform and the facilitation of provincial elections as well as of better relations between the provinces and the central government.

<+- • +>

The Petraeus-Crocker report to Congress will no doubt offer further evidence that the new approach is working but is far from having completed its assigned task. No fair-minded observer could conclude otherwise. Petraeus has already indicated that the central military element of the surge—the increase of 30,000 troops—will end by summer 2008. At that point, U.S. forces in Iraq are set to decline to pre-surge levels, roughly 130,000. The question Petraeus will now have to answer is: how long will troop levels need to stay there, and when can they start moving down?

What Petraeus must have uppermost in his mind is the record compiled by his predecessors in trying to produce results with just enough troops to come close but not enough to succeed. A premature drawdown would, by definition, cause the forfeiture of his hard-won gains. And the political reality is that once those troops left Iraq, they would not be coming back.

In a slide presentation that accompanied his September 2007 testimony to Congress, Petraeus gave a picture of what he considered an appropriate draw-down. In his reckoning, after remaining at 130,000 for some time, American troops could decline in number to approximately 115,000, then by slow and measured steps to around 100,000, then perhaps to 85,000, and so onward. The closer the troop levels came to 100,000 (or fewer) the more manageable the de-ployment would be militarily. At those levels, our ground forces would be able to return to a peacetime rotation schedule, which would put far less strain on the all-volunteer force.

In other words, a substantial American presence in Iraq is sustainable mili-tarily over the long term. The great unknown is whether such a commitment would be sustainable politically here at home.

The evidence of the past sixteen months is that the American people are likely to support, or at least tolerate, a reduction in American numbers grad-ual enough to preserve the gains of the surge. A President McCain, for exam-ple, would probably have no trouble taking advantage of this sustainable strategy and bringing our mission in Iraq to the most successful end achievable.

What of a President Barack Obama or a President Hillary Clinton? If one were to attempt an answer to this question from the two candidates' words and conduct during the long primary season, one would have reason to conclude that both, in promising a rapid "end" to the war with an equally rapid with-drawal of American forces, are bound and determined to snatch defeat from the jaws of at least partial victory.

But it is not impossible to imagine that these vital matters would appear dif-ferently to a Democratic President considering Iraq's and America's future from a seat at the desk in the Oval Office rather than from the stage of a college gym-nasium filled with delirious Democratic primary voters. One might even per-mit oneself to hope that, while continuing to speak derogatorily of George Bush's years as the shepherd of our Iraq policy, such a President would come to know, privately and in time, that he or she had been bequeathed something very different from a fiasco: the promise of a better outcome for Iraq, for the Middle East, and for the American people.

23

THE HISTORY BOYS

DAVID HALBERSTAM
Vanity Fair   August 2007

With last year's tragic and untimely death of David Halberstam, the world of journalism lost a giant. Halberstam earned a Pulitzer Prize at age thirty for his reporting on the Vietnam War and went on to write some twenty books on everything from global politics to pro basketball. One of Halberstam's great talents was historical reporting—an ability to shine a fresh light on recent events while simultaneously placing them in historical context. The Best and the Brightest, *his iconic book on how the Kennedy administration was ineluctably drawn into the Vietnam conflict, is universally regarded as one of the finest works of its kind.*

The following selection, written just before Halberstam's death, appeared posthumously in Vanity Fair. *In it, Halberstam draws on a lifetime of expertise as he takes direct aim at claims by the Bush White House that its unpopular decisions regarding Iraq will be vindicated by history.*

We are a long way from the glory days of Mission Accomplished, when the Iraq war was over before it was over—indeed before it really began—and the president could dress up like a fighter pilot and land on an aircraft carrier, and the nation, led by a pliable media, would applaud. Now, late in this sad, terribly diminished presidency, mired in an unwinnable war of their own making, and increasingly on the defensive about events which, to their surprise, they do not control, the president and his men have turned, with some degree of desperation, to history. In their view Iraq under Saddam was like Europe dominated by Hitler, and the Democrats and critics in the media are likened to the appeasers of the 1930s. The Iraqi people, shorn of their immensely complicated history, become either the people of Europe eager to be liberated from the Germans, or a little nation that great powerful nations ought to protect.

Most recently in this history rummage sale—and perhaps most surprisingly—Bush has become Harry Truman.

We have lately been getting so many history lessons from the White House that I have come to think of Bush, Cheney, Rice, and the late, unlamented Rumsfeld as the History Boys. They are people groping for rationales for their failed policy, and as the criticism becomes ever harsher, they cling to the idea that a true judgment will come only in the future, and history will save them.

Ironically, it is the president himself, a man notoriously careless about, indeed almost indifferent to, the intellectual underpinnings of his actions, who has come to trumpet loudest his close scrutiny of the lessons of the past. Though, before, he tended to boast about making critical decisions based on instinct and religious faith, he now talks more and more about historical mandates. Usually he does this in the broadest—and vaguest—sense: History teaches us . . . We know from history . . . History shows us. In one of his speaking appearances in March 2006, in Cleveland, I counted four references to history, and what it meant for today, as if he had had dinner the night before with Arnold Toynbee, or at the very least Barbara Tuchman, and then gone home for a few hours to read his Gibbon.

I am deeply suspicious of these presidential seminars. We have, after all, come to know George Bush fairly well by now, and many of us have come to feel—not only because of what he says, but also because of the sheer cockiness in how he says it—that he has a tendency to decide what he wants to do first, and only then leaves it to his staff to look for intellectual justification. Many of us have always sensed a deep and visceral anti-intellectual streak in the president, that there was a great chip on his shoulder, and that the burden of the fancy schools he attended—Andover and Yale—and even simply being a member of the Bush family were too much for him. It was as if he needed not only to escape but also to put down those of his peers who had been more successful. From that mind-set, I think, came his rather unattractive habit of bestowing nicknames, most of them unflattering, on the people around him, to remind them that he was in charge, that despite their greater achievements they still worked for him.

He is infinitely more comfortable with the cowboy persona he has adopted, the Texas transplant who has learned to speak the down-home vernacular. "Country boy," as Johnny Cash once sang, "I wish I was you, and you were me." Bush's accent, not always there in public appearances when he was younger, tends to thicken these days, the final g's consistently dropped so that doing becomes doin', going becomes goin', and making, makin'. In this lexicon Al Qaeda becomes "the folks" who did 9/11. Unfortunately, it is not just the speech that got dumbed down—so also were the ideas at play. The president's world, unlike the one we live in, is dangerously simple, full of traps, not just for him but, sadly, for us as well.

When David Frum, a presidential speechwriter, presented Bush with the phrase "axis of evil," to characterize North Korea, Iran, and Iraq, it was meant to recall the Axis powers of World War II. Frum was much praised, for it is a fine phrase, perfect for Madison Avenue. Of course, the problem is that it doesn't really track. This new Axis turned out to contain, apparently much to our surprise, two countries, Iraq and Iran, that were sworn enemies, and if you moved against Iraq, you ended up destabilizing it and involuntarily strengthening Iran, the far more dangerous country in the region. While "axis of evil" was intended to serve as a sort of historical banner, embodying the highest moral vision imaginable, it ended up only helping to weaken us.

◄◄ • ►►

Despite his recent conversion to history, the president probably still believes, deep down, as do many of his admirers, that the righteous, religious vision he brings to geopolitics is a source of strength—almost as if the less he knows about the issues the better and the truer his decision-making will be. Around any president, all the time, are men and women with different agendas, who compete for his time and attention with messy, conflicting versions of events and complicated facts that seem all too often to contradict one another. With their hard-won experience the people from the State Department and the C.I.A. and even, on occasion, the armed forces tend to be cautious and short on certitude. They are the kind of people whose advice his father often took, but who in the son's view use their knowledge and experience merely to limit a president's ability to act. How much easier and cleaner to make decisions in consultation with a higher authority.

Therefore, when I hear the president cite history so casually, an alarm goes off. Those who know history best tend to be tempered by it. They rarely refer to it so sweepingly and with such complete confidence. They know that it is the most mischievous of mistresses and that it touts sure things about as regularly as the tip sheets at the local track. Its most important lessons sometimes come cloaked in bitter irony. By no means does it march in a straight line toward the desired result, and the good guys do not always win. Occasionally it is like a sport with upsets, in which the weak and small defeat the great and mighty—take, for instance, the American revolutionaries vanquishing the British Army, or the Vietnamese Communists, with their limited hardware, stalemating the mighty American Army.

There was, I thought, one member of the first President Bush's team who had a real sense of history, a man of intellectual superiority and enormous common sense. (Naturally, he did not make it onto the Bush Two team.) That was Brent Scowcroft, George H.W Bush's national-security adviser. Scowcroft was so close to the senior Bush that they collaborated on Bush's 1998 presidential memoir, *A World Transformed*. Scowcroft struck me as a lineal descendant of Truman's secretary of state George Catlett Marshall, arguably the most extraordinary of the postwar architects of American foreign policy. Marshall was a formidable figure, much praised for his awesome sense of duty and not enough, I think, for his intellect. If he lacked the self-evident brilliance of George Kennan (the author of Truman's Communist-containment policy), he had a remarkable ability to shed light on the present by extrapolating from the past.

Like Marshall, I think, Scowcroft has a sense of history in his bones, even if his are smaller lessons, learned piece by piece over a longer period of time. His is perhaps a more pragmatic and less dazzling mind, but he saw all the dangers of the 2003 move into Iraq, argued against the invasion, and for his troubles was dismissed as chairman of the prestigious President's Foreign Intelligence Advisory Board.

I. THE TRUMAN ANALOGY

Recently, Harry Truman, for reasons that would surely puzzle him if he were still alive, has become the Republicans' favorite Democratic president. In fact, the men around Bush who attempt to feed the White House line to journalists have begun to talk about the current president as a latter-day Truman: Yes, goes the line, Truman's rise to an ever more elevated status in the presidential pantheon is all ex post facto, conferred by historians long after he left office a beleaguered man, his poll numbers hopelessly low. Thus Bush and the people around him predict that a similar Trumanization will ride to the rescue for them.

I've been living with Truman on and off for the last five years, while I was writing a book on the Korean War, *The Coldest Winter* [published in September 2007 by Hyperion], and I've been thinking a lot about the differences between Truman and Bush and their respective wars, Korea and Iraq. Yes, like Bush, Truman was embattled, and, yes, his popularity had plummeted at the end of his presidency, and, yes, he governed during an increasingly unpopular war. But the similarities end there.

Even before Truman sent troops to Korea, in 1950, the national political mood was toxic. The Republicans had lost five presidential elections in a row, and Truman was under fierce partisan assault from the Republican far right, which felt marginalized even within its own party. It seized on the dubious issue of Communist subversion—especially with regard to China—as a way of getting even. (Knowing how ideological both Bush and Cheney are, it is easy to envision them as harsh critics of Truman at that moment.)

Truman had inherited General Douglas MacArthur, "an untouchable," in Dwight Eisenhower's shrewd estimate, a man who was by then as much myth and legend as he was flesh and blood. The mastermind of America's victory in the Pacific, MacArthur was unquestionably talented, but also vainglorious, highly political, and partisan. Truman had twice invited him to come home from Japan, where, as Supreme Commander of the Allied Powers, he was supervising the reconstruction, to meet with him and address a joint session of Congress. Twice MacArthur turned him down, although a presidential invitation is really an order. MacArthur was saving his homecoming, it was clear, for a more dramatic moment, one that might just have been connected to a presidential run. He not only looked down on Truman personally, he never really accepted the primacy of the president in the constitutional hierarchy. For a president trying to govern during an extremely difficult moment in international politics, it was a monstrous political equation.

Truman had been forced into the Korean War in 1950 when the Chinese authorized the North Koreans to cross the 38th parallel and attack South Korea. But MacArthur did not accept the president's vision of a limited war in Korea, and argued instead for a larger one with the Chinese. Truman wanted none of that. He might have been the last American president who did not graduate from college, but he was quite possibly our best-read modern president. History was always with him. With MacArthur pushing for a wider war with China, Truman liked to quote Napoleon, writing about his disastrous Russian adventure: "I beat them in every battle, but it does not get me anywhere."

In time, MacArthur made an all-out frontal challenge to Truman, criticizing him to the press, almost daring the president to get rid of him. Knowing that the general had title to the flag and to the emotions of the country, while he himself merely had title to the Constitution, Truman nonetheless fired him.

It was a grave constitutional crisis—nothing less than the concept of civilian control of the military was at stake. If there was an irony to this, it was that MacArthur and his journalistic boosters, such as *Time*-magazine owner Henry Luce, always saw Truman as the little man and MacArthur as the big man. ("MacArthur," wrote *Time* at the moment of the firing, "was the personification of the big man, with the many admirers who look to a great man for leadership. . . . Truman was almost a professional little man.") But it was Truman's decision to meet MacArthur's challenge, even though he surely knew he would be the short-term loser, that has elevated his presidential stock.

⋘ • ⋙

George W. Bush's relationship with his military commander was precisely the opposite. He dealt with the ever so malleable General Tommy Franks, a man, Presidential Medal of Freedom or no, who is still having a difficult time explaining to his peers in the military how Iraq happened, and how he agreed to so large a military undertaking with so small a force. It was the president, not the military or the public, who wanted the Iraq war, and Bush used the extra leverage granted him by 9/11 to get it. His people skillfully manipulated the intelligence in order to make the war seem necessary, and they snookered the military on force levels and the American public on the cost of it all. The key operative in all this was clearly Vice President Cheney, supremely arrogant, the most skilled of bureaucrats, seemingly the toughest tough guy of them all, but eventually revealed as a man who knew nothing of the country he wanted to invade and what that invasion might provoke.

II. THE NEW RED-BAITING

If Bush takes his cues from anyone in the Truman era, it is not Truman but the Republican far right. This can be seen clearly from one of his history lessons, a speech the president gave on a visit to Riga, Latvia, in May 2005, when, in order to justify the Iraq intervention, he cited Yalta, the 1945 summit at which Roosevelt, Stalin, and Churchill met. Hailing Latvian freedom, Bush took a side shot at Roosevelt (and, whether he meant to or not, at Churchill, supposedly his great hero) and the Yalta accords, which effectively ceded Eastern Europe to the Soviets. Yalta, he said, "followed in the unjust tradition of Munich and the Molotov-Ribbentrop pact. Once again, when powerful governments negotiated, the freedom of small nations was somehow expendable. Yet this attempt to sacrifice freedom for the sake of stability left a continent divided and un-stable. The captivity of millions in Central and Eastern Europe will be re-membered as one of the greatest wrongs of history."

This is some statement. Yalta is connected first to the Munich Agreement of 1938 (in which the Western democracies, at their most vulnerable and well be-hind the curve of military preparedness, ceded Czechoslovakia to Hitler), then, in the same breath, Bush blends in seamlessly (and sleazily) the Molotov-Ribbentrop pact, the temporary and cynical agreement between the Soviets and Nazis allowing the Germans to invade Poland and the Soviets to move into the Baltic nations. And from Molotov-Ribbentrop we jump ahead to Yalta it-self, where, Bush implies, the two great leaders of the West casually sat by and gave away vast parts of Europe to the Soviet Union.

After some 60 years Yalta has largely slipped from our political vocabulary, but for a time it was one of the great buzzwords in American politics, the first shot across the bow by the Republican right in their long, venomous, im-mensely destructive assault upon Roosevelt (albeit posthumously), Truman, and the Democratic Party as soft on Communism—just as today's White House attacks Democrats and other critics for being soft on terrorism, less patriotic, defeatists, underminers of the true strength of our country. Crucial to the right's exploitation of Yalta was the idea of a tired, sick, and left-leaning Roo-sevelt having given away too much and betraying the people of Eastern Eu-rope, who, as a result, had to live under the brutal Soviet thumb—a distortion of history that resonated greatly with the many Eastern European ethnic groups in America, whose people, blue-collar workers, most of them, had voted solidly Democratic.

The right got away with it, because, of all the fronts in the Second World War, the one least known in this country—our interest tends to disappear for those battles in which we did not participate—is ironically the most impor-tant: the Eastern Front, where the battle between the Germans and Russians took place and where, essentially, the outcome of the war was decided. It began with a classic act of hubris—Hitler's invasion of Russia, in June 1941, three years before we landed our troops in Normandy. Some three million German troops were involved in the attack, and in the early months the penetrations were quick and decisive. Minsk was quickly taken, the Germans crossed the Dnieper by July 10, and Smolensk fell shortly after. Some 700,000 men of the Red Army, its leadership already devastated by the madness of Stalin's purges, were captured by mid-September 1941. The Russian troops fell back and moved as much of their industry back east as they could. Then, slowly, the Russian lines stiffened, and the Germans, their supply lines too far extended, faltered as winter came on. The turning point was the Battle of Stalingrad, which began in late August 1942. It proved to be the most brutal battle of the war, with as many as two million combatants on both sides killed and wounded, but in the end the Russians held the city and captured what remained of the German Army there.

In early 1943, the Red Army was on the offensive, the Germans in full retreat. By the middle of 1944, the Russians had 120 divisions driving west, some 2.3 million troops against an increasingly exhausted German Army of 800,000. By mid-July 1944, as the Allies were still trying to break out of the Normandy hedgerows, the Red Army was at the old Polish-Russian border. By the time of Yalta, they were closing in on Berlin. A month earlier, in January 1945, Churchill had acknowledged the inability of the West to limit the Soviet reach into much of Eastern and Central Europe. "Make no mistake, all the Balkans, except Greece, are going to be Bolshevized, and there is nothing I can do to prevent it. There is nothing I can do for Poland either."

Yalta reflected not a sellout but a *fait accompli*.

⊰⊷ • ⊶⊱

President Bush lives in a world where in effect it is always the summer of 1945, the Allies have just defeated the Axis, and a world filled with darkness for some six years has been rescued by a new and optimistic democracy, on its way to becoming a superpower. His is a world where other nations admire America or damned well ought to, and America is always right, always on the side of good, in a world of evil, and it's just a matter of getting the rest of the world to understand this. One of Bush's favorite conceits, used repeatedly in his speeches, is that democracies are peaceful and don't go to war against one another. Most citizens of the West tend to accept this view without question, but that is not how most of Africa, Asia, South America, and the Middle East, having felt the burden of the white man's colonial rule for much of the past two centuries, see it. The non-Western world does not think of the West as a citadel of pacifism and generosity, and many people in the U.S. State Department and the different intelligence agencies (and even the military) understand the resentments and suspicions of our intentions that exist in those regions. We are, you might say, fighting the forces of history in Iraq—religious, cultural, social, and inevitably political—created over centuries of conflict and oppressive rule.

The president tends to drop off in his history lessons after World War II, especially when we get to Vietnam and things get a bit murkier. Had he made any serious study of our involvement there, he might have learned that the sheer ferocity of our firepower created enemies of people who were until then on the sidelines, thereby doing our enemies' recruiting for them. And still, today, our inability to concentrate such "shock and awe" on precisely whom we would like—causing what is now called collateral killing—creates a growing resentment among civilians, who may decide that whatever values we bring are not in the end worth it, because we have also brought too much killing and destruction to their country. The French fought in Vietnam before us, and when a French patrol went through a village, the Vietminh would on occasion kill a single French soldier, knowing that the French in a fury would retaliate by wiping out half the village—in effect, the Vietminh were baiting the trap for collateral killing.

III. THE PERILS OF EMPIRE

You don't hear other members of the current administration citing the lessons of Vietnam much, either, especially Cheney and Karl Rove, both of them gifted at working the bureaucracy for short-range political benefits, both highly partisan and manipulative, both unspeakably narrow and largely uninterested in understanding and learning about the larger world. As Joan Didion pointed out in her brilliant essay on Cheney in *The New York Review of Books,* it was Rumsfeld and Cheney who explained to Henry Kissinger, not usually slow on the draw when it came to the political impact of foreign policy, that Vietnam was likely to create a vast political backlash against the liberal McGovern forces. The two, relatively junior operators back then, were interested less in what had gone wrong in Vietnam than in getting some political benefit out of it. Cheney still speaks of Vietnam as a noble rather than a tragic endeavor, not that he felt at the time—with his five military deferments—that he needed to be part of that nobility.

Still, it is hard for me to believe that anyone who knew anything about Vietnam, or for that matter the Algerian war, which directly followed Indochina for the French, couldn't see that going into Iraq was, in effect, punching our fist into the largest hornet's nest in the world. As in Vietnam, our military superiority is neutralized by political vulnerabilities. The borders are wide open. We operate quite predictably on marginal military intelligence. The adversary knows exactly where we are at all times, as we do not know where he is. Their weaponry fits an asymmetrical war, and they have the capacity to blend into the daily flow of Iraqi life, as we cannot. Our allies—the good Iraqi people the president likes to talk about—appear to be more and more ambivalent about the idea of a Christian, Caucasian liberation, and they do not seem to share many of our geopolitical goals.

◄– • –►

The book that brought me to history some 53 years ago, when I was a junior in college, was Cecil Woodham-Smith's wondrous *The Reason Why*, the story of why the Light Brigade marched into the Valley of Death, to be senselessly slaughtered, in the Crimean War. It is a tale of such folly and incompetence in leadership (then, in the British military, a man could buy the command of a regiment) that it is not just the story of a battle but an indictment of the entire British Empire. It is a story from the past we read again and again, that the most dangerous time for any nation may be that moment in its history when things are going unusually well, because its leaders become carried away with hubris and a sense of entitlement cloaked as rectitude. The arrogance of power, Senator William Fulbright called it during the Vietnam years.

I have my own sense that this is what went wrong in the current administration, not just in the immediate miscalculation of Iraq but in the larger sense of misreading the historical moment we now live in. It is that the president and the men around him—most particularly the vice president—simply misunderstood what the collapse of the Soviet empire meant for America in national-security terms. Rumsfeld and Cheney are genuine triumphalists. Steeped in the culture of the Cold War and the benefits it always presented to their side in domestic political terms, they genuinely believed that we were infinitely more powerful as a nation throughout the world once the Soviet empire collapsed. Which we both were and very much were not. Certainly, the great obsessive struggle with the threat of a comparable superpower was removed, but that threat had probably been in decline in real terms for well more than 30 years, after the high-water mark of the Cuban missile crisis, in 1962. During the '80s, as advanced computer technology became increasingly important in defense apparatuses, and as the failures in the Russian economy had greater impact on that country's military capacity, the gap between us and the Soviets dramatically and continuously widened. The Soviets had become, at the end, as West German chancellor Helmut Schmidt liked to say, Upper Volta with missiles.

At the time of the collapse of Communism, I thought there was far too much talk in America about how we had won the Cold War, rather than about how the Soviet Union, whose economy never worked, simply had imploded. I was never that comfortable with the idea that we as a nation had won, or that it was a personal victory for Ronald Reagan. To the degree that there was credit to be handed out, I thought it should go to those people in the satellite nations who had never lost faith in the cause of freedom and had endured year after year in difficult times under the Soviet thumb. If any Americans deserved credit, I thought it should be Truman and his advisers—Marshall, Kennan, Dean Acheson, and Chip Bohlen—all of them harshly attacked at one time or another by the Republican right for being soft on Communism. (The right tried particularly hard to block Eisenhower's nomination of Bohlen as ambassador to Moscow, in 1953, because he had been at Yalta.)

After the Soviet Union fell, we were at once more powerful and, curiously, less so, because our military might was less applicable against the new, very different kind of threat that now existed in the world. Yet we stayed with the norms of the Cold War long after any genuine threat from it had receded, in no small part because our domestic politics were still keyed to it. At the same time, the checks and balances imposed on us by the Cold War were gone, the restraints fewer, and the temptations to misuse our power greater. What we neglected to consider was a warning from those who had gone before us—that there was, at moments like this, a historic temptation for nations to overreach.

24

AFTER MUSHARRAF

JOSHUA HAMMER
The Atlantic Monthly   October 2007

Although Iraq has dominated the news from overseas in recent years, the U.S. military's fight to support Afghanistan's fledgling democracy has also turned into a quagmire, albeit on a smaller scale. Increasingly, it's clear that neighboring Pakistan holds the key to the region's long-term stability. The Taliban continues to use its safe haven in the tribal territories on Pakistan's side of the border to wage periodic offensives against U.S. and Afghan forces, while Osama bin Laden and his Al Qaeda lieutenants are purportedly hiding out in the same area. For its part, the Pakistani government has done little to root out the Taliban and Al Qaeda, and for good reason: Pakistan's president, Pervez Musharraf, while a nominal ally of the United States, can't afford to further alienate his country's already restive Muslim population.

In the following selection, Joshua Hammer—who spent twenty years writing for Newsweek—reports from inside Pakistan on what might be next for Musharraf and his critically important nation. [Note: In November 2007, not long after this article was published, Musharraf agreed to step down as Pakistan's top military commander. Benazir Bhutto, head of the Pakistan People's Party, was assassinated a month later.]

Last November, the Center for Strategic and International Studies, a bipartisan think tank in Washington, D.C., brought together more than two dozen former high-level United States government officials to take part in a half-day exercise on the future of Pakistan. In the room were former assistant secretaries of state and career ambassadors, as well as former senior officials from the Pentagon, the C.I.A., the Treasury, and USAID; it was a veritable who's who of Washington's Pakistan experts. The sponsors presented an escalating series of fictional crises—growing violence along the Pakistani-Afghan border, mass protests against the government by radical Islamists, the arrest of former Prime Minister Benazir Bhutto shortly after her return from exile—and asked participants how they would respond to rising chaos in the nuclear-armed state.

The exercise culminated with this scenario: In the aftermath of Pakistan's national elections in late 2007, Taliban forces attempt to assassinate Afghan President Hamid Karzai, then retreat to a hideout in western Pakistan. U.S. forces pursue them, and an American soldier is taken captive in South Waziristan, a tribal region in Pakistan's North-West Frontier Province. As the kidnappers post video images of the hostage on the Internet, Pakistani President Pervez Musharraf orders his army to attack the Taliban compound. The assault frees the American soldier, but leaves hundreds of militants, Pakistani troops, and civilians dead or wounded. Antigovernment riots spread across the country, peaking in a confrontation between civilians and Pakistani forces in Lahore that leaves a dozen people dead. That evening, in what looks like a coup attempt, troops surround the houses of both Musharraf and Shaukat Aziz, the prime minister. Hours later, the U.S. ambassador receives a call from a previously unknown Pakistani two-star general, "raising serious concerns," according to the scenario playbook, "over whether the chain of command in Pakistan has remained intact."

At this point, the policy makers broke into groups and tried to come up with a strategy to deal with the apparent change of leadership. But this proved difficult: The groups were unable to resolve critical questions with confidence. Though most agreed that the military would continue running the show, as it has for 33 of the last 60 years, there was widespread concern over whether the new army brass would likely be pro-American, anti-American, or something in between. There was also no consensus on whether the military—with Musharraf out of the picture—could hold the country.

With Pakistan reeling from the army's bloody assault on radical Islamists inside Islamabad's Red Mosque, and from a series of retaliatory attacks on Pakistani security forces, this scenario, conceived 11 months ago, seems more realistic every day. The military is demoralized by the bloody guerrilla war against the Taliban and Al Qaeda along the border. Islamist political parties, who hold power in one of the country's four provinces and share control in another, have become a disruptive and sometimes violent force. And Musharraf's life remains under constant threat.

Even some members of Musharraf's inner circle have warned him that he risks losing power unless he radically changes course. (It is conceivable that by the time you read this, he will already have fallen.) The beginning of the end may have come this past March, when the president, in what has come to be seen as a major blunder, fired and placed under house arrest the supreme court's chief justice, Iftikhar Muhammad Chaudhry, an independent-minded jurist who had challenged the military regime on sensitive cases. Demonstrations in support of the judge swelled through the spring, soon morphing into a broad-based pro-democracy movement. Since then, Musharraf has seemed unsteady in public, alternating shrill accusations against his opponents with apologetic pleas for support and understanding.

The longest-serving military ruler in Pakistan's history, Mohammed Zia ul-Haq, lasted 11 years, before he was killed in a plane crash, in August 1988. Musharraf might last longer (he has so far served eight years), but the rising unpredictability of when and how he might leave power has caused deep uncertainty—and anxiety—about what might follow him. One Western military liaison officer recounted a conversation he had with a general at staff headquarters in Rawalpindi the morning after last year's U.S. midterm elections. Coincidentally, the conversation took place just a day before the think-tank exercise on Pakistan's future, more than 7,000 miles away, and it puts the confusion of the exercise's participants in a better light. The general expressed his admiration for the constitutional process in the United States, and marveled at how, even after a sudden removal of a president—Kennedy's assassination, Nixon's resignation—the system continued to function. "If our president were to disappear tomorrow," the general admitted, "I have no idea in which direction our country would go."

⤛ • ⤜

The nightmare scenario for U.S. policy makers—and one reason they remain heavily invested in Musharraf—is an Islamic revolution in Pakistan. A tide of anti-American sentiment, some analysts fear, could bring to power Islamists, who would give free rein to the Taliban, spread nuclear technology to rogue states and terrorist groups, and support the mujahideen in Kashmir.

There's no doubt that Islamists have grown in numbers and prominence in Pakistan since 9/11. In 2002, six fundamentalist parties formed an alliance called Muttahida Majlis-e-Amal, or MMA, and rode a wave of anger at the American-led war in Afghanistan, taking 53 of the 342 seats in the National Assembly and forming the third-largest bloc in the parliament. The alliance won outright control of the provincial assembly in the North-West Frontier Province, and it now governs Balochistan in a coalition with Musharraf's ruling party. During the weeks that I spent in Islamabad earlier this year, the MMA repeatedly flexed its muscles in noisy protests—weekly demonstrations against legislation offering further legal protections to women, rallies against the government's razing of illegal makeshift mosques that have sprung up throughout the city. The demonstrations brought out hundreds of police officers and paralyzed traffic in the city for hours.

Moderate Muslims in Pakistan are worried about the Islamists' rising profile: Pervez Hoodbhoy, chairman of the Quaid-e-Azam University physics department, told me that the university has been "taken over" by Islamist fervor—more *hijabs* in the classrooms, more prayer, and "no bookstores, but three mosques with a fourth under construction" on campus. Hoodbhoy, a highly regarded nuclear physicist and a critic of military rule, told me that an Islamist takeover of the country, either by outright domination of the electoral process or in conjunction with a radical Islamist general, "is a real possibility."

Yet despite their clout in parliament and their seeming strength on the street, the Islamists are not widely popular: Their parties won only 11 percent of the vote in the 2002 elections (gerrymandering gave them a share of seats far greater than their numbers). Even in their stronghold, the North-West Frontier Province, they polled only 26 percent. Perhaps the biggest obstacle to the MMA's growth is its abysmal record of governance: In the North-West Frontier Province, which the alliance controls, social services are disintegrating. Unless anti-Western sentiment reaches sustained and unprecedented levels, the Islamists seem highly unlikely to muster enough votes to gain control of parliament in the next decade.

If this catastrophic scenario looks unlikely, so too does the potential for genuine democracy. Pakistan's largest opposition party, the Pakistan People's Party, or PPP, is run by former Prime Minister Benazir Bhutto. Bhutto fled to London in 1996 to escape corruption charges; her husband, Asif Ali Zardari, earned the nickname "Mr. 10 Percent" for allegedly taking kickbacks from foreign corporations. Though she remains by far the best-known civilian politician in Pakistan, her popularity is questionable. Many members of her party say she has stifled the emergence of fresh faces by clinging to leadership in exile, and a gulf is widening between the landowning elite that sets her party's agenda and the working class that constitutes the bulk of its support.

Bhutto's main civilian challenger, Nawaz Sharif, the chairman of the Pakistan Muslim League and another former prime minister, was deposed by Musharraf in 1999 (he had tried to fire Musharraf after the general orchestrated an ill-fated foray into Indian-controlled Kashmir); he now lives in Saudi Arabia, and had, before Musharraf's crisis, reportedly promised to remain outside Pakistan for 10 years in return for the commutation of a lifetime prison sentence he had been given for attempting to stop Musharraf's plane from landing in Islamabad during the coup. (The plane was low on fuel, and Sharif was convicted of terrorism and hijacking.) Beyond Bhutto and Sharif, there are virtually no national politicians of substance. "The sad thing is that we can't create a new civilian leadership in the country," one parliamentarian told me. "With 342 seats in the National Assembly, and 100 in the Senate, and the same in the provincial parliaments, we can't find one person, besides Benazir and Sharif, who can be a prime minister or a president. It is a shame for this country."

In late July, with his hold on power growing more tenuous, Musharraf met with Bhutto in Abu Dhabi to discuss her possible role in the next government (parliamentary elections are likely to be held this fall). A power-sharing arrangement, with Bhutto returning to become prime minister to offset Musharraf's presidency, might reduce political tensions, at least temporarily, and give civilians more say in governance. As this magazine went to press, no such deal had been struck. Even if one were achieved, it would be unlikely to greatly affect the underlying balance of power. As of this writing, Musharraf appeared likely to retain the presidency in the short run—either by reelection or by declaration of emergency rule. And although the presidency is nominally Pakistan's highest post, Musharraf derives greater power still from another position: chief of the army. His refusal to relinquish this second role has been a significant source of popular discontent. It is widely believed that he won't give it up because he realizes that without it, he could quickly be reduced to a figurehead by a rival general. And indeed, if he did give up his title, the real center of power would shift not to any civilian politician or political party, but to the new army chief.

◄─ • ─►

Whatever happens to Musharraf, the presidency, and the parliament, there is little doubt that the military will remain the dominant player in Pakistan for as long as it chooses. During the 11 years of democracy that followed Zia ul-Haq's death, the civilian prime ministers, Bhutto and Sharif, had diminishing influence over Pakistan's foreign policy and its nuclear program; Bhutto famously called the military-run Inter-Services Intelligence, or ISI, a "state within a state" and accused military intelligence of listening in on her phone calls. In 1990, the army, after charging her with corruption, engineered her removal by presidential decree. Sharif was tossed out nine years later, effectively at gunpoint. According to one senior Western diplomat in Islamabad, "If Musharraf should disappear from the scene tomorrow, you would have a meeting of senior military men, and a new chief of army staff, and that would be, either overtly or behind the scenes, your new government."

Throughout the ongoing crisis, the generals have played their cards close to the vest. Retired Lieutenant General Hamid Gul, the former head of the ISI, witnessed the transition from military to civilian rule after the death of Zia ul-Haq, in 1988, and he believes that after nearly eight years in power, the military is once again ready to recede into the background. "They will go back into the barracks, and they will be happy, because they would still be influencing the government," he told me. "The military casts a long shadow, and they would be protected."

Most American Pakistan-watchers, however, believe that many military officers—and certainly the privileged upper echelons—want just the opposite, and are less likely than ever to surrender power: They have grown accustomed to the perks and privileges of political life. "They don't have a game plan for a withdrawal from politics," says Stephen Philip Cohen, a fellow at the Brookings Institution, who has written frequently about the Pakistani military.

In the Western diplomat's view, the military's continued dominance would present no immediate danger to the United States or the region, because Musharraf's inner circle is secular, U.S.-trained, and at least nominally committed to the Bush administration's "war on terror." But these men are in their mid- and late 50s and moving toward the mandatory-retirement age of 60. (Musharraf himself turned 64 in August; he has ignored the mandatory-retirement rule.) The next tier of the military command is not nearly as well known. "We hope that this group would be Western-oriented, but there's no guarantee," says Derek Chollet, a participant in the Washington think tank exercise on Pakistan in November. "We simply don't know who they are."

≺- • ⤜

Islamabad, Pakistan's capital, is a clean, even sterile, city of wide boulevards, faux-Moghul architecture, and wooded parks. The army's presence is hardly overbearing; you rarely see uniformed officers or gun-toting soldiers on the streets. But as you become more attuned to the city's culture and commerce, you begin to realize that in fact the military is everywhere.

On my first evening in the capital, I got a taste of how the officer corps has insinuated itself into political life: A well-connected colleague brought me to a lavish wedding reception in the Hotel Serena for the daughter of the minister of the interior, Aftab Ahmad Khan Sherpao.

I expected to see bigwigs at the reception, and I did. The surprise—at a wedding for a civilian government official—was how many had military pedigrees. The reception was chock-full of generals and retired generals, including several corps commanders, the vice chief of army staff, Musharraf's press secretary, and—briefly—Musharraf himself. Almost all of them were, like Musharraf, wearing suits, not uniforms, but everyone knew who they were. My colleague, a newspaper editor based in Islamabad, pointed them out as they strutted about, nodding like dons to the other guests, the higher-ups accompanied by military secretaries and junior officers, also in civilian clothes. Musharraf himself moved serenely through the crowd, shaking hands and smiling beneficently. As we watched from a corner, my colleague observed wearily, "The line between military men and politicians has totally blurred in this country."

The army has dramatically increased its role in the public sector since Musharraf took over. "Thousands of officers are now employed in civil jobs; they have the best of everything," says retired General Aslam Beg, who served as chief of army staff under Benazir Bhutto from 1988 to 1991. One parliamentary opposition leader recently charged that 56,000 civil-service jobs had come into the hands of army personnel (other sources put this figure lower). Retired generals and brigadiers have taken over as chancellors and vice chancellors at Pakistani universities; they also run the post office, the tax authority, the housing authority, and the education department. Retired generals serve as the governors of two of Pakistan's four provinces.

The armed forces also control more than a hundred private-sector companies and have placed retired officers in the upper reaches of Pakistan's major businesses and industries. Rao Khalid Mehmood, former defense correspondent for the *Nation* newspaper in Islamabad and now the Islamabad bureau chief at a startup Pakistani television news channel, told me that at present, the military is the gateway to private-sector employment. Many people believe that "the only way to get a job is to know someone in the army," he says.

Ayesha Siddiqa, a well-known analyst in Islamabad and the author of *Military Inc.: Inside the Pakistani Military Economy,* says that the armed forces are major players in real estate, agribusiness, and several other industries. The empire includes banks, cable-TV companies, insurance agencies, sugar refineries, private security firms, schools, airlines, cargo services, and textile factories. The Fauji Foundation, for instance, is a "welfare trust" that is run by the defense ministry and spans 15 business enterprises. It provides cushy jobs for hundreds of retired officers (many retire in their late 40s), pays few taxes, and channels profits into a fund that is intended to benefit retired military personnel. And it is just one of several giant military-run foundations and companies that were set up decades ago and have grown steadily ever since.

The military's intrusion into commerce is quite visible in Islamabad, if you know what to look for. The logos of the Fauji Foundation and other military-run conglomerates appear on trucks, boxes, and buildings throughout the city. As Hoodbhoy told me, "They own gas companies. They make fertilizer, cement, soap, bottled water. They even make cereals, so when I have breakfast, I can't get away from them."

Midway through my stay in Pakistan, I attended a small dinner party in Islamabad. The guests included a handful of daily-newspaper reporters, a management consultant, and a young female member of parliament from

Musharraf's party. All of them—even the president's own party loyalist—were openly resentful of the military and its stranglehold on political and economic life. As we sat in a cramped dining room, eating *biryanis* and drinking tea, the group exchanged stories about military privilege. The consultant had recently returned after five years in the U.S., and he had landed a project at an army-run conglomerate that operates 41 companies and employs 15,000 people. He described his discovery that the corporation's top jobs, as well as those across many of the 41 companies, all were taken by retired officers with no formal business training and little understanding of basic economics. "Finance was managed by a colonel," he said. "Administration, risk management, human resources—these were jobs given as perks to retired officers." After several years of underperformance, the conglomerate had requested a bailout of nearly $100 million from the government. His firm had been hired to turn the business around. Speaking of the armed forces' role in Pakistan's economy, he said, "They have the power, and they can do whatever they want."

The parliamentarian added that the army was steadily helping itself to Islamabad's best land, often reselling it at a significant profit. The main vehicle for the landgrab, she told me, was the Defense Housing Authority, which purchases properties from private parties, for development and distribution to the officer corps. As a rule, she explained, the market value of the development escalates sharply once the military buys the property, because it is immediately regarded as prestigious and highly secure. "The corps commander gets a kickback from the real-estate developer," she said, and then "distributes the plots to lower-ranking officers [at government-subsidized prices], and sells what's left to civilians at a huge profit."

One afternoon, my driver, a 40-year-old Pashtun who had spent 20 years in the army as a chauffeur for the top brass, took me on a tour of his former employers' neighborhood. We drove 12 miles from Islamabad to Rawalpindi, an old city of mosques and bazaars that during colonial times was the site of a British cantonment. Today it is the location of Pakistan's general military headquarters, and large portions of the city have been taken over by housing developments for the retired military elite. Entering the city on the main Islamabad-Rawalpindi highway, we passed a large air-force base; the bridge where Al Qaeda operatives tried to blow up Musharraf's convoy in 2003; and a new McDonald's built on the site of the razed prison where former Prime Minister Zulfikar Ali Bhutto, Benazir's father, was hanged in 1979 on the order of Zia ul-Haq, the general who deposed him.

We turned into a gated community called "Askari 8," otherwise known as "Military Row." Our car crept along quiet residential lanes, planted with palm trees and lined with palatial villas of brick and marble. I might have thought we were in an exclusive Southern California suburb, except for the bronze plaques on the front gates identifying the owners: a former corps commander of Rawalpindi, a former vice chief of staff, a retired head of the ISI. Around the corner lay rows of smaller mansions. These belonged to brigadiers, my driver told me, officers one rank down from general.

The army's encroachment on civilian affairs has not inspired any kinship between the military and civilians, whom many officers view as inferior. A sense of entitlement is inculcated in the officer corps at the Pakistan Military Academy, in Kakul, a former base of the Indian army set among the pine-forested Himalayan foothills of the North-West Frontier Province. It was established shortly after partition in 1947, as a sort of home-grown version of Sandhurst, the British school where many Indian officers received their military education. In a tranquil setting dominated by snowy peaks, cadets culled from a huge pool of applicants spend two and a half years studying governance and political theory; the syllabus spans the canon of Western and Islamic literature and includes ancient Greek philosophers, Middle Eastern poets and historians, even the Indian military strategist Chanakya. Musharraf graduated from the academy in 1964; it is perhaps telling that since he came to power, the academy has begun offering courses in economics and business management.

The cadets spend as much time training their bodies as their minds. The climax of their athletic training is the "Acid Test," a multi-hour ordeal of running, climbing, and trudging over difficult terrain, while laden with heavy gear. At the finish, those who complete the test fire celebratory rounds at a target, and look up at an inscription that reads "VERILY THE POWER LIES IN FIREPOWER."

"Once you are through Kakul, you are the elect—you are a breed apart," says Tanvir Ahmed Khan, a former Pakistani foreign secretary. The military academy, he says, instills in cadets "a sense of pride and a genuine, deep-seated contempt for everyone outside the military." That contempt, says Khan, is rooted in a belief that civilian governments have proved uniformly inept and corrupt, repeatedly forcing the military to "rescue" the country from the clutches of incompetent civil servants and thieving politicians—a position that is increasingly ironic as the military dips ever deeper into the public trough.

⤛ • ⤜

The Pakistani military's relationship with the United States has been tempestuous. American and Pakistani soldiers began working together in the field in the 1950s, bound by mutual concerns about Soviet expansionism in the region. The relationship cooled after the United States imposed sanctions following Pakistan's 1965 war with India, but it warmed up again under the military dictatorship of Zia ul-Haq: The U.S. Department of Defense moved more than a thousand Pakistani officers through its International Military Education and Training program, or IMET, giving them months of training alongside American officers at elite American military institutions.

Major General Shaukat Sultan Khan, Musharraf's press secretary until March 2007, spent six months in infantry school at Fort Benning, Georgia, in 1983. He explained to me how the American training shaped the mentality of thousands of young officers of his generation. "It helps you to establish a better relationship and more understanding [of the U.S. perspective]," he said. "It broadens your outlook." At a recent gathering of regional commanders in Kabul, Shaukat Sultan formed an immediate bond with an American brigadier he had last seen during his Fort Benning days. "It gave us a connection," said Shaukat Sultan. "[Now] I can pick up the phone and call him directly."

Shaukat Sultan was among the last of a breed, however. In 1987, toward the end of the mujahideen campaign against the Soviets in Afghanistan, Congress threatened to impose sanctions if Pakistan continued to develop nuclear weapons. Three years later, the sanctions went into effect, and the United States suspended the IMET program. For the next 11 years, until 9/11, Pakistani officers had little or no contact with the U.S. military (IMET resumed in late 2001). "We lost a generation," the Western military liaison officer told me. That generation now overwhelmingly makes up the ranks of brigadier, colonel, and major—and includes some generals—in Pakistan's military.

By the early 1990s, as the Cold War was ending and the United States was disengaging from Central and South Asia, Pakistan's army had taken on a more Islamist character. Back in 1979, Zia ul-Haq—in an attempt to stir up zeal for the campaign in support of Afghanistan's mujahideen—had enacted a raft of Islamist ordinances, or *hudood,* posting an imam to every unit, encouraging prayer in the barracks, and installing a religious-affairs directorate at general headquarters. Banners outside army recruiting centers reportedly urged Pakistanis to enlist for the sake of Allah and jihad.

During this period the army and the ISI stepped up covert training of Islamist mujahideen to wage a guerrilla war against India in Kashmir, transforming what had been a largely secular struggle into a jihad—a war to liberate Islamic brethren from the yoke of the "Hindu occupiers." The Taliban's seizure of power in Afghanistan in 1996—also backed by Pakistan—furthered the military's goal of bleeding the Indian army in Kashmir; the Taliban allowed the Pakistani army to operate dozens of training camps in Afghanistan for the Kashmir struggle. The Taliban, who are ethnic Pashtuns with direct tribal links to Pakistan's own Pashtun population in the North-West Frontier Province and Balochistan, also provided a bulwark against Afghanistan's Tajik-dominated Northern Alliance and its key ally, India.

The military's support for Islamist causes was primarily tactical, and its inculcation of Islamist values in its troops appears to have been halfhearted. Shaukat Sultan told me, "There neither used to be orders during the Zia days that everyone come down for prayers, nor are there orders now. It all depends on the individual commanding officers." Nonetheless, in February 2000, Lieutenant General Mahmoud Ahmad, then the head of the ISI, claimed to an analyst at the Rand Corporation that "between 15 and 16 percent" of the Pakistani officer corps were Islamic extremists.

⤚ • ⤙

The United States, of course, took a renewed interest in Pakistan after 9/11. Faced with the now-infamous threat, supposedly delivered by Deputy Secretary of State Richard Armitage, that the country would be bombed "back to the Stone Age" if it failed to support the war on terrorism, Musharraf reversed course, dragging a sometimes-reluctant army along with him. In perhaps the most striking example of the country's about-face, Musharraf in December 2001 ordered a full army corps into the tribal areas to intercept Al Qaeda and sometimes Taliban militants fleeing across the Afghan border after the U.S.-led invasion; by the end of 2004, several hundred foreign militants had been captured.

Musharraf also cleaned house within the generals' rank. General Mahmoud, the ISI chief and a Taliban ally who had opposed the American invasion of Afghanistan, was sacked just weeks after 9/11. Musharraf downgraded the Islamic-affairs office from a directorate to a "section" run by a junior officer, and sought to dilute Islamist influence in the ranks. He began vetoing promotions of brigadiers and generals, and has put his own people in charge of the selection process at Pakistan Military Academy. He surrounded himself with a cadre of politically moderate generals, almost all of whom had been trained in the United States, including the army's vice chief, Lieutenant General Ahsan Saleem Hayat, the next in line for the army's top spot.

Nonetheless, the war along the border has opened a divide between the top military brass and junior officers. In 2006 alone, at least 300 Pakistani soldiers died in this campaign, most in roadside-bomb attacks or ambushes in the mountainous terrain; thousands of militants and civilians were also killed and injured. Tanvir Ahmed Khan, the former foreign secretary, recently addressed a gathering of mid-level officers at one of the army's premier training establishments about the war in Afghanistan, and found some uncertainty about Pakistani policy. I spoke with Khan for several hours at his comfortable house in Islamabad. An erudite figure in his early 70s who held senior positions during the Zia ul-Haq and Benazir Bhutto years, Khan has lectured and written widely on Pakistan's relations with its neighbors. He maintains ties with many of the country's most powerful military figures of the past three decades.

Khan recounted for me a telling conversation he'd had after his lecture at the training center. He was approached by an army major in his 30s who was confused about a Pakistani bombing raid in South Waziristan that had killed dozens of local Pashtun tribesmen who were fighting for the Taliban. The officer perceived the tribesmen not as terrorists but as Pashtun nationalists, whose targets were the Western occupiers and who had no quarrel with the Pakistani government. "He said, 'I am ashamed of what has been done there,'" Khan told me. The military has no love for Al Qaeda, Khan continued, at least as long as Al Qaeda can be defined as "'the Arabs,' as 'the other.'" But "when Musharraf claims that he has attacked these insurgents, and the media insist that dead bodies are those of tribesmen," Khan said, "it becomes a different story."

Near the end of my stay in Pakistan, a journalist friend in Islamabad introduced me to an old friend of his: a 35-year-old major in the Pakistani army, who had agreed to talk to me as long as I didn't use his name or identify his unit. We met in a small, smoky lounge at my friend's newspaper office. The major, who was wearing civilian clothes—jeans and a wool sweater thrown over a polo shirt—was a stocky, affable man who spoke colloquial English; he seemed relaxed and uninhibited, once I assured him that I'd protect his identity. "Major

Khaled," as I'll call him, grew up in northern Punjab—the "martial belt" that has traditionally provided the vast majority of soldiers and officers in the army—and he received his training at the Pakistan Military Academy. His career mirrored that of many other ambitious young Pakistani officers, and until recently, he had followed his orders without questioning them: He had participated enthusiastically, for instance, in the 1999 invasion of Kargil. All of that changed after Pakistani troops were deployed in the tribal agencies along the border to put down local insurgents and foreign fighters.

"I've met people of all ranks, in the line of fire, and nobody is happy with this way of solving the problem in Waziristan," he told me. "The terrain is hard. It's difficult to hold the ground. The insurgents know every inch of the area." Major Khaled told me he resented the implication, which he felt the U.S. government had fostered, that Pakistan was serving as the main refuge for Taliban and Al Qaeda fighters. "The terrain around Kabul is similar, so why do they say that the only hideouts are in Waziristan?" he said. "Why is Pakistan singled out? Pakistan has suffered a lot. I've lost colleagues in ambushes, to time bombs, to improvised explosive devices. The Pakistan army is bleeding for you people." I asked Khaled if his doubts about the mission had ever caused him to disobey the commands of higher-ups. He shook his head. "I'm not a policy maker. We just have to follow the orders, but people down below don't go into battle from their hearts. There could have been other options. This is not our battle. This is your battle, and we're paying the price."

Though Major Khaled told me that he admired American democracy and liked the American soldiers he had met, he had little confidence in the United States as an ally or benefactor. "We know that the United States tomorrow won't hesitate to forget us. They've done it before," he said. The only reason that Musharraf had signed on to the war on terrorism, he said, was that his government "has a gun to its head, and it has no other options." He returned to the theme that Pakistan was fighting a proxy war for an untrustworthy ally. "If we had to face bullets [to save Pakistan], we'd go, but why do that for someone who's not loyal to you [when Pakistan is not threatened]? This is not our war; Taliban, Al Qaeda are not criminals in our country."

The Western military liaison officer, who works closely with his Pakistani counterparts, says that the entire Pakistani military, from Musharraf on down, has been deeply ambivalent about the border campaign. He told me he thinks that Musharraf himself is beginning to realize that the Taliban and Al Qaeda could pose a threat to Pakistan's security if left untended, but that this view has not yet permeated the military leadership. In addition, he said, "They know that their initial army forays were largely unsuccessful, and that their army had never been in the [tribal areas] and was viewed as foreign—almost as much as our army would be. So they've backed away."

The Pakistanis, he says, often appear to turn a blind eye to insurgent infiltrations, fail to man border posts, and ignore American requests for cooperation. For months they have refused to establish a joint operations center in the border zone. "They say, 'We're thinking about it,' but it never happens," he says. He gave me an example of how Pakistani officers can sometimes work directly against U.S. interests on the border: On the afternoon of January 10, U.S. intelligence detected four "jingle trucks"—brightly painted vehicles adorned with jingling bits of metal, which typically serve as buses in both Pakistan and Afghanistan—transporting about 200 heavily armed insurgents to the border of the Kurram tribal agency, west of Peshawar.

Three Pakistani border posts were within a kilometer of where the trucks were off-loading fighters, but the fighters crossed into Afghanistan in broad daylight, unmolested. The Pakistanis ignored American requests to detain and interrogate the truck drivers. After the trucks had driven away, the Pakistani soldiers told the Americans that the drivers said they were innocent contractors. "We asked, 'Why didn't you arrest them? You could have interrogated them and asked them where they picked up the fighters, how much money they were paid, if they recognized foreign fighters.' But they didn't. They let them go."

The Americans' perceptions of the Pakistanis are shared by security officers in Kashmir. S.M. Sahai, the inspector general of the Jammu & Kashmir Police, the institution responsible for interdicting insurgents who cross the border from Pakistan, told me that Pakistani soldiers, especially enlisted men and "younger officers," are generally sympathetic to the Islamist insurgency. "If they have a face-to-face encounter with them along the border, they will arrest them," Sahai told me in Srinagar. "But the general attitude is to look the other way."

⤛ • ⤜

What might the United States lose if Musharraf were to fall from power, and what would it stand to gain? Curiously, on the issue that U.S. policy makers seem to care most about today—military action against Taliban and Al Qaeda operatives in the North-West Frontier Province and Balochistan—Musharraf's presence or absence might make little difference. As the United States has recently found, Pakistan's military is willing to push only so hard on this front; institutional resistance, popular opposition, and Pakistan's own strategic calculus are likely to limit action, no matter who is in charge. At the same time, some action and cooperation—intelligence sharing, covert assistance, low-grade military operations, and the rare high-profile strike—can probably be coaxed out of any regime that is likely to follow Musharraf's. The Pakistani army deeply values the American high-tech weaponry it receives; the equipment helps it keep pace with India's army. Benazir Bhutto, for her part, recently stated publicly that she wholeheartedly supported the war on terrorism. And the appetite of moderate Pakistanis for incursions against the militants has increased in the wake of the Red Mosque confrontation and the series of suicide attacks that followed.

The threat of an outright Islamist revolution—by gun or ballot—is low today, and so too is the threat that nuclear weapons could fall into the wrong hands. The army is not dominated by jihadists, and its controls on its missiles are strong. Yet the course of Pakistani politics remains vital to the United States. Military rule in Pakistan may have been helpful to U.S. interests for a time, but it isn't any longer. The benefits have diminished, while the corrosive effects on society have grown—and continue to grow.

The military's younger generation has exhibited some of the same unsavory tendencies as Musharraf: an inclination toward authoritarianism, contempt for civilians, indulgence of military corruption, and an unequivocal belief in the military as the country's savior. It also appears more sympathetic to Islamist causes and more hostile to India than is Musharraf. Pakistani officers in their 30s do not believe that the U.S. wants a long-lasting relationship with Pakistan; they have little camaraderie with U.S. soldiers, and they feel little empathy for U.S. political or diplomatic positions.

And while the military aims to do the opposite, it is slowly destabilizing Pakistan. Eight years of usurpation of power by Musharraf have weakened secular parties, corrupted the judiciary, and implanted army men in every facet of civilian life. Pakistan's population is now doubling every 38 years, creating severe social pressures. If the political process remains stunted, the Islamists may continue to gather strength until the country reaches a tipping point. "We are not going to collapse if Musharraf goes tomorrow; Pakistan will go on, *insha'allah*," I was told by Mohammed Enver Baig, a senator with the Pakistan People's Party. "But the 2007 elections could be a turning point for all of us. If the elections are not fair, don't be surprised if next time—after five years—you come and see me, I might have a long beard myself."

America may best serve its interests, then, by pulling off a balancing act: reinforcing ties to the existing power structure in Pakistan (the armed forces) while at the same time pushing hard for democracy. These two ends are not necessarily mutually exclusive. In August 1988, immediately after the death of the military dictator Zia ul-Haq, the vice chief of army staff, General Aslam Beg, summoned his naval and air chiefs, the head of the ISI, and the army judge advocate general to headquarters in Rawalpindi and informed them that he was turning over power to the chairman of the senate, a civilian, as Pakistan's constitution requires. There was no resistance, Beg recalls, and the new civilian president immediately called for multiparty elections. Those elections were among the freest and fairest in Pakistani history, and they ushered in 11 years of vibrant—if corrupt—civilian rule, ending only with Musharraf's coup. Given the prizes the army has since won under Musharraf, a quick and complete withdrawal from politics appears unlikely this time around—and therefore even a civilian democracy would find itself greatly constrained by military interests. But with careful management by Pakistan's politicians, and strong encouragement by the international community, the army might slowly disengage.

One important change in U.S. strategy that may already be having an effect is the reinstatement of the officer training program. Last year, the United States trained 112 Pakistani officers. Stepped-up military training could go a long way toward building trust, tamping down anti-American sentiment, and encouraging professionalism, respect for human rights, and a withdrawal to the barracks. "We lost 10 years," I was told by the Western military liaison official. "We need to make up for lost time."

Among junior officers, there is some support for relinquishing power. Major Khaled, the young officer I met in Islamabad, told me that back when he joined the army, "we went through villages during military exercises, and people welcomed us and gave us water, assistance. It's the opposite now. They think I'm a rich guy just because I'm a soldier. I feel the resentment; I see the bad looks. People say we've hung around too long." This widening gap between civilians and military has led to intense questioning among the junior officers, he told me. "A few days back, six of us were discussing the options, and we said, 'The army can exit and call for a fair and impartial election. Let the exiled leaders come back to Pakistan and install a civilian government. Democracy is the right way.'"

I wasn't sure whether Khaled was just spouting a line that he wanted me to hear, but the more he spoke, the more emphatic he became: "Our neighbor India has had democracy for 60 years. But the problem here persists. The courts are pathetic; judges are not independent; the police are illiterate, low-paid, and not fair; and corruption is rampant. A 50-year-old cop with five kids is getting $100 a month. What is he supposed to do?" The military, Major Khaled said, "should have strengthened the institutions instead of weakening them."

Restoring democracy in Pakistan is no guarantee of stability, or of a friendly attitude toward the United States. But a viable multiparty system could defuse the power of the Islamists and impose some checks on a military that controls every aspect of policy. And it would leave the United States less dependent upon the whims of a post-Musharraf general answerable only to the clique at headquarters. "I want restoration of political freedoms," Hoodbhoy told me. "Let people organize, hold political rallies; let there be trade unions, student unions, even if these unions would be ones you and I wouldn't like. Because when we have mobilization of society, we can have a Pakistan, down the line, where people matter. If I were an American president, I would make my support for Musharraf conditional on that."

25

THE BLACK SITES: A RARE LOOK INSIDE THE C.I.A.'S SECRET INTERROGATION PROGRAM

JANE MAYER
The New Yorker   August 13, 2007

Of all the changes wrought by the Al Qaeda attacks of September 11, 2001, and America's subsequent "war on terror," none has been more unsettling than the aggressive detention policies employed by the Bush administration against suspected terrorists, such as holding prisoners indefinitely without charging them or allowing them access to legal representation. Equally disturbing are the so-called "enhanced interrogation" techniques that President Bush has green-lighted at various

*times, up to and including the simulated-drowning technique known by the banal
name of "water-boarding."*

*Jane Mayer has consistently led the pack in reporting on our nation's post-9/11
detention practices; her series of* New Yorker *articles on the subject (and resulting
book,* The Dark Side) *are required reading for anyone interested in the state of
American democracy. In the following selection, Mayer continues to break new
ground with her report on the interrogation methods employed by U.S. forces—
which, if not outright torture, certainly seem to qualify as Torture Lite.*

In March, Mariane Pearl, the widow of the murdered *Wall Street Journal* re-
porter Daniel Pearl, received a phone call from Alberto Gonzales, the Attorney
General. At the time, Gonzales's role in the controversial dismissal of eight
United States Attorneys had just been exposed, and the story was becoming a
scandal in Washington. Gonzales informed Pearl that the Justice Department
was about to announce some good news: a terrorist in U.S. custody—Khalid
Sheikh Mohammed, the Al Qaeda leader who was the primary architect of the
September 11th attacks—had confessed to killing her husband. (Pearl was ab-
ducted and beheaded five and a half years ago in Pakistan, by unidentified Islamic militants.) The Administration planned to release a transcript in which
Mohammed boasted, "I decapitated with my blessed right hand the head of the
American Jew Daniel Pearl in the city of Karachi, Pakistan. For those who would
like to confirm, there are pictures of me on the Internet holding his head."

Pearl was taken aback. In 2003, she had received a call from Condoleezza
Rice, who was then President Bush's national-security adviser, informing her of
the same news. But Rice's revelation had been secret. Gonzales's announcement
seemed like a publicity stunt. Pearl asked him if he had proof that Mohammed's
confession was truthful; Gonzales claimed to have corroborating evidence but
wouldn't share it. "It's not enough for officials to call me and say they believe
it," Pearl said. "You need evidence." (Gonzales did not respond to requests for
comment.)

The circumstances surrounding the confession of Mohammed, whom law-
enforcement officials refer to as K.S.M., were perplexing. He had no lawyer.
After his capture in Pakistan, in March of 2003, the Central Intelligence Agency
had detained him in undisclosed locations for more than two years; last fall, he
was transferred to military custody in Guantánamo Bay, Cuba. There were no
named witnesses to his initial confession, and no solid information about what

form of interrogation might have prodded him to talk, although reports had been published, in the *Times* and elsewhere, suggesting that C.I.A. officers had tortured him. At a hearing held at Guantánamo, Mohammed said that his testimony was freely given, but he also indicated that he had been abused by the C.I.A. (The Pentagon had classified as "top secret" a statement he had written detailing the alleged mistreatment.) And although Mohammed said that there were photographs confirming his guilt, U.S. authorities had found none. Instead, they had a copy of the video that had been released on the Internet, which showed the killer's arms but offered no other clues to his identity.

Further confusing matters, a Pakistani named Ahmed Omar Saeed Sheikh had already been convicted of the abduction and murder, in 2002. A British-educated terrorist who had a history of staging kidnappings, he had been sentenced to death in Pakistan for the crime. But the Pakistani government, not known for its leniency, had stayed his execution. Indeed, hearings on the matter had been delayed a remarkable number of times—at least thirty—possibly because of his reported ties to the Pakistani intelligence service, which may have helped free him after he was imprisoned for terrorist activities in India. Mohammed's confession would delay the execution further, since, under Pakistani law, any new evidence is grounds for appeal.

A surprising number of people close to the case are dubious of Mohammed's confession. A longtime friend of Pearl's, the former *Journal* reporter Asra Nomani, said, "The release of the confession came right in the midst of the U.S. Attorney scandal. There was a drumbeat for Gonzales's resignation. It seemed like a calculated strategy to change the subject. Why now? They'd had the confession for years." Mariane and Daniel Pearl were staying in Nomani's Karachi house at the time of his murder, and Nomani has followed the case meticulously; this fall, she plans to teach a course on the topic at Georgetown University. She said, "I don't think this confession resolves the case. You can't have justice from one person's confession, especially under such unusual circumstances. To me, it's not convincing." She added, "I called all the investigators. They weren't just skeptical—they didn't believe it."

Special Agent Randall Bennett, the head of security for the U.S. consulate in Karachi when Pearl was killed—and whose lead role investigating the murder was featured in the recent film *A Mighty Heart*—said that he has interviewed all the convicted accomplices who are now in custody in Pakistan, and that none of them named Mohammed as playing a role. "K.S.M.'s name never came up," he said. Robert Baer, a former C.I.A. officer, said, "My old colleagues say

with one-hundred-per-cent certainty that it was not K.S.M. who killed Pearl."
A government official involved in the case said, "The fear is that K.S.M. is covering up for others, and that these people will be released." And Judea Pearl,
Daniel's father, said, "Something is fishy. There are a lot of unanswered questions. K.S.M. can say he killed Jesus—he has nothing to lose."

Mariane Pearl, who is relying on the Bush administration to bring justice in
her husband's case, spoke carefully about the investigation. "You need a procedure that will get the truth," she said. "An intelligence agency is not supposed
to be above the law."

⤛ • ⤜

Mohammed's interrogation was part of a secret C.I.A. program, initiated after
September 11th, in which terrorist suspects such as Mohammed were detained
in "black sites"—secret prisons outside the United States—and subjected to
unusually harsh treatment. The program was effectively suspended last fall,
when President Bush announced that he was emptying the C.I.A.'s prisons and
transferring the detainees to military custody in Guantánamo. This move followed a Supreme Court ruling, *Hamdan v. Rumsfeld*, which found that all detainees—including those held by the C.I.A.—had to be treated in a manner
consistent with the Geneva Conventions. These treaties, adopted in 1949, bar
cruel treatment, degradation, and torture. In late July, the White House issued
an executive order promising that the C.I.A. would adjust its methods in order
to meet the Geneva standards. At the same time, Bush's order pointedly did
not disavow the use of "enhanced interrogation techniques" that would likely
be found illegal if used by officials inside the United States. The executive order
means that the agency can once again hold foreign terror suspects indefinitely,
and without charges, in black sites, without notifying their families or local authorities, or offering access to legal counsel.

The C.I.A.'s director, General Michael Hayden, has said that the program,
which is designed to extract intelligence from suspects quickly, is an "irreplace-
able" tool for combatting terrorism. And President Bush has said that "this program has given us information that has saved innocent lives, by helping us stop
new attacks." He claims that it has contributed to the disruption of at least ten serious Al Qaeda plots since September 11th, three of them inside the United States.

According to the Bush administration, Mohammed divulged information
of tremendous value during his detention. He is said to have helped point the

way to the capture of Hambali, the Indonesian terrorist responsible for the 2002 bombings of night clubs in Bali. He also provided information on an Al Qaeda leader in England. Michael Sheehan, a former counterterrorism official at the State Department, said, "K.S.M. is the poster boy for using tough but legal tactics. He's the reason these techniques exist. You can save lives with the kind of information he could give up." Yet Mohammed's confessions may also have muddled some key investigations. Perhaps under duress, he claimed involvement in thirty-one criminal plots—an improbable number, even for a high-level terrorist. Critics say that Mohammed's case illustrates the cost of the C.I.A.'s desire for swift intelligence. Colonel Dwight Sullivan, the top defense lawyer at the Pentagon's Office of Military Commissions, which is expected eventually to try Mohammed for war crimes, called his serial confessions "a textbook example of why we shouldn't allow coercive methods."

The Bush administration has gone to great lengths to keep secret the treatment of the hundred or so "high-value detainees" whom the C.I.A. has confined, at one point or another, since September 11th. The program has been extraordinarily "compartmentalized," in the nomenclature of the intelligence world. By design, there has been virtually no access for outsiders to the C.I.A.'s prisoners. The utter isolation of these detainees has been described as essential to America's national security. The Justice Department argued this point explicitly last November, in the case of a Baltimore-area resident named Majid Khan, who was held for more than three years by the C.I.A. Khan, the government said, had to be prohibited from access to a lawyer specifically because he might describe the "alternative interrogation methods" that the agency had used when questioning him. These methods amounted to a state secret, the government argued, and disclosure of them could "reasonably be expected to cause extremely grave damage." (The case has not yet been decided.)

Given this level of secrecy, the public and all but a few members of Congress who have been sworn to silence have had to take on faith President Bush's assurances that the C.I.A.'s internment program has been humane and legal, and has yielded crucial intelligence. Representative Alcee Hastings, a Democratic member of the House Select Committee on Intelligence, said, "We talk to the authorities about these detainees, but, of course, they're not going to come out and tell us that they beat the living daylights out of someone." He recalled learning in 2003 that Mohammed had been captured. "It was good news," he said. "So I tried to find out: Where is this guy? And how is he being treated?" For more than three years, Hastings said, "I could never pinpoint anything." Finally, he received some classified briefings on the Mohammed interrogation. Hastings said that he "can't go into details" about what he found out, but, speaking of Mohammed's treatment, he said that even if it wasn't torture, as the Administration claims, "it ain't right, either. Something went wrong."

◄◄ • ►►

Since the drafting of the Geneva Conventions, the International Committee of the Red Cross has played a special role in safeguarding the rights of prisoners of war. For decades, governments have allowed officials from the organization to report on the treatment of detainees, to insure that standards set by international treaties are being maintained. The Red Cross, however, was unable to get access to the C.I.A.'s prisoners for five years. Finally, last year, Red Cross officials were allowed to interview fifteen detainees, after they had been transferred to Guantánamo. One of the prisoners was Khalid Sheikh Mohammed. What the Red Cross learned has been kept from the public. The committee believes that its continued access to prisoners worldwide is contingent upon confidentiality, and therefore it addresses violations privately with the authorities directly responsible for prisoner treatment and detention. For this reason, Simon Schorno, a Red Cross spokesman in Washington, said, "The I.C.R.C. does not comment on its findings publicly. Its work is confidential."

The public-affairs office at the C.I.A. and officials at the congressional intelligence-oversight committees would not even acknowledge the existence of the report. Among the few people who are believed to have seen it are Condoleezza Rice, now the Secretary of State; Stephen Hadley, the national-security adviser; John Bellinger III, the Secretary of State's legal adviser; Hayden; and John Rizzo, the agency's acting general counsel. Some members of the Senate and House intelligence-oversight committees are also believed to have had limited access to the report.

Confidentiality may be particularly stringent in this case. Congressional and other Washington sources familiar with the report said that it harshly criticized the C.I.A.'s practices. One of the sources said that the Red Cross described the agency's detention and interrogation methods as tantamount to torture, and declared that American officials responsible for the abusive treatment could have committed serious crimes. The source said the report warned that these officials may have committed "grave breaches" of the Geneva Conventions, and may have violated the U.S. Torture Act, which Congress passed in 1994. The conclusions of the Red Cross, which is known for its credibility and caution, could have potentially devastating legal ramifications.

Concern about the legality of the C.I.A.'s program reached a previously unreported breaking point last week when Senator Ron Wyden, a Democrat on the intelligence committee, quietly put a "hold" on the confirmation of John Rizzo, who as acting general counsel was deeply involved in establishing the agency's interrogation and detention policies. Wyden's maneuver essentially stops the nomination from going forward. "I question if there's been adequate legal oversight," Wyden told me. He said that after studying a classified addendum to President Bush's new executive order, which specifies permissible treatment of detainees, "I am not convinced that all of these techniques are either effective or legal. I don't want to see well-intentioned C.I.A. officers breaking the law because of shaky legal guidance."

A former C.I.A. officer, who supports the agency's detention and interrogation policies, said he worried that, if the full story of the C.I.A. program ever surfaced, agency personnel could face criminal prosecution. Within the agency, he said, there is a "high level of anxiety about political retribution" for the interrogation program. If congressional hearings begin, he said, "several guys expect to be thrown under the bus." He noted that a number of C.I.A. officers have taken out professional liability insurance, to help with potential legal fees.

Paul Gimigliano, a spokesman for the C.I.A., denied any legal impropriety, stressing that "the agency's terrorist-detention program has been implemented lawfully. And torture is illegal under U.S. law. The people who have been part of this important effort are well-trained, seasoned professionals." This spring, the Associated Press published an article quoting the chairman of the House intelligence committee, Silvestre Reyes, who said that Hayden, the C.I.A. director, "vehemently denied" the Red Cross's conclusions. A U.S. official dismissed the Red Cross report as a mere compilation of allegations made by terrorists. And Robert Grenier, a former head of the C.I.A.'s Counterterrorism Center, said that "the C.I.A.'s interrogations were nothing like Abu Ghraib or Guantánamo. They were very, very regimented. Very meticulous." He said, "The program is very careful. It's completely legal."

Accurately or not, Bush administration officials have described the prisoner abuses at Abu Ghraib and Guantánamo as the unauthorized actions of ill-trained personnel, eleven of whom have been convicted of crimes. By contrast, the treatment of high-value detainees has been directly, and repeatedly, approved by President Bush. The program is monitored closely by C.I.A. lawyers, and supervised by the agency's director and his subordinates at the Counterterrorism Center. While Mohammed was being held by the agency, detailed dossiers on the treatment of detainees were regularly available to the former C.I.A. director George Tenet, according to informed sources inside and outside the agency. Through a spokesperson, Tenet denied making day-to-day decisions about the treatment of individual detainees. But, according to a former agency official, "Every single plan is drawn up by interrogators, and then submitted for approval to the highest possible level—meaning the director of the C.I.A. Any change in the plan—even if an extra day of a certain treatment was added—was signed off by the C.I.A. director."

⤛ • ⤜

On September 17, 2001, President Bush signed a secret Presidential finding authorizing the C.I.A. to create paramilitary teams to hunt, capture, detain, or kill designated terrorists almost anywhere in the world. Yet the C.I.A. had virtually no trained interrogators. A former C.I.A. officer involved in fighting terrorism said that, at first, the agency was crippled by its lack of expertise. "It began right away, in Afghanistan, on the fly," he recalled. "They invented the program of interrogation with people who had no understanding of Al Qaeda or the Arab world." The former officer said that the pressure from the White House, in particular from Vice-President Dick Cheney, was intense: "They were pushing us: 'Get information! Do *not* let us get hit again!'" In the scramble, he said, he searched the C.I.A.'s archives, to see what interrogation techniques had worked in the past. He was particularly impressed with the Phoenix Program, from the Vietnam War. Critics, including military historians, have described it as a program of state-sanctioned torture and murder. A Pentagon-contract study found that, between 1970 and 1971, ninety-seven percent of the Vietcong targeted by the Phoenix Program were of negligible importance. But, after September 11th, some C.I.A. officials viewed the program as a useful model. A. B. Krongard, who was the executive director of the C.I.A. from 2001 to 2004, said that the agency turned to "everyone we could, including our friends in Arab cultures," for interrogation advice, among them those in Egypt, Jordan, and Saudi Arabia, all of which the State Department regularly criticizes for human-rights abuses.

The C.I.A. knew even less about running prisons than it did about hostile interrogations. Tyler Drumheller, a former chief of European operations at the

C.I.A., and the author of a recent book, *On the Brink: How the White House Compromised U.S. Intelligence,* said, "The agency had no experience in detention. Never. But they insisted on arresting and detaining people in this program. It was a mistake, in my opinion. You can't mix intelligence and police work. But the White House was really pushing. They wanted *someone* to do it. So the C.I.A. said, 'We'll try.' George Tenet came out of politics, not intelligence. His whole modus operandi was to please the principal. We got stuck with all sorts of things. This is really the legacy of a director who never said no to anybody."

Many officials inside the C.I.A. had misgivings. "A lot of us knew this would be a can of worms," the former officer said. "We warned them, It's going to become an atrocious mess." The problem from the start, he said, was that no one had thought through what he called "the disposal plan." He continued, "What are you going to *do* with these people? The utility of someone like K.S.M. is, at most, six months to a year. You exhaust them. Then what? It would have been better if we had executed them."

The C.I.A. program's first important detainee was Abu Zubaydah, a top Al Qaeda operative, who was captured by Pakistani forces in March of 2002. Lacking in-house specialists on interrogation, the agency hired a group of outside contractors, who implemented a regime of techniques that one well-informed former adviser to the American intelligence community described as "a *Clockwork Orange* kind of approach." The experts were retired military psychologists, and their backgrounds were in training Special Forces soldiers how to survive torture, should they ever be captured by enemy states. The program, known as SERE—an acronym for Survival, Evasion, Resistance, and Escape—was created at the end of the Korean War. It subjected trainees to simulated torture, including waterboarding (simulated drowning), sleep deprivation, isolation, exposure to temperature extremes, enclosure in tiny spaces, bombardment with agonizing sounds, and religious and sexual humiliation. The SERE program was designed strictly for defense against torture regimes, but the C.I.A.'s new team used its expertise to help interrogators inflict abuse. "They were very arrogant, and pro-torture," a European official knowledgeable about the program said. "They sought to render the detainees vulnerable—to break down all of their senses. It takes a psychologist trained in this to understand these rupturing experiences."

The use of psychologists was also considered a way for C.I.A. officials to skirt measures such as the Convention Against Torture. The former adviser to the intelligence community said, "Clearly, some senior people felt they needed a theory to justify what they were doing. You can't just say, 'We want to do what Egypt's doing.' When the lawyers asked what their basis was, they could say, 'We have Ph.D.s who have these theories.'" He said that, inside the C.I.A., where a number of scientists work, there was strong internal opposition to the new techniques. "Behavioral scientists said, 'Don't even think about this!' They thought officers could be prosecuted."

Nevertheless, the SERE experts' theories were apparently put into practice with Zubaydah's interrogation. Zubaydah told the Red Cross that he was not only waterboarded, as has been previously reported; he was also kept for a prolonged period in a cage, known as a "dog box," which was so small that he could not stand. According to an eyewitness, one psychologist advising on the treatment of Zubaydah, James Mitchell, argued that he needed to be reduced to a state of "learned helplessness." (Mitchell disputes this characterization.)

Steve Kleinman, a reserve Air Force colonel and an experienced interrogator who has known Mitchell professionally for years, said that "learned helplessness was his whole paradigm." Mitchell, he said, "draws a diagram showing what he says is the whole cycle. It starts with isolation. Then they eliminate the prisoners' ability to forecast the future—when their next meal is, when they can go to the bathroom. It creates dread and dependency. It was the K.G.B. model. But the K.G.B. used it to get people who had turned against the state to confess falsely. The K.G.B. wasn't after intelligence."

As the C.I.A. captured and interrogated other Al Qaeda figures, it established a protocol of psychological coercion. The program tied together many strands of the agency's secret history of Cold War–era experiments in behavioral science. (In June, the C.I.A. declassified long-held secret documents known as the Family Jewels, which shed light on C.I.A. drug experiments on rats and monkeys, and on the infamous case of Frank R. Olson, an agency employee who leaped to his death from a hotel window in 1953, nine days after he was unwittingly drugged with LSD.) The C.I.A.'s most useful research focused on the surprisingly powerful effects of psychological manipulations, such as extreme sensory deprivation. According to Alfred McCoy, a history professor at the University of Wisconsin, in Madison, who has written a history of the C.I.A.'s experiments in coercing subjects, the agency learned that "if subjects are confined without light, odors, sound, or any fixed references of time and place, very deep breakdowns can be provoked."

Agency scientists found that in just a few hours some subjects suspended in water tanks—or confined in isolated rooms wearing blacked-out goggles and earmuffs—regressed to semi-psychotic states. Moreover, McCoy said, detainees become so desperate for human interaction that "they bond with the interrogator like a father, or like a drowning man having a lifesaver thrown at him. If you deprive people of all their senses, they'll turn to you like their daddy." McCoy added that "after the Cold War we put away those tools. There was bipartisan reform. We backed away from those dark days. Then, under the pressure of the war on terror, they didn't just bring back the old psychological techniques—they perfected them."

The C.I.A.'s interrogation program is remarkable for its mechanistic aura. "It's one of the most sophisticated, refined programs of torture ever," an outside expert familiar with the protocol said. "At every stage, there was a rigid attention to detail. Procedure was adhered to almost to the letter. There was top-down quality control, and such a set routine that you get to the point where you know what each detainee is going to say, because you've heard it before. It was almost automated. People were utterly dehumanized. People fell apart. It was the intentional and systematic infliction of great suffering masquerading as a legal process. It is just chilling."

◄← • →►

The U.S. government first began tracking Khalid Sheikh Mohammed in 1993, shortly after his nephew Ramzi Yousef blew a gaping hole in the World Trade Center. Mohammed, officials learned, had transferred money to Yousef. Mohammed, born in either 1964 or 1965, was raised in a religious Sunni Muslim family in Kuwait, where his family had migrated from the Baluchistan region of Pakistan. In the mid-eighties, he was trained as a mechanical engineer in the U.S., attending two colleges in North Carolina.

As a teen-ager, Mohammed had been drawn to militant, and increasingly violent, Muslim causes. He joined the Muslim Brotherhood at the age of sixteen, and, after his graduation from North Carolina Agricultural and Technical State University, in Greensboro—where he was remembered as a class clown, but religious enough to forgo meat when eating at Burger King—he signed on with the anti-Soviet jihad in Afghanistan, receiving military training and establishing ties with Islamist terrorists. By all accounts, his animus toward the U.S. was rooted in a hatred of Israel.

In 1994, Mohammed, who was impressed by Yousef's notoriety after the first World Trade Center bombing, joined him in scheming to blow up twelve U.S.

jumbo jets over two days. The so-called Bojinka plot was disrupted in 1995, when Philippine police broke into an apartment that Yousef and other terrorists were sharing in Manila, which was filled with bomb-making materials. At the time of the raid, Mohammed was working in Doha, Qatar, at a government job. The following year, he narrowly escaped capture by F.B.I. officers and slipped into the global jihadist network, where he eventually joined forces with Osama bin Laden, in Afghanistan. Along the way, he married and had children.

Many journalistic accounts have presented Mohammed as a charismatic, swashbuckling figure: in the Philippines, he was said to have flown a helicopter close enough to a girlfriend's office window so that she could see him; in Pakistan, he supposedly posed as an anonymous bystander and gave interviews to news reporters about his nephew's arrest. Neither story is true. But Mohammed did seem to enjoy taunting authorities after the September 11th attacks, which, in his eventual confession, he claimed to have orchestrated "from A to Z." In April, 2002, Mohammed arranged to be interviewed on Al Jazeera by its London bureau chief, Yosri Fouda, and took personal credit for the atrocities. "I am the head of the Al Qaeda military committee," he said. "And yes, we did it." Fouda, who conducted the interview at an Al Qaeda safe house in Karachi, said that he was astounded not only by Mohammed's boasting but also by his seeming imperviousness to the danger of being caught. Mohammed permitted Al Jazeera to reveal that he was hiding out in the Karachi area. When Fouda left the apartment, Mohammed, apparently unarmed, walked him downstairs and out into the street.

In the early months of 2003, U.S. authorities reportedly paid a twenty-five-million-dollar reward for information that led to Mohammed's arrest. U.S. officials closed in on him, at 4 A.M. on March 1st, waking him up in a borrowed apartment in Rawalpindi, Pakistan. The officials hung back as Pakistani authorities handcuffed and hooded him, and took him to a safe house. Reportedly, for the first two days, Mohammed robotically recited Koranic verses and refused to divulge much more than his name. A videotape obtained by *60 Minutes* shows Mohammed at the end of this episode, complaining of a head cold; an American voice can be heard in the background. This was the last image of Mohammed to be seen by the public. By March 4th, he was in C.I.A. custody.

Captured along with Mohammed, according to some accounts, was a letter from bin Laden, which may have led officials to think that he knew where the Al Qaeda founder was hiding. If Mohammed did have this crucial information, it was time sensitive—bin Laden never stayed in one place for long—and officials needed to extract it quickly. At the time, many American intelligence officials still feared a "second wave" of Al Qaeda attacks, ratcheting the pressure further.

According to George Tenet's recent memoir, *At the Center of the Storm,* Mohammed told his captors that he wouldn't talk until he was given a lawyer in New York, where he assumed he would be taken. (He had been indicted there in connection with the Bojinka plot.) Tenet writes, "Had that happened, I am confident that we would have obtained none of the information he had in his head about imminent threats against the American people." Opponents of the C.I.A.'s approach, however, note that Ramzi Yousef gave a voluminous confession after being read his Miranda rights. "These guys are egomaniacs," a former federal prosecutor said. "They *love* to talk!"

⊰⊱ • ⊱⊰

A complete picture of Mohammed's time in secret detention remains elusive. But a partial narrative has emerged through interviews with European and American sources in intelligence, government, and legal circles, as well as with former detainees who have been released from C.I.A. custody. People familiar with Mohammed's allegations about his interrogation, and interrogations of other high-value detainees, describe the accounts as remarkably consistent.

Soon after Mohammed's arrest, sources say, his American captors told him, "We're not going to kill you. But we're going to take you to the very brink of your death and back." He was first taken to a secret U.S.-run prison in Afghanistan. According to a Human Rights Watch report released two years ago, there was a C.I.A.-affiliated black site in Afghanistan by 2002: an underground prison near Kabul International Airport. Distinctive for its absolute lack of light, it was referred to by detainees as the Dark Prison. Another detention facility was reportedly a former brick factory, just north of Kabul, known as the Salt Pit. The latter became infamous for the 2002 death of a detainee, reportedly from hypothermia, after prison officials stripped him naked and chained him to the floor of his concrete cell, in freezing temperatures.

In all likelihood, Mohammed was transported from Pakistan to one of the Afghan sites by a team of black-masked commandos attached to the C.I.A.'s paramilitary Special Activities Division. According to a report adopted in June by the Parliamentary Assembly of the Council of Europe, titled "Secret Detentions and Illegal Transfers of Detainees," detainees were "taken to their cells by strong people who wore black outfits, masks that covered their whole faces, and dark visors over their eyes." (Some personnel reportedly wore black clothes made from specially woven synthetic fabric that couldn't be ripped or torn.) A former member of a C.I.A. transport team has described the "takeout" of prisoners as a carefully choreographed twenty-minute routine, during which a suspect was hog-tied, stripped naked, photographed, hooded, sedated with anal suppositories, placed in diapers, and transported by plane to a secret location.

A person involved in the Council of Europe inquiry, referring to cavity searches and the frequent use of suppositories during the takeout of detainees, likened the treatment to "sodomy." He said, "It was used to absolutely strip the detainee of any dignity. It breaks down someone's sense of impenetrability. The interrogation became a process not just of getting information but of utterly subordinating the detainee through humiliation." The former C.I.A. officer confirmed that the agency frequently photographed the prisoners naked, "because it's demoralizing." The person involved in the Council of Europe inquiry said that photos were also part of the C.I.A.'s quality-control process. They were passed back to case officers for review.

A secret government document, dated December 10, 2002, detailing "SERE Interrogation Standard Operating Procedure," outlines the advantages of stripping detainees. "In addition to degradation of the detainee, stripping can be used to demonstrate the omnipotence of the captor or to debilitate the detainee." The document advises interrogators to "tear clothing from detainees by firmly pulling downward against buttoned buttons and seams. Tearing motions shall be downward to prevent pulling the detainee off balance." The memo also advocates the "Shoulder Slap," "Stomach Slap," "Hooding," "Manhandling," "Walling," and a variety of "Stress Positions," including one called "Worship the Gods."

In the process of being transported, C.I.A. detainees such as Mohammed were screened by medical experts, who checked their vital signs, took blood samples, and marked a chart with a diagram of a human body, noting scars, wounds, and other imperfections. As the person involved in the Council of Europe inquiry put it, "It's like when you hire a motor vehicle, circling where the scratches are on the rearview mirror. Each detainee was continually assessed, physically and psychologically."

According to sources, Mohammed said that, while in C.I.A. custody, he was placed in his own cell, where he remained naked for several days. He was questioned by an unusual number of female handlers, perhaps as an additional humiliation. He has alleged that he was attached to a dog leash, and yanked in such a way that he was propelled into the walls of his cell. Sources say that he also claimed to have been suspended from the ceiling by his arms, his toes barely touching the ground. The pressure on his wrists evidently became exceedingly painful.

Ramzi Kassem, who teaches at Yale Law School, said that a Yemeni client of his, Sanad al-Kazimi, who is now in Guantánamo, alleged that he had received similar treatment in the Dark Prison, the facility near Kabul. Kazimi claimed to have been suspended by his arms for long periods, causing his legs to swell painfully. "It's so traumatic, he can barely speak of it," Kassem said. "He breaks down in tears." Kazimi also claimed that, while hanging, he was beaten with electric cables.

According to sources familiar with interrogation techniques, the hanging position is designed, in part, to prevent detainees from being able to sleep. The former C.I.A. officer, who is knowledgeable about the interrogation program, explained that "sleep deprivation works. Your electrolyte balance changes. You lose all balance and ability to think rationally. Stuff comes out." Sleep deprivation has been recognized as an effective form of coercion since the Middle Ages, when it was called *tormentum insomniae.* It was also recognized for decades in the United States as an illegal form of torture. An American Bar Association report, published in 1930, which was cited in a later U.S. Supreme Court decision, said, "It has been known since 1500 at least that deprivation of sleep is the most effective torture and certain to produce any confession desired."

Under President Bush's new executive order, C.I.A. detainees must receive the "basic necessities of life, including adequate food and water, shelter from the elements, necessary clothing, protection from extremes of heat and cold, and essential medical care." Sleep, according to the order, is not among the basic necessities.

In addition to keeping a prisoner awake, the simple act of remaining upright can over time cause significant pain. McCoy, the historian, noted that "longtime standing" was a common K.G.B. interrogation technique. In his 2006 book, *A Question of Torture,* he writes that the Soviets found that making a victim stand for eighteen to twenty-four hours can produce "excruciating pain, as ankles double in size, skin becomes tense and intensely painful, blisters erupt oozing watery serum, heart rates soar, kidneys shut down, and delusions deepen."

Mohammed is said to have described being chained naked to a metal ring in his cell wall for prolonged periods in a painful crouch. (Several other detainees who say that they were confined in the Dark Prison have described identical treatment.) He also claimed that he was kept alternately in suffocating heat and in a painfully cold room, where he was doused with ice water. The practice, which can cause hypothermia, violates the Geneva Conventions, and President Bush's new executive order arguably bans it.

Some detainees held by the C.I.A. claimed that their cells were bombarded with deafening sound twenty-fours hours a day for weeks, and even months. One detainee, Binyam Mohamed, who is now in Guantánamo, told his lawyer, Clive Stafford Smith, that speakers blared music into his cell while he was handcuffed. Detainees recalled the sound as ranging from ghoulish laughter, "like the soundtrack from a horror film," to ear-splitting rap anthems. Stafford Smith said that his client found the psychological torture more intolerable than the physical abuse that he said he had been previously subjected to in Morocco, where, he said, local intelligence agents had sliced him with a razor blade. "The C.I.A. worked people day and night for months," Stafford Smith quoted Binyam Mohamed as saying. "Plenty lost their minds. I could hear people knocking their heads against the walls and doors, screaming their heads off."

Professor Kassem said his Yemeni client, Kazimi, had told him that, during his incarceration in the Dark Prison, he attempted suicide three times, by ramming his head into the walls. "He did it until he lost consciousness," Kassem said. "Then they stitched him back up. So he did it again. The next time, he woke up, he was chained, and they'd given him tranquilizers. He asked to go to the bathroom, and then he did it again." This last time, Kazimi was given more tranquilizers, and chained in a more confining manner.

The case of Khaled el-Masri, another detainee, has received wide attention. He is the German car salesman whom the C.I.A. captured in 2003 and dispatched to Afghanistan, based on erroneous intelligence; he was released in 2004, and Condoleezza Rice reportedly conceded the mistake to the German chancellor. Masri is considered one of the more credible sources on the blacksite program, because Germany has confirmed that he has no connections to terrorism. He has also described inmates bashing their heads against the walls. Much of his account appeared on the front page of the *Times*. But, during a visit to America last fall, he became tearful as he recalled the plight of a Tanzanian in a neighboring cell. The man seemed "psychologically at the end," he said. "I could hear him ramming his head against the wall in despair. I tried to calm him down. I asked the doctor, 'Will you take care of this human being?'" But the doctor, whom Masri described as American, refused to help. Masri also said that he was told that guards had "locked the Tanzanian in a suitcase for long periods of time—a foul-smelling suitcase that made him vomit." (Masri did not witness such abuse.)

Masri described his prison in Afghanistan as a filthy hole, with walls scribbled on in Pashtun and Arabic. He was given no bed, only a coarse blanket on the floor. At night, it was too cold to sleep. He said, "The water was putrid. If you took a sip, you could taste it for hours. You could smell a foul smell from it three metres away." The Salt Pit, he said, "was managed and run by the Americans. It was not a secret. They introduced themselves as Americans." He added, "When anything came up, they said they couldn't make a decision. They said, 'We will have to pass it on to Washington.'" The interrogation room at the Salt Pit, he said, was overseen by a half-dozen English-speaking masked men, who shoved him and shouted at him, saying, "You're in a country where there's no rule of law. You might be buried here."

According to two former C.I.A. officers, an interrogator of Mohammed told them that the Pakistani was kept in a cell over which a sign was placed: "The Proud Murderer of 3,000 Americans." (Another source calls this apocryphal.) One of these former officers defends the C.I.A.'s program by noting that "there was absolutely nothing done to K.S.M. that wasn't done to the interrogators themselves"—a reference to SERE-like training. Yet the Red Cross report emphasizes that it was the simultaneous use of several techniques for extended periods that made the treatment "especially abusive." Senator Carl Levin, the chairman of the Senate Armed Services Committee, who has been a prominent critic of the Administration's embrace of harsh interrogation techniques, said that, particularly with sensory deprivation, "there's a point where it's torture. You can put someone in a refrigerator and it's torture. Everything is a matter of degree."

⊶ • ⊷

One day, Mohammed was apparently transferred to a specially designated prison for high-value detainees in Poland. Such transfers were so secretive, according to the report by the Council of Europe, that the C.I.A. filed dummy flight plans, indicating that the planes were heading elsewhere. Once Polish air space was entered, the Polish aviation authority would secretly shepherd the flight, leaving no public documentation. The Council of Europe report notes that the Polish authorities would file a one-way flight plan out of the country, creating a false paper trail. (The Polish government has strongly denied that any black sites were established in the country.)

No more than a dozen high-value detainees were held at the Polish black site, and none have been released from government custody; accordingly, no first-hand accounts of conditions there have emerged. But, according to well-informed sources, it was a far more high-tech facility than the prisons in Afghanistan. The cells had hydraulic doors and air-conditioning. Multiple cameras in each cell provided video surveillance of the detainees. In some ways, the circumstances were better: the detainees were given bottled water. Without confirming the existence of any black sites, Robert Grenier, the former C.I.A. counterterrorism chief, said, "The agency's techniques became less aggressive as they learned the art of interrogation," which, he added, "*is* an art."

Mohammed was kept in a prolonged state of sensory deprivation, during which every point of reference was erased. The Council on Europe's report describes a four-month isolation regime as typical. The prisoners had no exposure to natural light, making it impossible for them to tell if it was night or day. They interacted only with masked, silent guards. (A detainee held at what was most likely an Eastern European black site, Mohammed al-Asad, told me that white noise was piped in constantly, although during electrical outages he could hear people crying.) According to a source familiar with the Red Cross report, Khalid Sheikh Mohammed claimed that he was shackled and kept naked, except for a pair of goggles and earmuffs. (Some prisoners were kept naked for as long as forty days.) He had no idea where he was, although, at one point, he apparently glimpsed Polish writing on a water bottle.

In the C.I.A.'s program, meals were delivered sporadically, to insure that the prisoners remained temporally disoriented. The food was largely tasteless, and barely enough to live on. Mohammed, who upon his capture in Rawalpindi was photographed looking flabby and unkempt, was now described as being slim. Experts on the C.I.A. program say that the administering of food is part of its psychological arsenal. Sometimes portions were smaller than the day before, for no apparent reason. "It was all part of the conditioning," the person involved in the Council of Europe inquiry said. "It's all calibrated to develop dependency."

The inquiry source said that most of the Poland detainees were waterboarded, including Mohammed. According to the sources familiar with the Red Cross report, Mohammed claimed to have been waterboarded five times. Two former C.I.A. officers who are friends with one of Mohammed's interrogators called this bravado, insisting that he was waterboarded only once. According to one of the officers, Mohammed needed only to be shown the drowning equipment again before he "broke."

"Waterboarding works," the former officer said. "Drowning is a baseline fear. So is falling. People dream about it. It's human nature. Suffocation is a very scary thing. When you're waterboarded, you're inverted, so it exacerbates the fear. It's not painful, but it scares the shit out of you." (The former officer was waterboarded himself in a training course.) Mohammed, he claimed, "didn't resist. He sang right away. He cracked real quick." He said, "A lot of them want to talk. Their egos are unimaginable. K.S.M. was just a little doughboy. He couldn't stand toe to toe and fight it out."

The former officer said that the C.I.A. kept a doctor standing by during interrogations. He insisted that the method was safe and effective, but said that it could cause lasting psychic damage to the interrogators. During interrogations, the former agency official said, officers worked in teams, watching each other behind two-way mirrors. Even with this group support, the friend said, Mohammed's interrogator "has horrible nightmares." He went on, "When you cross over that line of darkness, it's hard to come back. You lose your soul. You can do your best to justify it, but it's well outside the norm. You can't go to that dark a place without it changing you." He said of his friend, "He's a good guy. It really haunts him. You are inflicting something really evil and horrible on somebody."

Among the few C.I.A. officials who knew the details of the detention and interrogation program, there was a tense debate about where to draw the line in terms of treatment. John Brennan, Tenet's former chief of staff, said, "It all comes down to individual moral barometers." Waterboarding, in particular, troubled many officials, from both a moral and a legal perspective. Until 2002, when Bush administration lawyers asserted that waterboarding was a permissible interrogation technique for "enemy combatants," it was classified as a form of torture, and treated as a serious criminal offense. American soldiers were court-martialed for waterboarding captives as recently as the Vietnam War.

A C.I.A. source said that Mohammed was subjected to waterboarding only after interrogators determined that he was hiding information from them. But Mohammed has apparently said that, even after he started cooperating, he was waterboarded. Footnotes to the 9/11 Commission report indicate that by April 17, 2003—a month and a half after he was captured—Mohammed had already started providing substantial information on Al Qaeda. Nonetheless, according to the person involved in the Council of Europe inquiry, he was kept in isolation for years. During this time, Mohammed supplied intelligence on the history of the September 11th plot, and on the structure and operations of Al Qaeda. He also described plots still in a preliminary phase of development, such as a plan to bomb targets on America's West Coast.

Ultimately, however, Mohammed claimed responsibility for so many crimes that his testimony came to seem inherently dubious. In addition to confessing to the Pearl murder, he said that he had hatched plans to assassinate President Clinton, President Carter, and Pope John Paul II. Bruce Riedel, who was a C.I.A. analyst for twenty-nine years, and who now works at the Brookings Institution, said, "It's difficult to give credence to any particular area of this large a charge sheet that he confessed to, considering the situation he found himself in. K.S.M. has no prospect of ever seeing freedom again, so his only gratification in life is to portray himself as the James Bond of jihadism."

⤙ • ⤚

By 2004, there were growing calls within the C.I.A. to transfer to military custody the high-value detainees who had told interrogators what they knew, and to afford them some kind of due process. But Donald Rumsfeld, then the Defense Secretary, who had been heavily criticized for the abusive conditions at military prisons such as Abu Ghraib and Guantánamo, refused to take on the agency's detainees, a former top C.I.A. official said. "Rumsfeld's attitude was, *You've* got a real problem." Rumsfeld, the official said, "was the third most powerful person in the U.S. government, but he only looked out for the interests of his department—not the whole Administration." (A spokesperson for Rumsfeld said that he had no comment.)

C.I.A. officials were stymied until the Supreme Court's Hamdan ruling, which prompted the Administration to send what it said were its last high-value detainees to Cuba. Robert Grenier, like many people in the C.I.A., was relieved. "There has to be some sense of due process," he said. "We can't just make people disappear." Still, he added, "The most important source of intelligence we had after 9/11 came from the interrogations of high-value detainees." And he said that Mohammed was "the most valuable of the high-value detainees, because he had operational knowledge." He went on, "I can respect people who oppose aggressive interrogations, but they should admit that their principles may be putting American lives at risk."

Yet Philip Zelikow, the executive director of the 9/11 Commission and later the State Department's top counselor, under Rice, is not convinced that eliciting information from detainees justifies "physical torment." After leaving the government last year, he gave a speech in Houston, in which he said, "The question would not be, Did you get information that proved useful? Instead it would be, Did you get information that could have been usefully gained only from these methods?" He concluded, "My own view is that the cool, carefully considered, methodical, prolonged, and repeated subjection of captives to physical torment, and the accompanying psychological terror, is immoral."

Without more transparency, the value of the C.I.A.'s interrogation and detention program is impossible to evaluate. Setting aside the moral, ethical, and legal issues, even supporters, such as John Brennan, acknowledge that much of the information that coercion produces is unreliable. As he put it, "All these methods produced useful information, but there was also a lot that was bogus." When pressed, one former top agency official estimated that "ninety percent of the information was unreliable." Cables carrying Mohammed's interrogation transcripts back to Washington reportedly were prefaced with the warning that "the detainee has been known to withhold information or deliberately mislead." Mohammed, like virtually all the top Al Qaeda prisoners held by the C.I.A., has claimed that, while under coercion, he lied to please his captors.

In theory, a military commission could sort out which parts of Mohammed's confession are true and which are lies, and obtain a conviction. Colonel Morris D. Davis, the chief prosecutor at the Office of Military Commissions, said that he expects to bring charges against Mohammed "in a number of months." He added, "I'd be shocked if the defense didn't try to make K.S.M.'s treatment a problem for me, but I don't think it will be insurmountable."

Critics of the Administration fear that the unorthodox nature of the C.I.A.'s interrogation and detention program will make it impossible to prosecute the entire top echelon of Al Qaeda leaders in captivity. Already, according to the *Wall Street Journal*, credible allegations of torture have caused a Marine Corps prosecutor reluctantly to decline to bring charges against Mohamedou Ould Slahi, an alleged Al Qaeda leader held in Guantánamo. Bruce Riedel, the former C.I.A. analyst, asked, "What are you going to do with K.S.M. in the long run? It's a very good question. I don't think anyone has an answer. If you took him to any real American court, I think any judge would say there is no admissible evidence. It would be thrown out."

The problems with Mohammed's coerced confessions are especially glaring in the Daniel Pearl case. It may be that Mohammed killed Pearl, but contradictory evidence and opinion continue to surface. Yosri Fouda, the Al Jazeera reporter who interviewed Mohammed in Karachi, said that although Mohammed handed him a package of propaganda items, including an unedited video of the Pearl murder, he never identified himself as playing a role in the killing, which occurred in the same city just two months earlier. And a federal official involved in Mohammed's case said, "He has no history of killing with his own hands, although he's proved happy to commit mass murder from afar." Al Qaeda's leadership had increasingly focused on symbolic political targets. "For him, it's not personal," the official said. "It's business."

Ordinarily, the U.S. legal system is known for resolving such mysteries with painstaking care. But the C.I.A.'s secret interrogation program, Senator Levin said, has undermined the public's trust in American justice, both here and abroad. "A guy as dangerous as K.S.M. is, and half the world wonders if they can believe him—is that what we want?" he asked. "Statements that can't be believed, because people think they rely on torture?"

Asra Nomani, the Pearls' friend, said of the Mohammed confession, "I'm not interested in unfair justice, even for bad people." She went on, "Danny was such a person of conscience. I don't think he would have wanted all of this dirty business. I don't think he would have wanted someone being tortured. He would have been repulsed. This is the kind of story that Danny would have investigated. He really believed in American principles."

26

EUPHEMISM AND AMERICAN VIOLENCE

DAVID BROMWICH
The New York Review of Books   April 3, 2008

The final selection in this year's anthology is devoted explicitly to how we "talk about war." As David Bromwich notes, George Orwell was the first to describe in depth the technique of using deliberately colorless language to desensitize ordinary citizens to the inherent violence of warfare. Bromwich, a professor of literature at Yale University, effectively illustrates how this time-honored practice has been

employed by the Bush administration—with the media's cooperation—to shape
American public opinion on Iraq, the war on terror, and other hot-button issues.

In Tacitus' *Agricola*, a Caledonian rebel named Calgacus, addressing "a close-packed multitude" preparing to fight, declares that Rome has overrun so much of the world that "there are no more nations beyond us; nothing is there but waves and rocks, and the Romans, more deadly still than these—for in them is an arrogance which no submission or good behavior can escape." Certain habits of speech, he adds, abet the ferocity and arrogance of the empire by infecting even the enemies of Rome with Roman self-deception:

> A rich enemy excites their cupidity; a poor one, their lust for power. East and West alike have failed to satisfy them. . . . To robbery, butchery, and rapine, they give the lying name of "government"; they create a desolation and call it peace.

The frightening thing about such acts of renaming or *euphemism,* Tacitus implies, is their power to efface the memory of actual cruelties. Behind the façade of a history falsified by language, the painful particulars of war are lost. Maybe the most disturbing implication of the famous sentence "They create a desolation and call it peace" is that apologists for violence, by means of euphemism, come to believe what they hear themselves say.

On July 21, 2006, the tenth day of the Lebanon war, Condoleezza Rice explained why the U.S. government had not thrown its weight behind a cease-fire:

> What we're seeing here, in a sense, is the growing—the birth pangs of a new Middle East, and whatever we do, we have to be certain that we're pushing forward to the new Middle East, not going back to the old one.

Very likely these words were improvised. "Growing pains" seems to have been Rice's initial thought; but as she went on, she dropped the "pains," turned them into "pangs," and brought back the violence with a hint of redemptive design: the pains were only *birth pangs.* The secretary of state was thinking still with the same metaphor when she spoke of "pushing," but a literal image of a woman in labor could have proved awkward, and she trailed off in a deliberate anticlimax: "pushing forward" means "not going back."

Many people at the time remarked the incongruity of Rice's speech as applied to the devastation wrought by Israeli attacks in southern Lebanon and Beirut. Every bombed-out Lebanese home and mangled limb would be atoned for, the words seemed to be saying, just as a healthy infant vindicates the mother's labor pains. Looked at from a longer distance, the statement suggested a degree of mental dissociation. For the self-serving boast was also offered as a fatalistic consolation—and this by an official whose call for a cease-fire might well have stopped the war. "The birth pangs of a new Middle East" will probably outlive most other phrases of our time, because, as a kind of metaphysical "conceit," it accurately sketches the state of mind of the President and his advisers in 2006.

◄← • →►

The phrase also marked a notable recent example of a turn of language one may as well call *revolutionary euphemism.* This was an invention of the later eighteenth century, but it was brought into standard usage in the twentieth— "You can't make an omelet without breaking eggs"—by Stalin's apologists for revolution and forced modernization in the 1930s. The French Revolutionist Jean-Marie Roland spoke of the mob violence of the attack on the Tuileries as *agitation* or *effervescence,* never as "massacre" or "murder"—improvising, as he went, a cleansing metaphor oddly similar to Rice's "birth pangs."

It was natural, said Roland, "that victory should bring with it some excess. The sea, agitated by a violent storm, roars long after the tempest." The task of the revolutionary propagandist, at a temporary setback, is to show that his zeal is undiminished. This he must do with a minimum of egotism, and the surest imaginable protection is to invoke the impartial authority of natural processes.

If one extreme of euphemism comes from naturalizing the cruelties of power, the opposite extreme arises from a nerve-deadening understatement. George Orwell had the latter method in view when he wrote a memorable passage of "Politics and the English Language":

> Defenceless villages are bombarded from the air, the inhabitants driven out into the countryside, the cattle machine-gunned, the huts set on fire with incendiary bullets: this is called *pacification.* Millions of peasants are robbed of their farms and sent trudging along the roads with no more than they can carry: this is called *transfer of population* or *rectification of*

frontiers. People are imprisoned for years without trial, or shot in the back of the neck or sent to die of scurvy in Arctic lumber camps: this is called *elimination of unreliable elements.* Such phraseology is needed if one wants to name things without calling up mental pictures of them.

Orwell's insight was that the italicized phrases are colorless by design and not by accident. He saw a deliberate method in the imprecision of texture. The inventors of this idiom meant to suppress one kind of imagination, the kind that yields an image of things actually done or suffered; and they wanted to put in its place an imagination that trusts to the influence of larger powers behind the scenes. Totalitarianism depends on the creation of people who take satisfaction in such trust; and totalitarian minds are in part created (Orwell believed) by the ease and invisibility of euphemism.

◄◄• • •►►

Before launching their response to Islamic jihadists in September 2001, members of the administration of George W. Bush and Dick Cheney gave close consideration to the naming of that response. The President has been reported by Bob Woodward and Robert Draper to have said to his staff that they should all view the September 11 attack as an "opportunity."* His sense of that word in this context is hard to interpret, but its general bearings are plain. Imaginative leadership, the President was saying, must do far more than respond to the attack, or attend to the needs of self-preservation. Better to use the attack as an opportunity to "go massive," as Donald Rumsfeld noted on September 11. "Sweep it all up. Things related and not." A similar sense of Bush's purpose has recently been recalled by Karl Rove. "History has a funny way of deciding things," Rove said to an audience at the University of Pennsylvania on February 20, 2008. "Sometimes history sends you things, and 9/11 came our way." But so, all the more pressingly: how to name the massive and partly unrelated response to a catastrophe which was also an opportunity?

The name must admit the tremendousness of the task and imply its eventual solubility, but also discourage any close inquiry into the means employed.

---

* Bob Woodward, *Bush at War* (Simon and Schuster, 2002), p. 32; Robert Draper, *Dead Certain: The Presidency of George W. Bush* (Free Press, 2007), p. 166.

They wanted to call it a war; but what sort of war? The phrase they agreed on, *the global war on terrorism,* was at once simple-sounding and elusive, and it has served its purpose as nothing more definite could have done.

The "global war on terrorism" promotes a mood of comprehension in the absence of perceived particulars, and that is a mood in which euphemisms may comfortably take shelter. There is (many commentators have pointed out) something nonsensical in the idea of waging war on a *technique* or *method,* and terrorism was a method employed by many groups over many centuries before Al Qaeda—the Tamil Tigers, the IRA, the Irgun, to stick to recent times. But the "war on crime" and "war on drugs" probably helped to render the initial absurdity of the name to some degree normal. This was an incidental weakness, in any case. The assurance and the unspecifying grandiosity of the global war on terrorism were the traits most desired in such a slogan.

Those qualities fitted well with a style of white-lipped eloquence that Bush's speechwriter Michael Gerson had begun to plot into his major speeches in late 2001. It made for a sort of continuous, excitable, canting threat, emitted as if unwillingly from a man of good will and short temper. Gerson, from his Christian evangelical beliefs and journalistic ability (he had worked for *US News & World Report* and ghostwritten the autobiography of Chuck Colson), worked up for the President a highly effective contemporary "grand style" that skated between hyperbole and evasion. The manner suggested a stark simplicity that was the end product of sophisticated analysis and a visionary impatience with compromise.

This was exactly the way President Bush, in his own thinking, turned his imaginative vices into virtues, and he intuitively grasped the richness of a phrase like "the soft bigotry of low expectations" or "history's unmarked grave of discarded lies"—resonant formulae which he approved and deployed, over the challenges of his staff. What did the phrases mean? As their creator knew, the mode of their nonmeaning was the point. Like "pacification" and "rectification of frontiers," these markers of unstated policy were floating metaphors with a low yield of fact. But they left an image of decisiveness, with an insinuation of contempt for persons slower to pass from thought to action.

Euphemism has been the leading quality of American discussions of the war in Iraq. This was plain in the run-up to the war, with the talk of "regime change"—a phrase welcomed by reporters and politicians as if they had heard it all their lives. Regime change seemed to pass at a jump beyond the predictable either/or of "forced abdication" and "international war of aggression." Regime change also managed to imply, without saying, that governments do, as a matter of fact, often change by external demand without much trouble to anyone. The talk (before and just after the war) of "taking out" Saddam Hussein was equally new. It combined the reflex of the skilled gunman and the image of a surgical procedure so routine that it could be trusted not to jeopardize the life of the patient. It had its roots in gangland argot, where taking out means knocking off, but its reception was none the worse for that.

⪻ • ⪼

Are Americans more susceptible to such devices than other people are? Democracy exists in continuous complicity with euphemism. There are so many things (the staring facts of inequality, for example) about which we feel it is right not to want to speak gratingly. One result is a habit of circumlocution that is at once adaptable and self-deceptive. "Their own approbation of their own acts," wrote Edmund Burke of the people in a democracy, "has to them the appearance of a public judgment in their favor." Since the people are not always right but are by definition always in the majority, their self-approbation, Burke added, tends to make them shameless and therefore fearless. The stratagems of a leader in a democracy include giving the people a name for everything, but doing so in a way that maintains their own approbation of their own acts. Thus a war the people trust their government to wage, over which we have no control, but about which we would prefer to think happy thoughts, gives the widest possible scope to the exertions of euphemism.

There has sprung up, over the past five years, a euphemistic contract between the executive branch and many journalists. "A short, sharp war," as Tony Blair was sure it would be, has become one of the longest of American wars; but the warmakers have blunted that recognition by breaking down the war into stages: the fall of Baghdad; the Coalition Provisional Authority; the insurgency; the election of the Assembly; the sectarian war. In this way the character of the war as a single failed attempt has eluded discovery; it has come to seem, instead, a many-featured entity, difficult to describe and impossible to judge. And to assist the impression of obscurity, two things are consistently pressed out of view: the killing of Iraqi civilians by American soldiers and the destruction of Iraqi cities by American bombs and artillery.

Slight uptick in violence is a coinage new to the war in Iraq, and useful for obvious reasons. It suggests a remote perspective in which fifty or a hundred deaths, from three or four suicide bombings in a day, hardly cause a jump in the needle that measures such things. The phrase has a laconic sound, in a manner popularly associated with men who are used to violence and keep a cool head. Indeed, it was generals at briefings—Kimmitt, Hertling, and Petraeus—who gave currency to a phrase that implies realism and the possession of strong personal shock absorbers.

A far more consequential euphemism, in the conduct of the Iraq war—and a usage adopted without demur until recently, by journalists, lawmakers, and army officers—speaks of mercenary soldiers as *contractors* or *security* (the last now a singular-plural like the basketball teams called Magic and Jazz). The Blackwater killings in Baghdad's Nissour Square on September 16, 2007, brought this euphemism, and the extraordinary innovation it hides, suddenly to public view. Yet the armed Blackwater guards who did the shooting, though now less often described as mere "contractors," are referred to as *employees*—a neutral designation that repels further attention. The point about mercenaries is that you employ them when your army is inadequate to the job assigned. This has been the case from the start in Iraq. But the fact that the mercenaries have been continuously augmented until they now outnumber American troops suggests a truth about the war that falls open to inspection only when we use the accurate word. It was always known to the Office of the Vice President and the Department of Defense that the conventional forces they deployed were smaller than would be required to maintain order in Iraq. That is why they hired the extracurricular forces.

Reflect on the prevalence of the mercenaries and the falsifying descriptions offered of their work, and you are made to wonder how much the architects of the war actually wanted a state of order in Iraq. Was this as important to them as, say, the assurance that "contracting" of all kinds in Iraq would become a major part of the American economy following the invasion? We now know that the separate bookkeeping and accountability devised for Blackwater, Dyn-Corp, Triple Canopy, and similar outfits was part of a careful displacement of oversight from Congress to the vice-president and the stewards of his policies in various departments and agencies. To have much of the work of this war parceled out to private companies, who are unaccountable to army rules or military justice, meant, among its other advantages, that the cost of the war could be concealed beyond all detection. What is a contractor? Someone contracted to do a job by the proper authority. Who that hears the word "contractor" has even asked what the contract is for?

There was a brief contest over *surge*—so ordinary yet so odd a word. The rival term emphasized by critics of the war was "escalation": a word that owes its grim connotations to Vietnam. The architects of the surge—Frederick Kagan and Retired General Jack Keane—fought hard to stop the mass media from switching to *escalation*. Their wishes were granted almost without exception, and to clinch the optimistic consensus, the *New York Times* on July 30, 2007, published an extraordinary Op-Ed by Kenneth Pollack and Michael O'Hanlon praising the progress of the surge. The authors, supporters of the war who were permitted falsely to describe themselves as skeptics, wrote, as they confessed, after an eight-day army-guided tour, from which they had neither the enterprise nor the resources to step out and seek information on their own. But it now seems likely that, with the help of the surge, the word as much as the thing, 2008 will end with as many American troops in Iraq as 2006. Meanwhile, as the mass media approved of the surge, they lost interest in Iraq, and that was the aim. The strategists of the surge may have taken some pleasure in putting across a word that sounds like a breakfast drink but that insiders at the American Enterprise Institute, the Brookings Institution, and the Pentagon would recognize as shorthand for counterinsurgency.

When Seymour Hersh broke the story of Abu Ghraib, Secretary of Defense Rumsfeld was keen on excluding the word *torture* from all discussions of the coercive interrogations and planned humiliations at the prison. His chosen word was *abuse*: a word that has been devalued through its bureaucratization in therapies against spousal abuse, child abuse, and so on. "Torture," by comparison, still sets teeth on edge, and the word had been avoided for a long time.

Yet there were many, and not only in the inner circle of the vice-president, in the panic months after September 2001 who eagerly approved the breaking of old restrictions in the global war on terrorism. Alfred McCoy in *A Question of Torture* recalls that in late 2001 and early 2002 "a growing public consensus emerged in favor of torture."* And lawmakers were not to be outdone by legal theorists; Representative Jane Harman said, "I'm OK with it not being pretty."

---

* Alfred W. McCoy, *A Question of Torture: CIA Interrogation from the Cold War to the War on Terror* (Metropolitan, 2006).

What did the new tolerance encompass? "Interrogation in depth" was one way of putting it; "professional interrogation techniques" were spoken of (perhaps with a view to the professionalism of the contractors). With the apparent acceptance of torture, the inversions of euphemism began to be extended to grammar as well as diction. Thus Alan Dershowitz argued in January 2002 for "torture warrants," to be issued by judges, and later spoke of the legitimation of torture as "bringing it within the law" (where, he implied, the torturer, the tortured, and the law would all be more secure). By bringing torture within the law, what Dershowitz meant was breaking the law out of itself to accommodate torture.

This argument was always about two things: the truth of words and the reality of violence. The statements to House and Senate committees, in late January and early February 2008, by Attorney General Michael Mukasey and Director of National Intelligence Mike McConnell oddly converged on the following set of propositions. A method of interrogation known as "waterboarding" would feel like torture if it was done to them (Mukasey and McConnell offered different but parallel versions of the same personal formula, pretty clearly in coordination). The method had been used by American interrogators after September 11, 2001, they said, but it was not in use at present. Whether it constituted torture was a matter under investigation—an investigation so serious that no result should be expected soon—but authorization of the practice was within the powers of the President, and he reserved the right to command interrogators to waterboard suspects again if he thought it useful. The attorney general added his assurance that, in the event that the practice was resumed, he would notify appropriate members of Congress, even though Congress had no legal authority to restrain the President.

It would be hard to find a precedent for the sophistical juggle of these explanations. The secret in plain view was not a judgment about present or future policy, but an imposed acceptance of something past. President Bush, in 2002 and later, sought and obtained legal justifications for ordering the torture of terrorism suspects, and it is known that American interrogators used methods on some suspects that constitute torture under international law. If these acts had been admitted by the attorney general to meet the definition of torture, those who conducted the interrogations and those who ordered them, including the President, would be liable to prosecution for war crimes. Because the legacy of the Nuremberg Trials remains vivid today, the very idea of a war crime has been treated as a thing worth steering clear of, no matter what the cost in overstretched ingenuity. Thought of a war crime does not lend itself to euphemistic reduction.

Yet "waterboarding" itself is a euphemism for a torture that the Japanese in World War II, the French in Indochina, and the Khmer Rouge, who learned it from the French, knew simply as the drowning torture. Our American explanations have been as misleading as the word. The process is not "simulated drowning" but actual drowning that is interrupted. Clarifications such as these, in the coverage of the debate, did not emerge from news reports on the Mukasey and McConnell testimony; they had to be found in the rival testimony, either in public discussions or before Congress, of opponents like Lieutenant Commander Charles D. Swift (the JAG Corps defense counsel who was denied promotion after his public criticism of the Guantánamo tribunals) and Malcolm W. Nance (a retired instructor at the U.S. Navy SERE school).

The contrast between the startling testimony of men like these and the speculative defense of waterboarding offered by semiofficial advocates such as David B. Rivkin, the Reagan Justice Department lawyer and journalist, has been among the most disquieting revelations of these years. A group of men who think what they want to think and pay little attention to evidence have been running things; and they are guided not by experience but by words that were constructed for the purpose of deception.

◂◂ • ▸▸

Americans born between the 1930s and the 1950s have a much harder time getting over the shock of learning that our country practices torture than do Americans born in the 1970s or 1980s. The memory of the Gestapo and the GPU, the depiction of torture in a film like *Open City*, are not apt to press on younger minds. But the different responses are also a consequence of the different imaginings to which people may fall prey. Many who fear that their children might be killed by a terrorist bomb cannot imagine anyone they know ever suffering injustice at the hands of the national security state.

This complacency suggests a new innocence—the correlative in moral psychology of euphemism in the realm of language. And if you take stock of how little *general* discussion there has been of the advisability of pursuing the global war on terrorism, you realize that this country has scarcely begun to take stock of the United States as an ambiguous actor on the world stage. Those who said, in the weeks just after the September 11 attacks, that the motives of the terrorists might be traced back to some U.S. policies in the Middle East were understandably felt to have spoken unseasonably. The surprising thing is that six and a half years later, when a politic reticence is no longer the sole order of the day, discussion of such matters is still confined to academic studies like Chalmers Johnson's *Blowback* and Robert A. Pape's *Dying to Win,** and has barely begun to register in the *New York Times,* in the *Washington Post,* or on CNN or MSNBC. Ask an American what the United States may have to do with much of the world's hostility toward us and you will find educated people saying things like "They hate the West and resent modernity," or "They hate the fact that we're so free," or "They hate us because this is a country where a man and a woman can look at each other across a table with eyes of love." Indeed, the single greatest propaganda victory of the Bush administration may be the belief shared by most Americans that the rise of radical Islam—so-called Islamofascism—has nothing to do with any previous actions by the United States.

Nothing can excuse acts of terrorism, which are aimed at civilians, or those acts of state terror in which planned civilian deaths are advertised as "collateral damage." Yet the uniformity of the presentation by the mass media after 2001, to the effect that the United States now faced threats arising from a fanaticism with religious roots unconnected to anything America had done or could do, betrayed a stupefying abdication of judgment. The protective silence regarding the 725 American bases worldwide, and the emotions with which these are regarded by the people who live in their shadow, cover up a clue in the fact that fifteen of the nineteen hijackers on September 11 were Saudis. The presence of thousands of American troops on Arabian soil was hotly resented. To gloss over or ignore such facts only obstructs an intelligent discussion of the reaction likely to follow from any extended American occupation of the Middle East.

"Baghdad is calmer now; the surge is working." The temporary partial peace is an effect of accomplished desolation, a state of things in which the Shiite "cleansing" of the city has achieved the dignity of the status quo, and been

* Chalmers Johnson, *Blowback: The Costs and Consequences of American Empire* (Metropolitan, 2000); Robert A. Pape, *Dying to Win: The Strategic Logic of Suicide Terrorism* (Random House, 2005). *Dying to Win* was reviewed in these pages [*The New York Review of Books*] by Christian Caryl, September 22, 2005.

ratified by the walls and checkpoints of General Petraeus. "The surge is working" is a fiction that blends several facts indistinguishably. For example: that
Iraq is a land of militias and (as Nir Rosen has put it) the U.S. Army is the
largest militia; that in 2007 we paid 80,000 "Sunni extremists" to switch sides
and then call themselves The Awakening. Americans have suggested that the
members of this militia make up neighborhood watch groups, and have assigned them euphemistic cover-names such as Concerned Local Citizens and
Critical Infrastructure Security. In fact, many of them are "increasingly frus-
trated with the American military," according to Sudarsan Raghavan and Amit
R. Paley in a *Washington Post* story that ran on February 28 [2008].

⤛ • ⤜

"If a Power coerces once," wrote H.N. Brailsford in his great study of imperial-
ism *The War of Steel and Gold*, "it may dictate for years afterwards without re-
quiring to repeat the lesson." This was the design of the American "shock and
awe" in Iraq. Looking back on the invasion, one is impressed that so clear-cut
a strategy could have evaded challenge under the casual drapery of "democracy." But say a thing often enough, so as to subdue the anxiety of a people and
flatter their pride, and, unless they have come to know better with their own
eyes and their own hands, they will accept the illusion.

"History begins today" was a saying in the Bush White House on September
12, 2001—repeated with menace by Deputy Secretary of State Richard Armitage to the director of Pakistani intelligence Mahmoud Ahmad—a statement that on its face exhibits a totalitarian presumption. Yet nothing so much
as language supplies our memory of things that came before today; and, to an
astounding degree, the Bush and Cheney administration has succeeded in persuading the most powerful and (at one time) the best-informed country in the
world that history began on September 12, 2001. The effect has been to tran-
quilize our self-doubts and externalize all the evils we dare to think of. In this
sense, the changes of usage and the corruptions of sense that have followed the
global war on terrorism are inseparable from the destructive acts of that war.

—March 5, 2008

PERMISSIONS

CONTRIBUTORS

Jon Lee Anderson is a staff writer for *The New Yorker*. His work has also appeared in the *New York Times, Harper's, Life,* and *The Nation*. He's the author of several books, including, most recently, *The Fall of Baghdad*.

Steve Brodner is a freelance illustrator specializing in political satire. His works have appeared in numerous publications, including *The New Yorker, Esquire, Harper's, National Lampoon, Playboy, Sports Illustrated, Spy,* and the *New York Times Book Review*. His political work is collected in the book *Freedom Fries*.

David Bromwich is the Sterling Professor of English at Yale. In addition to *The New York Review of Books*, his work has appeared in *The New Republic, The Nation,* and other magazines. He is editor of Edmund Burke's selected writings, *On Empire, Liberty, and Reform,* and coeditor of the Yale University Press edition of *On Liberty*.

Jonathan Chait is a senior editor at *The New Republic*. He has also written for the *New York Times Magazine*, the *Wall Street Journal, The American Prospect, Time, Slate,* and other publications. He's the author of *The Big Con: The True Story of How Washington Got Hoodwinked and Hijacked by Crackpot Economics*.

Tim Dickinson is a contributing editor to *Rolling Stone* magazine and the author of *Rolling Stone*'s National Affairs Daily blog. He previously was an editor at *Mother Jones*.

Peter D. Feaver is the Alexander F. Hehmeyer Professor of Political Science and Public Policy at Duke University and director of the Triangle Institute for Security Studies. He is the coauthor of *Getting the Best Out of College*.

Amanda Fortini has written for *New York, The New Yorker,* and the *New York Times Magazine* and is a regular contributor to *Slate*.

Joshua Green is a senior editor at *The Atlantic Monthly* and a contributing editor to *Washington Monthly*. His work has also appeared in *Esquire, The New Yorker,* and *Rolling Stone* magazine.

David Halberstam was the author of numerous books, including *The Best and the Brightest,* his classic study of the origins of the Vietnam War. His most recent book, published after his death in 2007, is *Coldest Winter: America and the Korean War.* He shared the 1964 Pulitzer Prize for national reporting for his coverage of the Vietnam War as a reporter for the *New York Times.*

Joshua Hammer is a freelance foreign correspondent. A longtime reporter for *Newsweek,* where he served most recently as Jerusalem and Africa bureau chief, he is the author of several books, including, most recently, *Yokohama Burning: The Deadly 1923 Earthquake and Fire That Helped Forge the Path to World War II.*

John Heilemann is a contributing editor to *New York* magazine.

Linda Hirshman is a retired distinguished professor of philosophy and women's studies at Brandeis University. In addition to the *New York Times Magazine,* she has written for *Glamour, Tikkun, Ms.,* the *ABA Journal, The American Prospect,* and the *Boston Globe* and is the author of *Get to Work: A Manifesto for Women of the World.*

Chris Jones is a writer at large for *Esquire* and the author of *Too Far from Home: A Story of Life and Death in Space.*

Tom Junod is a writer at large for *Esquire.* His work has also appeared in *Life, Sports Illustrated,* and *GQ,* where his writing has won two National Magazine Awards.

Ryan Lizza is *The New Yorker*'s Washington correspondent. Formerly the White House correspondent for *The New Republic,* he has also been a correspondent for *GQ* and a contributing editor to *New York* and has written for the *New York Times, Washington Monthly,* and *The Atlantic Monthly.*

David Mamet has written over two dozen plays, including *Glengarry Glen Ross,* for which he received the 1984 Pulitzer Prize for drama. He has also written or cowritten numerous screenplays and has directed ten films. A contributing blogger to the *Huffington Post*, he's the author of a number of books, including *Bambi vs. Godzilla: On the Nature, Purpose, and Practice of the Movie Business*.

David Margolick is a contributing editor to *Vanity Fair*. Formerly a correspondent for the *New York Times*, he's the author of several books, including, most recently, *Beyond Glory: Joe Louis vs. Max Schmeling, and a World on the Brink*.

Jane Mayer is a staff writer for *The New Yorker*. She's the author of several books, including, most recently, *The Dark Side: The Inside Story of How the War on Terror Turned into a War on American Ideals*.

George Packer is a staff writer for *The New Yorker*. His work has also appeared in *Mother Jones, The Nation, Harper's,* and the *New York Times Magazine*. He's the author of several books, including, most recently, *The Assassin's Gate: America in Iraq,* and a play, *Betrayed,* based on his work as a journalist in Iraq.

Rick Perlstein has written for *The Nation, The Village Voice, The New Republic Online,* and other publications. He's the author of several books, including, most recently, *Nixonland: The Rise of a President and the Fracturing of America*.

Todd S. Purdum is national editor at *Vanity Fair* and a former Washington correspondent for the *New York Times*. He is the lead author of *A Time of Our Choosing: America's War in Iraq*.

Jennifer Senior is a contributing editor to *New York* magazine.

Joseph E. Stiglitz is a professor of economics at Columbia University, where he also holds appointments in the schools of business and international and public affairs. A former senior vice president and chief economist at the World Bank, he was awarded the Nobel Prize for economics in 2001. He has authored or coauthored numerous books, including *Globalization and Its Discontents*.

Andrew Sullivan is a senior editor at *The Atlantic Monthly*. He's the author of several books, including *The Conservative Soul: Fundamentalism, Freedom, and the Future of the Right*.

Clive Thompson is a contributing writer for the *New York Times Magazine* and a columnist for *Wired* magazine, and he publishes his own blog, collisiondetection.net. His work has also appeared in *New York, Discover, Fast Company,* and other publications.

Drew Westen is a professor of psychology, psychiatry, and behavioral science at Emory University. The author of *The Political Brain: The Role of Emotion in Deciding the Fate of the Nation,* he's also a guest blogger on the *Huffington Post,* a contributor to National Public Radio's *All Things Considered,* and the founder of Westen Strategies, a political and corporate consulting firm.

Alexis Lipsitz

Royce Flippin is the series editor of *Best American Political Writing*. A former senior editor at *American Health* magazine, he has written for various publications, including the *New York Times*, *Men's Journal*, *Self,* and *Parents* magazine. This is his seventh year as the editor of the series.

PublicAffairs is a publishing house founded in 1997. It is a tribute to the standards, values, and flair of three persons who have served as mentors to countless reporters, writers, editors, and book people of all kinds, including me.

I. F. STONE, proprietor of *I. F. Stone's Weekly*, combined a commitment to the First Amendment with entrepreneurial zeal and reporting skill and became one of the great independent journalists in American history. At the age of eighty, Izzy published *The Trial of Socrates*, which was a national bestseller. He wrote the book after he taught himself ancient Greek.

BENJAMIN C. BRADLEE was for nearly thirty years the charismatic editorial leader of *The Washington Post*. It was Ben who gave the *Post* the range and courage to pursue such historic issues as Watergate. He supported his reporters with a tenacity that made them fearless and it is no accident that so many became authors of influential, best-selling books.

ROBERT L. BERNSTEIN, the chief executive of Random House for more than a quarter century, guided one of the nation's premier publishing houses. Bob was personally responsible for many books of political dissent and argument that challenged tyranny around the globe. He is also the founder and longtime chair of Human Rights Watch, one of the most respected human rights organizations in the world.

·   ·   ·

For fifty years, the banner of Public Affairs Press was carried by its owner Morris B. Schnapper, who published Gandhi, Nasser, Toynbee, Truman, and about 1,500 other authors. In 1983, Schnapper was described by *The Washington Post* as "a redoubtable gadfly." His legacy will endure in the books to come.

Peter Osnos, *Founder and Editor-at-Large*